The Third Reich's Celluloid War

THE THIRD REICH'S CELLULOID WAR

PROPAGANDA IN NAZI FEATURE FILMS, DOCUMENTARIES AND TELEVISION

IAN GARDEN

The History Press

*This book is dedicated to the memory of our good friend, Tom Durrheim
(1957–2011)*

First published 2012
This paperback edition published 2016

The History Press
The Mill, Brimscombe Port
Stroud, Gloucestershire, GL5 2QG
www.thehistorypress.co.uk

British Library Cataloguing in Publication Data.
A catalogue record for this book is available from the British Library.

ISBN 978 0 7509 6817 1

Typesetting and origination by The History Press
Printed and bound by CPI Group (UK) Ltd

Contents

Acknowledgements   7
Author's Note   8
Introduction   9

I. Propaganda and its Significance for Hitler   11

II. The Control of Film Propaganda under the Nazis   16

GERMAN FEATURE FILMS (1933–45)

III. Anti-British Propaganda   23
    Background   23
    Der Fuchs von Glenarvon   28
    Das Herz der Königin   36
    Mein Leben für Irland   46
    Ohm Krüger   52
    Titanic   62

IV. Anti-Semitic Propaganda   72
    Background   72
    Die Rothschilds   78
    Jud Süss   85

V. Anti-American Propaganda   92
    Background   92
    Der verlorene Sohn   98
    Der Kaiser von Kalifornien   104
    Sensationsprozess Casilla   110

VI. Anti-Eastern Europe Propaganda   117
    Background   117
    Heimkehr   122
    G.P.U.   129

VII. Nationalistic and Pro-Nazi Propaganda 137
    Background 137
    Hans Westmar 145
    Wunschkonzert 153
    Kolberg 160

VIII. Films for Entertainment 170
    Background 170
    Der Mann, der Sherlock Holmes war 176
    Münchhausen 181
    Die Feuerzangenbowle 187

IX. Comparative Anti-Nazi Propaganda in the Allies' Feature Films
    (1938–45) 193

X. Nazi Documentaries (1933–45) 210
    Background 210
    Triumph des Willens 217
    Olympia 226
    Feldzug in Polen 232
    Der ewige Jude 238
    Der Führer schenkt den Juden eine Stadt 247
    Rund um die Freiheitsstatue 255

XI. Television as a Propaganda Weapon for the Nazis (1934–44) 259

XII. Conclusion 269

Select Bibliography 276
Index 280

ACKNOWLEDGEMENTS

This book has been researched and written over a number of years, and I would like to acknowledge the valuable assistance provided by a number of individuals and institutions without which it could not have been completed.

In terms of research, I would like to thank Christiane Eulig and her team at the Deutsches Filmmuseum in Frankfurt for providing me with access to their film library and archives; Inge Kempenich of the FSK in Wiesbaden for specific information about the dates of film censorship approval; Matthew Lee and the Film Archive team at the Imperial War Museum in London for allowing me to view a number of rare war films; and staff at the National Library of Scotland in Edinburgh.

The inclusion of the vast number of images and photo stills used to illustrate the text would not have been possible without the assistance and provision of material by André Mieles of the Deutsches Filminstitut in Frankfurt; Dave McCall of the British Film Institute in London; Christian Unucka of the Verlag für Filmschriften for the use of cover images from the *Illustrierter Film-Kurier* and *Illustrierte Film-Bühne* film programmes; Malcolm Hay and Eleanor Whitney of the Curator's Office at the Palace of Westminster; Professor Randall Bytwerk of Calvin College, Grand Rapids, USA; Geoffrey Swindells of Northwestern University, USA; Petra Faitsch of the Friedrich Wilhelm Murnau Stiftung in Wiesbaden; Danièle Guerlain of Transit Film; Tanja Schwankl of Movieman Productions; Massimo Moretti of Canal + Image UK; Giuseppe Petrucelli of ITV Studios Global Entertainment; Hans-Peter Blechinger of Jupiter-Film; the United States Holocaust Memorial Museum; the Library of Congress; The Bundesarchiv-Bildarchiv; and the Kobal Collection. Every effort has been made to contact the copyright holders of all material used but, notwithstanding, I express my apologies for any omissions.

The technical and legal assistance from Campbell Black, Fraser Edwards, Mark Buckland and Graeme West has also been invaluable.

A large number of specific individuals also deserve special mention for their practical assistance, guidance and suggestions in the completion of this book. These include Helen Gillard, Brian Taylor, Jo de Vries, Fiona Scott, Jim Dunnigan, Ed Furgol, Yvonne Burgess, Hilary Swanston, Tom Durrheim, Bill Kantor, Kevin Horgan, Joyce and Kay Matthew, Julie Mair, George Dickson, Lucina Prestige, John Mackintosh, Bobby Wood, Gary Cooper, Professor Jo Fox, David Mackenzie, Ian Lewis and, above all, my ever-supportive parents.

Author's Note

Websites

thethirdreichscelluloidwar.com
Supplementary information about Nazi film propaganda and the films analysed in this book.

battlingwiththetruth.co.uk
As a follow-up to *The Third Reich's Celluloid War*, my latest book – *Battling with the Truth* – explores which side was more truthful in its newsreel and press coverage of key events in the Second World War. It reveals how both sides were rather 'economic with the truth' in their reporting of the war, often failing to comment on incidents which were particularly embarrassing or likely to undermine the morale of the general public.

iangarden.co.uk
My personal website, which provides details of forthcoming speaking engagements and the film courses which I run in Edinburgh each year.

Introduction

A lie told often enough becomes the truth.

– Vladimir Ilyich Lenin (attributed)

This book's primary purpose is to tell the truth about the nature of Nazi film propaganda.

Born out of the frustration and despair arising from Germany's defeat in the First World War, the Nazi regime was ultimately to unleash a terrible whirlwind. It would not only result in the incarceration and death of millions of civilians in prisons and camps across Europe, but would also provoke a second war which would wreak havoc across the whole world and in which many tens of millions would ultimately die.

The awesome influence of propaganda was one of the major drivers of that whirlwind, and it became just as much a key weapon of the Nazis, both in their elevation to a position of authority and in their garnering of support from the German people for another war, as any power wielded by their secret police or Germany's armed forces.

Although several excellent books have been written on the subject of propaganda in German cinema during the period of the Third Reich, many of these are very academic in nature, and there are few books which examine in any great detail the precise content and history of those films which might be of most interest to a modern-day audience. Most of the general public have heard of Leni Riefenstahl and her documentaries about Hitler and the 1936 Olympic Games. They have perhaps also read about some of the anti-Jewish films or *Kolberg*, the Nazis' last completed film, but few are aware, for example, of the nature of the anti-British and anti-American feature films that were released, many of which still make historically fascinating viewing today.

This book aims to address this knowledge gap by examining the content of a cross-section of the most interesting feature and documentary films produced in Germany during the Nazi regime, particularly from a British, Irish and American perspective. It briefly sets each group of films in context and then analyses in detail the plot and key points of curiosity surrounding each film, such as production problems, censorship difficulties, propaganda effectiveness, the personal involvement of Goebbels or even the subsequent fate of actors and directors who appeared in these films. The book also includes a chapter which provides a comparison with the sort of propaganda being promoted in the Allied feature films of the same period, and a section on Nazi television which continued to broadcast until 1944, unlike in the UK where transmission ceased as soon as war was declared.

In my childhood, I can well remember being fascinated by the patriotic content of so many British and American Second World War feature films screened on television, and even more so when I later discovered that many of these had actually been produced during the war, when the final outcome was still far from certain. One of the most notable examples is the 1942 film, *Went the Day Well?* which opens in an English churchyard sometime in the future, but where the narrator is talking as if the war is already over and Hitler has had his just desserts. Such fictional war-based plots, charged with largely unfounded optimism, were a recurrent feature of the Allied films at the time. I was gradually to discover that the Allies' focus on this type of propaganda film was to contrast sharply with the character and far more varied subject matter of the feature films being viewed by the German public during the same period.

In my investigation of the subject, it also came as a surprise to learn that, while Nazi Germany might have been able to wage a war which would over-run most of Europe and North Africa and create the most effective and frightening weapons of war, when it came to making film propaganda, the Nazis were certainly not omnipotent and, although they had a lot of successes, they also made a lot of mistakes.

Sometimes films were produced which had the exact opposite effect on the audience to that which had been intended. Sometimes, it took so long to produce a film that, by the time it was finished, it had to be withdrawn because the war had moved on and the content was no longer relevant. Other times, they even banned films themselves despite the original concept carrying official support and, on at least two occasions, the directors of the films were seemingly executed before their films were even ready for release.

Given the terrible destruction and suffering to which the policies and beliefs of the Nazis were to lead, it is quite understandable that many post-war documentaries have tended to analyse the subject by beginning with the premise that any films released during the Nazi period were the product of an evil, authoritarian regime and must be full of blatant political propaganda and untruths. In reality, while some very nasty, propaganda-laden films were produced, the vast majority of feature films were devoid of overt political content. Several feature films were classics in their own right, even if the reader might take issue with some of the films' content and biased portrayal of history. Many of the comedies were very amusing, and some of the colour epics were as spectacular as anything being produced by Hollywood at the time and deserve to be acknowledged as such. Even some of the famous documentaries contained scenes which were actually rather unflattering in their portrayal of Nazi Germany.

Consequently, this book serves to expose some of the myths which have emerged about Nazi film propaganda and, by dispassionately examining the content and background of a film as a whole, rather than by concentrating on specific excerpts, it highlights both the triumphs and the failures, the truth and the lies, in a search for hard facts among the myriad of conflicting reviews which often exist.

Many of the films examined in this book were banned by the Allies at the end of the war, but as time has passed and new generations arise with no direct association with that period, several of these films, although often censored versions, are now becoming more generally available. Given that increasing numbers of these films are also now being released with German or English subtitles, it is to be hoped that many readers will be sufficiently intrigued as to watch some of the films for themselves. Even with the benefit of hindsight as to the nature of Nazism and the outcome of the Second World War, it is important to judge for one-self the good, bad and ugly elements of the films and not be unduly influenced by what might be written in this or other books.

I would hope that the lasting message which the book conveys to the reader is a recognition of how every film can be made to serve a propagandistic purpose, and that it is imperative to stay alert to this possibility when viewing virtually any film or newsreport on any subject released today.

Propaganda and its Significance for Hitler

... in every great revolutionary movement that is of world importance, the idea of this movement must always be spread abroad through the operation of propaganda.

– Adolf Hitler, Mein Kampf

What is propaganda?

The noun propaganda derives from the Latin verb '*propagare*' and came to refer to the pre-cutting process employed in the propagation of plants. Early reference to the word is found in the mechanism of the Catholic Church in the seventeenth century with the '*Congregatio de propaganda fide*' (literally, the '*Congregation for the Propagation of the Faith*') and, thereafter, the term tended to be applied to any device used for the promotion of a particular cause.

There are numerous elaborate definitions of what is meant by propaganda today but, in its simplest form, these can best be summarised as follows:

The presentation of information on a particular subject in such a manner as to seek to guide the recipient towards a certain way of thinking or course of action.

Propaganda was initially intended as a positive concept, and it is really only its persistent misuse, primarily in a political context, which has served to devalue its meaning. Consequently, the concept of propaganda nowadays invariably tends to be associated with information which is, at best, misleading or, in the worst case, entirely fallacious.

In order to explore what is actually meant by propaganda in practical terms, it is necessary to begin by dispelling a number of myths as to its nature. Above all, propaganda does not necessitate telling lies, although it can undoubtedly include such methods. Nor does propaganda necessarily involve distorting the truth, although this is a common occurrence. In fact, propaganda frequently involves making statements which might be absolutely true, but where only selected facts are reported and in the most negative or positive manner, so as to evoke a specific response from the reader or viewer.

The following is a non-political example of negative propaganda. Let us assume that a particular newspaper has been undertaking a concerted campaign with the specific aim of

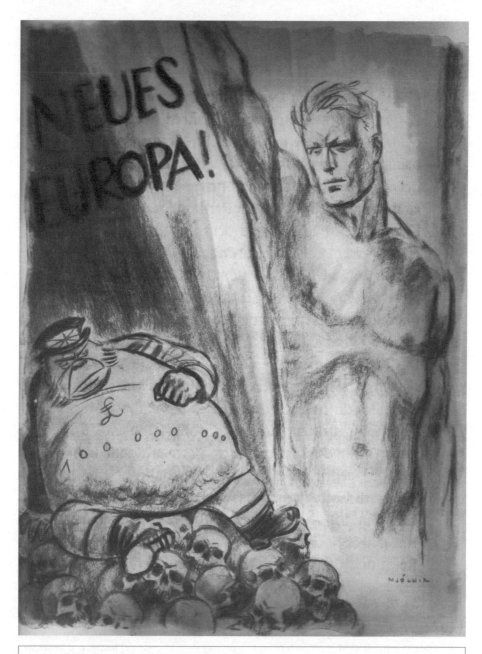

Inner cover of a special edition of the *Illustrierter Beobachter*, the Nazis' weekly illustrated magazine. This edition, issued shortly after the outbreak of the Second World War, shows Britain growing fat on the corpses of other nations and roundly condemns England for provoking the war. France was to receive similar criticism in other editions. (*Randall Bytwerk*)

discrediting a football coach. When his team is heavily beaten, the newspaper heaps abuse on the unfortunate coach for poor team selection, poor tactics and a lack of leadership, and includes quotes from fans supporting this view. The fact that half of the regular team was ill with influenza and that the manager was in hospital with appendicitis on the day of the match is simply not reported. Therefore, while the newspaper was factually correct, it plainly failed to provide a balanced report as to the reasons for the defeat. In a free society, another newspaper should be able to give the whole story, allowing the general public to reach its own objective conclusions. However, in a society where there is absolute control over media production, then the true facts might well be successfully concealed.

In a political context, during the Falklands War in 1982 between Britain and Argentina, the British government decreed that only a limited number of journalists would be permitted to travel on board the British aircraft carrier accompanying the task-force and to participate in the official press briefings. The Ministry of Defence tightly controlled the flow of information, and the journalists were largely dependent on access to the satellite communications controlled by the military for the submission of reports back to the UK. Journalists' reports were pre-censored and they were occasionally fed false information by the British authorities, designed to mislead the Argentineans as to their true intentions. The journalists were often prevented from witnessing the actual fighting and it was fifty-four days before any photographs of the conflict emerged. When HMS *Coventry* was sunk, it took more than twelve hours for the information to be released in the House of Commons. If anyone tried to gain an unbiased impression of the true situation by listening to news reports from foreign radio or TV stations, then they were going to be sadly disillusioned, since the same reports were often translated word for word from the original accounts in English. Consequently, the rest of the world could never be certain that it was being provided with an objective assessment of the progress of that war.

Even today, propaganda is still at the forefront of almost every aspect of modern existence, be it from the reporting of the wars in Iraq and Afghanistan or in government election broadcasts in America or Britain, and all despite the widespread use of the internet and satellite technology for the dissemination of information. One can only imagine how much easier it was for the Nazis to dictate propaganda output in Germany in the 1930s and 1940s, often for far more sinister purposes, and when there were far greater limitations on the types of media to which the masses could turn for information and entertainment.

What did the concept of propaganda mean for Hitler?

Quite simply, if it had not been for his generally effective use of propaganda, it is doubtful whether Hitler would ever have been able to gain power in Germany, let alone achieve and retain support for another war.

Poster for the promotion of *Mein Kampf* by Adolf Hitler. *(BArch, Bild 003-002-005/FR)*

Propaganda meant everything to the Nazis and, when it came to war, was considered by Hitler to be a weapon of the first order, playing just as important a role as more traditional weapons of destruction. It was such an important concept in the mind of Hitler that two chapters of his book, *Mein Kampf* (My Struggle), contain the word in their title, and passing reference is also made to its importance in other sections of the book.

As a disillusioned veteran, Hitler is quick to highlight the importance of Allied propaganda in the defeat of Germany in the First World War and, conversely, Germany's complete naïvety in the employment of such an important weapon in support of its own cause.

He complains how the British and French had been far more effective in using propaganda to blame Germany for the Great War, depicting the Germans as barbarians with terrible weapons of destruction, while making no reference to their own such weapons. The English propaganda war against German soldiers, which began in 1915, had swollen into a storm flood by 1918. Hitler explains how, at first, the Germans had laughed at the content of the enemy leaflets, but gradually they became more influential, and, by the end, the Germans believed that anything they heard from their own side was untrue. The position was not helped by negative letters from home, criticism from their own press and the outbreak of a number of damaging strikes when the German nation could least afford them. He firmly believed that the strikes encouraged the enemy and indirectly led to the deaths of many thousands of German soldiers.

Hitler also blames Germany's downfall on much of the information pedalled by the press and is obsessed by the fact that, with only a rare exception, the press was controlled by Marxists and Jews.

By far the most effective branch of political education, which in this connection is best expressed by the word 'propaganda', is carried on by the press.

Ironically, such was his perception of the influence of the press that, once he came to power, Hitler simply sought to ensure that all the media were subsequently controlled by the Nazis for expounding their own messages.

HITLER'S VIEWS ON EFFECTIVE PROPAGANDA

The art of propaganda consists in putting a matter so clearly and forcibly before the minds of the people as to create a general conviction regarding the reality of a certain fact, the necessity of certain things and the just character of something that is essential.

Hitler clearly recognised that propaganda was simply a means to an end, and its success could only be judged by the end it was intended to serve. His war experiences did lead him to deduce that the first condition of propaganda is that it should *not* be objective, but rather that it display a systematically one-sided attitude towards every problem that has to be handled.

He compares the exercise to a poster for soap, whereby the onlooker would naturally shake his head if an advert for some new brand of soap insisted on highlighting the excellent qualities of competitive brands. He concludes that the aim of propaganda is not to try to pass judgement on conflicting rights, but rather to emphasise exclusively the right which your side is asserting.

Accordingly, he felt that the sole responsibility for the First World War should have been attributed to England, rather than tacitly accepting that Germany shared some responsibility for the war. Whereas English propaganda prevented any comment which might have raised doubt as to who was to blame for the war, he was conscious that the Germans became hesitant and distrustful when they were led to believe by their own people that the enemy might have some right on his side.

'The Führer is always right'. A typical weekly quotation poster issued by the Nazis – designed to inspire the masses. (*Randall Bytwerk*)

Much of Hitler's views on propaganda also arose from his sneaking admiration for the masterly way the Marxist Socialists employed propaganda, and he accepted that the correct use of propaganda is an art in itself. He had been mesmerised by their hour-long processions through the city and the impassioned speeches, and was determined that his movement could learn from their example.

This also taught him the importance of audience differentiation. While it was quite appropriate to employ logical, reasoned propaganda to persuade intellectuals to a certain way of thinking, he realised that, for the masses, cruder methods had to be adopted, whereby only constant repetition succeeds in imprinting an idea on the memory of the general populace.

Hitler's many insightful reflections on propaganda provide a fascinating background to the propaganda films which will be reviewed later in this book and, in summary, his key observations are:

◊ Propaganda should be focused
◊ Propaganda has to be consistent and persistent
◊ Propaganda should never be weakened through objective analysis
◊ Propaganda should be limited to a few simple themes or slogans, and these should be repeated time and again

It is worth noting how confident Hitler had been when he entered the German Labour Party in 1921, as he had immediately taken charge of their propaganda campaign and evidently had tremendous belief in his own ability to utilise propaganda effectively.

> ... I was tormented more than once by the thought that if Providence had put the conduct of German propaganda into my hands, instead of into the hands of incompetent and even criminal ignoramuses and weaklings, the outcome of the struggle [i.e. the Great War] might well have been different.

It was a shortcoming which he was absolutely determined would not be repeated in 1939.

CHAPTER II

THE CONTROL OF FILM PROPAGANDA UNDER THE NAZIS

THE REICH'S MINISTRY FOR PUBLIC ENLIGHTENMENT AND PROPAGANDA

Given the importance which Hitler placed on the value of propaganda, it comes as no surprise that when the Nazis did gain power in January 1933, one of their top priorities was to establish the *Reichsministerium für Volksaufklärung und Propaganda* (Reich's Ministry for Public Enlightenment and Propaganda).

Headed by Dr Joseph Goebbels, the ministry was responsible for controlling all media and culture, with the intention of manipulating the 'spiritual' direction of Germany according to

Nazi ideology and beliefs. From fairly humble beginnings, the ministry was to employ more than 2,000 employees in seventeen different departments by the outbreak of war, and its budget was to increase to 187 million Reichsmarks by 1941.

The ministry wielded direct power over every aspect of media and culture through which the general populace might be influenced, including the German and foreign press, literature, art, music, theatre, films, radio and television. While Goebbels had always considered the radio to be the most effective means of reaching and influencing the masses, he did recognise the propaganda potential of large-screen cinema, as it was easy to comprehend and had more appeal to the emotions.

The Ministry for Public Enlightenment and Propaganda (Mauerstraße, Berlin, in 1939). (*BArch, Bild 146-1985-013-24/Hagemann, Otto*)

Dr Joseph Goebbels: As head of the Propaganda Ministry, Goebbels often re-wrote film scripts and personally selected directors and cast members. (*BArch, Bild 146-1968-101-20A/Hoffmann, H.*)

Within the ministry, the *Reichsfilmkammer* (Reich's Film Chamber) was charged with exercising control over the whole film industry across Germany. As Hitler had argued in *Mein Kampf* that it was the Jewish control of media which was largely to blame for Germany's defeat in the First World War, the Nazis were determined to remove their 'treacherous influence' this time round. Therefore, by stipulating that only those of German descent and nationality were allowed to become members of the chamber, such a restriction ensured the indirect removal of the vast majority of Jews from the film industry as producers, directors or actors.

Control was absolute. Scripts had to be submitted prior to the commencement of filming, and nothing could be released for public consumption without the prior approval of the Propaganda Ministry. Notwithstanding, more than thirty feature films were actually well into production or actually completed before the decision was taken for them to be banned – either because of the quality and content of the films or because they were at odds with Nazi ideology. The press coverage of feature films was also strictly controlled. Since Goebbels had banned film criticism, reviews tended simply to guide readers as to what to expect from a film and psychologically prepared them for how they might respond to the content.

Not only would Goebbels indicate to the film companies the sort of films he was seeking at any moment in time, such as more anti-British films during the early war years, but he also frequently intervened in the selection of directors and actors for these films. Indeed, he blatantly abused his position of authority in respect of the choice of actresses for key roles, where a refusal to succumb to his advances could ensure an actress's subsequent failure as a film star.

In an early speech of guidance to film producers, Goebbels demanded that films should capture the spirit of the times while avoiding endless military parades. This was undoubtedly a reference to earlier documentary-type films, with which presumably both the ordinary civilians and the Nazi hierarchy had had their fill.

Having worked as a journalist and bank clerk, and having had his early novels rejected by publishers, it is somewhat ironic that Goebbels should now take an active role in determining the nature and content of films which would be screened in Germany, often personally rewriting scripts and demanding scenes be edited or even re-shot. He even established the German Film Academy in 1938 to ensure that future film directors would recognise what was expected of them by the Nazi regime, and to meet the shortfall of personnel resulting from the increasing exclusion of Jewish employees.

THE REORGANISATION OF THE GERMAN FILM INDUSTRY UNDER THE NAZIS

The German film industry had been in financial difficulty for some time, not helped by the cost of introducing talking movies and subsequent strikes by live musicians concerned that sound films would make them redundant. Consequently, in order to assist the film industry, a *Filmkreditbank* was established on 1 June 1933 to lend money to production companies at competitive rates. Finance was generally available if the producer could raise at least 30 per cent of the production costs elsewhere and could present a good business case as to why the film would enjoy box office success. Of course, such dependence by the industry on state finance also had a direct influence on each film's content and subject matter.

New cinema laws were gradually passed for the positive encouragement of acceptable films through the introduction of a more rigorous censorship regime. Such censorship controls required the pre-submission of scripts, introduced an increased number of film ratings and widened the circumstances according to which a film could be banned. In practice, a film could now be banned for the most spurious of reasons if it could be said to endanger public order, the interests of the state or offend National Socialist, religious, moral or artistic feeling. Such rules did not leave much room for manoeuvre. Apart from the kudos brought by the award of the highest film ratings known as *Prädikate*, such ratings also carried varying financial incentives for the producers in terms of reduced entertainment taxes and an increased share of profits. The highest rating which could be awarded to a film was defined, rather clumsily, as 'politically valuable and artistically especially valuable' and, by 1938, there was a requirement that any film which enjoyed a 'politically valuable' rating had to be screened by cinemas.

Although the reorganisation of the German film industry by the Nazis did initially lead to its increased financial success, German film exports declined significantly from 1935 onwards. The decline was partly due to politically motivated boycotts of German films by the rest of the world, and also to the censorship office's increasing refusal to screen many foreign films on political or racial grounds, resulting in a reciprocal ban on the import of German films by other countries. By early 1941, for example, all American films had been banned from being screened in Germany. The Nazis were forced to act to support the industry by the establishment of a trust company in 1936 which was designed to take a majority shareholding and administer the assets of struggling film companies. By 1939, all the major film companies, i.e. Ufa, Tobis, Terra, Bavaria, Wien-Film and Prag Film AG, had become state-funded companies. Attendance figures at German cinemas did increase significantly and, by 1940, the average citizen was visiting the cinema thirteen times a year compared with only seven visits in 1937–38.

Despite improved profits, however, the industry still failed to resolve all its production problems, and a report released in September 1941 highlighted that the main difficulties besetting the industry were rocketing production costs and delays in the completion of films. In turn, these failings were blamed on the scale of the films being demanded and the constant official intervention in script and scene content. There is no doubt that the combination of a shortage of raw materials such as film stock, key personnel being called away to the war effort and frequent air-raid interruptions, all had an increasingly negative impact on film production. In the belief that further centralisation and the sharing of production facilities would help improve efficiency, the industry was ultimately to become completely nationalised in February 1942, when a new state-owned holding company, Ufa-Film GmbH (known as Ufi), was established to take control of the production and finance of the whole German film industry.

GOEBBELS' PRINCIPLES OF PROPAGANDA

Like Hitler, Goebbels had his own very distinct views on the importance of propaganda and, in his article on 'Goebbels' Principles of Propaganda' (*Propaganda*, Macmillan Press, 1995), Leonard Doob contends that it is possible to deduce from Goebbels' writings a number of principles of propaganda to which he adhered. From the point of view of film propaganda, the most relevant of these principles include:

Propaganda must be planned and executed by only one authority.

Goebbels, himself, was to review a film or newsreel at least three evenings a week.

To be perceived, propaganda must evoke the interest of an audience and must be transmitted through a communication medium which attracts attention.

Apart from the radio, the cinema was considered to be of paramount importance in this regard, with special attention being taken to ensure that bombed cinemas were re-opened again as soon as possible.

Credibility alone must determine whether propaganda output should be true or false.

While Goebbels accepted that truth should be used as often as possible, he also recognised that lies were equally useful if they could not be disproved.

Propaganda must be carefully timed.

While the timing and content of news reports could be carefully controlled, Goebbels did become increasingly frustrated that feature films were delayed in completion and frequently emerged too late to make the impact which had been originally desired.

Propaganda must label events and people with distinctive phrases and slogans, and these must be continually repeated.

This was a principle which Goebbels clearly shared with Hitler. Consequently, in anti-British films, for example, the British/English are repeatedly accused of being untrustworthy and ruthless. Likewise, the Jews are always portrayed as being dirty, devious, greedy and immoral.

Propaganda must avoid the raising of false hopes for your own people and must reinforce a certain degree of anxiety concerning the consequences of defeat.

Without causing undue panic, it was important to strike a balance whereby the enemy was depicted as being a vile and merciless aggressor to whom Germans would not want to consider defeat.

Propaganda should aim to funnel German aggression against specific hate objects.

The list of hate objects was extensive and certainly included Jews, Bolsheviks, Marxists and capitalists.

THE CHANGING NATURE OF FEATURE FILMS AND DOCUMENTARIES DURING THE NAZI ERA

Between 1933 and 1945, more than 1,300[1] feature films, of which more than a hundred were specifically state-commissioned, were produced by German film companies. The focus and degree of propaganda input in each film constantly shifted to reflect the Third Reich's changing priorities throughout its existence. Only around 10 per cent of the films were specifically political in content, and the remaining 90 per cent were a mixture of comedies, revues, adventure and detective films, and musicals. While such entertainment films may not always have contained any direct political message, Goebbels recognised that they were still politically important and rested secure in the knowledge that such works would at least attract the public to the cinemas, where he could control the content of the newsreel and documentary films which would precede or follow the main features.

Promotion of Hitler and the Nazi Party to the German people

On their assumption of power, the Nazis urgently needed films which would extol the virtues of Hitler as Germany's leader and constantly demonstrate to the ordinary people how the Nazis' policies were in the best interests of Germany. As part of the process of persuasion that the removal of democracy in favour of those with the greatest intelligence was a marked benefit, there was extensive film coverage of the impressive special Party Days, where hundreds of thousands of soldiers and spectators would gather to listen to the arousing speeches of Hitler and the main party leaders. Numerous documentaries would feature great public works projects which would remind people how Hitler had successfully reduced unemployment and restored a sense of pride in being German. Life was shown to be far better than under the Weimar Republic, and several feature films creatively documented the stories of the sacrifices made by embellished Nazi heroes in the early struggles (*Kampfzeit*) against the communists.

Promotion of key facets of Nazi ideology

In parallel with the promotion of Hitler, a series of 'educational' documentaries and information films was produced to support key aspects of Nazi philosophy, such as the portrayal of Aryans as a superior race and of Jews as being vile parasites who had always wielded a negative influence on the world. Typically, such films featured disturbing images of asylum inmates and provided countless statistics to support the contention that the compulsory sterilisation of those suffering from hereditary diseases and the introduction of euthanasia would not only protect the superiority of Aryan stock but also have considerable economic benefit, through the closure of many special care homes and hospitals. Such instructional films were also screened to the youth of Germany both through events held for the Hitler Youth and also through regular film periods in school for which attendance was compulsory. Films were also produced to provide guidance to women as to how they should support their country and their husbands in time of war by not just producing more offspring, but also by gradually assuming more civilian and military tasks which had hitherto been the sole preserve of men.

Work honours the woman, as it does the man, but the child ennobles the mother.

---

1   This figure is taken from Dr Alfred Bauer's *Deutsche Spielfilmalmanach 1929–1950* and includes all German-speaking feature films either produced in Germany and Austria, or produced by German companies abroad. It also includes some longer documentary and cultural films screened as part of a general evening programme.

Promotion of Nazi Germany to the rest of world

If it were important to use propaganda to maintain public support for their policies on the Home Front, it was equally important for the Nazis to present an appropriate image to the rest of the world. Pre-war feature films contained little open criticism of the British or American regimes, since these were countries with which Germany was not yet at war and with which it did not even necessarily plan to go to war.

Documentaries would proudly present the rebirth of Germany as a successful nation seemingly at one with itself and where all people were united in support of their great leader. Before the war, the Nazis were keen to present themselves as a peaceful country with no aggressive tendencies other than for self-protection, and the world could not help but be impressed by the scale and logistical prowess of the Germans in their organisation of the 1936 Olympics in Berlin. Even at the very height of the war in 1943, the ability of Germany to release such an epic film as *Münchhausen*, in stunning Agfacolor and full of special effects, earned the admiration of many countries, even those at war with Germany.

Justification of war to the German people

In contrast to the reasonable image presented to the rest of the world before 1939, once war had actually commenced, the Nazis saw a need for the production of a series of feature films justifying why they were at war. It was important to demonstrate to their people how an unjust world had exploited Germany through the Versailles Treaty, and how war was necessary to address their legitimate and reasonable demands. Films which showed Poles ill-treating

'What we are due to lose!' Poster graphically illustrating how much territory and possessions Germany would forfeit as a result of the infamous Versailles Treaty. (*BArch, Plak 002-008-015/Oppenheim, L.*)

their minority German communities were designed to arouse German anger while, through a series of historical films, the British were invariably presented as being wicked imperialists and bullies of smaller nations, who deserved their comeuppance, and against whom war was primarily a means of self-defence.

Morale-boosting films

At the height of the war, a few feature films showed military personnel happily going about their duty at the front, while others were designed to show the unity between the fighting men at the front with civilians back home, signifying that they were locked together in a common struggle. At the same time, many escapist films were primarily produced for entertainment purposes and to divert attention from the war. As the war progressed, Goebbels was increasingly to make a distinction between the outward behaviour of people (*Haltung*) and their inner spirit (*Stimmung*). By 1943, and the war in the Soviet Union having turned against them, Goebbels was to accept that, generally, *Stimmung* was all but dead and that even the German people's outward conduct was becoming a matter of concern. In reality, many Germans believed the war was lost when America entered the war in December 1941 and, although the introduction of the V weapons and early successes in the Battle of the Bulge did bring some encouragement, there was little convincing news which would help to raise morale.

Ultimately, in the final throes of the war, attention turned to producing films which would motivate the citizens towards one final, heroic sacrifice, culminating in the release of *Kolberg* in January 1945. Rather than suffer the ignominy of defeat, this film sought to encourage the general populace to resist the enemy to the very last man and woman, inspired by the supposedly glorious example of the town of Kolberg's successful stand against Napoleon in the early nineteenth century.

Propaganda theory in practice

Having established the theory of propaganda and how the Nazis set in place the structure necessary to deliver the required results, the following chapters will consider a number of specific examples of the various categories of films which were released during the Nazi era and the extent to which the theory was successfully converted into practice. The analysis will reveal that, although many excellent films were produced in terms of artistic merit and even of successful propaganda prowess, there were several instances where the process did not run smoothly and where a combination of factors contributed to some films singularly failing to achieve their intentions.

Chapter III

German Feature Films: Anti-British Propaganda

Background

The notion of producing a number of propagandistic feature films which were specifically anti-British or, more often, anti-English in nature, created a certain dilemma for the Nazis. Hitler had never really wished to go to war with Britain and, indeed, it was actually Neville Chamberlain who had been forced to declare war on Germany on 3 September 1939 because of the failure by the Germans to withdraw from Poland.

In fact, regardless of what might have been said publicly, it is evident that Hitler secretly admired the British for their imperialist successes, and particularly for the way they had managed to govern India and surrounding countries, an area with a population of more than 300 million at the turn of the twentieth century, with only around 70,000 British soldiers.

It is perhaps no surprise, therefore, that one of Hitler's favourite films was *The Lives of a Bengal Lancer* (1935), an American film starring Gary Cooper about heroic British soldiers defending the borders of British India against mutinous tribesmen.

Consequently, German feature films produced prior to 1939, such as *Die Reiter von Deutsch-Ostafrika* (*The Riders of German East Africa*) (1934), which is actually set during the First World War, tended to be more respectful of Britain as an enemy and referred more to the parallels between the British and the Germans as individuals locked in a common struggle, where the sense of patriotic duty forces the participants to behave in an uncharacteristically ruthless manner.

Hitler was fascinated with *The Lives of a Bengal Lancer*. (*Verlag für Filmschriften*)

July 1941: Anti-British cartoon from *Lustige Blätter* showing Churchill nailing Britain together with lies and promises. 'Caution, don't disturb!' (*Randall Bytwerk*)

There were phases between 1932 and 1938 when Hitler was quietly confident that Britain could be persuaded to join Germany in a war across Europe, especially because of Britain's historical pedigree as a colonial power. However, even by 1937, he was starting to reconcile himself to the fact that even if Britain would not unite with Germany, it could at least remain neutral. This optimistic outlook was reinforced by the firm insistence of his foreign minister, Von Ribbentropp, that Britain would never go to war over Poland. Even after September 1939, Hitler still hoped that a peaceful accommodation could be reached with Britain and, while this was the case, it would have been counter-productive to release any particularly vitriolic anti-British propaganda which might have prevented such an agreement or conveyed conflicting messages to the German people.

Nevertheless, just as Goebbels was to request his film production companies to create anti-Semitic films in 1938, likewise, as soon as Britain declared war on Germany, Goebbels asked the film companies to come forward with ideas for anti-British films. But many of these films took some time to come to fruition, and the situation was not helped by Hitler's constant reluctance to undertake such an anti-British propaganda campaign. Goebbels became increasingly frustrated by Hitler's continued hesitancy, especially after Britain refused to accept Germany's offer of peace in July 1940 and, therefore, Goebbels determined to step up anti-British film production, regardless of Hitler's views. Goebbels was quite convinced that ordinary Germans were sympathetic to Britain's complete defeat, and he wanted to exploit such aggressive emotions.

Goebbels made very clear his own view of the English in an article entitled '*Englands Schuld*' (England's Guilt), which appeared in a special edition of *Illustrierter Beobachter* in the autumn of 1939, in which he ruefully complained that England had forced the war on Germany – 'England is responsible for the war and will have to pay for it!'

By April 1941, he declared that the German propaganda war against Britain was entering a new phase, and he encouraged the media to emphasise that England's history was based on three themes – lies, the breaking of promises and brute force. Indeed, a number of earlier films did not have an anti-British plot focus, but nevertheless hinted at the unsporting nature of the British. *Morgenrot* (*Sunrise*) (1933), the first film released during the Nazi era, shows a First World War U-boat being lured into a trap by a flagless sailing ship manned by British sailors in civilian clothes. The British eventually hoist a Danish flag and switch this for a British ensign only at the very instant that they open fire with a cannon concealed behind the rigging. In *Pour le Mérite* (1938), when a captured British First World War pilot requests permission to go to the rest room, the Germans do not ask him to give his word of honour not to try to escape since he is a 'gentleman'. However, he does take the opportunity to escape, illustrating how little the British could be trusted to conduct themselves in an honourable fashion.

Goebbels' final request was that he wanted film-makers to draw a clear distinction between the ordinary British citizens, their government and war-mongers. These were distinctions which the Allies were also often to draw in their films and speeches at that time.

ANTI-BRITISH FILMS REVIEWED

In order of chronological release, the five anti-British or anti-English films analysed in the following pages are: *Der Fuchs von Glenarvon* (1940), *Das Herz der Königin* (1940), *Mein Leben für Irland* (1941), *Ohm Krüger* (1941) and *Titanic* (1943).

These particular films have been chosen because they are representative of the type of anti-English material produced at the time, the varying degrees of intensity of propaganda they exhibit and because these films are likely to be of most interest to the modern English-speaking viewer or reader. The first four films condemn the excesses of English imperialism and all the films attack almost every aspect of the English character. The bulk of their venom, however, is deliberately directed towards the English ruling classes rather than against the ordinary working man.

As their names suggest, *Der Fuchs von Glenarvon* (*The Fox of Glenarvon*) and *Mein Leben für Irland* (*My Life for Ireland*) are both set in Ireland, and have as their theme the oppression of the Irish by the English/British and the resistance shown by the Irish to gain their freedom. *Der Fuchs von Glenarvon* is entirely fictional while *Mein Leben für Irland* is clearly centred on the events surrounding the Dublin uprisings of 1921.

Dr Carl Peters winning the support of local tribes in his bid for the German colonisation of East Africa in *Carl Peters*. (*Deutsches Filminstitut, Frankfurt/ Friedrich – Wilhelm-Murnau Stiftung (FWM)*)

Luis Trenker, Lotte Koch and Peter Petersen trying to distribute medicine to the African natives in *Germanin* in the face of British opposition. (*Deutsches Filminstitut/FWM*)

Both are entertaining thrillers and enjoyed considerable box office success. The launch of these two Irish films was to occur either side of the release of another film in November 1940, which also focused on England's alleged historic abuse of its power on the other nations of the British Isles, namely *Das Herz der Königin* (*The Heart of the Queen*). On this occasion, the film recounts the story of England's intervention in Scottish affairs with Queen Elizabeth I's cruel betrayal and then ultimate execution of Mary, Queen of Scots.

Apart from England's abuse of its closest neighbours, the Nazis were keen to condemn Britain's wider imperialist ambitions, and its cruel and ruthless activities are recorded in a number of films set in Africa, including *Carl Peters* (1941) and *Germanin – Die Geschichte einer Kolonialen Tat* (*Germanin – The Story of a Colonial Deed*) (1943).

Set towards the end of the nineteenth century, *Carl Peters* recounts the legend of Dr Carl Peters, who had been determined to establish colonial possessions for the Germans in Africa so as to guarantee Germany's future supply of raw materials. While his main adversaries are the British, who already control much of Africa, Peters also faces hostility from a high-ranking official, Leo Kayser, and a German Member of Parliament, both of whom are Jews and fearful for their own positions if he should succeed. Undertaking a first expedition at his own expense, Peters soon wins the support of a number of tribes in East Africa. They are all willing to enter into a treaty with Germany when he promises to protect them from the dreaded slave traders who, until then, have been given permission by the British to undertake such business. The English are shown to be devious colonialists who try to steal the treaties before they reach the German authorities and even plot to have Peters murdered. Despite his many successes and his eventual appointment as commissioner for German East Africa, Peters is ultimately forced to resign by his Jewish enemies, primarily because he had authorised the execution of a couple of natives for murdering his colleagues. Ashamed of his own people for kowtowing to the English, Peters takes comfort in the knowledge that he has played his part in opposing British supremacy in the region and in establishing a strong German base in East Africa.

Germanin tells the story of Professor Dr Achenbach, who had been working in Africa on a cure for the sleeping sickness spread by the Tsetse fly. His research is interrupted by the outbreak of the First World War and the resultant destruction of his laboratory by the British. Even after the war, the British refuse to allow him to distribute *Germanin*, the trade name for Germany's cure for the virus, because they are concerned that this will harm Britain's colonial dominance. The British deliberately feed false information to the natives about the drug and even have it destroyed. Ironically, both Achenbach and the British Colonel Crosby, simultaneously fall victim to the disease and, with only one undamaged dose of the drug remaining, Achenbach sacrifices his own life for Crosby's, on the condition that Crosby will allow *Germanin* to be distributed across Africa. Throughout the film, the British are depicted as arrogant, heartless colonialists who show no human compassion for their African subjects, while the sympathetic Germans are prepared to sacrifice their own lives for the sake of the whole African nation.

Ohm Krüger, however, is far and away the most controversial and extravagant of the Africa-based films. Completed in April 1941, it was one of the most expensive films produced during the Nazi era and recounts the depressing story of Britain's early exploitation of South Africa and portrays the British/English in an exceptionally vile and despicable manner.

Titanic, which was released in 1943, is a re-working of the well-known disaster but with the introduction of a number of fictitious German characters and a harsh condemnation of the English/American capitalist behaviour which had provoked the tragedy and led to such a loss of life. The review exposes how events associated with the film are almost as heart-rending as the tragedy on which the film is based and includes the death of the film's director in a Gestapo prison prior to the film's completion.

The irony of all these films is that their primary audience was always going to be either German civilians or military personnel, and possibly also inhabitants of those countries which the Germans had invaded, although, as will be explained later, the screening of such films in occupied countries occasionally had unexpected consequences for the Nazis.

These films were never released in the likes of Ireland, which remained neutral during the war, or in South Africa, which eventually sided with the Allies, and it is, therefore, impossible to gauge how the films would have been received in those countries. Nevertheless, it seems unlikely that the screening of these films would have incited such patriotic, anti-English sentiments as to have led to those nations being actually prepared to side with the Nazis against Britain and the Allies. At worst, the films might have fostered some indifference as to the outcome or perhaps even some resentment towards the British, but such is the fickle nature of propaganda that they might just as easily have become a source of amusement for apparently giving such one-sided representations of history.

Film title: *Der Fuchs von Glenarvon*
Year of release: 1940
Type: Feature film
Primary purpose: Anti-English/British and pro-Irish propa-
      ganda/entertainment
Director: Max W. Kimmich
Principal stars:

Karl Ludwig Diehl	(Baron John Ennis of Loweland)
Tim Elsholtz	(Tim Malory)
Richard Häussler	(Major McKenney)
Werner Hinz	(Sir John Tetbury)
Ferdinand Marian	(Justice of the Peace Grandison)
Olga Tschechowa	(Gloria Grandison)

INTRODUCTION

Der Fuchs von Glenarvon (*The Fox of Glenarvon*) is the first of two specifically pro-Irish and, by implication, anti-British films produced on the orders of Goebbels. The film is based on a 1937 book by Nicola Rohn and was directed by Max Kimmich, who just happened to be Goebbels' brother-in-law.

It is a thrilling tale about the struggle by the Irish to win back their freedom after 800 years of oppressive British[2] control, and every opportunity is taken to paint the English in a poor light and to arouse the viewer's sympathy for Ireland and its long-suffering people.

It is somewhat ironic, therefore, that by the time this film was screened in 1940, Ireland had already virtually regained its full independence in a process that began in 1922, and the 'crimes' of which the English are accused are exactly the same misdemeanours for which the Nazi regime would be charged by the Allies both during and after the war.

PLOT SUMMARY

The film is set in early twentieth-century Ireland, with the prologue explaining the background and influencing the viewer as to what to expect from the film.

> *Ireland – the green island is one of the oldest victims of forced rule by the English! For eight hundred years, the methods of British politics have been deceit, forgery, robbery, murder and arson. The millions who were starved, expelled or executed bear witness to the passion*

---

2   As with virtually all of the Nazis' anti-British films, there is no attempt to distinguish between the terms 'British' and 'Eng-
     lish' and quotations given in this book simply translate the actual German word used in the film.

Ennis, Grandison and Gloria in discussion after the sinking of the New Zealand. (Deutsches Filminstitut/FWM)

of this people. But the pride and love of freedom of the Irish could not be broken.

After an initial scene in which a group of dark 'Ribbonmen' recite an oath about England being their enemy, the action moves to the house of the Justice of the Peace, an Englishman called Grandison. Two of the Ribbonmen are seeking Grandison's intervention on behalf of their colleagues who are to be transported to the death cell in Belfast the following day. Grandison appears sympathetic, but the viewer soon discovers that he is playing a double game, since he warns the prison governor to transport the prisoners early the following morning so as to avoid any trouble. Grandison tries to conceal his duplicity from his charming Irish wife, Gloria, but admits that being an official in the service of the King of England makes it difficult for him to find a middle way between his duty and her soft heart.

The following day, a coach containing Baron John Ennis of Loweland comes upon an abandoned prison transport wagon in the swamplands from which the prisoners have been freed. Other police arrive and explain that the wagon had been attacked by the Ribbonmen, as is evident from the tell-tale bunch of ribbons which has been left beside the bodies of two dead policemen. Grandison arrives and is introduced to Sir Ennis whom it transpires has been abroad for seven years. The reason for his departure is linked to the death of his wife, who had been struck down by English machine-gun fire while Ennis had been involved with the Irish independence movement.

Later, Ennis agrees to lend the Ribbonmen two horses for a funeral cortège and is subsequently welcomed by their leader as someone who had a good reputation as a fighter for Ireland. Ennis then attends the wake for the dead, during which a woman, who turns out to be Gloria, sings a very moving lament.

The action moves to a ballroom where a rather heated debate ensues regarding Irish politics, and Ennis voices his disquiet about the rumoured arrival of the notorious Sir John Tetbury, who is being sent from England to keep order in Ireland. Requested to sing during the ball, Gloria is immediately recognised by Ennis as the woman who had attended the secret funeral, although she insists he is mistaken. He is enchanted by her and shocked to learn that she is married to Grandison. On returning home, it becomes obvious that, although Grandison is madly in love with his wife, the feeling is not reciprocated and she does not really trust him.

The scene changes swiftly to a stormy night, when despite the best efforts of Ennis, Gloria and a rescue team, a ship, the New Zealand, is wrecked on the rocks with the loss of thirty lives. Ennis reports to Grandison that no light had been shining from the lighthouse, and Grandison concludes that the ship had been deliberately lured towards the rocks, asserting that this was the work of the Ribbonmen who knew that Tetbury was meant to be on-board.

The viewer soon learns that Grandison, probably for insurance reasons since we later learn that he had a financial interest in the ship, had actually arranged for one of his employees,

The notorious Sir John Tetbury played by
Werner Hinz. (*Deutsches Filminstitut/FWM*)

Malory, to lure the ship onto the rocks by shining a diversionary lamp from the former light house. Although neither Grandison nor Malory knew that Tetbury was going to be on board the ship, this turns out to be rather fortuitous since it firmly points all suspicion towards the Ribbonmen. Grandison also arranges for an eagle-eyed coastguard to be murdered to conceal the true cause of the wreck.

In the meantime, Ennis, who is in love with Gloria, asks her to warn the Ribbonmen that they are under suspicion. While she refuses to accept that her husband is hostile to the Ribbonmen, she does contend that the marriage has helped prevent a lot of evil. Despite her own feelings for Ennis, she is resolute that she and Ennis should not see each other any more. Shortly thereafter, Ennis is arrested by the authorities for the murder of the coastguard, primarily because he was the only outsider who knew the coastguard was going to be examining the former light house, and because a bullet from Ennis's Winchester had been found.

Gloria eventually reveals to Grandison that Ennis cannot be guilty as she had been with Ennis at the hunting lodge at the very time of the shooting. After a short argument, Grandison agrees to convey her testimony, provided that she never sees Ennis again. Ennis is subsequently released from prison on condition that he leaves Ireland and never returns.

Having arrived safely on a later ship, Tetbury is determined to introduce more ruthless methods of control. He remarks to Grandison that the latter has been somewhat unlucky, what with the freeing of prisoners from the transport, the sinking of the *New Zealand* and the release of Ennis because of an alibi which Grandison had provided himself. There is also an implicit threat when Tetbury mentions that Grandison is married to an Irish woman. Grandison pleads for his wife not to be implicated in the affair, and this is seemingly agreed, provided that Grandison supplies the names of suspected rebels and the places where they congregate.

Presumably as a result of a tip-off from Grandison, Tetbury and his men then violently disrupt a church service, but the Ribbonmen, who had been holding a meeting in the sacristy of the church, manage to escape just in time. Gloria finally accepts that her husband was the informer and tells him that she is leaving him.

The final action moves to the tavern where a kangaroo court is assembled by the Ribbonmen to determine who has betrayed them. Earlier, Malory had planted blame on Ennis as he had been arrested but then released again for no apparent reason. Both Grandison and Ennis agree to participate in the proceedings and, in what is a blatant lie, Grandison supports Malory's account and confirms to the court that Tetbury had told him that Ennis had been released as a stool pigeon. Ennis's fate seems sealed despite his protestations of innocence and his claim that it is actually Grandison who had betrayed them in the church, sunk the *New Zealand* and had arranged for the murder of the coastguard.

Fortunately, Gloria arrives at that very moment to warn them all that it is a trap and that the English soldiers are approaching. She is asked to swear an oath of loyalty to the Ribbonmen

A secret meeting of the Ribbonmen under the church. (*Deutsches Filminstitut/FWM*)

and, as tension mounts, she reluctantly concedes that her husband had been behind the attack by the soldiers in the church. Grandison is seized by the Ribbonmen and a rope placed round his neck, so that when the soldiers eventually arrive at the burning tavern, they find 'the fox' hanging dead from a beam. Several of the soldiers and their horses then become trapped in the swamp and some die, leaving the Ribbonmen, Gloria and Ennis to escape. While their leader contends it is too early to celebrate and that freedom is still some way away, Ennis is quick to add, 'but this will be a sign for all Ireland!'

The film finishes on a high note with rousing music as the Ribbonmen, Gloria and Ennis march in step across the marshes, their burning torches raised high as they join together in the inspiring chorus of a freedom song.

CRITICAL REVIEW

While *Der Fuchs von Glenarvon* is primarily an exciting piece of fiction, its aim is not just to entertain but also to portray the English as ruthless oppressors of Ireland, and to create in the mind of the viewer a common bond between the Germans and the Irish in their fight for victory over the English.

The film moves at speed, although there are instances where the sub-plots seem to have been hastily contrived simply to allow the focus of the main plot to succeed. For example, there is no clear explanation as to why Grandison arranged for Malory to lure the ship on to the rocks or why it was so important to prevent the coastguard revealing that a false light had been shone from the old lighthouse. After all, the coastguard's revelations would still have allowed the Ribbonmen to be named as the likely culprits. Consequently, we can only surmise that the only reason why the coastguard has to be killed is so that suspicion can be directed towards Ennis, because his subsequent arrest and all that arises from that arrest is central to the whole storyline. This criticism apart, the film is certainly an effective vehicle of propaganda against the English.

Nature of the anti-English propaganda contained in the film

In terms of anti-English propaganda, the case against the English is constructed in three ways.

Historical context
The first means of vilifying the English is to paint a damning picture of what English rule has meant for the beautiful island of Ireland and its innocent people. The opening captions leave the viewer in no doubt that the English have been merciless oppressors who have resorted to deceit and murder to achieve their ends, and that the film will proceed to provide

Tetbury rounding up suspects in the church. (*Deutsches Filminstitut/FWM*)

continuing examples of such crimes.

There are repeated references to the 'English methods' of keeping order, which are obviously considered to be inhumane and draconian. Such oppression ranges from the confiscation of horses to the execution of ordinary citizens simply 'for loving their country'. Ennis's manservant neatly summarises the current position in his complaint to his master:

> *The English burnt down a whole village because farmers hid a few men. It is much harder to be a good Irishman than it used to be.*

Characterisation of the English masters

The second form of propaganda relates to the deliberately negative portrayal of the characters of *all* the individual English personalities in the film.

Grandison, the Justice of the Peace, is utterly unprincipled and is guilty of crimes which range from mendacity to murder. He pretends to be sympathetic to the Irish cause while all the time alerting the authorities to their activities, either through duty or for personal gain. He lies to his wife about trying to assist the Irish and gives false testimony against Ennis in the trial scene, when he claims that Tetbury had released Ennis as a stool pigeon.

Devoted to his Irish wife, Grandison is so desperate to prevent her from being investigated by the English authorities that he is even prepared to betray the names of the Irish conspirators and their meeting places to Tetbury. However, his duplicity stretches far beyond what might reasonably be expected of an English official, as can be seen by his responsibility for the callous sinking of the *New Zealand* and the cold-blooded murder of the coastguard. Apart from his hopeless infatuation with Gloria, he does not possess a shred of decency.

The English military authorities are just as ruthless, and are rightly feared and hated. The officer who demands that Ennis must leave Ireland for an exile 'without a prescribed timescale' resembles Lord Kitchener and behaves in an officious, arrogant and threatening manner. There is a menacing undertone that if Ennis continues to complain about their judgement, then something even worse will happen to him.

If Grandison is lacking in any moral decency, then the dreaded Sir John Tetbury is shown to be even more cunning and brutal. He has absolutely no qualms about using excessive force and underhand tactics to achieve his ends, as is evidenced by his nickname the 'Hangman of India' due to his activities in the colonies. By hinting at Grandison's incompetence and making veiled accusations against Grandison's Irish wife, he virtually blackmails Grandison, who is, after all, supposed to be on his side, into revealing where the Irish conspirators hold their meetings. Tetbury's brutal intervention in the midst of the church service, with innocent worshippers being shot or knocked to the ground, is another example of his ruthless determination to achieve success at any cost.

The secret romance between Ennis and Gloria. (*Deutsches Filminstitut/FWM*)

It is worth noting that both the Allies and the German film-makers were keen to portray attacks within places of worship as particularly heinous crimes, and it is a frequent motif in films of the period, including *Freedom Radio* (1941) and *Went The Day Well?* (1942) when the Nazis were cast as the evil perpetrators instead of the British.

The creation of a common bond between the Irish and the Germans

The third form of propaganda is the empathy which gradually develops throughout the film towards the Irish and the feeling that the Germans share a common bond with the Irish in their struggle against the English.

In contrast to the negative depiction of the English, the Irish are characterised as kind-hearted, generous, God-fearing people, who seek nothing more than freedom for their country. Specific individuals such as Gloria and Ennis are shown to be honourable, coura-geous and altruistic.

It would appear that Gloria never really loved her husband but has sacrificed her happi-ness for the sake of Ireland:

It is not a question of what is good for me. I am Irish and I have a duty to fulfil.

She still accepts, however, that falling in love with Ennis is wrong and is torn between her duty as a patriot and as a wife when she has to admit, under oath, that it was her husband rather than Ennis who had betrayed the Ribbonmen to the English authorities.

Sir John Ennis is the respectable aristocrat who has already suffered for Ireland through the murder of his wife by the English. He is very discreet in his dealings with Gloria so as to protect her from any scandal. He displays a total lack of concern for his own welfare by lending horses to the Ribbonmen, risking his life to try to save the *New Zealand* and by agreeing to participate in the kangaroo court proceedings, even though all the suspicion pointed towards him.

A number of more subtle insertions are also employed to reinforce the German viewer's feelings of solidarity with the Irish and their shared cause. In the opening scenes, the Ribbonmen are shown reciting an oath of unity which concludes with the question, 'Who is our enemy?' to which they all respond in unison, 'England!' It is evident that most German viewers would have had no difficulty in swearing the same oath, as England was indeed perceived to be the common enemy. This 'link' with the Nazis is also to be found in the dark clothes and long boots worn by the Ribbonmen, in their various oaths and ceremonies, in the ribbons being adopted as a symbol of their existence, just like the swastika, and in the final marching scene with lit torches, where the rousing freedom songs are all very evocative of Nazi night-time parades in Nürnberg.

Likewise, at the ball, the viewer has to admire the pluckiness of the handsome, young man (reminiscent of an archetypal Nazi Youth member) who boldly makes his political feelings known to Grandison:

Where does England get the right to be involved here? We, Irish, were a free people when England was governed by Rome!

In the final denouement, when the English soldiers become trapped in the swamp and the Ribbonmen are able to escape, Ennis exclaims, 'It is a sign for all Ireland', because the Irish have been able to win at least one battle with the English. However, it might as well have read that it was a sign for all of Germany, as the German audience will leave the cinema in good spirits as if, through this example of the Irish, the Germans too will achieve victory over the wicked English.

Underlying irony of the film

It is somewhat ironic that the film should be so enthusiastic in supporting this small Irish nation against its English oppressors. How could such condemnation of English techniques really stack up when compared with a ruthless Nazi regime which was prepared to force its authority on large and small nations across the whole of Europe?

The ultimate paradox is found in the callous manner that Tetbury and his fellow officers achieve their ends. Showing no mercy or respect for holy places, fabricating evidence and banishing people from their own country without just cause were certainly characteristics which the Allies would have more readily identified with the worst excesses of Nazi power. The scene where Grandison is intimidated because his wife is Irish can have differed little from 1940s Germany, where having a Jewish wife would have been just as dangerous. Similarly, Ennis's complaint during the interview before his arrest that he did not know it was a crime to express reservations about English methods must have struck some chord with those subject to a Nazi-controlled state.

One has to ask whether a German audience would have been completely oblivious to such apparent parallels, even if they would not have dared to voice such an opinion openly, or whether, flushed with Hitler's early military successes, they were indeed blinded to the reality of the tyrannical regime under which they now existed.

POINTS OF NOTE CONCERNING THE PRODUCTION OF THE FILM AND ITS RECEPTION

Was the film a financial and propaganda success?

The actual filming for this production commenced in December 1939 and was completed within a remarkably short period of only three months. However, even though the film was directed by his brother-in-law, Goebbels still insisted on re-working a number of scenes before its initial screening in Berlin on 24 April 1940. Goebbels was very satisfied with the final result and commented in his diary that month:

Fuchs von Glenarvon ... is wonderful now, and will come in very useful for our propaganda.

Assisted by its prestigious cast, the film was well received in Germany, and it certainly achieved Goebbels' primary aim of combining entertainment with a convincing propaganda message, while the censors awarded it an 'artistically worthy' rating. Press comment was quick to emphasise how the film told the truth about the oppression of the Irish people by the unscrupulous English. However, this enthusiasm by Goebbels for such pro-Irish films was not to last and following the release of *Mein Leben für Irland* in 1941, Goebbels decreed that no more films of this type should be produced.

What became of the director and the principal actors in the film?

The director, Max Kimmich, had married Goebbels' youngest sister in 1938 and, although already a successful screenwriter, his career as a director only really advanced under the Nazis, for whom he was to work on a number of anti-British films. After the war, the ban on his films imposed by the Allies was eventually lifted in the early 1950s, and he continued to work in a variety of capacities in the film industry.

The career of Olga Tschechowa (Gloria) blossomed under the Nazis and she never concealed that she was close friends with both Hitler and Goebbels, the latter considering her to be a 'charming lady'. As her name suggests, however, she was of Russian descent and, following her death, the Soviets released information which suggests that she had, in fact, served as a secret agent for the communists during the war years.

Ferdinand Marian (Grandison) was one of the most well-known actors of the period, appearing in countless propaganda films and almost exclusively in the role of the villain. He was to die in a suspicious car crash in 1946.

Despite starring in a number of other anti-British Nazi propaganda films, the acting career of Werner Hinz (Sir John Tetbury) was to continue to flourish after the war, including a key role in *The Longest Day* in 1962.

CONCLUSION

Der Fuchs von Glenarvon incorporated many features which make a film commercially successful – tension, courage, mystery, love and an uplifting ending – and it just so happened that it also made effective anti-English propaganda. In style, it is far more akin to the sort of propaganda films being produced by the Allies, that is to say 'pure fiction', albeit placed in a semi-historical setting, and it is little wonder that it was well received at the German box office. Undoubtedly, England did operate an oppressive regime in Ireland for many years, which rightly deserves to be acknowledged but, quite understandably from a German view-point, the film is careful to avoid any reference to German methods of occupation. The oppression to which the Irish had been subjected by the English bore no comparison with the treatment which the Nazis were meting out in the countries which they were currently conquering across Europe and even against their own opponents within Germany. It was, therefore, important that the English/British should always be considered an even more despotic nation than Germany, rather than an innocent victim struggling for survival against Nazi tyranny.

In the final analysis, propaganda is not about giving a balanced perspective but about achieving the desired response from the viewer and, in respect of a German audience at least, *Der Fuchs von Glenarvon* certainly realised that objective.

Film title: *Das Herz der Königin*
Year of release: 1940
Type: Feature film
Primary purpose: Anti-English propaganda/
          entertainment
Director: Carl Froelich
Principal stars:

Axel von Ambesser	(Lord Henry Darnley)
Enrico Benfer	(David Riccio)
Willy Birgel	(Lord Bothwell)
Lotte Koch	(Johanna Gordon)
Maria Koppenhöfer	(Queen Elizabeth I)
Zarah Leander	(Mary, Queen of Scots)
Will Quadflieg	(Olivier)
Walther Suessenguth	(Lord Jacob Stuart)

INTRODUCTION

Released in November 1940, *Das Herz der Königin* (*The Heart of the Queen*) tells the sad story of the life of Mary, Queen of Scots and boasted one of Germany's most celebrated actresses, Zarah Leander, in the key role. With little alteration to the true events to which the story relates, the Nazis sought to manipulate the account for their own anti-English propaganda purposes, depicting Queen Elizabeth's treatment of Mary and Scotland as yet another historical example of English belligerence and unwarranted meddling in the affairs of other nations.

While the film was not particularly successful at the box office at the time, the Allies still felt that it was sufficiently contentious to have it banned from further screening in Germany at the end of the war, primarily because the film was regarded as being unjustifiably negative in its condemnation of the English and falsified history. However, by November 1952 the film was permitted to be screened again and is still freely available as a DVD in Germany today.

PLOT SUMMARY

The film begins with a brief explanation of how there had once been a time when Scotland and England were separate independent nations and how Mary, Queen of Scots (Maria Stuart) had returned from France to assume the throne of Scotland. Driven by hatred and jealousy, Queen Elizabeth of England plotted Mary's downfall and eventually succeeded in having her imprisoned in England.

The action begins in Fotheringhay Castle, where Mary is singing a gentle melody about the unpredictability of life. The song ends abruptly when Mary sings the line 'tomorrow freedom or death', as the dreadful reality of those words hits home. Nevertheless, Mary is convinced that Elizabeth will release her from prison when she reads her latest letter. The viewer soon

Queen Mary finds herself obliged to marry the dandy, Lord Darnley. (*Deutsches Filminstitut/FWM*)

discovers, however, that Elizabeth and her court have determined that Mary is guilty of adultery, the death of her husband and of conspiracy against the throne of England. She is to be beheaded the following morning. Mary insists she is innocent and cannot believe that Elizabeth would sign her death warrant. In praying to the Virgin Mary for help, she looks back to her initial arrival in Scotland and how her heart had awakened when she had returned to her beloved homeland.

In a flashback, the viewer is shown how Mary, being a woman and a Catholic, receives a cold welcome from the Scottish nobles and even from her half-brother, Jacob, who has been acting as regent in her absence. Lord Bothwell, in particular, refuses to serve a woman and urges her to return to France. Even Johanna, the last survivor of the Clan Gordon, is initially of a mind to poison Mary, because the Stewarts had been responsible for the death of her three brothers. However, moved by Mary's words, Johanna knocks the goblet from Mary's hand at the last moment and vows obedience to the Queen. Bothwell is eventually imprisoned for insulting the Queen, but it soon becomes obvious that he has a sneaking admiration for Mary's bravery and wisdom, and also that she is in love with him.

In England, meanwhile, there is a fear that Mary may have her sights set on the Crown of England and, although the English have already been bribing the Scottish nobles to support Elizabeth, the decision is taken to send Lord Henry Darnley to present himself at the Scottish court. Although he is a Scot, he had pledged allegiance to Elizabeth, and his role is to ensure that it is the Scottish nobles who are in charge of the country rather than Mary.

Darnley looks and acts like a dandy and earns little respect from the Scottish nobles other than for the financial 'presents' which he brings them, courtesy of Elizabeth. Nevertheless, he soon falls in love with the beautiful Mary. The Scottish nobles continue to try to force her to abdicate, but relent on the basis that she marries and provides them with a Scottish 'king'. Mary has it in mind to marry Bothwell, with whom she is in love and because she knows that their union would make Scotland stronger and easier to control.

However, when she discovers that Johanna has already persuaded Bothwell to enter into a marriage of convenience with her, Mary accepts the advice of her Italian secretary, Riccio, that she

Lord Bothwell entices Mary to his bed chamber. (*Deutsches Filminstitut/FWM*)

should marry Darnley, as this will provide a Scottish king but still allow Mary to continue as the true ruler with Riccio's assistance.

Jacob is so upset by this marriage that he appeals to Elizabeth for assistance, since the country is really being ruled by Riccio. When he shows Elizabeth a picture of Mary's son, she is filled with jealousy and Elizabeth agrees to send another noble, Sir John, to plot Riccio's downfall.

In any event, upset by Riccio's influence over Mary and by malicious rumours that Riccio might be the true father of Mary's son, Darnley eventually assists some of the other nobles in the murder of Riccio.

Having been alerted to the intended murder, Bothwell arrives on the scene and moves Mary to his own castle for her safety. He tells her that he has left Johanna and the viewer is left to assume that Bothwell and Mary spend the night together. Elizabeth is furious at this unforeseen development and fears a Scotland which is now in strong hands. She arranges for Jacob to advise Darnley that she will provide him with an army of 5,000 men if he will fight Bothwell. However, Darnley, who is suffering from the pox, will not hear any more ill spoken of Mary as he now realises that it was a lie that she had slept with Riccio.

Johanna produces the love letters which will help seal Mary's fate. (*Deutsches Filminstitut/FWM*)

Bothwell arranges for Darnley to be killed, ostensibly in a mysterious explosion, and this provides an excuse for Bothwell and Mary to be married under the auspices of the Catholic Church, which does not recognise the validity of Bothwell's earlier Protestant marriage to Johanna.

While Mary is actually quite content with her current position, Elizabeth sends a letter to Mary, offering her and her son refuge in England in her time of distress, and sends Jacob with an army to restore order.

At Mary's wedding, Johanna, driven by jealousy and revenge, hands over love letters between Mary and Bothwell which will eventually be used at Mary's trial. Bothwell is dragged away, and Mary is forced to go to England where, instead of being safe, she is imprisoned by Elizabeth.

The action then returns to the present and Mary's incarceration and impending execution. Mary conducts herself with great dignity throughout, accepting that she has had a hand in the death of Riccio, Darnley and her servant, Olivier. However, she seeks solace in the belief that earthly death will make her pure and free again. In a very moving scene with all her supporters sobbing as she is led away, the film ends with Mary standing nobly before the executioner's block voicing words of prayer and looking to the heavens for justice.

CRITICAL REVIEW

Reminiscent of a Shakespearean tragedy with copious servings of romance, intrigue, murder and suspense, *Das Herz der Königin* is an excellent film. The contrast between the two queens is clearly exposed, with Mary being tender and resolute and Elizabeth ruthless and unforgiving.

As a piece of entertainment, what gives the film added appeal are the numerous melodies which the Swedish actress, Zarah Leander, playing the role of Mary, sings so tenderly. Each song reflects the mood of a particular scene in the film, be it joy or despair, and brings relief from the intensity of the underlying drama. It is little wonder that the songs were released as records in their own right.

However, what makes this film particularly interesting as a piece of propaganda is that little had to be changed from the true story to achieve propaganda impact. It was always going to be an impossible task for Mary to reconcile her desire to be a caring ruler of Scotland with Scotland's need for a strong and powerful leader to control the nobles. Add the complications of religious tensions between Catholicism and Presbyterianism, historic clan rivalries, Mary's own search for personal happiness and the meddling in Scottish affairs by Elizabeth, and it was obvious that Mary's reign was always destined to be short-lived.

From an anti-English standpoint, the story was a god-send for the Nazis as, in their seemingly ignominious treatment of the pious and innocent Mary, the English could be portrayed, once again, as merciless imperialists who ruthlessly dominate smaller nations and stop at nothing to achieve their ends.

Vilification of the English

The assassination of the English character derives from two sources, namely the actions of Queen Elizabeth and those of her court. The actions of the latter seem to be driven by paranoia that Scotland and Mary pose a threat to England and herald a forced return to Catholicism:

> *Elizabeth's Advisor: – 'She [Mary] has her eyes set on the crown of England.'*
> *Another Advisor: – 'Today Scotland – tomorrow perhaps even England.'*
> *Elizabeth: – 'But the French would applaud and the Pope declare his blessing!'*

The behaviour of Elizabeth is driven by a mixture of self-interest and English national interest, and she exhibits a whole series of unpleasant character traits which often overlap.

Treachery, lies and duplicity

The most obvious aspect of Elizabeth's treacherous nature is her promise to Mary of safe refuge in England, when, in reality, Mary is subjected to a long period of imprisonment before being executed on the very orders of Elizabeth. The film has no hesitation in openly condemning the actions of Elizabeth. But the true horror of the crime is perhaps most forcibly displayed in Mary's own despair at the injustice of her treatment as revealed towards the end of the film:

> I am not England's enemy. The charges are false. Elizabeth has lied. The Queen of England has lied!

However, Elizabeth's treachery and duplicity are also evident on a number of other occasions during the film. For example, it transpires that under her guidance the English have been bribing the Scottish nobles for some time, and when her advisors express concern that giving Darnley an army to fight Bothwell may make him too strong, Elizabeth's ruthlessness is revealed in her ominous answer:

> Anyone who allows himself to be helped by England will die!

Jealousy

Some of Elizabeth's most vicious verbal outbursts and drastic decisions derive from her jealousy of Mary. When Lord Jacob shows her a picture of Mary's son and heir, Elizabeth is so jealous that she immediately determines to cause disruption to Mary's seemingly happy love life by plotting the death of Riccio. Then there is the occasion when Sir John returns to advise her that Darnley has been killed and that Bothwell and Mary are in love with each other. Elizabeth cries out in frustration, 'love, love, love' when she learns that Mary has not only been loved by Darnley and probably Riccio but also Bothwell, whereas she has had no such joy in her life.

Indeed, when Sir John naïvely mentions that Mary is pretty and that, while taller than Elizabeth, not too tall, he fails to realise that this description so infuriates Elizabeth that this is perhaps the primary reason why he is led away to be beheaded for failure.

Elizabeth is displeased to learn of Mary's superior height and beauty. (*Deutsches Filminstitut/ FWM*)

Cunning

Elizabeth also possesses an evil shrewdness. It is Elizabeth who tells her advisors that the tree should not be shaken until the fruit is ripe and that in Scotland the harvest is late. It is she who sends Darnley to 'encourage' the Scottish nobles in their opposition to Mary and who sends Sir John to arouse jealousy in Darnley, which later results in the murder of Riccio.

It is Elizabeth who panders to Jacob's lust for power by promising to make him her regent in Scotland if he helps defeat Mary, while at the same time assuring her lord chancellor that Jacob will not remain her regent for long!

Cowardice

Elizabeth's cowardice is evident in her refusal to open Mary's final letter and to give an excuse for not being present at the court's decision to execute Mary. She hides behind a signature and is happy to let others do her dirty work for her. She never meets Mary face to face and is not even present at the execution.

Depiction of Mary as a martyr

The constant portrayal of Mary as an innocent victim is an equally effective means of deepening the viewer's loathing of Elizabeth and all she stands for.

Mary is the true heroine of the story, devout in her service to the Virgin Mary and finally raised to martyrdom in the manner of her death. In all that she does, she speaks like a benevolent ruler and is depicted as acting out of the purest of motives. She is the complete antithesis of the vile and selfish Elizabeth:

> I only ever lived for Scotland, only followed my heart. My heart slept when I came to France as a child, and my heart slept when I left France but when I saw Scotland again, as its Queen, then it awoke.

It is this dedication to Scotland which leads her to marry Darnley, even though she does not love him. When Riccio suggests that duty is holier than love and that it is a question of the throne, not of the heart, Mary unhesitatingly responds, 'I will do my duty!' At a time when Germany was looking for all its citizens, including its womenfolk, to be prepared to make great sacrifices for their country, what better example than the Scottish Queen?

German viewers' impression of Britain?

What impression of the British would German viewers gain from this film? They would have considered Britain to be a divided nation. The Scots are portrayed as being bedevilled by internal strife, disunited, and treacherous to their own people at the prospect of financial gain, power or religious reasons. Likewise, the English leaders have no redeeming features whatsoever. They are likely to be guided by irrational personal interest and certainly cannot be trusted to keep their promises.

Despite all the underhand tactics which Elizabeth employs, the German viewer is also likely to have taken comfort from the fact that the English rulers are far from omnipotent. Elizabeth certainly made a poor choice in sending Darnley and Sir John to carry out her work in Scotland.

Likewise, while the film does not reflect particularly well on the Scots, who are prepared to accept bribes and who maintain a low opinion of women, they are certainly not so naïve as to trust England or Elizabeth. Even though Jacob is prepared to hand over Mary to Elizabeth, he has more sense than to let her son, James, be sent with her:

England must not get him – he is Scotland's heir.

To what extent was the film based on historical fact?

In terms of historical accuracy, the facts contained in the film are generally correct. Mary did want the best for her subjects and, although a Catholic, she did encourage wide religious freedom and had many Protestant friends and contacts. The marriage with Darnley was indeed an attempt by Mary to maintain some sort of stability, but Darnley's dissatisfaction with his role as a consort gradually resulted in Mary placing undue reliance on Riccio, making him unpopular with the Scottish nobles and precipitating his murder. Ironically, the Scottish nobles subsequently soon became equally disenchanted with Darnley, and Bothwell is believed to have been one of the main conspirators implicated in Darnley's murder. Given that Elizabeth was childless, in the event of her death, Mary would have been the rightful heir to the throne of England. English fear as to Mary's ambitions and the threat of Catholic domination was the main reason for Mary's long imprisonment in England and, ultimately, Elizabeth was responsible for signing her death warrant.

However, while much of the story is based on fact, one or two key details have been altered or omitted, partly for dramatic effect but also for greater propaganda impact.

Firstly, although related to Mary, Darnley was born in England and, despite suggestions to the contrary, it appears that Mary was very much in love with him rather than the other way round. Furthermore, the fact that he was Catholic and had interests in England increased concern in England that the marriage was an attempt by Mary to strengthen her claim to the throne of England. Secondly, Mary's marriage to Bothwell was actually conducted in the Protestant rather than the Catholic tradition, but the film version allows greater emphasis to be placed on the tensions caused by the conflict between the two religious sects in Scotland and England at that time. Thirdly, and most importantly, it was really only after defeat in battle that Mary travelled to England to seek help from Elizabeth. It was the frustration born of her subsequent nineteen-year forced imprisonment which eventually resulted in Mary's becoming inveigled into the Babington Plot with English and foreign Catholics to assassinate Elizabeth and place Mary on the throne of England. Ultimately, it was primarily because of incriminating correspondence relating to this and other conspiracies that Mary was eventually executed.

From a propaganda angle, the most significant changes are Mary's 'escape' to England being of her own volition and the fact that she did indeed contrive to have Elizabeth murdered. Such truths would have reduced the viewer's sympathy for Mary and made Elizabeth's execution order seem more justifiable – hence, presumably, why this information was withheld from the German audience in 1940.

Indeed, the film could have had a more upbeat ending by mentioning how Mary would have the last victory when her son became James VI of Scotland and James I of England, and would arrange for Fotheringhay Castle to be wiped from the map and for a magnificent monument to be erected in Mary's honour at Westminster Abbey. However, this would have detracted from the viewer's impression that Mary was an unavenged martyr and that England deserved to be punished for its previous crimes.

How was the film received?

Given that the film boasted such famous stars as Zarah Leander and Maria Koppenhöfer, it is rather surprising that it was not a box office hit with German audiences. Even the film censors at the time considered the film to be sufficiently worthy to be categorised as being of 'artistic

Queen Elizabeth I of England and Ireland. (*'Elizabeth I' oil on panel painted in the circle of Richard Burchett, 1854–60. WOA 3199, © Palace of Westminster Collection*)

Mary, Queen of Scots. ('*Mary, Queen of Scots*' oil on panel in the circle of Richard Burchett, 1854–60. *WOA 3211, © Palace of Westminster Collection*)

and cultural merit'. From a propaganda angle, Goebbels was never satisfied with the film, although it is difficult to understand his complaint that while the film was intended to be anti-English and anti-Church, it ended up being pro both!

After the war, fellow actors such as Will Quadflieg, who played Olivier, criticised the casting of Leander as Mary and dismissed the film as superficial and pure kitsch.

While it is certainly true that the film does simplify what was a very complicated period in British history, it would be unfair to criticise the film for its concentration on the romantic aspects of Mary's life and Elizabeth's role in her downfall, because there is no doubt that these, together with religious tension and internal power struggles, were the primary factors in the tragedy, all of which are mentioned in the film. Indeed, one has to ask whether the post-war criticisms were driven as much by a desire to discredit any positive association with anything emanating from the Nazi era, as by an intention of giving a balanced review of the artistic merits of the film.

However, the combination of the fact that it was primarily a woman's film because of the love interest, was considered unsuitable for minors, and was ultimately a tragedy, meant that the film was always going to be a little too heavy for an audience which was just starting to become accustomed to the demands of the war and who might well have preferred lighter entertainment.

CONCLUSION

While *Das Herz der Königin* may not have been considered a classic film at the time, the story of Mary, Queen of Scots did provide the Nazis with another useful example of how England had behaved in its historic relationship with other nations. Just as Britain was shown to have abused the Irish and deprived them of their independence, this Scottish story was yet another instance of England using its military might and financial strength to act with the harsh and unfeeling temperament of an imperialist bully.

If this is how England had treated one of its closest neighbours, then how could it possibly be trusted in its dealings with other nations? The film sought to stoke up further resentment against Britain and to help promote the notion that Britain deserved its comeuppance and that the war against Britain was justifiable. After all, it was actually Britain that had declared war on Germany.

Whatever its shortcomings in absolute historical accuracy, *Das Herz der Königin* is still a moving narrative of a troubled time in British history, and the melodies sung by Mary and the scenes with the travelling players are still quite captivating today. Given that the film is now more readily available, modern viewers have the opportunity to judge for themselves whether Leander was miscast and to what extent the film went beyond the reporting of historical fact and became an unbalanced piece of anti-English propaganda.

Film title: *Mein Leben für Irland*
Year of release: 1941
Type: Feature film
Primary purpose: Anti-English/British propaganda
Director: Max W. Kimmich
Principal stars:
Anna Damman   (Maeve Fleming)
René Deltgen   (Robert Devoy)
Werner Hinz   (Michael O'Brien Senior)
Eugen Klöpfer   (Duffy)
Heinz Ohlsen   (Patrick O'Connor)
Will Quadflieg   (Michael O'Brien Junior)
Paul Wegener   (Sir George Beverley)

INTRODUCTION

Mein Leben für Irland (*My Life for Ireland*) was the second of the anti-British propaganda films produced by the Nazis which were inspired by the Irish War of Independence. The film was released early in 1941 and was very well received at the box office in Germany, partly because it was an exciting action thriller and, partly, because its themes of love, self-sacrifice and heroism were always going to be popular, especially when they revolved around a small nation's struggle against the imperialist British. However, the negative reaction which such films produced towards the Nazis in those countries occupied by the Germans was to result in this being the last such Irish-focused film to be commissioned by Goebbels.

PLOT SUMMARY

The film begins on the outskirts of Dublin in 1903, where a sheriff acting on behalf of the British government is shown aggressively harassing a poor family for two years' non-payment of rent. Some Irish rebels try to come to the assistance of the farmer, and a gun battle ensues in which the leader of the rebels, Michael O'Brien, and five of his men are captured. After a mock trial, they are all sentenced to death for belonging to a secret society dedicated to breaking Ireland away from the United Kingdom. In a moving scene prior to their execution, O'Brien is permitted to marry his beautiful fiancée, Maeve, and she confesses to him that she is pregnant and bearing his son.

The action then moves swiftly to 1921, at St Edward's School which has all the appearance of an English boarding school but is located in Dublin. Sir George Beverley, a high-ranking English official is in conversation with the headmaster. It transpires that the English authorities have been deliberately financing the private education of a number of Irish boys whose fathers have caused problems for England in the past, in the hope that, by mixing them with English boys, the Irish boys will begin to think like the English.

Maeve's moving farewell to Michael O'Brien prior to his execution by the British. (*Deutsches Filminstitut/FWM*)

After a brawl following a rugby match, two of the boys, Michael O'Brien (son of the executed rebel) and Patrick O'Connor, become very close friends, and Michael invites Patrick home to visit his mother one weekend. Patrick, who lost his parents at an early age, instantly falls in love with the beautiful and charming Maeve, regarding his day spent with her as the best day of his life. Subsequently, he steals a photo of her from Michael and sneaks out from school one night to catch a glimpse of her at her house. However, when he notices another man in her bedroom, he is filled with jealousy, confiding his adventure to another pupil, Henry Beverley (Sir George's nephew), who had spotted him sneaking out of the school.

Unaware that the man he had seen was the wounded rebel, Robert Devoy, Patrick gives Henry a full description of the man. Henry, who is acting as an informant for his uncle, immediately reports his findings, and Maeve is subsequently arrested for harbouring a criminal, although Devoy had actually managed to escape in the interim.

Later, Patrick is overcome with remorse when he realises that, however unwittingly, he is responsible for betraying the whereabouts of Devoy and for Maeve's subsequent arrest.

Determined to put matters right, Patrick eventually manages to contact Devoy and confesses what had happened. Devoy is seeking to find a way of freeing Maeve from prison and, when Patrick explains that the Secret Service had tried to employ him to work for them and had told him of a secret entrance to the prison, Devoy decides to trust Patrick and use him to pass false information to the Secret Service. Devoy and Patrick agree to keep their arrangement secret and, to help inspire Patrick, Devoy gives him the special silver cross which O'Brien Senior had originally passed to Maeve before his execution, on which is inscribed the motto, '*Mein Leben für Irland*' (My life for Ireland).

The other boys believe that Patrick is a traitor and torture him to tell the truth but, given his vow of secrecy to Devoy, he refuses to reveal his secret. The British authorities are indeed duped by the false information they received and reduce their troop numbers, thereby enabling the rebels to launch their own attack on the city at a pre-arranged time. Simultaneously, O'Brien leads the other boys in the school in revolt, seizing the rifles held in the school's armoury and taking these to the rebels. A fierce battle around the prison ensues, during which Devoy is killed, but Patrick manages to lead the rebels through the secret passageway into the prison. The rebels are victorious, and Maeve and the other prisoners are freed. However, Patrick is shot in the process, and it is only when Maeve discovers the silver cross around his neck as she cares for him that she and Michael realise that Patrick was not a traitor after all. As Patrick lies dying in Maeve's arms, Michael movingly declares that Patrick deserves to keep the cross because:

You gave more than your life, you sacrificed your honour!

The film concludes to the sound of a rousing Irish freedom anthem and a close-up of the cross and its 'My Life for Ireland' inscription.

CRITICAL REVIEW

As with many of the Nazis' propaganda films, *Mein Leben für Irland* does have a clear focus in its disparaging attitude towards anything associated with the British. Where it differs from many other such films is that it actually has quite an exciting plot which keeps the viewer entertained right to the last scene. The film falls more into the genre of historical fiction, and although there was a series of risings in Dublin in 1921, no claim is made that the screenplay is based on historical events.

Britain's treatment of the Irish

From the very opening scenes, the sheriff and police working for the British authorities are portrayed as lacking any form of compassion for their Irish neighbours. It is obvious that the farmer is poor and cannot afford to pay any taxes, but the authorities are unmoved by his arguments or by the fact that thousands of Irish people are dying of starvation. The rough treatment of a young boy and the womenfolk shows that the British are no better than savage brutes in their treatment of the Irish, and the viewer's sympathy immediately lies with O'Brien and his band of freedom fighters as they try to stand against their British overlords.

In the subsequent military trial scene, during which the prisoners are denied any defence counsel or right of appeal, great care is taken to depict the rebels as representing a wide cross-section of Irish society. The six prisoners are composed of a goldsmith, a writer, a transport worker, a university professor, a student and a clerk. When they are accused of murder, this provides an opportunity for O'Brien to retort with some very hard-hitting lines regarding the oppression of the Irish:

> We fought for our country's freedom, which you English have betrayed and sold out. You have driven us from our homes, fenced us in. You left no tree for us to hang ourselves from; no water to drown ourselves in; not enough soil to bury our dead. Thousands and thousands starving to death each year – that's *murder!*

The viewer hopes that the prisoners will be rescued but, when they are led out for execution and the silhouette of three gallows is shown against the prison wall, it is obvious that they are going to die. This will leave the viewer feeling that the Irish nation as a whole has been treated unfairly and that the execution of these ordinary men is totally unjust.

There are also several occasions when the Irish are shown to have been exploited by the English for their own ends, such as the former Sergeant Duffy, now in charge of the armoury at the school, who had fought for the English in India and how Sir George Beverley, his then commanding officer, had abandoned him when wounded to save his own life.

Denigration of the English character and culture

The opportunity is also taken to condemn or belittle almost every aspect of English culture. For example, the devious nature of the English character is apparent in their infiltration of Irish society with informers and in bribing people to work for them. The horrifying extent of such deviousness is further illustrated in their attempts to indoctrinate the Irish pupils into an English way of thinking by their controlled education in an 'English' environment. Some of the most disparaging comments are to be found in the classroom scenes. When Michael O'Brien coughs violently to indicate his displeasure with his master's teaching that, 'only those who understand the deeper sense of the claim of English rule and accept it unconditionally will have a free and easy life', he is obliged to recite what he has been taught about English foreign policy, even though it is clear to all that he does not believe what he is reciting by heart:

English colonialism has always been marked by its Christian charity. If ruthless force had to be used then it was only against those immature tribes who resisted. The measures taken were in their best interests.

Such an attack on the origins of the British Empire is a common theme in the anti-British films, especially in *Ohm Krüger*, where it is claimed that the murder of missionaries is used as an excuse by the English to invade a country and then never to leave.

Furthermore, in their harsh treatment of Maeve, the English invent rumours that she is Devoy's mistress, so as to try to alienate his supporters. One of the rebels makes it clear that such underhand practices by the English are far from rare:

Typical English – the old methods – they fight with lies and slander.

The film demeans what it regards as elitist – upper-class activities such as rugby and golf and the English concept of fair play – with a suggestion that what the English really mean by 'playing the game' is that it is acceptable to cheat so long as you don't caught. Even the worth of the Victoria Cross is devalued as it transpires that it had been awarded to Sir George Beverley for bravery in the face of the enemy, when he had actually been a coward, stealing the wounded Duffy's water to save his own life. Belonging to the right social background is revealed to be the key to a successful career in England, rather than progression through personal merit.

In reality, it is apparent that the Germans' understanding of many of the British customs was rather sketchy. Instead of using an oval ball, rugby is played with a ball more the shape and size of a round leather medicine ball, and the golfers have little idea of how to hold a golf club. Similarly, the so-called old English ritual of 'the burning of books and papers' at the end of term seems rather contrived and less than convincing. While the Nazis certainly sanctioned their own burning of inappropriate books in May 1933, it would seem rather unlikely that the English school masters in this film would have endorsed the burning of the very text books which they were using to justify English foreign policy to their Irish students. Nevertheless, as this scene neatly coincides with the timing of the rebellion, it provides an opportunity for the students to throw *all* their 'English-orientated' text books and even Britain's supposed flag for Ireland, which contained a Union Jack in one corner, onto the fire with great relish.

Above all else, the authorities are shown to be stupid and naïve. How could the English allow themselves to be outwitted by a bunch of school boys or believe that young Irish school children could be so easily indoctrinated into the English way of thinking?

Michael soon becomes aware of his betrayal of Maeve in his conversations with Sir George Beverley. (*Deutsches Filminstitut/FWM*)

Effectiveness as a work of propaganda

The film was very popular in Germany. It had an exciting plot with themes of love and sacrifice and where the underdog Irish heroes ultimately emerge victorious. In many ways, the content was more akin to the type of fictional propaganda film which was so successful in Britain at that time. Even the Allied Control Commission, which was established at the end of the war to pronounce on the suitability of the screening of films in Germany, declared the film to be 'a very good production with excellent acting, [albeit] full of anti-British propaganda'.

Consequently, the film did serve as an effective piece of propaganda for the Nazis both in terms of arousing anti-British feelings and in inspiring their own citizens to greater sacrifice.

There is no doubt that many Germans still felt resentment against the French and British for the harsh reparations imposed after the First World War and for the constraints subsequently placed on Germany regarding the control of its own affairs. Not only did the film allow the Germans to feel an empathy with the Irish, who were to remain officially neutral during the war, but it also helped justify Germany's own reason for being at war with Britain. By depicting the British as employing such tactics as indoctrination, cruelty, deception, bribery and murder in pursuit of their imperialistic ambitions, it was easy to arouse feelings of hatred and anger in the viewer towards the hegemonic British. Again, it is somewhat ironic that history would record such tactics as being more readily identifiable with the Nazis rather than the British in the control of both their own people and the nations they conquered.

However, the film also served, through the examples of the heroic Irish characters, to reinforce and glorify those character traits which the Nazis so admired and wished to engender in their own people.

Maeve would serve as a glorious example to all German women of a character stoically resolute in the face of her husband's death, determined to continue the fight for the freedom of her country through her offspring. Every Hitler Youth member would certainly have wanted to play the part of Michael or Patrick. The boys are strong, courageous and quick-witted, and in his death, Patrick is clearly portrayed as a martyr figure. The older leaders, such as Devoy and O'Brien Senior, are all prepared to sacrifice their own lives for the sake of the greater cause. For the Nazis, these were all magnificent role models whose behaviour would certainly be required to be copied by all Germans when the war turned against them.

How was the film received?

A report issued by the SS in May 1940 contended that any film which portrays an oppressed people's struggle for freedom will generally find a good reception and, for the reasons already mentioned above, this film was certainly well received in Germany when it was released in February 1941. An accompanying report about the film in the *Filmwoche* magazine of 19 February 1941 talked of the tragedy of Ireland and how there was no better example of the role of antipathy between two peoples than in the century-long hatred which existed between the Irish and the British. In an impassioned account of English/Irish history, the article proudly asserted that the IRA was continuing its attacks on England even though Ireland had adopted a neutral position in the current war.

Both *Der Fuchs von Glenarvon* and *Mein Leben für Irland* were directed by Goebbels' brother-in-law, Max Kimmich. While the latter film was rated as being of 'political and artistic merit', Goebbels was generally less impressed with *Mein Leben für Irland*, and his ultimate scepticism as to the effectiveness of either of the Irish films as a means of wider propaganda was reinforced by reports that, when screened in the likes of Poland and Czechoslovakia, local resistance movements had identified the Irish films as being more akin to their own struggle for freedom against the Nazis rather than arousing anti-British hostility.

Consequently, by the time *Mein Leben für Irland* was close to completion, Goebbels had already made up his mind that he did not want to see any more Irish-themed films produced, since, 'the theme was not sufficiently convincing'.

POINT OF NOTE CONCERNING THE PRODUCTION OF THE FILM

Michael's interrogation in the headmaster's study. (*Deutsches Filminstitut/FWM*)

Towards the climax of the film, there is an exciting battle scene with tanks and machine guns. An explosives expert had been employed to set up the charges for a number of explosions but he was called up to military service before the battle scene was filmed, and inadequate instructions had been left regarding the use of the explosives. As a consequence, during the filming of this scene, several extras set off the explosives by mistake and were injured in the process. Nevertheless, filming continued uninterrupted, and this does help to explain some rather odd actions by an apparently injured man sitting behind the main action, who presumably had been genuinely wounded in the recording of the battle scene. The accident was only made public after the war.

With regard to the key actors in the production, it is interesting to note that the part of the hero, Michael O'Brien Senior, is played by Werner Hinz. Paradoxically, in the earlier Irish film, *Der Fuchs von Glenarvon*, Hinz had played the part of the ruthless and hated English officer, Sir John Tetbury. Hinz evidently did not wish to be typecast in the role of a villain.

CONCLUSION

In terms of entertainment, *Mein Leben für Irland* was as exciting a thriller as anything produced by any country in 1941. The examples of Michael O'Brien Junior and Senior, Devoy, Patrick and Maeve served as clear models for German soldiers, the Hitler Youth and womenfolk in Germany, and the portrayal of British oppression of the Irish provided ample justification to the ordinary German as to why Britain's imperialist ambitions had to be prevented at all costs.

However, there was undoubtedly a naïvety in Nazi Party circles if it were ever believed that the film would be a successful form of propaganda anywhere other than in Germany. The inspiration which it provided to rebel groups in Nazi-occupied countries in their struggle against German control is another example of how, when it comes to producing propaganda films, the audience has to be chosen carefully, as it is only too easy for the desired intention to backfire. Having been banned by the Allies at the end of the war, despite its anti-English bias, the film was again cleared for viewing in Germany in 1980 for those aged sixteen and over.

Film title: *Ohm Krüger*
Year of release: 1941
Type: Feature film
Primary purpose: Anti-English/British propaganda
Director: Hans Steinhoff
Principal stars:

Gustav Gründgens	(Joseph Chamberlain)
Werner Hinz	(Jan Krüger)
Emil Jannings	(Paul Krüger)
Ferdinand Marian	(Cecil Rhodes)
Gisela Uhlen	(Jan's wife)
Hedwig Wangel	(Queen Victoria)
Otto Wernicke	(Camp Commandant)

INTRODUCTION

It is hard to find any propaganda film released during the Nazi era which contains a more venomous and systematic tirade of anti-English abuse than is presented by the 1941 feature film, *Ohm Krüger* (*Uncle Krüger*).

Loosely based on the events surrounding the Second Boer War between the British and the Boers of the Transvaal in South Africa, the film takes the opportunity to condemn the British Empire and every aspect of the English character. No class, rank or occupation in English society is exempt from the film's condemnation or ridicule.[3]

Joseph Goebbels was closely involved in its production, and it is little wonder that in his diary note of 2 April 1941, he was pleased to report that the film provided fantastic excitement and was, 'the kind of anti-English film you can only dream of!'

PLOT SUMMARY

The film opens in a hotel in Switzerland where the old President of the Boers, Paul Krüger, affectionately known to his people as Ohm (Uncle) Krüger, has sought refuge as he fights with blindness and ill-health. In one long flashback, he recounts to his nurse how the current state of affairs has arisen and why he did not negotiate with the English with whom the Boers have now concluded a peace treaty.

Through the flashback, it is explained how tensions had arisen between the Boers and the English when Cecil Rhodes, Prime Minister of the Cape Colony, had discovered that the land around Pretoria contained some of the purest gold in the whole world. The English were

---

3   Once again the terms 'British' and 'English' tend to be applied on a random basis, notwithstanding, for example, that
    many of the soldiers were Scots wearing kilts.

determined to secure this gold at any price and had not only bribed many of the deputies in the Boer government, but had also contrived via Dr Jameson (actually a Scot but persistently referred to as English throughout the film) to incite a riot among the black tribes. Aware of what the English are plotting, Jameson is captured and, in the meantime, Krüger buys £2 million worth of arms to protect the Boer lands from the English. Having already had military successes in the First Boer War, Krüger is fairly upbeat about warding off any unwanted approaches from the English:

> We are a peaceful nation but if the English force us we will beat them a second time and God will be with us.

In the meantime, Queen Victoria has been advised by her colonial secretary, Joseph Chamberlain (father of Neville Chamberlain), that he is determined to gain access to the gold mines in the Transvaal, even if this means going to war with the Boers. For the sake of appearances, it is agreed that, in the first instance, they will try to get Krüger formally to agree that the English will be given the right to mine for gold in the Transvaal. Distrusting the English, Krüger does eventually agree to go to England to sign such an agreement. Nevertheless, Krüger is a shrewd man and has engineered matters in such a way that the miners are crippled by exorbitant taxes for the gold they mine and are forced to buy their dynamite from local suppliers at ten times the true rate for explosives.

However, on returning home and facing contrived opposition from some of his parliamentary colleagues as well as antagonism from his son, Jan, Ohm Krüger resolves to resign as president. Rhodes arrives and tries to make one last attempt to show how war could be avoided if one man, i.e. Krüger, could find common ground whereby the Boers keep their independence but allow the English to mine their gold. Rhodes makes the fatal error of trying to bribe Krüger to accept such a role in the belief that 'everything has its price'. This so infuriates the noble Krüger that he tears up his resignation letter and resolves to lead his nation to war against the English if that is what is necessary to retain their lands and freedom. As Krüger later explains in an impassioned argument with his Anglophile son:

> This is a battle of life and death ... it's either the English or us. To negotiate with England means giving up our freedom and becoming English slaves!

War does ensue and, frustrated by some initial Boer victories, the English appoint General Kitchener to take charge of the campaign. He resorts to far more ruthless tactics which include designating all Boer civilians and fighting men as 'rebels', burning houses and farms, and the removal of women and children to concentration camps.

Jan, a hitherto pacifist and supporter of England, joins the revolution after he accidentally kills an English soldier whom he caught trying to rape his wife. However, the war starts to go badly for the Boers and no other nation is prepared to offer them practical help against the English. The women and children are deliberately kept incarcerated in poor conditions, with many dying of hunger and typhoid. Jan is captured while plotting to rescue his wife, and when he is executed in front of the camp internees, the women rise in uproar, and many are shot by the English soldiers.

The flashback ends, and we return to the hotel, where Krüger explains in a very moving final scene that his countrymen then had no alternative other than to sign a treaty but that, some day, a higher power will ensure that vengeance is delivered on the English:

> That was how England subdued our small nation by the cruellest of means, but eventually the day of retribution will come! I don't know when, but all that blood could not have been spilt in vain. We are just a small, weak nation. But great and powerful nations will revolt against the British tyranny. They will knock England to the ground. God will be with them and this will clear the way for a better world.

CRITICAL REVIEW

Ohm Krüger is a very powerful film where almost every conceivable outrage is blamed upon the English. The case against the character of the English is cleverly constructed throughout each successive scene by means of a number of very moving speeches and dramatic images.

Propagandistic character assassination

Royalty

As the head of the British Empire, Queen Victoria is subjected to the most unflattering of portrayals.

Admittedly, at first, she is seen to be more sympathetic towards the Boers as she queries with Chamberlain why the government wants to make changes which could mean a conflict with the Boers, especially when it is a poor country with too many friends. She feels that the British already have enough problems in India, but at least it is a rich country. However, this seemingly more pragmatic approach to the issue is soon abandoned when Chamberlain explains that the country is rich in gold. This changes everything, and she can be seen to be almost salivating at the prospect of securing this gold as she knocks back her 'whisky' medicine like an alcoholic:

> If there is gold to be found there, then this land belongs to us!

She does eventually recover some of her composure in suggesting that Chamberlain should still try to find a solution which avoids war, such as that the Boers agree to hand over the gold and, in return, England will 'look after' their country. However, in accepting Chamberlain's prognosis that it will be impossible to negotiate with Krüger, she suggests that they trick him by getting him to visit the Queen to sign an agreement. If he does not come or refuses to

sign the agreement then, at least, England will have been able to show its good intentions to the whole world before it goes to war, and the appearance of justice will be on their side.

The Queen's cunning mind is also revealed in her deathbed scene later in the film when she explains to her son, the Prince of Wales:

> We have to end this war with the Boers quickly ... You have to be very clever and careful. Always make sure that nations hate each other. For the day they stop arguing with each other will be the day of our downfall. I am so afraid.

It is difficult to tell what she means by her final words. Is she afraid that she will be judged harshly by God or is she afraid of what will happen to Britain? Perhaps the German

Queen Victoria, Empress of India. (*Library of Congress*)

Joseph Chamberlain, father of Neville Chamberlain. (*Deutsches Filminstitut/FWM*)

audience is meant to interpret this as a premonition that Britain will lose the Second World War.

Above all else, in painting Queen Victoria in such a bad light, it is no wonder that the film fails to mention that Victoria was almost entirely of German descent.

Politicians

Chamberlain is also depicted as a conspiring diplomat who cannot be trusted. Of course, this was actually, Joseph Chamberlain, father of Neville Chamberlain, who tried to negotiate with Hitler. For many Germans, there would have been an assumption that this was the same Chamberlain and it was a name for which they held little respect. The fact that he is portrayed as belonging to the aristocracy, and his patronising and offensive attitude towards the Boers when he tries to justify military intervention to the Queen, are sufficient reasons for him to be disliked by all viewers:

> Destiny has called upon England to educate the small and underdeveloped nations. This is an old and approved principle of our politics. The Boers are backward. They resist being subjects of your Majesty. They'd rather die than become English.

Such reluctance was obviously crime enough for the Boers to deserve to be defeated in a war against the might of the British Empire.

Generals

If the English royalty and politicians were not portrayed as sufficiently vile, these traits are shown to transcend all levels of society. In the early years, the war goes badly for the British, so General Kitchener (who was actually Irish) is appointed to take control. Again, Kitchener is a name that was probably well known to the Germans who had fought in the First World War. So, little wonder that this unfeeling 'criminal' should be shown to be adopting the most vicious and underhand of tactics to win the war:

> War must be fought with colonial methods ... it means no more humanitarian sentimentality. Burn their farms, separate women and children from men and place them in concentration camps. All Boers are outlaws. We won't discriminate between armed forces and civilians.

Officers and soldiers

The rot continues through the ranks. Evil officers abuse their power in the concentration camps by depriving the women and children of proper food and medical attention, and ordering the massacre of many women in the camp when they rebel at the hanging of Jan Krüger. The other officers and NCOs are not much better as they callously carry out their orders to set fire to civilian farms and houses.

Lord Kitchener. (*Library of Congress*)

The Church

One might have expected the Church to be seen in a more favourable light, but this is not the case. Early in the film, the viewer is presented with a strange scene where, to the accompaniment of 'God Save the Queen', missionaries are shown to be handing out Bibles and guns at one and the same time to black natives whom the British wish to revolt against the Boers. The English are repeatedly mocked for giving the outward appearance of being Christians but acting in a totally un-Christian manner. For example, when Ohm Krüger is recounting to the nurse the back-ground to his sad story, he explains:

Did you know my ancestors lived happily in Cape Land for more than 200 years and then the English came and took away their farm? It can't be the will of God that our whole nation should live in slavery!

Businessmen

Cecil Rhodes, managing director of the British South Africa Company, and Dr Jameson, his

A British officer (who resembles Winston Churchill) about to sanction the hanging of Jan Krüger and the massacre of some of the other prisoners. (*Deutsches Filminstitut/FWM*)

administrator, also attract a good deal of criticism. Rhodes is seen to be both a ruthless businessman and a cunning rogue who declares:

Being a capitalist and being an Englishman is the same thing.

Even Queen Victoria describes Rhodes as a shady character whom she does not really trust.

When he learns about the gold reserves, he and Jameson plot to start border riots which will give the English an excuse to invade the Boer lands. Likewise, when he discovers that Krüger has thwarted their plans by imposing huge taxes on the gold they mine, he determines that he will have to take care of Krüger himself. The impetuous Jameson wants to assassinate Krüger as it would be cheap and quick, but Rhodes is wilier, wanting to appear peaceful at first.

Rhodes goes to visit Krüger and tries to appeal to his vanity by suggesting that he could avoid conflict by becoming president of a great South Africa, an independent land where the Boers and English could live together in peace. However, when Krüger refuses the role of a 'puppet' leader, Rhodes resorts to financial bribery. This unsubtle approach serves only to infuriate Krüger, who tears up his proposed resignation letter in anger and leads his country to war.

Ordinary British citizens

No one is spared the film's wrath. Cecil Rhodes' wife is charming but, when she hears about the gold, even she knows what must be done. She asserts that England must declare war on the Boers, and her keen insight pleases her husband. Also, it is this apparent 'she-devil' who raises the Boer women's hopes by offering better prison conditions, but only on the condition that they sign a declaration asking their husbands to give up the senseless fight.

Even when Paul Krüger comes to meet the Queen to sign the first agreement, there is a comment from an ordinary bystander that Chamberlain will fool him all right.

Rhodes tries to tempt Krüger to come to an agreement with the British. (*Deutsches Filminstitut/FWM*)

From all these negative descriptions, the viewer seems to be left to ask whether there is a single Briton who is not conniving, greedy or inhuman, and the answer is 'seemingly not!'

In contrast to the dreadful British, Paul Krüger is depicted as a caring father figure (somewhat reminiscent of Hitler) who is in charge of a small, fiercely independent nation. The viewer is encouraged to side with the underdog against the ruthless might of the British Empire and cannot fail to join in the enthusiasm of the Boers' marching song, 'Boer Land is a Free Land', and share the joy of their early military successes against the English.

Irony of the content

With the benefit of hindsight, one cannot watch this film without immediately identifying a whole series of instances where the very crimes of which the English/British were being accused are the same crimes which the Nazis would ultimately commit. It is a blatant attempt to justify the crimes of the Nazis, especially in respect of concentration camps, by claiming that they were acting no worse than the British. One can only surmise as to whether a German audience would have been so blind as not to see the parallels with their own country. Key examples of these double standards are found in the implicit condemnation of:

◊   The British contriving to start a war with the Boers if they did not sign an agreement or attempt to negotiate. (Compare this with Hitler's 'negotiations' over the Sudetenland and dressing up Germans in Polish uniforms to give Germany an excuse for invading Poland.)

◊   The fact that it is impossible to negotiate with the English as they never keep their promises. (The same could certainly be said for Hitler in the piece of paper he signed for Neville Chamberlain and his lie that Germany had no further expansionist ambitions after Czechoslovakia.)

◊   The British introduction of concentration camps. (These were really planned as internment camps and, unlike the Nazis, these were never intended for the deliberate mass extermination of 'undesirables'.)

◊   Kitchener's decree that there would be no distinction between the treatment of civilians and fighting men, and that his soldiers were just 'carrying out orders' in burning down the farms. (Compare this with the Nazis' bloody and ruthless destruction of Poland and the Soviet Union in what increasingly became 'Total War', and where the excuse was 'Befehl ist Befehl' – 'orders are orders'.)

Separating fact from fiction

The opening credits of the film freely admit that Ohm Krüger is adapted from themes taken from the novel, 'Man without a Nation' by Arnold Krieger. With deeper insight, this might almost be a triple warning that much of the content might be pure fiction.

However, it is certainly true that the discovery of vast deposits of good quality gold in the Transvaal in 1886 resulted in a vast influx of foreigners (mainly British) looking to exploit the resource. It is quite correct that, as apprehension mounted over the number of foreigners, Jameson was responsible for trying to encourage an uprising in an attempt to uphold their rights. It is also true that economic and political tensions intensified until the Boers declared war on Britain. This developed into a protracted guerrilla war which only ceased in 1902 with the Treaty of Vereenigung.

Nor can it be denied that under Kitchener, the British adopted a scorched earth policy and moved civilians into internment/concentration camps where more than 21,000 women and children died of starvation and typhoid.

What is the nature of the propaganda in this film?

If so much of the story is based on truth, the viewer might well question where the propaganda in the film is found? The answer lies in the fact, as was discussed in Chapter I, that propaganda does not necessarily necessitate telling a lie; it simply often involves not telling the whole truth.

And so, in this film, the propaganda exists both in the totally biased way in which history is reported, and in the host of absolute and exaggerated statements which simply cannot be sustained.

Biased reporting

It is often said that history is written by the victors, but if we try to examine the Second Boer War objectively, then the following facts should also be taken into account, though they are deliberately ignored in the film.

First, it should be recognised that the Boers themselves were foreigners in this region and that there had always between tensions between the British, who took possession of the Cape Colony in 1806, and the Boers, which culminated in the First Boer War and a rather uneasy peace.

Second, tensions actually rose because of the vast volumes of new foreigners arriving to exploit the gold, and it was probably inevitable that a second war was going to ensue unless the Boers agreed to some sort of compromise which respected the rights of the new foreigners. By introducing punitive taxes and high explosive costs, it could be argued that the Boers actually broke the spirit of the initial agreement reached with Britain, prompting a war which the Boers could never win.

Third, by adopting guerrilla tactics, it was almost unavoidable that the Boer women and children who had been lending support to the male fighters would have to be interned. The British had no experience of caring for hundreds of thousands of people in such camps, and poor administration as much as deliberate punishment meant that poor shelter, overcrowding and a shortage of food led to the spread of a number of contagious diseases and a high death rate, especially among children. However, there was never any plan for the deliberate mass extermination of the women and children, and even nations ill-disposed towards Britain never made any such assertions at the time. The problems were actually exacerbated by the Boers' use of traditional medicines which often carried other diseases. Such problems also affected the British forces which, although losing up to 7,000 men in battle, actually lost a further 14,000 through disease.

Indeed, such was the public outcry in Britain about the conditions in the camps and the excessive tactics adopted by Kitchener, the British were forced to offer peace terms on a number of occasions before the Boers eventually signed an agreement in May 1902. The film deliberately chooses to ignore the compassion and humanity which were displayed by a growing percentage of the British population towards the fate of the Boers, which forced a swifter end to the war.

Use of absolute statements and hyperbole

Apart from deliberately distorting the true characters of many of the leading players, such as showing Queen Victoria downing a bottle of whisky, the film excels in dialogue containing exaggerated statements which are clearly wrong or cannot be proven. Such comments include:

Ohm Kruger:
You can never negotiate with the English
The English never keep their agreements

Do you think I ever expected you to abide by the Agreement? That would have been a first in English history!

Queen Victoria:
We English have no friends

Chamberlain:
The men who made England great have always had a bad reputation

Likewise, *all* missionaries were not bad people, and the truth is that neither side wanted to give arms to the black natives. *All* civilians would not have had the same views and, indeed, it was outraged public opinion in Britain which forced the British to sue for peace.

However, there is no doubt that the combination of biased dialogue and a persistently negative portrayal of all the English characters and their actions must have instilled a feeling of hatred towards the British, especially in Germany, given that many Boers were of German descent.

POINTS OF NOTE CONCERNING THE PRODUCTION AND CONTENT OF THE FILM

Production and reception

At a cost of 5.5 million Reichsmarks, *Ohm Krüger* was the third most expensive film produced during the Nazi era and was premiered on 4 April 1941. Most of it was filmed in and around Berlin, and there are some outstanding battle and crowd scenes which required many thousands of extras. Consequently, although the film did achieve top attendance figures after only a few weeks, the cost of production and advertising was such that Tobis, the producers, were never able to earn a profit from the film.

Goebbels wrote Krüger's final prophetic speech predicting England's future downfall, and he was so impressed with the film that, in addition to its receiving an 'especially valuable' rating from the censors both for 'political and artistic' merit, he created a special award for it called 'Film of the Nation'.

While the film won the Mussolini Cup at the Venice Film Festival in 1941 as the best foreign film, it actually received a mixed reception in Germany. Nazi posters promoting the film featured prisoners in the concentration camp, and Goebbels records in his diary that, although some viewers found the film too horrific, he felt that this was what was required if the film were going to have an effective impact on the public.

Director and cast

The director, Hans Steinhoff, who was involved in the production of a number of other propaganda movies, including *Hitlerjunge Quex*, was killed in 1945 when his plane was shot down by the Soviets as he was fleeing back to Berlin from Prague. The cast included a number of actors who were to star in other Nazi propaganda movies and many who were added to the 'divinely gifted' list of performers which would excuse them from active military service. Emil Jannings, who plays Paul Krüger, had been a successful silent movie actor in Hollywood before the war. Given his closeness to the Nazi hierarchy, he was prevented from resuming a film career after the war and died a bitter man in 1950. Married to a Jew, Otto Wernicke (concentration camp commandant) was allowed to work as an actor only with special permission from the state, although he was to star in a number of other famous Nazi propaganda films including *Kolberg*. Ferdinand Marian (Cecil Rhodes) also played a whole host of villainous roles in other propaganda films before his death in 1946.

CONCLUSION

As a piece of anti-English propaganda, this film is second to none, aided by the fact that much of the content was loosely based on historical fact.

The propaganda arises from the fact that the film gives only one side of the story, and this leads the viewer to draw the conclusion that the story is symbolic of the whole of British history and of the character of all Britons. Consequently, it encourages the viewer to agree that a war against Britain is justified as the British deserve to be punished for the many sins which the British Empire has committed in the past. With the constant reference to God being on the side of the Boers, the Second World War almost becomes portrayed as a holy crusade.

Thus, while the film was primarily intended for a German audience, it would also have had an impact on the many other nations who held a grudge against the British Empire, and on anyone who was looking for a good reason to feel antagonistic towards the British.

In any event, the film was banned from being shown in Germany when the Allies took control in 1945, although it was subsequently screened in East Germany in 1953. In Germany today, it can still be obtained only on loan and under strict conditions.

Film title: *Titanic*
Year of release: 1943
Type: Feature film
Primary purpose: Anti-English/British propaganda/
     entertainment
Directors: Herbert Selpin & Werner Klingel
Principal stars:

Ernst F. Fürbringer	(Sir Bruce Ismay)
Kirsten Heiberg	(Gloria)
Hans Nielsen	(First Officer Petersen)
Sybille Schmitz	(Sigrid Olinsky)
Karl Schönböck	(Lord Astor)
Charlotte Thiele	(Lady Astor)
Otto Wernicke	(Captain Smith)

INTRODUCTION

The history surrounding the film *Titanic* makes it one of the most interesting and intriguing feature films produced during the Nazi era. It was actually banned from being screened in Germany shortly after its release, and events associated with this film, both during and post production, were just as dramatic and heart-breaking as the events surrounding the tragedy of *Titanic* itself.

The film *Titanic* was produced in 1943 with the aim of providing both entertainment and anti-English and pro-German propaganda. At that time, it was one of the most expensive feature films which had ever been produced in Germany, incorporating a mix of special effects using models and clever camera photography. It was filmed in Berlin and on a passenger ship in the Baltic. While many of its ideas were copied by later film-makers, this version is unique because of its uncompromising attack on the English, and wealthy English capitalists in particular, for being directly responsible for the sinking of the *Titanic* and subsequent loss of life. It also introduces a number of imaginary German characters whose heroic and dignified actions were designed to serve as commendable examples to a German audience.

Its premiere was to take place in Paris in November 1943, but its first screening in Germany would not occur until February 1950.

PLOT SUMMARY

Having warned the viewer in the opening credits and to the accompaniment of dark and foreboding music that the film is going to depict the fateful maiden voyage of the *Titanic*, the action opens with Sir Bruce Ismay, president of the White Star Line, addressing the shareholders. He solemnly explains that, while the construction of the *Titanic* has just been completed, unforeseen delays have increased the construction costs, and this has resulted in a sharp fall in the share price.

The main protagonists in heated discussion on board the *Titanic* – Sigrid Olinsky, First Officer Petersen, Gloria Ismay and Sir Bruce Ismay. (*Deutsches Filminstitut/FWM*)

However, in a subsequent meeting with key board members, we see a quite different side to Ismay's character. Almost smiling with enthusiasm, he urges them to sell their shares so as to force the price even lower, assuring them that they will be able to buy back the shares on the cheap in the future. He guarantees that something will happen on the maiden voyage of the *Titanic* which will force the price higher again.

The scene switches to the *Titanic*, and the viewer is introduced to the principal protagonists in the ensuing tragedy. First, there is Ismay, already in discussion with Captain Smith about the reward the latter could earn if the ship arrives in New York ahead of schedule, and Ismay's beautiful girlfriend, Gloria. Then, in turn, we have Sigrid Olinsky, a wealthy, unmarried Baltic lady, and examples of the British aristocracy in the form of the Duchess of Canterville and Lord Douglas. There are also a couple of 'ordinary' Germans, Professor Bergmann and his assistant, Doctor Lorenz, and, finally, we are presented with the American, Lord Astor, the richest man on board, and his beautiful wife, Lady Madeleine.

Ismay makes a short speech revealing that the *Titanic* is not only the largest but also the fastest ship in the world, already sailing at a record speed of 26.5 knots. This is the surprise news which it is hoped will send the share price rocketing again.

Later, we are introduced to First Officer Petersen, a handsome and diligent German, who is a last-minute replacement for an English officer with appendicitis and who will become the hero of the film.

In view of ice warnings from other ships, Petersen, who had some emotional attachment to Sigrid on a previous voyage, first appeals to Sigrid and then to Gloria to use their influence to persuade Ismay to reduce speed and avoid catastrophe. However, it is all in vain and, halfway through the film, the ship hits the infamous iceberg. It gradually emerges that the ship has been badly damaged and, despite the belief that it was 'unsinkable', it will eventually succumb. Given that the ships responding to its calls for help will be too far away to reach *Titanic*

The real Captain Smith. (*Keele University's Warrilow Collection*)

before it sinks, it is decided to offload as many passengers into the lifeboats as possible, with women and children receiving priority. To avoid panic, the passengers are informed that they are undertaking a lifeboat drill, and the orchestra is ordered to keep playing throughout.

When Sigrid explains to Petersen that she has feelings for him and that she had tried to get Ismay to reduce speed, Petersen's romantic feelings towards her return and, in a very moving scene, he eventually persuades her to board a lifeboat, giving her his coat to keep her warm. Panic below deck results in some officers being overpowered by male passengers, and an officer is forced to shoot two passengers to try to stop the rabble. Hopes are raised when the lights of a nearby ship, the SS *Californian*, are spotted, but are soon dashed again when it fails to respond to their white flares which are not a recognised emergency signal.

Throughout all of the commotion, Astor has remained ignorant of what has been happening and is congratulating himself on having secured 52 per cent of the White Star Line at a good price. Ismay is still confident that he will obtain a place in a lifeboat and offers to save Astor's life as well if he will allow him to remain president of the company. However, Astor's fate appears sealed when his assistant rushes in with the fateful news that men who try to get into the lifeboats are being shot. Astor ruefully exclaims, 'Ismay, I sense you won't be able to keep your side of the bargain!'

Captain Smith refuses to give Ismay a place in a lifeboat, but help comes from an unexpected source in the form of Petersen, who has decided to save Ismay in order that he may be brought before the Maritime Board to answer for his actions. Action intensifies as the ship fills with water, and it becomes increasingly evident who will be saved. Gloria will survive, but Lord Douglas will perish. Petersen also seems destined to die but, in a final heroic gesture of rescuing a young girl trapped in her bedroom, the girl and he are eventually plucked from the water by the very lifeboat on which he had placed Sigrid.

The final scene is in the court of inquiry back in London, where Petersen, in giving his evidence, is adamant that only one man was responsible for the catastrophe – the president of the White Star Line. But, the court eventually determines, somewhat surprisingly, that it was the captain who was responsible for the fate of his ship, and Ismay is acquitted without punishment.

The film concludes with a final damning declaration appearing in German across the screen:

THE DEATHS OF 1500 PEOPLE REMAINED UNATONED FOR – AN ETERNAL CONDEMNATION OF ENGLAND'S QUEST FOR PROFIT!

CRITICAL REVIEW

Like all the subsequent *Titanic* movies, the story of this 1943 film is centred on the relationships between certain passengers and the human tragedy which emerges from the collision

Such was the quality of the special effects that later films about the *Titanic* were to incorporate footage from this 1943 version. (*Deutsches Filminstitut/FWM*)

with the iceberg and the subsequent loss of so many lives. What makes this film very different, however, is the deliberate focus on the actions of the president of the White Star Line, the introduction of fictitious German characters and the condemning conclusion that the loss of the ship was due to greedy English capitalists.

By today's standards, the special effects used for the ship's voyage and its actual sinking would be considered fairly routine, but they were very advanced and dramatic for their time. The action in the lifeboats was filmed in the Baltic Sea and, for a number of reasons, the film was to exceed budget considerably. Nevertheless, it is quite noticeable that there is no 'bobbing' sea motion in the early internal scenes either in the ballroom or the cabins. Most of the real cinematic action arises once the ship has struck the iceberg, and it is only towards the end of the film that passengers are shown being thrown around as the ship lurches to one side or sinks into the water. Much use is made of models, and the camera keeps returning to scenes which show the engine room and ballroom gradually filling with water. On deck, however, there is a much more vivid impression of the panic and loss of life, as passengers rush around trying to secure a place in lifeboats. The ship's warning siren sounds persistently in competition with the screams of the passengers. Tension mounts as there is a real feeling that time is running out for many on board.

Effectiveness as a work of propaganda

The film *Titanic* is very successful in influencing the viewer to draw the conclusion that the accident could have been avoided and carefully constructs a case not only against Ismay, but also against capitalism in general and England in particular.

Portrayal of Sir Bruce Ismay, president of the White Star Line

Though Ismay is outwardly a very influential and highly respected gentleman, the film undertakes a complete assassination of his character by depicting him as treacherous, greedy and a coward.

SS *Titanic*.
(*Gary Cooper*)

From the earliest scenes, he is shown to be plotting to find a way to make personal gain out of the current fall in the White Star Line's share price, even if this is at the expense of the other shareholders. Indeed, when it later becomes apparent that someone else is deliberately short-selling to force the price down, Ismay rather ironically complains that someone is doing to him exactly what he wanted to do to everyone else.

The audience is not inclined to feel particularly sympathetic. He had hoped that the share price would soar if the *Titanic* could win the Blue Riband by becoming the fastest ship to cross the Atlantic. To ensure success, he is seen trying to appeal to Captain Smith's own greed by offering him $5,000 for the ship's arrival on schedule in New York and a further $1,000 for every hour in advance. He is keen to emphasise that the faster Smith pushes the ship, the greater the reward.

His ruthless and irresponsible attitude is reinforced by his constant refusal to allow the ship to reduce speed, even when Petersen reports that drift ice has been reported in the vicinity. Ismay responds angrily:

Danger – that is ridiculous. The Titanic *is unsinkable!*

Despite Petersen's warnings that he is putting 2,000 lives at risk because of the shortage of lifeboats, Ismay abuses his authority by demanding that Captain Smith maintain a direct course at full speed. Ismay also fails to listen to other approaches by Sigrid, Petersen and Astor. He is even prepared to sacrifice personal morality for financial gain, as is evident in his false display of affection towards the rich Sigrid and his guilty confession to Gloria, albeit that Gloria seems to accept his assurance that it is only a business relationship.

When the ship does hit an iceberg and Ismay is informed by Petersen that the ship is sinking, panic sets in and he tries to bribe Petersen with the offer of $10,000 to secure him a place on a lifeboat. Like Gloria, the viewer is sickened by his cowardice, and disdain for his capitalist greed grows even deeper when he attempts to bargain with Astor by offering that he will secure a place for Astor, too, if Astor will let Ismay remain president of the White Star Line. Despite the fact that priority for the lifeboats should be given to women and children, Ismay is eventually forced to try to persuade the captain to secure him a place, and we are again reminded that it is Ismay who is responsible for the accident when the captain quietly declares:

I believe nature placed you and your people above me. I followed your orders to the letter. But I was wrong, President Ismay.

The viewer still hopes that Ismay will be punished for all his crimes at the Maritime Board and, therefore, feels cheated when he walks free. Our hatred for this man and all he represents is complete.

Portrayal of the upper classes

If the film condemns Ismay, then it also paints the characters of most of the other well-to-do American or English personalities in a very poor light. In fact, the desire to distinguish the upper classes from the third class passengers in the film is deliberately accentuated by giving Ismay and Astor, respectively, a knighthood and peerage which they never, in fact, possessed.

Astor is shown to be little better than Ismay. Business means more to him than his wife, and he is apparently so caught up in his enthusiasm to gain control of the White Star Line that he seems quite oblivious to the sirens and screams of passengers. His wife and Gloria are little different. They seem calmer and more self-assured than their respective partners in private, but it is obvious that their only reasons for staying with these men are the power and the wealth which they possess.

Comments about England are always negative. For example, there are a number of arrogant statements by Ismay which would certainly have riled the German viewer. In speaking to his fellow board members, Ismay states:

> But I ask all of you to trust me ... just as we trust our Titanic – the proudest ship ever to sail – soon to set to sea for the honour of the White Star Line and for the glory of England.

Likewise, in his opening address to the passengers, he boasts, 'You also know that English experts say she is the world's safest ship!'

Consequently, the downfall of both Ismay and the *Titanic* comes to be equated with the reckless arrogance and greed of the English upper classes as a whole. Even the court's decision to allow Ismay to walk free is a sad indictment of English justice, and this is emphasised by the words which appear on the screen as a final damning conclusion to the film.

Nevertheless, the middle and working classes are portrayed in a much more benign manner. The wireless operators will not accept tips and keep broadcasting right to the end. The naval officers and crew also carry out their duties effectively with no thought to their personal safety. There is a touching moment as the officers salute each other respectfully when the captain relieves them of their duty once all the lifeboats have been lowered. Despite the general panic, there are also several individuals in steerage who do try to come to the assistance of their fellow passengers.

Portrayal of German characters

One of the most interesting aspects of the film is the propaganda opportunity exploited through the introduction of a number of heroic German characters who never actually existed.

Every German viewer would certainly have wanted to model himself on First Officer Petersen, who undertakes his duties flawlessly and does not care whom he upsets in his attempts to prevent the ensuing disaster. He acts in a gentlemanly manner at all times in his dealings with Sigrid, and this provides the main romantic interest in the film. When he orders her to join a lifeboat, and we see her head slowly disappearing below the deck line, the viewer assumes that they will not see each other again. However, it is only fitting that he should survive the cold waters and be the one to give evidence at the trial. If anyone was to be blamed for their actions on that fateful night, then it certainly was not going to be Petersen.

Another love element is provided in the whirlwind romance between two employees, Heidi and Franz, whose names alone reveal a clue as to their nationality. They show such enthusiasm in all they do and smile at each other right to the end. They are truly good people, and

Heidi and Franz, two fictional employees of the *Titanic* whose whirlwind romance provides a welcome distraction from the main action. (*Deutsches Filminstitut/FWM*)

the viewer cannot help but feel that Franz does not deserve to die. We never actually see what happens to him.

Even Professor Bergmann and his assistant are depicted as admirable Germans. The professor stoically accepts that he is an old man and will not survive, but that what is more important is his research and that his young assistant *will* survive to carry on his work. It is certainly an admirable example for a Germany deep in war and dependent on the young to continue to fight for the cause.

POINTS OF NOTE CONCERNING THE CONTENT AND PRODUCTION OF THE FILM

Was Ismay directly responsible for the sinking of the ship?

Where is the dividing line between fact and fiction? The film suggests that it is primarily Ismay's reckless ambition to win the Blue Riband by reaching New York ahead of schedule, which resulted in the collision with an iceberg and the consequent loss of life. This biased account seems to lack validity. Despite the 26.5 knot speed reported in the film, *Titanic*'s top speed was actually only around 23 knots. Consequently, Ismay would have known that the *Titanic* would never have been able to beat the Atlantic crossing record as it was not taking the most direct route, and *Mauritania* had already made a crossing in 1909 at an average speed of 26.06 knots, a record which was to stand for twenty years.

Likewise, no evidence was ever provided by any of the surviving officers to support the charge that Ismay ordered Smith to disregard the iceberg warnings and to proceed to New York at breakneck speed. While good publicity could have been expected from an early arrival in New York, the priority was to ensure that the ship arrived safely without any undue incident. The film also fails to mention that a further six ice warnings were received by the wireless operators on the day of the collision, but that the operators were so busy with transmitting messages for passengers that these ice warnings were never reported to the captain.

The builders of *Titanic* never actually claimed it was unsinkable. However, given its system of supposedly watertight bulkheads and fuelled by press comment and some early advertising literature, many, including Ismay, certainly believed that the *Titanic* was *practically* unsinkable. Consequently, Ismay might well have been less likely to have been concerned by potential drift ice warnings, even if they had been reported.

Nonetheless, it could well be argued that Ismay was indirectly responsible for the loss of life arising *after* the collision. It was reported that such was Ismay's desire to provide the very highest level of luxury for the rich and famous that he had ordered the original design of the ship to be altered, reducing the number of lifeboats from forty-eight to sixteen. It is surprising that the film-makers failed to note this. Of course, the Board of Trade must also share some of the responsibility since this number was still regarded as satisfactory for a ship of the *Titanic*'s tonnage.

In reality, the combination of bad luck in encountering an iceberg on a still sea in mid-spring, ill-judgement on the part of the first officer for putting the engines in reverse when the iceberg was sighted, the failure of the SS *Californian* to respond to radio messages and distress flares, and the lack of lifeboats were the real reasons for the disaster.

Was Ismay a coward?

With regard to the claim that Ismay was a coward, it is certainly true that he managed to board the last lifeboat to leave the ship as it was being lowered, albeit after having apparently assisted with the boarding of some women and children. He subsequently claimed that he had not realised that there were other women and children who were still on the ship. Whatever the truth, his reputation was certainly ruined and, for the rest of his life, he was to be hounded by the press and haunted by his memories of the deaths of other passengers.

Did the German characters portrayed in the film actually exist?

While there is plenty of evidence of examples of heroism and self-sacrifice in the final hours of this tragedy, there is nothing to support the contention that any of the acts of heroism which we witness were displayed by Germans. According to the country of residence section of *Encyclopedia Titanica*, there were only five German and Austrian passengers on the ship. Of these five, only the woman and one of the men, who had travelled under an assumed name and acted in a far from gentlemanly manner, survived. The first officer was actually a Scotsman called Murdoch, and even the chief officer was an Englishman. Both were reported to have assisted with the boarding of women and children into lifeboats, and neither survived.

Consequently, a great deal of poetic licence has been adopted to derive any pro-German propaganda out of a film which would otherwise have been quite depressing and of little direct interest to a German audience, other than to give them further justification for despising everything which England represented.

HOW WAS THE FILM RECEIVED?

While we know that Goebbels was critical of the poor acting in the film, we shall never know how the film would have been received by the general public as it did not have much of a chance to be a box office success. Only completed early in 1943, the film was eventually banned by the censors from being screened in Germany in April 1943, out of concern for reaction to the panic and death scenes associated both with the sinking and the shooting of the passengers by an officer. There was unease that this would cause unnecessary anguish in a cinema audience and perhaps even elicit some sympathy for the ordinary English passengers who were to die. This seems somewhat ironic since, by 1943, most German civilians would have been aware of the horrors of war, and the deaths in the film must have appeared rather routine compared to the real world in which they lived.

Perhaps the real reason is that by 1943, the authorities desired a film which would provide entertainment, and they needed to be sure it would inspire an audience rather than cause more depression. This aim was obviously seen to outweigh any benefit that might be derived from the anti-English propaganda element which it contained. Nevertheless, after extensive editing and cutting, the film was shown in Paris and at a few military installations by late 1943, before it was banned completely by Goebbels.

We can only surmise that although the film was quite exciting, had some love interest, was more or less based on a true historical incident and did portray the German characters in a good light, it was never going to be a 'feel good' movie, and perhaps the greatest surprise is that it was ever allowed to be commissioned in the first instance.

THE FATE OF THE DIRECTOR AND THE POST-PRODUCTION DISASTERS ASSOCIATED WITH THE FILM

If the story of the 1912 *Titanic* disaster were not tragic enough, this 1943 version was fated to be associated with almost as much ill-luck and personal tragedy as the real event.

First, Herbert Selpin, the film's original director, known to be short-tempered, was overheard complaining one day about the ineffectiveness of the army and how the war was delaying the completion of his movie. This was reported to the Gestapo. Selpin was arrested and, having refused to withdraw his remarks in a subsequent meeting with Goebbels, Selpin was found hanged in his cell on 1 August 1942. There are conflicting reports as to whether he committed suicide or was executed, although the balance of evidence suggests that he was murdered. The film had to be completed by Werner Klingel.

Second, the film was due to be premiered in Berlin early in 1943, but the premiere had to be postponed because the building in which the film print was held was bombed the night before the event.

Third, much of the outside action had been filmed on board a cruise ship called the *Cap Arcona*. Only days from the end of the war, this ship was itself deliberately bombed by the Allies who were unaware that it was transferring prisoners from German concentration camps

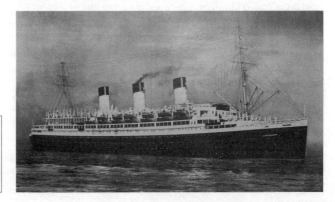

The *Cap Arcona*: the tragic cruise ship used for filming outside scenes on the *Titanic*. (*Wikimedia Commons*)

to Amsterdam. Many thousands were to die when the ship sank, in what is regarded as one of the cruellest naval tragedies in history.

Finally, in addition to being banned by the Germans from being screened during the war, the film was banned again by the Western Allies in April 1950, due to its anti-British characterisation and the fact that well-to-do English passengers are shown to be saved while German lower deck passengers are left to drown. Ironically, the Soviet Union allowed public viewing of the film in East Berlin and East Germany from March 1950, presumably for exactly the same reasons. It continued to be banned in most Western countries after the war because of its anti-capitalist and anti-English sentiments, and it was only in 1955 that a censored version was released for general viewing across the whole of Germany.

CONCLUSION

In terms of dramatic action, the film *Titanic* is certainly very effective and holds the viewer's attention throughout. As a piece of propaganda, it cleverly places the blame for the collision and loss of life on greedy English capitalists, while ensuring that almost all the acts of stoic heroism and self-sacrifice are reserved for the imaginary German characters introduced to the story. Nevertheless, it was never going to be other than a 'disaster' movie and was bound to evoke conflicting emotions from a German audience who might well have decided that they would prefer to watch a comedy rather than a tragedy at that time. Even so, whether the fears about its negative impact on an audience were so great that it deserved to be banned is open to question. This film had nothing to do with the war, and the German characters in the film should have served as uplifting role models in the difficult times ahead.

The greatest tragedy is that the overall history associated with this film is almost as depressing as the historical disaster of the *Titanic* itself, and it was ten years before any other film company would be brave enough to produce another film on this subject.

CHAPTER IV

GERMAN FEATURE FILMS:
ANTI-SEMITIC PROPAGANDA

BACKGROUND

Given that a key aspect of Nazi ideology centred on Aryan supremacy and the contention that the Jews were parasites who had to be removed from positions of authority if Germany were to flourish, it is perhaps rather surprising that relatively limited numbers of anti-Semitic films were actually produced during the Nazi era, and the bulk of these appeared after 1939.

While the open oppression of the Jews in Germany, through the gradual removal of their rights as German citizens, had begun as soon as the Nazis came to power in 1933, *Kristallnacht* (Night of the Broken Glass), which took place from 9 to 10 November 1938, is widely regarded as the commencement of the Final Solution. Apart from the mass burning of synagogues and Jewish businesses, it signalled the beginning of forced deportations and the removal to concentration camps of millions of Jews across Europe.

However, the early shortage of blatant anti-Semitic films to support such attacks on the Jewish population partly reflects Hitler's own initial ambivalence towards the Jews. In the early pages of *Mein Kampf*, Hitler actually declares that in his innocent years in Linz, he had thought that the Jews were persecuted only because of their faith, and he claims that he not only

WENN·ES·DEM INTERNATIO/ NALEN·FINANZJUDEN/ TUM·GELINGEN SOLLTE/DIE·VÖLKER NOCH·EINMAL·IN EINEN·WELTKRIEG ZU·STÜRZEN/DANN WIRD·DAS·ERGEB/ NIS·NICHT·DER·SIEG DES·JUDENTUMS SEIN·SONDERN DIE VERNICHTUNG·DER·JÜ/ DISCHEN·RASSE IN EUROPA

A D O L F　HITLER

A Nazi slogan poster issued in September 1941 taken from Hitler's speech of 30 January 1939, blaming the Jews in advance for any world war. It reads: 'If International Finance Jewry should once again succeed in plunging the peoples into a world war, then the result will not be the victory of Jewry, but rather the destruction of the Jewish race in Europe.' (*Randall Bytwerk*)

The synagogue in Aachen after its destruction on *Kristallnacht*. (*US Holocaust Memorial Museum courtesy of Stadtarchiv, Aachen*)

abhorred remarks against them but was also unhappy with the anti-Semitic stance of some of the newspapers. Nevertheless, within a few short pages of his book, Hitler seems to undergo a complete character transformation. He asserts that he began to realise that these Jewish Germans did not just have a different religion but were also a different people whose aim was to assert the national character of Judaism. He complains about Jews being 'water shy' and the key proponents of vulgar art and literature, prostitution and the white slave trade. Ultimately, there is hardly any aspect of moral decadence which he does not lay at their door:

> And so I believe today that my conduct is in accordance with the will of the Almighty Creator. In standing guard against the Jew I am defending the handiwork of the Lord.

Goebbels' views on the Jews were just as contradictory. In a letter written in 1919 to his girlfriend, Anka, Goebbels wrote:

> As you know, I can't stand this exaggerated anti-Semitism. I can't claim that many of my best friends are Jews, but my view is that you don't get rid of them by huffing and puffing, let alone by pogroms. And even if you could do so, that would be highly ignoble and unworthy.

However, by 1921, Goebbels had completed a novel about his own life story under the title of *Michael*, which provides a valuable insight into his changed opinion of the Jews:

> Jews make me physically sick – the mere sight of them does this ... the Jew has raped our people, soiled our ideals, weakened the strength of the nation, corrupted morals ... Either he destroys us or we destroy him!

In reality, despite such hostile views, the lack of openly antagonistic anti-Jewish films in the early Nazi years was very much a deliberate political ploy not to arouse the hostility of the rest of the world. Germany was not yet at war, and the Nazis recognised that the Jews did wield tremendous international power, especially in finance, and that any propagandistic attacks on the Jewish race had to be carefully co-ordinated.

Consequently, there is some uncertainty as to whether it was Hitler or Goebbels who finally took the initiative in urging the production of anti-Semitic films and, indeed, as to when that initiative first occurred. There was certainly no public mention of producing anti-Semitic films when Goebbels launched the Nazis' vicious campaign against the Jews in November 1938. In fact, it is only in Hitler's speech at the Reichstag on 30 January 1939 that there is a blatant threat that the Nazis will specifically produce anti-Jewish films if Hollywood continues to pro-duce anti-Nazi films. Whatever the truth, there was also some doubt as to what would make an acceptable anti-Semitic film, with Goebbels being particularly unhappy with the crude and naïve style of some of the early Jewish documentary films.

When it comes to feature films, *Robert und Bertram* (*Robert and Bertram*), which was released in July 1939, is generally regarded as the first anti-Semitic film produced by the Nazis. It is primarily an entertaining musical farce based on an earlier stage play and is devoid of any specifically hostile anti-Jewish comments. It is a love story about two mischievous vaga-bonds, Robert and Bertram, who use their dubious skills to find a way of removing financial difficulties which would otherwise prevent Lenchen from marrying her beloved Michel.

The Jewish contribution to the tale does not arise until the second half of the film with the introduction of the successful Jewish businessman, Ipelmeyer, and his ridiculous wife, daughter and servants. While there are certainly stereotypical presentations of the Jewish characters in the film, such as a comment that Ipelmeyer has made his fortune at other peo-ple's expense, the way Jews speak German and in the manner they conduct themselves, there is nothing particularly offensive about these portrayals. Indeed, it is more reminiscent of the clichéd portrayal of the national characteristics of say the Scots or the French and is more akin to a Molière or Shakespeare comedy where fun is derived from mocking an individual's excessive personal characteristics such as being miserly or a hypochondriac.

One notable line does occur when Ipelmeyer is speaking in confidence to one of the vaga-bonds. He whispers to the vagabond that he is an Israeli, to which the vagabond responds that he also would share a secret in that he has a large stomach. The implication is that, visu-ally, it is obvious whether or not someone is a Jew.

However, just as much fun is poked at non-Jewish characters, and the real villains of the peace are the two non-Jewish vagabonds who steal jewellery from Ipelmeyer, but who are still accepted into heaven because their crimes were not committed for personal gain but to ensure the happiness of the two lovers, Lenchen and Michel. The only slightly more sinister portrayal of the Jews is the suggested loose sexual morality of both Ipelmeyer and his wife. In the former case, Ipelmeyer is eager to seduce a pretty young ballerina, but even this vain attempt ends in comedy as Ipelmeyer has been slipped a sleeping draught by his wife's lover, and it is while Ipelmeyer is asleep that he is relieved of his valuables by the two vagabonds. All in all, the film is a light-hearted fairytale, and the ordinary viewer was never likely to leave the cinema filled with any hostility towards, or fear of, the Jews. It is little wonder, therefore, that Hitler and Goebbels were both dissatisfied with the style and effectiveness of this film.

A further anti-Semitic comedy, *Leinen aus Irland* (*Linen from Ireland*), was released just two months later. However, this time the lines are far more acerbic and the action less farcical than in *Robert und Bertram*.

The 1929 play on which the film was based recounts an attempt to permit the cheap import of linen from Ireland, which would have benefited local textile manufacturers and resulted in increased unemployment for Czech citizens. Brennstein, a non-Jew, is the owner of one

Film programme for the 1939 comedy, *Robert und Bertram*. (*Author's Collection /Verlag für Filmschriften*)

particular manufacturing company, Libussa, and he enters into a business arrangement with a Jewish businessman, Schlesinger, for the sale of ladies' lingerie to the Balkans. The whole plot is complicated by Brennstein's attempts to have his daughter, Lilly, who is in love with a civil servant called Goll opposed to the lifting of tariffs, make him change his mind. In return, her father will permit her marriage to Goll. While there is some mockery of Schlesinger as a typical financially astute Jewish businessman, the treatment of the Jews in the play is generally quite gentle. Indeed, Lilly is later to express some sympathy for her father's Jewish secretary, Dr Körner, who is finding it difficult to be a gentleman given that he comes from the ghetto. Nevertheless, the film plot is deliberately manipulated to maximise negative sentiments towards Jews. First, the setting is moved to a border town in the Sudetenland, where the Sudeten-German owner of a textile company is deceived into handing control of his business to Libussa, which is based in Prague. Second, rather than Brennstein, who is director of Libussa, the takeover is masterminded by Kuhn, Libussa's Jewish general secretary, who is also the primary driver behind persuading officials to remove the tariffs from imported Irish linen. The smarmy Kuhn, together with his less sophisticated uncle Sigi, are portrayed as particularly vile and unpleasant characters and bear similarities to the key Jewish characters who would appear in *Jud Süss* the following year. The final insult is for the Jew, Kuhn, to seek permission from Brennstein to marry his daughter, Lilly. Not only is his ridiculous proposal declined, but Kuhn is summarily dismissed when Brennstein becomes aware of the sort of underhand activity in which Kuhn has been engaged.

While Goebbels had had little direct involvement in the production of *Leinen aus Irland*, he was to declare himself satisfied with the final version of this film.

ANTI-SEMITIC FILMS REVIEWED

Critical references to the Jews are to be found in a good number of other films of the period, including *Hans Westmar*, *S.A. Mann Brand*, *Heimkehr* and *G.P.U.*, but this was not the primary propaganda focus of those films. Indeed, it was only towards the end of 1938 that each of the film companies was issued with a directive from the Propaganda Ministry to produce a major anti-Semitic work.

In order of chronological release, the most influential of the films subsequently produced were: *Die Rothschilds* (July 1940), *Jud Süss* (September 1940) and *Der ewige Jude* (November 1940).

These three films are by far the most infamous anti-Jewish films ever screened by the Nazis, and yet each is completely different in style and subject matter.

Die Rothschilds (*The Rothschilds*) is a supposedly accurate historical account of the attempts by Nathan Rothschild to ingratiate himself into the higher echelons of English business society, and recounts how the Rothschild family across Europe contrived to ensure that they were the financial beneficiaries of Britain's war with Napoleon. Comic in parts, the film succeeds in attacking Jews, the English and capitalists all in one go, but with the result that viewers are left with conflicting emotions as to which side is most worthy of their disdain or sympathy.

Jud Süss (*Jew Süss*) is another historical film, but this time set in eighteenth-century Stuttgart and gives an account of how the Jew Süss Oppenheimer abused his influence over the Duke of Württemberg to impose draconian taxes on the general populace for his own personal gain. In the process he commits murder, torture and rape and is eventually hanged for his crimes. It is the most disturbing, racially motivated feature film produced by the Nazis.

While of feature length, *Der ewige Jude* (*The Eternal Jew*) is really a documentary using actual footage from the Warsaw Ghetto, and so, for this reason, its detailed analysis has been reserved for Chapter X of this book. The film abuses the innocent involvement of civilians in posing for the camera to support a portrait of the Jews as filthy, lazy parasites who, like a plague, have spread their corrupt influence across the whole world. It is a truly vile and upsetting depiction of the Jewish race and their role in world history.

These films were to have a lasting impact, not just on the Germans who viewed the films at the time, but also because of the outrage which the films were to evoke when screened to the wider world, and the devastating consequences for the careers of many of the actors and directors who had collaborated in the production of these films.

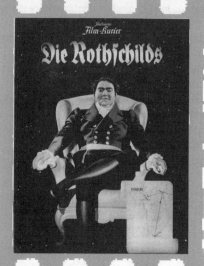

Film title: *Die Rothschilds Aktien auf Waterloo*
Year of release: 1940
Type: Feature film
Primary purpose: Anti-Jewish and anti-English/capital-
      ism propaganda
Director: Erich Waschneck
Principal stars:

Albert Florath	(Bearing)
Walter Franck	(Herries)
Herbert Hübner	(Turner)
Carl Kuhlmann	(Nathan Rothschild)
Waldemar Leitgeb	(Wellington)
Hans Stiebner	(Bronstein)
Gisela Uhlen	(Phyllis)
Hilde Weissner	(Sylvia Turner)
Herbert Wilk	(George Crayton)

Introduction

Originally released in the summer of 1940, *Die Rothschilds* (*The Rothschilds*) was the first of the films produced in response to Goebbels' directive that every film company should produce an anti-Semitic film. Despite some early box office success, the film was withdrawn after only two months, partly because of internal political differences and partly because its screening would soon clash with the launch of *Jud Süss*, which was to prove to be a far more influential production. After some editing, the film was eventually re-released in July 1941 under the expanded title of *Die Rothschilds Aktien auf Waterloo* (*The Rothschilds' Shares in Waterloo*).

Whilst primarily an anti-Semitic film, it is also very critical of the English and English capitalism in particular, and it is this confused lack of focus which prevents the film from becoming an effective propaganda instrument.

Public screening of the film in Germany today is only permitted under certain conditions, and the film is still not available for general purchase.

Plot summary

As the full title of this film suggests, the plot of *Die Rothschilds Aktien auf Waterloo* is centred on the financial role played by the Rothschild family in the Battle of Waterloo.

The film opens at an informal gathering of influential City of London bankers, where the key figures, Bearing[4] and Turner, are discussing how much their consortium should bid for a shipment of gold which has just arrived from the East Indies. In the subsequent auction, they are outbid by Nathan Rothschild, and they are so incensed that an immigrant Jew should

---

4   Whether or not deliberately, the name 'Bearing' appears written with this spelling in the opening credits, although it was presumably a reference to the famous 'Baring' banking family which still exists today.

Nathan Rothschild shows his frustration when no guests arrive to attend his banquet. (*BFI/FWM*)

'muscle-in' on their business that they lodge a formal complaint with Herries, the treasury high commissioner. Herries, however, is quite indifferent to their protests, and it later transpires that even Herries is prepared to reach an agreement with Rothschild for the delivery of the gold to Spain for the campaign which Wellington is going to wage against Napoleon.

Meanwhile, prior to leaving for battle, Lieutenant George Crayton and Bearing's daughter, Phyllis, who are besotted with each other, meet in secret, as her father is totally opposed to any such relationship, given that Crayton is not a man of substance.

Throughout the film, Rothschild resorts to a number of devious stratagems as he tries to worm his way into influential English society. First, he attempts to ingratiate himself with Turner's wife, Sylvia, by offering her the use of his coach when her horses run wild. Then, he endeavours to come to a private arrangement with Wellington regarding the delivery of the minted gold. Later, he seeks to win the support of Sylvia by showing affection and generosity towards Phyllis, who has been disowned by her father for bearing an illegitimate child to Crayton. Finally, he tries to host an elaborate banquet to which all the great and the good of British society are invited, but this is a complete failure as Turner deliberately hosts a rival reception at the same time, which all Rothschild's invitees attend instead. Indeed, throughout the film, most of Rothschild's attempts to be accepted by 'English' society are doomed to failure.

Nevertheless, in his financial dealings, he does successfully manipulate his Jewish contacts to transport the minted gold through France to Spain, albeit with the deduction of exorbitant fees.

Napoleon is eventually forced to sue for peace, and this gives Rothschild the opportunity to provide financial assistance to the exiled Duke of Orleans in return for Rothschild's brother, James, being allowed to conduct the business of state finance in France, once the Duke becomes the next king. However, Napoleon's subsequent escape from Elba and his renewed military activities threaten to thwart Rothschild's plans, and so he is forced to resort to other means to protect his position. Crayton, in the mistaken belief that he is serving Wellington, agrees to provide Rothschild with up-to-date reports by courier pigeon regarding the course of the war.

In reality, Turner, Bearing and their cronies are also seeking to make a profit from the war by buying British government bonds, in the firm belief that Wellington will again defeat Napoleon. Consequently, while Rothschild disposes of his bonds when he learns that Napoleon is attacking the Prussians, the other city gents continue to buy as many of these bonds as are available.

When Crayton realises that, rather than assisting the war effort, he has only been helping speculators in the stock market, he releases the rest of the pigeons in anger and, initially, this leads Rothschild to believe that Napoleon has won the war and that he is ruined. However, one of Rothschild's other agents has been able to rush back from the continent and confirms that Napoleon actually lost the Battle of Waterloo. Rothschild then deliberately feeds false rumours to the Stock Exchange to the effect that the British have lost the war. Turner and his colleagues are forced to sell their bonds at knock-down prices and Rothschild purchases these in secret, so that by the time the truth regarding the outcome of the war emerges, he is worth more than £11 million and claims that he is 'rich enough to buy all of England!'

The film concludes by showing Rothschild, while in discussion with Herries, proudly marking on paper the influence of the Jews from Jerusalem and across all the financial centres of Europe. There is one final menacing slogan added to the re-released version of the film which seeks to bring the history of the Rothschilds up-to-date and make clear to the viewer that both the Jews and the English are considered Germany's enemies:

> By the completion of this film, the last of the Rothschilds will have left Europe as refugees
> – the struggle against their accomplices in England – the British Plutocracy – continues ...

CRITICAL REVIEW

While the primary focus of the propaganda in this film is undoubtedly directed against the Jewish race, much of the film is also highly critical of English capitalism and the ruling classes of both England and France.

Portrayal of the Jews

In his attempts to be accepted by the higher echelons of English business society, Nathan is shown to be ruthlessly ambitious, greedy and opportunistic. He pays over the odds for the shipment of gold so as to win the commission to transport minted gold to Wellington in Spain. In his provision of financial support to the Duke of Orleans, his proposed lavish banquet for the city elite, the gift of rare flowers to Sylvia and even in the gifts he bestows on Phyllis, Rothschild is shown to be prepared to speculate shrewdly if he believes this will eventually

Nathan tries to ingratiate himself with English business society by making a good impression on the wives of the rich and powerful. (BFI/FWM)

allow him to make a handsome profit from such investments. By acting as the secret benefactor of the beautiful Phyllis, there is a definite suggestion that Rothschild's intentions might be less than honourable and not merely in a financial sense.

However, above all else, it is the actions of the whole Rothschild family and, by implication, the International Jewish Movement, in their involvement in the war with Napoleon, which is so roundly condemned by the film. Politically, it is quite apparent that the Rothschilds are indifferent to the outcome of the war and that their only concern is to profit as much as possible from helping to finance the war and from any stock market speculation resulting from the war. First, in a series of stereotypical representations of shabbily dressed Jews with long, unkempt hair, we see each intermediary in the transport of gold coin from England to Spain greedily deducting his own commission. Then, in the war itself, the various European branches of the Rothschild family have no scruples about reaching local agreements with the competing sides in the conflict. Nevertheless, Nathan Rothschild is the principal culprit, both in his deceitful

The Duke of Wellington, who was in fact of Irish descent. ('*Arthur Wellesley, Duke of Wellington*' oil on canvas by John Lucas, 1851–52. WOA 3157, © Palace of Westminster Collection)

misuse of Crayton to obtain advance information about the progress of the war and also in his completely immoral manipulation of the Stock Exchange for his own ends, by deliberately arranging for false information to be circulated about the outcome of the Battle of Waterloo. The film's condemnation of the horrifying extent of the Rothschilds' power is clearly highlighted in the final scenes of the film where the Star of David ominously illustrates the Jewish influence across all the key European finance centres, and a map depicts Britain as being completely under the control of the Jews.

Portrayal of the English capitalists and ruling classes in England and France

The film ridicules the English from the very opening scenes, as is evident in the seemingly innocent badinage between Bearing and his business acquaintances about the dangers of being a missionary. This story gives an excuse for the throw-away comment that when a missionary is killed, the British government sends out a punishment expedition which gives it the opportunity to examine the country further and then never leave. It is an obvious criticism of Britain's imperialistic, expansionist ambitions.

The practices of the well-to-do, influential, financial families are also roundly condemned by the film. Turner and Bearing are seen to be almost as ruthless and deceitful as Nathan in business matters, both in their determination not to allow the Rothschilds, as a Jewish family, to break into their cosy business relationships, and in their attempts to profit from the war by maximising their holdings in government bonds. Ironically, the most convincing criticism arises from a conversation which takes place between Sylvia and the businessmen early in the film, when she is recounting how her horses had run wild and how she had been rescued by Mr Rothschild. Her complaints about their unkind comments regarding Rothschild evoke the response, 'Madam, you were born in Ireland!' She quickly responds, 'Not only born ... I have always realised here in England how fortunate I am to be Irish!' Her husband goes on to explain how, for Sylvia, being English is as good as having a character defect. She continues by condemning the pious hypocrisy of Bearing for considering Lieutenant Crayton good enough to die for England as a soldier, but not of sufficient standing to marry his daughter. This attempt to differentiate between the characters of the Irish and the English in the eyes of the Germans is a common theme in Nazi propaganda films and most evident in the two pro-Irish films, *Der Fuchs von Glenarvon* and *Mein Leben für Irland* which were analysed earlier in this book.

The attack on the English continues in the negative portrayal of Wellington, whom the Germans obviously recognised as being regarded as one of Britain's greatest military heroes. He is depicted as a shameless womaniser, so profligate in his reckless lifestyle that his creditors are never far from his door. Indeed, when he voices outrage at the discovery that of the 10,600 guineas of minted gold which left England, only 5,512 guineas arrived in Spain, it is made clear that he is really no better than the Jewish intermediaries when he asks the paymaster to reserve another 500 guineas for his own secret account. Above all, there is a deliberate attempt to undermine Wellington's place in history, with Crayton's constant insistence, rightly or wrongly, that Wellington was beaten and that it was only the intervention of Blücher and his Prussians which won the Battle of Waterloo for Wellington. It is somewhat ironic that having gone to great lengths to differentiate between the Irish and the English in the Sylvia scenes, the film blatantly ignores the fact that Wellington was, in fact, of Irish descent, although this would have been clear from any encyclopaedia entry of the time. Indeed, there is even a comment that Wellington's family has been English for more than 300 years. Obviously, any attack on the character of Wellington as a typical Englishman would have been greatly diluted by the revelation that he was actually Irish.

Nathan Rothschild
(right) plotting
with his agent,
Bronstein.
(*Deutsches
Filminstitut/FWM*)

Effectiveness as a work of propaganda

Notwithstanding a comment in the *Berliner Lokal-Anzeiger* newspaper at the time that the story was based on facts, there is no doubt that the effectiveness of the film as a means of promoting anti-Jewish propaganda is constantly undermined by the film's simultaneous attacks on the English and French ruling classes and its condemnation of the character of influential City of London businessmen.

Consequently, the unreasonable attitude of the English bankers towards Rothschild, simply because he is a Jew, actually evokes a certain sympathy and admiration from the viewer for his perseverance in the face of such adversity. Even Bearing admonishes Turner for his blatant, anti-Jewish racism in his complaint to Herries about Rothschild's business practices, and Turner's cruelty and arrogance in arranging a rival banquet on the same day as the one Rothschild had planned is quite astounding. Given that so many of his projects backfire, there are times when he almost becomes a figure of fun, such as his visit to Sylvia with his collection of exotic tulips. He is eventually obliged to beat an undignified retreat, chased out of the door by her bulldog, and the humour is reinforced in his subsequent relating of the unfortunate incident to his Jewish confidant, Bronstein:

> Nathan: You said she would be alone!
> Bronstein: I told you to visit Mrs Turner. I didn't say to visit her dog!

In practice, it is only in the later scenes that the utterly ruthless aspects of Rothschild's character come to the fore in his deception of Crayton and in the deliberate feeding of false information to the Stock Exchange. Indeed, it is the English capitalist classes which are subjected to more persistent criticism for their racist attitude towards the Jews, for their hypocritical stance to those of a lower social rank, for their lack of compassion for Phyllis and her child and, ultimately, for their own reckless speculation for financial gain. It is somewhat ironic that the viewer is inclined to feel pity for Phyllis and Crayton and their illegitimate child when, with a slight change of emphasis, Crayton might just as easily have been condemned for acting in such a dishonourable fashion. But such an approach would certainly have detracted from the effectiveness of the desired criticism of the English city gentlemen.

The condemnation of English society as a whole is neatly summarised towards the end of the film when Crayton reveals to the sympathetic Sylvia that he, Phyllis and their son are going to leave the country:

Crayton: There must be a place where you can breathe freely. Everything has a price here. Your dignity, your fortune, even death pays out in this ...
Sylvia: ... land of freedom!
Crayton: ... Freedom! Even God is not free in this country. He's a business partner, nothing more.

But even these harsh observations are undermined by earlier scenes in the film when the English bankers and the ordinary people who have invested with these bankers are portrayed as victims, both because of the severe financial losses which they have incurred through the actions of the treacherous Jews and also because the Aryan British have allowed themselves to become a nation ruled by Jews.

The Nazis' own views on the film

While Goebbels was initially greatly impressed by the screenplay, he became increasingly uncomfortable with the film itself and, quite justifiably, was dubious about its likely effect on the viewer. Unlike *Jud Süss*, which was far more vitriolic in its denunciation of the whole Jewish race, *Die Rothschilds* was never awarded a highly acclaimed rating by the authorities. Admittedly, the timing, both of the production and of the initial release of the film, was somewhat unfortunate since, in the summer of 1940, Hitler was still wrestling between trying to reach peace with Britain and condemning the British for being imperialist oppressors with whom he could never negotiate. Disagreements concerning the content arose with Hess and other party members, hastening the film's initial withdrawal, and a restriction was imposed on the media from reporting on the film in any detail.

Conclusion

As a work of entertainment, *Die Rothschilds Aktien auf Waterloo* is actually quite successful, with some intermittent humour to counter the tension which arises as the viewer awaits the outcome of the underlying financial battle between the Rothschilds and the English bankers.

Despite the title and its apparent anti-Jewish focus, Mirko Jelusich, who provided the original idea for the film, indicated that the original script had an anti-British bias, and there is little doubt that the conflict which emerged between competing objectives and changing political priorities had an adverse effect on the overall effectiveness of the film as a work of propaganda. As Goebbels declared, a propaganda message should always be simple and consistent, and the main failing of this film is an overambitious attempt to satisfy a number of propaganda objectives at the same time.

On the one hand, the film wanted to arouse hatred against the Jews for making money out of the Napoleonic War and, indeed, for a war in which so many Prussians had lost their lives. But, on the other hand, the film *also* wished to condemn the English for their arrogant, capitalist ways *and* for allowing themselves to be outwitted by the Jews. In practice, any film with multiple and, at times, conflicting objectives, which actually evoked some sympathy for Germany's enemies, was never going to achieve its propaganda aims, even though it was reasonably successful at the box office. While banning the film at the end of the war, even the Allied Control Commission seemed relatively unperturbed in their closing analysis of the content:

An excellent production with anti-British tendency meant for popular consumption by the uninformed.

It would be left to the shortly-to-be released *Jud Süss* and *Der ewige Jude* to achieve the more direct anti-Semitic impact which the Nazis so desired.

Film title: *Jud Süss*
Year of release: 1940
Type: Feature film
Primary purpose: Anti-Jewish propaganda
Director: Veit Harlan
Principal stars:
Heinrich George   (Duke of Württemberg)
Werner Krauss   (Rabbi Loew & Secretary Levy)
Ferdinand Marian   (Jud Süss)
Kristina Söderbaum   (Dorothea Sturm)

INTRODUCTION

It is no exaggeration to claim that *Jud Süss* (*Jew Süss*) represents one of the most disturbing racially motivated feature films produced during the Nazi era. It is not a horror film nor does it contain particularly explicit scenes of violence, although there are some elements of torture, but what makes it particularly disquieting is how the viewer is systematically persuaded that the Jew, Süss Oppenheimer, and, therefore, all Jews are treacherous and immoral creatures driven solely by personal interest and financial greed.

What is perhaps most disconcerting is that the film declares itself to be 'based on historical fact', and it was specifically shown to concentration camp guards and to SS units, which were about to be deployed in Jewish areas. It was a huge box office success, being viewed by more than 20 million people in Germany alone between 1940 and 1943, and was awarded the Golden Lion award at the Venice Film Festival in 1940. It even played to full houses when screened in France. Box office receipts for the four years to 1944 exceeded 12 million Reichsmarks, an astronomical sum for the time.

PLOT SUMMARY

The film is set in Stuttgart in 1733 and begins with the popular Prince Karl Alexander assuming the role of Duke of Württemberg from his recently deceased cousin. He solemnly binds himself to his beloved Swabians, swearing an oath to govern the land strictly according to the constitution in conjunction with the People's Council.

However, it is soon obvious that he is really an uncouth rogue and, short of money, he sends his aide to Frankfurt to call on Süss Oppenheimer to see if he can obtain some jewellery for his wife as a belated coronation gift. Oppenheimer offers him a necklace for the vastly reduced price of 10,000 thalers, but with the rather ominous aside that, 'We'll come to an understanding in Stuttgart!' However, Oppenheimer also insists that he wants to meet the Duke personally in Stuttgart, which would be difficult as all Jews were banned from the city. So, armed with appropriate entry documents supplied by the aide and having taken the drastic step of disguising his Jewishness by shaving off his sideburns and beard and wearing non-Jewish clothes, he gains entry to the city. In the course of his journey, he comes to meet the beautiful Dorothea Sturm, with whom he becomes infatuated. However, she is already in love with Faber, secretary to her father, who is the head of the People's Council.

Given that the People's Council refuses to finance the Duke's more whimsical excesses, Oppenheimer wins over the Duke with flattery, and he gives him money for a ballet. Eventually, the Duke is in debt for more than 340,000 thalers, and Oppenheimer persuades him to transfer the administration of the duchy's cities and villages to him, as minister of finance, for ten years, during which he will claim taxes from the citizens for the use of the streets and bridges, and will share the tolls with the Duke. This extra burden obviously provokes anger among the people towards the Jews and this, together with the Duke's and Oppenheimer's licentious behaviour with young girls, including Dorothea, almost leads to open revolt. However, the incidents do give Oppenheimer the chance to convince the Duke both to agree to lift the ban on Jews in Stuttgart and also to give him a letter of proxy to the effect that all operations performed by Oppenheimer carry the Duke's authority. He also persuades the Duke to agree to hang the blacksmith for his insolence.

As opposition grows, the Duke agrees to dissolve the council and to establish a more loyal ministry. Oppenheimer tries to convince Sturm to head up the ministry and also makes vague threats if he won't consent to his marrying Dorothea. However, a swift marriage with Faber is arranged in the interim, which allows Sturm to tell Oppenheimer that he is too late and that his daughter will bring no Jewish children into the world! In the meantime, Oppenheimer persuades other Jews to supply the 500,000 thalers necessary to borrow an army from another state to keep the Duke in power.

The council continues to plot revolution and to incite others to rise in riot, but Faber is captured. He is tortured, and his cries of pain result in Dorothea allowing herself to succumb to the Jew's advances, so as to gain his release. However, she is immediately horrified by what she has done and drowns herself. In a moving scene, Faber carries her body to the court

Oppenheimer pleading for his life in court. (*Deutsches Filminstitut/FWM*)

Oppenheimer, played by the infamous Ferdinand Marian, resorts to guile and flattery to win the support of the Duke. (*BFI/FWM*)

to demand justice. The Duke becomes angry, suffers a heart attack and dies, which allows Oppenheimer to be captured and charged with blackmail, usury, abuse of office, procurement and treason. However, he appeals, 'What am I guilty of here? I only followed the desires and orders of my Duke!' In pleading for his own life, he is portrayed as a miserable coward for whom the viewer has little sympathy when he is eventually condemned to be hanged until dead.

Sturm reads out one final chilling message:

All Jews must leave Stuttgart within three days. May our descendants forever hold fast to this law so that they can be spared much harm and keep their property and their lives and the lives of their children and their children's children!

The moral for a 1940 audience in Hitler's Germany could not have been clearer.

CRITICAL REVIEW

Effectiveness as a work of propaganda

In terms of anti-Jewish propaganda, it is hard to conceive that a more effective film could have been produced. From the earliest scenes, it is made clear that true Germans should feel ashamed to be seen in Jewish areas. The Jews are all made to look like tramps with scraggy beards and are dressed in unusual Caftan clothes. When the Duke's aide comes to visit Oppenheimer, the other Jews surmise that he can only have come for one thing:

He wants money like everyone else. First he's got to give and then we can take and take and take!

The scene fades away to the sound of their evil, hollow laughter, reminiscent of Shakespeare's Shylock demanding his pound of flesh.

For years, the Nazi regime had been distributing material showing Aryan Germans how they could identify Jews. It is, therefore, significant that from his first meeting with Oppenheimer, the hero, Faber, is able to identify him as a Jew despite the latter's attempts to disguise his appearance and Faber is immediately antagonistic towards him.

Sentimental feelings towards the *Heimat* (the home or place you come from) is a common theme in Nazi films, and the surprise that Dorothea shows when Oppenheimer reveals that he has no '*Heimat*' serves to reinforce the viewer's disdain for these wandering people with no real roots of their own. When the ban on Jews entering Stuttgart is lifted, this homeless motif is repeated in the depressing scene of hordes of Jews streaming into the city like diseased locusts about to strip it bare.

The portrayal of the Jew, Süss Oppenheimer

With regard to Oppenheimer himself, the viewer's hatred grows in intensity as he tends to exhibit some new excess of depravity in each successive scene. It is hard to find any good features in Oppenheimer, as he allows nothing to prevent the achievement of his goals. From fairly innocent beginnings, where he simply uses weasel words to gain the support of the Duke and displays false charm towards the Duke's wife and Dorothea, the seriousness of his crimes gradually increases. These range from his ruthless money-making schemes at the expense of ordinary citizens to the rape of a married woman which results in her suicide.

He is often referred to in the third person by the Duke, which is another effective way of distancing us from regarding him as a sensitive human being. Indeed, his evil-doing is repeatedly portrayed as being symbolic of the Jewish race. When Sturm is trying to encourage others to look for a way to hit back at Oppenheimer, his comments are directed towards all Jews:

The Jews are not at all clever – they are just sly! We have to be cleverer than them.

Role of religion

If the evil deeds of Oppenheimer alone were not sufficient to arouse the viewer's disgust, the opportunity is taken on a number of occasions to use religious imagery to justify the viewer's hatred.

On the one hand, the case is made that Christians almost have a duty to be anti-Jewish. In the People's Council meetings, in order to support their opposition to Oppenheimer, a couple of references are made to Martin Luther's views on the Jews:

You will have no more deadly enemy than a true Jew. First you should set fire to their synagogues, then take away their writings and ban them from usury.

The Nazis made reference to Luther on numerous occasions as justification for their attacks on the Jews. While Luther did indeed make these specific comments, it should be remembered that he was writing in the early sixteenth century when all religious figures were far more outspo-

ken in their beliefs. In 1523, Luther actually recommended that kindness should be shown towards the Jews, as Christ himself was born a Jew, and it was only because he failed to convert them to Christianity that Luther gradually became more openly critical and antagonistic towards them. Luther's influence persisted long after his death, however, and did lead to the expulsion of Jews from many German cities. Nevertheless, it is a matter for debate as to whether he would ever have gone so far as to argue for the systematic annihilation of the whole Jewish race.

On the other hand, the viewer is deliberately made to feel very uneasy about

Oppenheimer is sentenced to death for all his crimes. (BFI/FWM)

Judaism and what it stands for. Not only do the Jews look and dress differently, but in their religious ceremony we are confronted with the chanting of the worshippers as the urn containing the Torah is processed around the synagogue, all of which would have been very alien to the majority of the German population. In a later scene, when Oppenheimer tries to force Dorothea to succumb to his will, he shouts out in frustration, 'We Jews have a God of wrath who promises an eye for an eye and a tooth for a tooth!' This contrasts strongly with the far more measured Christian comments made by Sturm at Oppenheimer's trial. Despite listing all the heinous charges against Oppenheimer for which the people have suffered, Sturm claims that he is still looking only for what is just – 'Two wrongs don't make a right! An eye for an eye is not our way!'

However, he continues by quoting from their old Criminal Code to the effect that if a Jew lies with a Christian, then he shall be condemned to die. This is accepted as an incontrovertible matter of fact and, therefore, Oppenheimer's fate is sealed.

Ironic content

The film contains several incidences of irony, most of which probably escaped the viewing audience of the time.

The greatest irony is that the heroes in this film are the members of the People's Council and their supporters, while the Duke, initially received with great enthusiasm, gradually becomes the arch villain as, incited by Oppenheimer, he becomes more and more draconian, dismissing the council and assuming absolute power. In 1940, the reality in Germany was that Hitler had similarly been welcomed into power and had acted in such a way as to dismiss the Reichstag and become an absolute ruler. In practice, the parallels between the Duke and Hitler are obvious, as both became absolute dictators, abolishing democracy and removing anyone who dared to oppose them. Perhaps the difference was that, in 1940, Hitler was still seen as a benevolent dictator to whom many Germans owed employment and a source of pride in their nation.

It is also somewhat ironic that for all the disgust which the viewer is made to feel towards Oppenheimer and, in many cases, the Jewish race as a whole, the theoretically more influential Rabbi Loew, with whom Oppenheimer engages, is actually seen to be more down-to-earth. He condemns Oppenheimer for becoming as vain as a peacock and seems reluctant to mislead the Duke or to support rebellion, although this is ultimately what occurs.

The final interesting role reversal is the fact that the People's Council relies on a black Egyptian servant in the Royal Palace to keep it advised as to what plots are being concocted between Oppenheimer and the Duke. Hitler was always dismissive of non-whites, as was evident in his reaction to the American Jesse Owens winning the medals in the sprint events of the 1936 Olympic Games in Berlin. How unfitting then, from a Nazi view point, that the fate of the heroes of this film should be dependent on information fed to them in secret by a black man.

POINTS OF NOTE CONCERNING THE CONTENT AND PRODUCTION OF THE FILM

Was the film based on fact?

Zarah Leander, the famous Swedish actress, mentioned in an interview after the war that Goebbels once told her over dinner that he was toying with the idea of producing a film, called *Jud Süss*, as a direct response to Chaplin's satirical comedy, *The Great Dictator*. The film was loosely based on a book by Lion Feuchtwanger which was published in 1925 and actually banned by the Nazis in 1933. The book tells the story of Josef Süss Oppenheimer, a Jew who lived from 1698 to 1738 and who was indeed financial advisor to the Duke of Württemberg which gave him, *inter alia*, the authority to collect taxes and tolls. When the Duke died suddenly, Oppenheimer was arrested and hanged. This much was true but having seen a 1934 British film version of the book, starring Conrad Veidt, which was actually condemning anti-Semitism, Goebbels himself took personal responsibility for a complete refocus of the story to suit his own purposes. He concentrated on the fateful consequences which can arise from Jewish greed and ambition, by identifying Oppenheimer as being directly responsible for the hanging of a blacksmith, the torture of Faber and the rape of a married Christian woman.

Ironically, Feuchtwanger was a German Jewish novelist who had always been fiercely critical of the Nazis before they came to power. Consequently, he was constantly persecuted by the Nazis and was forced to flee to the United States for refuge. His works were included in the infamous burning of books by inappropriate authors in 1933 and, therefore, it must have been particularly galling for Feuchtwanger that the Nazis should adapt one of his books as a source for one of the most anti-Semitic films ever produced.

How were the director and principal actors selected, and what became of them?

Given the nature of the film, it is hard to believe that anyone would have been enthusiastic about being associated with this film, and this was indeed the case, with many actors and producers claiming to have deliberately made excuses for not participating. Even Veit Harlan, the eventual director, who was involved in making several other propaganda movies for the Nazis, had tried to use the poor quality of the script as a reason for not proceeding. He volunteered for active military service as an alternative, but Goebbels made it clear that failure to produce the film would be seen as the equivalent of desertion, and Harlan had no alternative other than to succumb. Nevertheless, Harlan did try to portray Oppenheimer in a more generous light, making revenge the main motivation for Oppenheimer's rape of Dorothea and writing a moving final speech for Oppenheimer in which he denounces the court before going heroically to his death. However, Goebbels was so enraged by the content of the speech that he had it replaced with one where Oppenheimer is seen as a miserable coward, paradoxically left begging for his own life, when throughout the film it was obvious he would have ended the lives of others without a second thought. Even Harlan's Swedish wife, Kristina Söderbaum, who played Dorothea, had tried to use the recent birth of her baby as an excuse for non-involvement, but instead Harlan was permitted to stop work on the film whenever his wife needed to breastfeed the baby.

In the trials held after the war, Harlan was required to defend himself against a number of charges, including crimes against humanity. He was able to escape punishment largely on the basis that he was carrying out orders and that

Veit Harlan (right) photographed at his own trial for crimes against humanity in 1949. (*BArch, Bild183-2007-1022-508*)

the Nazis controlled what he produced, although others continued to call for all his films to be boycotted.

It was even harder to find someone to play the role of the hated Oppenheimer and, having failed to entice a number of renowned actors to take the part, Goebbels eventually persuaded Ferdinand Marian, an Austrian actor, well liked by German film audiences, that it would be in his best interests to accept the part. Indeed, Marian had a half-Jewish daughter from his wife's first marriage, and this was well known to Goebbels. Of course, the fact that he was already a well-known actor added considerable credibility both to the role and the film. Given his reluctance to star in the film, it is reported that during production Marian sought to sabotage the intention of the film in a number of areas. Nevertheless, despite the despicable character he portrayed, he became even better liked in Germany after the film and received standing ovations at a number of cinema screenings which he attended. Reminiscent of Vincent Price both in appearance and film character, he went on to star in a number of other blatant propaganda movies during the war years, often adopting the 'villain' role as a Jew or an Englishman, and also in less obviously political films such as *Münchhausen* in 1943.

Having fled back to Austria after the war, he was initially banned by the Allies from pursuing a film career. He tragically died in a mysterious car crash in August 1946; this was rumoured to have been a drink-induced suicide, although there were two other passengers in the car who surprisingly escaped uninjured. It is also worth noting that shortly after Veit Harlan's trial in 1950, Marian's wife was found drowned in Hamburg, also as an apparent suicide.

Heinrich George, who played the part of the Duke of Württemberg, was arrested for his involvement in this and other propaganda films, such as *Kolberg*. He died in 1946, after an appendix operation while imprisoned by the Soviets in the former Sachsenhausen concentration camp outside Berlin.

Werner Krauss, who played the role of the Rabbi Loew and Oppenheimer's secretary, did support Nazi beliefs and was made an 'Actor of the State' by Goebbels. After the war, although he was only considered to have played a minor supporting role in expounding Nazi ideology, he was forced to undertake a long process of denazification.

Although the key roles were not played by Jews, even though several actors had Jewish spouses or relatives, many other Jews were forcibly drafted in to provide the extras for the procession into Stuttgart and the synagogue scenes, both of which were actually filmed in Prague.

CONCLUSION

The effectiveness of this film as a successful work of anti-Jewish propaganda is unquestionable, although Goebbels always claimed in public that the film was not meant to be a piece of propaganda and that viewers had simply drawn their own conclusions from the production. The most revealing comment is left to Goebbels himself, who was so satisfied with the final version that he wrote in his diary:

> *A quite extraordinary success – a work of genius. The sort of anti-Semitic film that we could only wish for. I'm really pleased with it!*

With viewers particularly distressed by the rape scene and the image of Jews streaming into Stuttgart, it is little wonder that the screening of the film resulted in an increase in anti-Jewish violence in Germany, demonstrations in Hungary and led to its being banned in Sweden in 1941. The content of this film is considered so subversive that the sale of a DVD of the film is still prohibited in Germany and across most of Europe.

Chapter V

German Feature Films:
Anti-American Propaganda

Background

Given that the USA's entry into the war was one of the primary reasons for Germany's ultimate defeat, it is somewhat surprising that the Nazis did not produce a whole host of anti-American feature films, just as they had produced specifically anti-British and anti-Jewish films. There were a number of reasons for this reticence.

Firstly, many millions of people of German ancestry lived in America, and the Nazis did not want to do anything to alienate this sizeable community, many of whom, other than the most recent immigrants who had fled Nazi persecution, were potentially well disposed towards the new Germany. Hitler was advised not to place too much reliance on ethnic Germans living in America, but it was support which was to grow while Hitler was successful and even more so when he announced, after the *Anschluss* with Austria, that all Germans worldwide were to be considered citizens of the Third Reich. There was certainly a sizeable Fifth Column operating within America, and the trial of a German spy ring in 1938, on which the film *Confessions of a Nazi Spy* is based, reveals the level of underlying support for Germany in some quarters at that time. Consequently, if anti-American films were going to be produced, then they had to be very precisely focused so as not to alienate this tacit support.

Secondly, the longer that America could be kept out of the war the better, since it would obviate the need for the Nazis to fight a war on yet another front. In this regard, the Nazis were fortunate in having the support of such influential American citizens as the aviator, Charles Lindbergh, who was instrumental in campaigning against America being drawn into another European war. Therefore, unless seriously provoked, Hitler was unwilling to allow Goebbels *carte blanche* in the production of anti-American films.

Thirdly, given that the USA did not formally enter the war until December 1941, and as a feature film could easily take twelve months from conception to completion, it was always going to take time for suitable films to emerge. By then, the Nazis' film priorities had undoubtedly changed as Germany was fighting a war on several fronts and needed to produce more entertainment films to raise the morale of its civilian population.

This does not mean that there were no directly anti-American films; it is just that many of these were produced long before the war commenced and were, by nature, more critical of

November 1943: Anti-American cartoon from *Lustige Blätter* showing truth standing on its head when Uncle Sam is giving out information. (*Randall Bytwerk*)

Aviator Charles Lindbergh was staunchly opposed to America being dragged into Europe's war. (*Library of Congress*)

the American way of life, of capitalist greed, of unemployment and of the apparent failings of the democratic system.

Anti-American feature films can be divided into two categories. First, there are the films produced after 1933, but before the war in Europe had actually commenced. Key films include the mountain and homeland-type films of Arnold Fanck, Leni Riefenstahl and Luis Trenker. While these films were not specifically commissioned by the Nazis, their content was particularly timely, especially in their portrayal of powerful individuals as rebels and leaders, comparable with Hitler's role in the new Germany. When it came to anti-American sentiments in particular, the Trenker films often presented an idealised vision of a simple and ordered lifestyle – usually characterised by rural Germany – and contrasted this with the decadent and heartless reality of capitalist America. While Trenker would claim that he never deliberately produced such works in order to promote Nazi ideology, and, indeed, he was later to fall out of favour with Goebbels, it was certainly convenient for the Nazis that his early films neatly adhered to their own vision of the world.

Then, there are the later feature films and documentaries which were deliberately produced in response to what was considered the unprovoked criticism by America of the German way of life, and the release of overtly anti-Nazi films by Hollywood.

Already aware that films like *Confessions of a Nazi Spy* were in the course of production, Hitler publicly lost his temper with America when, in an impassioned speech on 30 January 1939, he threatened to produce anti-Jewish films if Hollywood continued to release anti-Nazi films. The fact that most of the major Hollywood film production companies were owned by Jewish families made this section of American society a particularly convenient target for the Nazis. As early as 1933, American film companies had been obliged to remove 'objectionable' material from any films they planned to screen in Germany and only to distribute such revised versions across Europe. In September 1937, a camp held in New Jersey for 18,000 supporters of the German American Bund encouraged a boycott of Hollywood films which were considered to be the creation of ignoble Jews. Indeed, many German-based Nazis would willingly have introduced an immediate ban on American films, but the practical reality was that Hollywood films, which between 1933 and 1938 accounted for 52 per cent of Germany's film imports, were still required to satisfy the needs of their cinema-goers.

Consequently, it was really only after Hitler's Reichstag speech that the prohibition of American films significantly intensified, and it was not until July 1940, and well after war had commenced, that the most brutal of the Nazis' anti-Semitic feature-length films started to appear. Of these, it is only *Der ewige Jude* (November 1940) which makes any direct reference to the Jewish influence in America.

Despite such provocation, and conscious of forthcoming American elections where the electorate was still lukewarm about another war, President Roosevelt staunchly refused, in public at least, to make direct criticism of the Nazis by name. It was only after the election was won that he felt prepared to be far more aggressive in his speech of 29 December 1940:

> The Nazi masters of Germany have made it clear that they intend not only to dominate all life and thought in their own country, but also to enslave the whole of Europe, and then use the resources of Europe to dominate the world … the experience of the last two years has proven beyond doubt that no nation can appease Nazis.

Apart from the early anti-American and anti-Jewish films, there were two other feature films which the Allies considered to be sufficiently anti-American as to be banned after the war. In both cases, it would seem that the Allies were looking for almost any excuse to impose such a ban. *Fünf Millionen suchen einen Erben* (*Five Million Looking for an Heir*) was first released in April 1938 and, as a comedy starring the popular Heinz Rühmann, it seems an unlikely film to have been prohibited. It was officially denounced for ridiculing the American way of life and American institutions, but was only banned, retrospectively, in 1950, following objections raised by the American High Commission. Watching the film today, the only possible aspect with which one might take offence is the use of the word 'Negro' to describe Joshua, a black American man-servant, and the visible anxiety shown towards him by a German woman who has obviously never seen a black man before. The ban was subsequently repealed, and the film is still very popular and now freely available on DVD in Germany.

The other film is *Pedro soll hängen* (*Pedro Will Hang*), which was released in July 1941. Set in South America, it tells the story of a shepherd, Pedro, who seemingly commits a murder which he bitterly regrets. His pregnant girlfriend persuades him to plead for mercy, and he is

Mabel (Leni Marenbach) who almost sabotages Peter's (Heinz Rühmann) claim to his inheritance in *Fünf Millionen suchen einen Erben*. (*Deutsches Filminstitut / Jupiter-Film GmbH*)

The murderer, Pedro, with his beloved Pepita in Veit Harlan's *Pedro soll hängen*. (*Deutsches Filminstitut/ FWM*)

eventually freed. Although the film was banned by the Allies because of some anti-American allusions, it seems more likely that the primary reason for its prohibition was the fact that it was directed by Veit Harlan, who was associated with so many of the Nazis' most offensive films, including *Jud Süss*. Harlan actually regarded the film as his masterpiece and the one for which he wanted to be best remembered.

By 1942, although Hitler was still reluctant to allow Goebbels to produce any particularly hard-hitting anti-American feature films, several short documentaries were released. These include *Rund um die Freiheitsstatue* (*Around the Statue of Liberty*), which is reviewed in Chapter X, and *Amerika sieht sich selbst* (*America Looks at Itself*). Both films employed news-reel and real feature film footage, albeit often out of context, to create a depressing image of American society compared with the ordered, crime-free presentation of Nazi Germany. An indication of Goebbels' own low opinion of Americans at that time can be gauged from his diary entry of 27 May 1942:

> A report on the interrogation of American prisoners is really gruesome. These American sol-
> diers are human material which can in no way stand comparison with our own people. One
> has the impression we are dealing with a band of savages. The Americans are coming to
> Europe with a spiritual emptiness that really makes you shake your head. They are unedu-
> cated and know nothing. For instance they ask whether Bavaria belongs to Germany and
> such like. I have reviewed statistics about the number of Jews in the American radio, film
> and press industries. The percentage is truly terrifying. Jews are 100% in control of films and
> 90–95% in control of the press and radio.

Goebbels was later offered an idea for an anti-American film by the Reich's cultural minister, Friedrich Bethge. It involved converting Bethge's drama, *Marsch der Veteranen*, into a film and he conveyed his idea to Goebbels in a letter in July 1944:

I consider that the time has arrived to release the March of the Veterans *as a big film, but not set in the Russia of Napoleon, but rather in the country and the time where the idea for the drama originates, namely Washington, in 1932. I can think of few film subjects that show the mendacity of 'civilised' America more convincingly and at the same time place before the eyes of the world what the treatment of the American participants in the war by their own Fatherland was like at that time and which would probably not be much different at the end of this war.*

However, even if Hitler or Goebbels had agreed with the concept, it was far too late to produce a film with the primary purpose of demoralising American soldiers and even the American public. Given that the Allies would ensure that the film would never be screened to Americans, its production would surely have been a complete waste of time.

ANTI-AMERICAN FILMS REVIEWED

The three films chosen to be analysed in detail in this chapter extend across a broad range of themes and time periods, although, for the reasons previously noted, only the third film was first screened after the outbreak of the Second World War. In order of chronological release they are: *Der verlorene Sohn* (*The Prodigal Son*) (1934), *Der Kaiser von Kalifornien* (*The Emperor of California*) (1936) and *Sensationsprozess Casilla* (*Sensation Trial: Casilla*) (1939).

Der verlorene Sohn (*The Prodigal Son*) is typical of many of the homeland-type films starring Luis Trenker and owes much of its style to the silent movie era. Attracted by the lure of New York, the naïve mountain shepherd discovers that life in depression-hit America is far removed from the land of hope and opportunity he had expected, and the film is considered anti-American because of its particularly negative portrayal of the American way of life.

Also featuring Trenker in the star role, *Der Kaiser von Kalifornien* (*The Emperor of California*) is a Western which recounts the story of Johann Suter's pioneering exploits in the early development of America and the impact of the California Gold Rush of 1841. Several details of the story have been exaggerated for dramatic effect, and these changes undoubtedly have a propaganda impact.

Finally, *Sensationsprozess Casilla* (*Sensation Trial: Casilla*), which was released just after the outbreak of war in Europe, is a courtroom drama set in America and follows the case of a German accused of the murder of a child film star. It is an entertaining and fast-moving film, but its real claim to fame lies in its highly disparaging portrayal of the American justice system and the dubious values of its citizens.

All three films were initially banned from further screening in Germany at the end of the war, although the two Trenker films are now readily available again on DVD.

Film title: *Der verlorene Sohn*
Year of release: 1934
Type: Feature film
Primary purpose: Anti-American propaganda/
     entertainment
Director: Luis Trenker
Principal stars:
Maria Andergast   (Barbl Gudauner)
Jimmy Fox   (Hobby)
Paul Henckels   (School teacher)
Marian Marsch   (Lilian Williams)
F.W. Schröder-Schrom   (Mr Williams)
Luis Trenker   (Tonio Feuersinger)

INTRODUCTION

Fresh from the success of *Der Rebell* (*The Rebel*), Luis Trenker's next great offering was *Der verlorene Sohn* (*The Prodigal Son*). Released in 1934, the film was not actually commissioned by the Nazis, but for Goebbels the subject matter was very much in keeping with Nazi ideology and beliefs, with the added benefit that the film was anti-capitalist and, in this case, specifically anti-American in its representation of the wider world.

Set in the Tyrol and New York, it is a typical '*Heimat*' film, which paints an idealistic picture of the simple life of the mountains in contrast to the squalor of an America suffering from the rigours of the Great Depression.

PLOT SUMMARY

The film opens in the Tyrolean mountains with Tonio and his girlfriend, Barbl, quietly relaxing among the cows and sheep. Tonio is a simple woodcutter and is well respected in his peasant community, but he has a great desire to explore the wider world and especially America. He is also an accomplished sportsman and, on winning a skiing competition, he becomes acquainted with Lilian, the highly sophisticated daughter of Mr Williams, a rich American who had provided Tonio's prize.

Much to Barbl's disquiet, Lilian is obviously impressed by the athletic Tonio and persuades him to take her on a trip into the mountains. The weather suddenly turns, and they are caught in an avalanche, resulting in the death of Tonio's fellow guide, and Tonio is so upset by the accident that he resolves not to climb the mountains again.

In the next scene, Tonio is seen arriving in New York, fascinated by the skyscrapers which resemble giant mountains. Discovering that Mr Williams is away for the winter, Tonio is forced

Tonio, relaxing with his girlfriend, Barbl, in the idyllic setting of the Tyrolean mountains. (*Deutsches Filminstitut/MOVIEMAN*)

to search for a job. Not only does he find it difficult to secure any employment but he soon runs out of money and is thrown out of his apartment for non-payment of rent. He has to sleep rough and meets up with an unemployed American, Hobby, and they both eventually obtain temporary work on the construction of a new skyscraper. When Hobby is escorted away by the police, Tonio is left to provide for his own survival, stealing a loaf and narrowly avoiding arrest. Tonio finally obtains work as a ringside assistant in Madison Square Gardens and is so incensed when a boxer punches the referee that he jumps into the ring and, to the great delight of the audience, knocks out the offending boxer himself.

Spotted by Williams and Lilian, who are spectators at the fight, Tonio is rescued from his life on the streets and is next seen enjoying life at a party at the Williams' house. Following Lilian's confession of love for Tonio, he has to admit that he could not live in America and he rushes back to the Tyrol where they are celebrating the *Rauhnacht* spirit festival, with all the townspeople disguised in masks and the spirits giving praise to the Sun King. The film ends on a happy note as Tonio and Barbl are reunited and enter the church together to join in the festivities.

CRITICAL REVIEW

Der verlorene Sohn is a deceptively simple tale, and in form and content, is greatly influenced by the previous silent movie era. Much of the film is devoid of dialogue and filled instead with moving music. Indeed, the first half hour of the film is more in keeping with the various mountain movies in which Luis Trenker was involved in some capacity, such as *Der Berg des Schicksals* (*The Mountain of Destiny*), *Der heilige Berg* (*The Holy Mountain*) and *Der grosse Sprung* (*The Big Jump*). They all contain spectacular film photography of the mountains and revolve around a struggle with the forces of nature, such as the tragic death sequence in this particular film.

Luis Trenker, as the unemployed Tonio, seeking fame and fortune in New York. (*Deutsches Filminstitut/ MOVIEMAN*)

Dramatic realism

The scene of the storm on the mountain is very effective and there is one very clever touch as the Tyrolean mountains fade into New York skyscrapers when Tonio arrives in the States, symbolic of the fact that the new world which Tonio is entering is just as dangerous as the one he has left behind.

It is also notable that all the dialogue in the scenes set in New York is in English with no German subtitles which, while certainly making the action far more authentic, must surely have been difficult for many of the German viewing public to follow at that time. Perhaps this was a deliberate ploy to emphasise just how isolated a German seeking work might feel in a large city in the United States.

How did Trenker and his films come to the attention of the Nazis?

On 28 March 1933, Goebbels made a speech in which he named four films he considered to be of particular merit, and which he wished to see emulated by the German film industry, namely *Battleship Potemkin*, *Anna Karenina*, *Die Nibelungen* and *Der Rebell*.

Goebbels had been particularly impressed by the 1932 film, *Der Rebell* (*The Rebel*), in which Trenker had not only played the leading role but which he had also written and co-directed. Set in 1809, the film tells the story of a student, Severin, returning home to his Tyrolean village to find his house burnt to the ground, his mother and sister murdered and the village controlled by Napoleon's troops. Severin leads the villagers in a heroic guerrilla-type struggle against the French and, although he is eventually captured and executed, the film ends with his rising victoriously from the dead against the vision of the glorious future of one united Germany. Such a plot was like manna from heaven for the Nazis, and the closing 'victory through death' sequence was to be copied and repeated in their own films, *Hans Westmar* and *Hitlerjunge Quex*.

The release of *Der verlorene Sohn* in September 1934 was equally fortuitous, since a story which combined a nostalgic love of the German '*Heimat*' and a renunciation of the American way of life was just the sort of propaganda which Goebbels desired.

Why did this film hold such an appeal for the Nazis?

First, *Der verlorene Sohn* presents the idyllic image of the life of a typical rural, hard-working Aryan, with their simple customs and superstitions. Indeed, the film provides a remarkable insight into both their pagan and Christian traditions. While the film begins with the figure of Christ hanging from a cross on a mountain-side altar and concludes with all the villagers happily entering a church, the film is punctuated with scenes depicting their spirit festival, with the masked villagers dressed to represent the Sun King and the spirits of the earth, forest, wind and fire.

Second, at a time when many Europeans were seduced by the prospect of a better life abroad, and Tonio can certainly be seen to share in such enthusiasm, this film clearly emphasises the advantages of remaining in familiar German surroundings, rather than venturing out to the dangerous, lonely existence likely to be encountered in a big city overseas.

Despite Barbl's concern that Tonio will never return from America, the school teacher recites a German saying, which is repeated later in the film, '*Wer nie fortkommt, kommt nie heim*' ('Who never goes away will never come home'). It is a rather philosophical observation that everyone should be allowed to get 'wanderlust' out of their system so that they can ascertain for themselves that 'east, west, home's best'. This was certainly going to be the case for Tonio who will return home to Germany as 'the prodigal son', but a much wiser man into the bargain.

Third, although Goebbels was displeased with some of the film's religious imagery, he was still more attracted by the anti-American propaganda aspects of the film. While it was going to be many years before Germany would be at war with America, the Nazis were becoming increasingly frustrated by the mounting criticism of their regime by what they perceived as America's Jewish-controlled media. By blaming international capitalism for all of Germany's woes, including their defeat in the First World War, the film's anti-American bias was a godsend for the Nazis.

Whatever the other excesses of the Nazi regime, there is no doubt that Hitler did reduce unemployment levels in Germany and did much to re-establish a feeling of national pride among the Germans. In such circumstances, the Nazis were amazed that Roosevelt could have the effrontery to criticise life in Germany when the American way of life had so spectacularly failed to provide work for the masses and had created such a divide between the rich and the poor.

Tonio's excitement in learning about other parts of the world from the village school teacher. (*Deutsches Filminstitut/ MOVIEMAN*)

Tonio's life on the streets reveals that there is plenty of food for everyone, but only if you can afford to buy it. Instead, the unemployed are forced to rely on the charity of the food kitchens. There is even covert criticism that good, white, hard-working, upright citizens like Tonio cannot obtain work, with preference even given to American blacks over non-Americans.

With only rare exceptions, the American people are shown to be uncaring and unsympathetic towards those out of work. There is the landlady who does not hesitate in throwing Tonio out for failing to pay his rent and, as if it were a police state, there is the constant harassment by police officers. The exceptions are his friend, Hobby, who ironically had fought against the Germans in the First World War, and even the policeman who chases Tonio for stealing bread from the market, only seemingly to let him go when he realises that Tonio had merely stolen to satisfy his desperate hunger.

The American way of life is seen to generate a corrupting influence in that otherwise perfectly upright citizens like Tonio are forced to resort to immoral practices such as stealing milk and bread to survive. Even American pastimes are shown to be decadent and degrading. The great appeal of boxing, where brute force wins the day, depicts the American public as savages baying for blood. Once again, there appears to be a disproportionate focus on the black spectators who seem to be particularly excited by the violence in the ring.

Tonio's ultimate rejection of the prospect of a wealthy, pretty American wife and all that America stands for, and his preference to return home to his simple life in the Tyrol and marry a faithful local girl, provides a neat conclusion from a Nazi standpoint. The call of the homeland is shown to rank above all other distractions.

Did Trenker have Nazi sympathies?

As with so many other leading German film directors and actors of the time, it is difficult to judge the true extent of Luis Trenker's support for the Nazi regime. There is no doubt that the

A scene from *Der Rebell*, which brought Trenker and his films to the attention of the Nazis. (*Deutsches Filminstitut/MOVIEMAN*)

content of *Der Rebell* and Trenker's earlier First World War film, *Berge in Flammen* (*Mountain in Flames*), contained just the sort of heroic, nationalistic vision of Germany which was so in keeping with the philosophy of the Nazis, and which made them very favourably disposed towards him. Indeed, Trenker was one of several leading film directors who, in March 1933, became a founder member of the Directors' Section of the National Socialist Factory Cell Organisation (NSBO) before formally joining the Nazi Party in 1940. However, it is also true that the sort of films he was producing had evolved long before the Nazis came to power. Trenker always claimed that he was not a Nazi and was actually denounced as early as 1934 for agreeing that it was a scandal that the Germans were burning books and expelling the Jews. Whether or not Trenker deliberately took advantage of the attention shown to him by the Nazis is open to question but, as will be shown in the analysis of the next film in this chapter, he was soon to fall foul of Goebbels and was eventually prevented from directing any more films for the Nazis.

Conclusion

Ostensibly an innocent film about a villager's experiences of the Great Depression in New York, *Der verlorene Sohn* is beautifully filmed and combines many of the best elements of silent movies with modern cinema techniques. Tonio's experience of poverty in New York can either be regarded as an accurate portrayal of life in the Thirties, or it can be interpreted as direct criticism of the American way of life.

Although the film had a Jewish producer, Paul Kohner, who had already forsaken Europe for Hollywood, the Nazis still considered the film to be sufficiently significant as to award it a rating of 'artistically especially worthy'. The film was an outstanding success in Germany, receiving rapturous ovations at its premieres in Stuttgart and Berlin, and winning the prize at the Venice Film Festival in 1935 as 'the most significant foreign film'. Nevertheless, the film was not distributed in the United States and was regarded as sufficiently anti-American to be banned by the Allies at the end of the war, although it has been freely available on DVD in Germany since 2004.

Film title: *Der Kaiser von Kalifornien*
Year of release: 1936
Type: Feature film
Primary purpose: Anti-American propaganda/
    entertainment
Director: Luis Trenker
Principal stars:

Viktoria von Ballasko	(Anna Sutter)
August Eichhorn	(Harper)
Luis Gerold	(Ermattinger)
Bernard Minetti	(Ghostly stranger)
Reginald Pasch	(Marshall)
Luis Trenker	(Johann August Suter)
Paul Verhoeven	(Bar-tender Billy)

INTRODUCTION

Der Kaiser von Kalifornien (*The Emperor of California*) is a Western which was set and filmed in the United States. Indeed, it is one of only a handful of feature films produced during the Nazi era in which the plot was set in the United States.

In a most dramatic and entertaining manner, the film recounts the life story of Johann Suter (or John Sutter), an early pioneer of the west coast of North America. The film was released in Germany in 1936 and was awarded the prize of 'Best Foreign Film' at the Venice Film Festival in the same year, before being screened around the world.

While produced long before war in Europe and even some five years before Germany was to declare war on the United States, it was considered to be sufficiently *anti*-American as to be banned by the Western Allies at the end of the war from further screening in West Germany. Somewhat ironically, at the same time, the director of the film claims that it was banned by the Soviet Union from being shown in Vienna because it was considered to be *pro*-American. In reality, the lessons of the film can be interpreted in various different ways, and some aspects could even be considered to be anti-Nazi in content. Such ambiguity suggests that the film was far from being an effective propaganda vehicle for the Nazis.

PLOT SUMMARY

The initial credits explain how the film is based on the life of Johann August Suter, who was born in the town of Kandern before becoming a Swiss citizen and moving to the USA, where he was to become inextricably linked with the development of California.

The story opens in Germany where Suter is busy printing subversive posters, complaining about the lack of freedom which the German state affords its citizens. Whilst evading arrest

Suter with his wife, Anna, about to flee Germany for the opportunities and freedom presented by America. (*Deutsches Filminstitut/FWM*)

in the high tower of the church, a ghostly stranger appears before him and encourages him to conquer the great lands which exist in other parts of the world. After a tearful farewell to his beautiful and supportive wife, Anna, and his two young sons, Suter does indeed leave for America, initially earning money from selling furs. He is reunited with his old friend, Ermattinger, and together with the bartender, Billy, they undertake to make the long journey west where they have heard stories that the soil is so fertile that corn can be harvested three times a year.

They are robbed en route by three crooked desperados led by Harper. However, when Suter and his friends subsequently care for an Indian who has been wounded by Harper's men, they are soon befriended by the Indians, the crooks are captured, and Suter and his friends recover their possessions and continue on their journey.

The route west is long and difficult and, as they cross the desert, one by one, they have to leave their horses to die; when Billy collapses with exhaustion Suter walks on alone. Suter and his colleagues are very fortunate to be rescued by a wagon train led by Marshall, although the wagon train is in almost as much difficulty because of a lack of food and water. Once recovered, Suter sets out alone and, after climbing across a mountain, discovers a river on the other side. Everyone is saved, and they all proceed to Sacramento which is under the control of the Mexican authorities. Suter eventually persuades the authorities to let him cultivate the land outside the town for ten years and, before long, he successfully grows crops and fruit, and rears cattle, sheep and horses, thereby providing work for thousands of people. He is so successful that the land is formally gifted to him by the Mexicans and he virtually becomes the emperor, or Kaiser, of California, being recognised as one of the richest and most powerful men in the area.

All seems idyllic, but then two events occur which threaten this happy existence. First, the US government occupies California, claiming that, by being part of the Union of the United States, peace to the area can be restored and an end put to the unrest and civil wars which have disrupted the country. Second, Marshall advises him that he has discovered gold in the riverbed

Suter wins approval from the Mexican authorities to cultivate the land outside Sacramento for a period of ten years. (*Deutsches Filminstitut/FWM*)

and, despite Suter's exhortations that Marshall should conceal his find for at least five years, Marshall soon leaks out the truth and before long the whole area is caught up with gold fever. Most of Suter's workers abandon their day-to-day farming tasks to pan for gold and, as Suter had predicted, many succumb to poverty, robbery and death.

His bankers soon insist that either he joins one of their gold syndicates to repay his debts or they will put up his farm for auction. Suter, however, vows to continue cultivating the land with his closest colleagues and to try to ignore the hunt for gold. His wife and sons have arrived from Germany to join him in the interim. While he is farming the land one day, his sons innocently try panning for gold themselves in the very area which is controlled by Harper and his men, although, theoretically, the land still belongs to Suter. Harper sees an opportunity for revenge on Suter and pays a colleague to have the two boys shot. Such is Anna's grief on learning of this tragedy that she collapses beside the corpses of the boys and dies from a broken heart.

Suter is left to continue alone, his court case against the American authorities, in which he seeks the return of his lands, dragging on for many years.

The story moves on and the viewer sees Suter being cheered through the town of San Francisco as part of the city's celebration of the tenth anniversary of its foundation. Suter is officially thanked for all he had done to help the development of the town, and he is named as senator for California and made a general in the American army. The mayor also announces that the United States' courts have determined to recognise the technical validity of Suter's claim to the lands. Given the hostile reception which this decision evokes, the officials hope that Suter will renounce his claims, but instead he insists on his rights and demands the immediate removal of all the gold diggers living on his land. A riot ensues in which Suter is lucky to escape with his life, and Harper and Marshall are among those keen to burn down the whole town. In the anarchy which follows, Marshall is seized by the crowd and lynched. Suter returns to his ranch house to discover that it has already been set alight by Harper and his cronies. In a short gun fight, Harper is shot dead by Suter, but Ermattinger is also killed, intercepting a bullet intended for Suter.

The final action takes place on the steps of the Capitol in Washington, where a poor and elderly Suter is once again confronted by the ghost he had encountered at the beginning of the film. The ghost tells Suter that his journey is at an end and that he should be content that he has served the world faithfully. The ghost leaves him with a vision of how America will look in the future, with skyscrapers, large housing developments and powerful machinery, and the film concludes with a moving flashback to the three riders who had been responsible for the whole development of the region in the first place.

Johann Suter becomes the archetypal cowboy and developer of California. (*Deutsches Filminstitut/FWM*)

CRITICAL REVIEW

Der Kaiser von Kalifornien is an exciting story which contains all the elements found in a good Western, such as man's struggle against the elements, conflicts between good and bad cowboys, romance and, above all, a few gun fights. What makes the film more credible is that it is, indeed, based on the life story of Johann Suter who moved to California in the 1830s and whose land was overrun in the Gold Rush of 1841. What is perhaps most interesting is that Luis Trenker, who plays the part of Suter, was also responsible for writing the book on which the film is based and for producing and directing the film itself.

The film was first screened in Germany in July 1936, and was even shown in the United States in 1937, receiving favourable reviews despite its lack of commercial success. However, as a piece of propaganda, the film evokes a number of conflicting responses ranging from anti-American to pro-American to anti-Nazi.

Potential Anti-American propaganda

The fact that Suter was of German/Swiss descent was a blessing for the Nazis as he could be depicted as a simple citizen standing against the corruption of the wider world. He is portrayed as a hard-working, God-fearing individual whose sole aim is to make the world a better place, so that anything which damages the idyllic world which Suter tries to create in the States is seen as being ungodly. Indeed, the appearance and utterances of the ghostly stranger reinforce the notion that he is doing God's work.

This almost makes him appear superhuman, especially given his survival in the desert and his determination to find the river on the other side of the mountains. Such is God's favour, that Suter is rewarded with vast lands in California which he is soon able to cultivate for the production of crops and the rearing of animals. He can almost be regarded as a messianic Führer who uses his skills to turn the country into a land of plenty.

The proclamation that California has moved from the control of Spain into the Union of the United States is so low key that it appears more like a death sentence. What ultimately destroys Suter's 'Eden' is the greed created by the Gold Rush and, despite earlier assurances that the United States would bring peace to the region, it is evident that order is not maintained.

Indeed, the American way of life is condemned as one where decent values are soon overwhelmed by man's more basic instincts and financial greed. Faced with instant prosperity, individuals are only too willing to abandon the laborious work necessary to grow food and raise animals.

When Suter asks Marshall what he intends to do with his new-found wealth, his response is immediate:

At any rate – not work with you any more – I'm going to dig for gold and lodge claims until I become the richest man in the world.

However, it is not just the ordinary people who are overcome by avarice; the disease soon spreads to the American bankers who had been supporting Suter. When these treacherous capitalists threaten to force the sale of his property if he won't join one of the syndicates created to exploit the gold reserves, Suter becomes almost apoplectic with rage.

There is an implied criticism that while gold fever may bring initial wealth for some, it will force others into poverty and lead to death and robbery, the destruction of property and a lowering of moral standards. The latter consequence is most evident in the scene in the saloon where the viewer is confronted with examples of the debauchery and loose-living which money can promote. There are close-ups of a number of the good-time girls in the saloon being of African origin and there is an obvious, if unspoken, condemnation of such interracial relationships.

Even the concluding comments by the ghostly stranger about America are rather ambiguous. Although he tells Suter to be content with the way he has served the world, he also reveals a vision of a future America powered by huge machines and covered with skyscrapers and housing developments, adding the ominous words, 'rightly or wrongly'.

Potential Pro-American propaganda

It is hard to understand how the Soviet Union could ever have conceived of the film as being pro-American, other than in its depiction of the potential rewards of free enterprise and of the successful industrialised nation which then existed in America. It is more likely that the Russians would have been hostile to any film which featured America as its subject matter, as they were concerned that it might have provoked unrest among viewers striving for the freedoms which America offered, compared to the repressive communist regime to which they were now subjected.

Potential Anti-Nazi propaganda

The film, strangely, could just as easily be seen to convey some criticism of the Nazi regime at that time.

Ironically, the primary reason why Suter flees from Germany is because he believes the citizens are being exploited and denied freedom of thought and speech by tyrannical rulers. His claims that the days of Napoleon and Metternich are still 'alive and well' could well have been seen as overt criticism of Hitler, as a modern-day dictator.

Likewise, there are several occasions in the film when Suter becomes so angry that he is quite frightening and rants and raves like a dictator, reminiscent of Hitler himself. Such examples of his unbalanced behaviour include his threatening Marshall with a gun so as to persuade him not to reveal his gold find; when he shouts abuse at the bankers who are demanding the repayment of his loans; and when he stands up in the hall in San Francisco and forcibly explains that he wants the gold diggers removed from his land. Indeed, it could be argued that it is his very failure to compromise which indirectly leads to the destruction of his own property and the deaths of his friends and family.

However, given that the film was completed in 1936 and that much of the populace was still entranced by Hitler and the national pride which he had restored, any such negative parallels were likely to be ignored by the majority of viewers.

Suter's Fort in California. (*Library of Congress*)

How do the events in the film compare to the true life story of Johann Suter?

While much of the basis of the story contained in the film is correct, other aspects have evidently been altered for dramatic effect.

First, Suter was not entirely the angel which the story suggests. It would appear that his true reason for leaving Switzerland was the fact that he was being sought by the police for suspected business fraud. Second, although the Gold Rush did hasten his downfall, this was mainly because the American authorities did *not* recognise his full rights to his lands and, while he was awarded damages, these never emerged, leaving him to die a poor man. Finally, Suter actually predeceased his wife, his first son became a successful businessman, and there is no note of any of his children having been murdered. All of these features were presumably omitted or added to the film simply to increase the viewers' sympathy for Suter and all that befalls him in America.

CONCLUSION

Der Kaiser von Kalifornien is a splendid Western. The various action scenes are very effective, and the special effects used in the ghost and desert scenes all help add to the viewers' enjoyment of the film. As a famous alpinist, director and actor, Trenker was already very popular in Germany. In his early days, he was often entertained by the Nazis who had been particularly impressed by his earlier film, *Der Rebell*, which he had directed and played the leading star. Hitler actually attended a premiere of *Der Kaiser von Kalifornien* in his Reich Ministry, and the film was classified by the Nazis as being of 'special political and artistic merit'. Nevertheless, and despite the film's success at the Venice Film Festival in 1936, Trenker had started to fall out of favour with the Nazis by the following year. They were very disappointed with the content of his next film, *Condottieri*, where it was considered that too much was made of the Catholic faith, and Italian knights (actually SS men) were shown to kneel before the Pope. The final nail in his coffin occurred in 1940 with his reported reluctance to sacrifice his South Tyrolean identity and move back to Germany when South Tyrol was handed to Italy. His initial hesitation was to earn both Goebbels' and Hitler's lasting displeasure, and served as an impediment to his producing and directing any further films during the Nazi era.

In any event, whatever its merits as a Western, *Der Kaiser von Kalifornien* was not a particularly satisfactory piece of Nazi propaganda. However, now that the film is once again available in Germany on DVD, it is probably best left to modern viewers to assess for themselves to what extent the film can be considered either anti-American, pro-American or anti-Nazi, or, indeed, a mixture of all three.

Film title: *Sensationsprozess Casilla*
Year of release: 1939
Type: Feature film
Primary purpose: Anti-American propaganda/
    entertainment
Director: Eduard von Borsody
Principal stars:

Lissy Anna	(Ines Brown)
Erich Fiedler	(Attorney Salvani)
Jutta Freybe	(Jessie, Vandegrift's daughter)
Heinrich George	(Attorney Vandegrift)
Richard Häußler	(State Prosecutor)
Albert Hehn	(Peter Roland)
Käte Pontow	(Binnie)
Dagny Servaes	(Sylvia Casilla)
Alice Treff	(Almar, Vandegrift's secretary)

Introduction

Although courtroom films were a common feature of the Nazi era, *Sensationsprozess Casilla* (*Sensation Trial: Casilla*) is rather unusual because of its setting in a modern courtroom in the United States. First screened in Berlin in September 1939, it is considered to be an anti-American film because of its hostile portrayal of the American legal system and the American way of life.

Based on a book by Hans Possendorf, the film tells the story of a German cameraman who is accused of the murder of a child film star and who, as a foreigner, would have found it difficult to secure a fair trial in America had it not been for the intervention of a renowned defence attorney.

Plot summary

The film begins rather dramatically with the pilots of a passenger plane flying over Casablanca having suddenly fallen seriously ill. Among the passengers are a famous American attorney, Cäsar Vandegrift, his daughter, Jessie, and Peter Roland, a prisoner being escorted back to the United States to stand trial for the abduction of a child film star ten years previously. As Peter is the only other person on board capable of flying the plane, the passengers have little choice other than to put their faith in him to fly the plane to safety. Primarily through gratitude for their eventual safe landing and partly because he believes Peter's claim that he is innocent of the murder of Binnie Casilla, Vandegrift takes a personal interest in his case and arranges for an attorney called Salvini to represent Peter in court.

Given the wide media attention which the case will bring, it transpires that the general manager of PPC films is planning to re-release some of Binnie's earlier films and to split the profits with Binnie's stepmother, Sylvia Casilla. Both Binnie's natural mother, Anna, and her father

Peter Roland (right) succeeds in convincing Vandegrift of his innocence while making an emergency landing in Casablanca. (*Deutsches Filminstitut/FWM*)

had died in the intervening years. Sylvia is concerned by Vandegrift's interest in the case and arranges for her shifty servant, James, to keep track of the defence by courting the affections of Vandegrift's secretary, Almar. Meanwhile, Peter confesses to Vandegrift that while he did abduct the girl, this was done to protect her from mistreatment by her parents who had been stunting her growth so that she could remain a child star. Peter claims that Binnie is alive and living in South America, and Jessie is secretly dispatched to bring the girl to the trial. Unfortunately, Almar inadvertently lets slip Jessie's movements to James, who follows Jessie to Columbia and manages to reach Binnie's house in advance. Consequently, when Jessie eventually arrives at the house, she discovers that it has been burned to the ground and there is no sign of Binnie.

Back in the wild frenzy of the courtroom in Stockford, where proceedings were being broadcast live on American television, various witnesses are called to the stand. First, Sylvia's black maid, Ines Brown, claims that she had heard Peter declare his love for Anna, a claim which he vehemently denies. Next, Sylvia recounts how a foreigner had telephoned her husband three nights before the abduction demanding $100,000 to prevent the seizure of the child. It was only later that they were convinced it was the voice of Peter, who was employed as a cameraman by PPC films. While Peter quietly admits to Salvani that he had written a letter warning the family to stop abusing Binnie, he had never sent a ransom demand and he had certainly never phoned the Casillas' house. It also emerges that when the abduction did take place, Sylvia had fired two shots at the kidnapper and from blood-stained clothes left at the scene of the crime it would appear that Binnie had been wounded in the process.

Vandegrift eventually assumes the role of defence attorney himself, casting doubt on the evidence of the handwriting expert who, although convinced that the blackmail letter was written by Peter, cannot confirm that he has examined every single word in the letter. Even though the fresh disappearance of Binnie is a setback, Vandegrift proceeds to try to demolish the prosecution's case point by point. First, the evidence of Ines is shown to be unreliable because when she is asked to reiterate her earlier claims concerning Peter's love for Anna, she uses exactly the same words as in her earlier testimony. Second, Vandegrift manages to imply that the Casillas had invented the story of a phone call from a blackmailer, rather than take Peter's letter to the police as

Vandegrift (Heinrich George) cunningly succeeds in proving that the maid's testimony is unreliable. (*Deutsches Filminstitut/FWM*)

its content would have been embarrassing for them.

The defence's case is also strengthened by a statement from Binnie's nanny that there was a book in the house on glandular research, and that she had heard Sylvia say to her husband that Binnie must not grow any more otherwise there would be no more film deals with PPC. Knowing that Peter was fond of the child and vice-versa, she had reported her concerns to Peter, who was horrified at the thought of Binnie being deliberately mistreated in this way.

Following Binnie's original abduction, it transpired that Binnie's father and stepmother had made various attempts to have a death certificate issued so that they could inherit the fortune being kept in trust for her. This fact allows Vandegrift to make the damning assertion that the only person who had anything to gain from Peter going to the electric chair was Sylvia Casilla!

When Peter is brought to the stand, he describes how, on witnessing a doctor secretly giving injections to Binnie each night, he had resolved to abduct the child and force her parents to admit their misdeeds. He explains how he had started to write a letter, but that he must have dropped it in the garden and now assumes the Casillas had discovered the letter and had forged an ending, thereby making it appear as a blackmail letter. However, despite the growing evidence of ill-doing by Binnie's parents, the failure of the defence to produce Binnie herself results in Peter's being judged guilty of her murder and sentenced to death.

Just as all hope for Peter seems lost, it emerges that Binnie had managed to escape and soon arrives in Stockford. Now, Sylvia claims that she does not recognise Binnie and implies that she may be an imposter, despite the apparent scar on her shoulder from a bullet wound. However, X-rays reveal that a bullet is still lodged in Binnie's shoulder which, once removed, is shown to fit neatly into the revolver fired by Sylvia at the fleeing abductor. With Binnie's identity having been proven, Peter is immediately released from prison. The film has a happy conclusion with Binnie and Peter sailing off to Peter's parents in Germany, and the certainty of future romance between Jessie and Peter.

CRITICAL REVIEW

Sensationsprozess Casilla is a fast-moving film which combines mystery and romance as the truth surrounding the disappearance of Binnie is gradually revealed. The viewer's attention is not only held by the dramatic outbursts of the lawyers and witnesses in the court, but also by the constant uncertainty as to the final outcome of the case, since the defendant's prospects of success ebb and flow as more information comes to light. The fact that the testimony of the key witnesses is placed in doubt, and that it is obvious that the Casilla family was more interested in monetary gain than Binnie's welfare, really does little to weaken the case against

Sylvia refuses to recognise Binnie as her stepdaughter. (*Deutsches Filminstitut/FWM*)

Peter, especially when he admits that he had abducted the child. Even the defence team believes that Binnie really has been murdered in the interim. Any hope gained from the eventual appearance of Binnie is immediately dashed when Binnie cannot prove her own identity, only to be rekindled with the revelation that the bullet extracted from her shoulder was fired from Sylvia's gun.

As a piece of detective fiction, however, the plot is not without its flaws. Why didn't the Casillas go to the police as soon as they received the supposed blackmail phone call? How were Peter and the wounded Binnie ever able to flee the States in the first place? Given that everyone is agreed that Binnie had been hit by a bullet during her kidnap, why does no one consider that she might indeed have been killed by that bullet rather than murdered by Peter? Even press reviews at the time complain that the film does not reveal the fate of Sylvia's dangerous servant, James. With regard to proving the identity of Binnie, would not her blood-type, dental and other medical records also have served to clarify the position without the need for a potentially dangerous operation to remove the bullet? In today's world, Peter's seemingly undue interest in the young Binnie would have appeared rather unhealthy and would possibly have given rise to other charges as to the reason for the abduction. However, all of this can be overlooked in that the film provides good entertainment and a happy ending.

Nature of Anti-American propaganda

It would, nevertheless, be naïve to consider *Sensationsprozess Casilla* as nothing more than a piece of innocent entertainment, since the film contains a good deal of material which is clearly anti-American. The denigration of the American way of life is found both in the negative portrayal of its legal system and in the values and behaviour of its citizens.

Condemnation of the American legal system
Any German viewer of the time would clearly have been shocked by this graphic presentation of the adversarial nature of American legal procedure compared to the more measured and

inquisitorial style of the German system. The courtroom appears more like a theatre, with the key participants performing as actors on a stage and whose actions are applauded or jeered by the watching public. The fact that the proceedings are being transmitted live, and that journalists can constantly intervene to take photographs, clearly suggest that it is sensationalism rather than justice which will be the winner. The radio broadcast is frequently interrupted by an announcement that the programme is sponsored by the best milk chocolate company in the world, a fact which seems more important than the fate of the defendant.

The whole system seems to be corrupt or at best open to abuse. Even the judge is a bit of a maverick whose seemingly whimsical decisions as to which questions might be permitted sometimes inconvenience the defence and at other times the prosecution, although at no time does he seem prepared to intervene to prevent the intimidation of the witnesses who have taken to the stand.

For both the prosecutor and the defence attorney, winning the case seems more important than the actual guilt or innocence of the accused. The state prosecutor is even shown trying to manipulate the outcome of the case in his pre-court briefing with Sylvia Casilla. He asks her to show some reluctance to condemn Peter when she is asked if she thinks he is guilty, as this will make a better impression on the press and the jury. Likewise, Vandegrift is not averse to hiring some rough-looking villains to obtain copies of information which will help his client.

The impression that the whole process is a sham is reinforced by the oath which witnesses are supposed to swear before they give their testimony. This should be a solemn and significant element in the proceedings, but as the clerk speaks in such a monotone manner, either shortening the oath or reciting it so quickly that its significance is lost, it only serves as a piece of meaningless ritual.

In the courtroom itself, both sides resort to underhand tactics when interviewing witnesses and speaking to the jury. In his opening remarks, the prosecutor is particularly adept at playing to his 'jury audience' as he dramatically lists the reasons why Peter deserves the electric chair. He almost explodes with anger as he points to the accused, and he puts extra pressure on the ultimate verdict of the jury by adding, as if the case is already won, that it is 'the world' against Peter Roland.

However, the defence is depicted to be just as devious. When Ines claims that Peter had been in love with Anna, Salvani immediately starts his cross examination in a very intimidating manner by demanding how much Ines had been paid. Before he can complete his question, Ines falls to her knees and claims she had not been paid, obviously assuming that he was

accusing her of having been bribed by Sylvia Casilla to make such a statement. The whole public gallery bursts into laughter when Salvani calmly claims that he had only been going to ask her how

Vandegrift, his daughter, Jessie and Salvani work together to achieve Peter Roland's acquittal. (*Deutsches Filminstitut/FWM*)

much she was paid as a maid by *Anna* Casilla. The damage to the reliability of the witness is thus assured. Similarly, Vandegrift bullies the handwriting expert by refusing to let him answer his questions with nothing other than a simple 'yes or no', thereby evoking misleading answers. There is also an amusing moment when, having admitted to his own team that the case seems lost because of the non-appearance of Binnie, Vandegrift still has the audacity to stand up in court and bluff that the case is 'as good as won'. To the German cinema viewer, the American justice process must have seemed entirely farcical.

The most passionate denunciation of the system is voiced by the defendant himself. When asked why he had not gone to the police about the Casillas' mistreating their daughter, he responds that the police would have thought he was mad, that the Casillas were influential people with lots of money and, above all else, because he was a foreigner. Indeed, he was a German! Even the evidence provided by the nanny in support of Peter is cast into doubt when it is revealed that she is also a German. What more damning condemnation of the American legal system than the assertion that only an American would receive fair treatment in America, and that influence and money carried more weight than the truth!

Condemnation of American values
However, the film goes much further than simply condemning the American legal system; it also derides American values and priorities.

Morbid curiosity
The depraved curiosity of the average American citizen is demonstrated by the very fact that this trial aroused sufficient public interest to be broadcast live, and important events in the case make front-page news simply because it concerns the fate of a film star. Their interest is not so much for the fate of the accused, but for the sensational revelations about the lives of the key participants which they hope will emerge from the proceedings.

This morbid curiosity is also reflected in the number of sightseers visiting the house where the abduction occurred. Plaques have been erected to show where key incidents took place and the guide revels in describing all the gory details. The sightseers act like lemmings with their heads turning from side to side as the guide points to various scenes of the crime, and it is amusing how they all stand up in unison to take compulsory photographs. There is absolutely no sensitivity for the feelings of the real human beings involved in the case. Such curiosity may be commonplace in today's world with such easy access to the media, but this was not the case in most of the world at that time and hence why it is America, ironically, which falls prey to so much criticism, primarily because of the very openness of its society.

Society governed by financial greed and power
Time and again, examples are provided of how every level of American society is dominated by the power and influence which wealth brings. The film illustrates how the greed for money has led to the moral corruption of ordinary citizens prepared to go to any lengths for financial reward.

The fact that parents would deliberately conspire with a corrupt doctor to have their child's growth stunted is a clear indictment of the relative value placed on money and morality in American society. Such is the extent of Sylvia's greed that she is prepared to bribe her maid to commit perjury and to arrange for her servant, James, to go to South America and remove all evidence of Binnie's existence. Indeed, she is even ready to, as it were, 'commit murder' by allowing Peter to go to the electric chair just so that she can be certain of inheriting the fortune left in trust for Binnie.

Likewise, the facts that the tour guide not only makes money out of selling lurid photographs of both Peter Roland and the electric chair, but will also charge extra to allow tourists to visit the rooms in which the abduction took place, demonstrate that there are no depths to which people will not sink for the sake of profit.

Even the general manager of Binnie's film company is determined to make an unexpected windfall from the interest in the court case by re-releasing Binnie's earlier films. Given that the Nazis perceived the American film industry as being run by Jews, which in many cases was indeed true, it is very convenient that this general manager should be seen to be greedily grabbing every last 'pound of flesh' in this way.

CONCLUSION

Completed in less than six months, the German censors were happy to approve the screening of *Sensationsprozess Casilla*, a film which neatly reflected the Nazi vision of the wider world and which pokes fun at an America whose President Roosevelt had become increasingly outspoken in criticising Germany's internal policies. Hitler had been particularly incensed by the Warners' release of *Confessions of a Nazi Spy* in April 1939, and the Nazis had threatened to produce a series of retaliatory films exposing life in the United States as being one of greed, corruption, crime and unhappiness. This film, which, in the eyes of the Nazis, showed a flawed American legal system as indicative of a failed society, achieved many of these aims. Indeed, there is a disparaging aside early in the film from Sylvia's servant about the whole concept of democracy – the very form of government which is so applauded by Roosevelt.

By focussing on the apparent failings of the American legal system, the Nazis were naturally happy to divert attention away from the brutal nature of National Socialist justice and its courtrooms, which were to send thousands of citizens to imprisonment or death, often for the most spurious of reasons.

At the end of the war, *Sensationsprozess Casilla* was one of the films immediately banned by the Allies, partly because it was considered very anti-American and partly because it starred Heinrich George, who featured in a number of the Nazis' more controversial films. Rather surprisingly, the director of the film, Eduard von Borsody, who was involved in the production of a number of even more explicit Nazi propaganda films such as *Wunschkonzert*, had no difficulty resuming his career in films after the war. It is possibly a reflection of the fact that the Allies themselves really saw little to condemn in *Sensationsprozess Casilla*, which in many ways was perhaps a fair reflection of American society at that time, even if they were reluctant to make such an admission. In fact, earlier American films such as *Stranger on the Stairs* (1940), starring Peter Lorre, had already exposed the failings of American justice with its depiction of an absent-minded judge, a jury which is half-asleep and a bullying prosecutor. By 1957, the film was again cleared for general screening primarily on the grounds that, by then, a whole raft of American-produced films openly critical of America's legal system had been released.

Chapter VI

German Feature Films:
Anti-Eastern Europe Propaganda

Background

Films containing propaganda against nations and peoples situated to the east of Germany fall into two key categories.

On the one hand, the Nazis required films designed to highlight how people of German descent who had moved abroad to find work and fortune were often mistreated by the majority native population where they settled. These German emigrants needed to be rescued and welcomed back to the Fatherland, and such romanticised tales were eventually to be used as a pretext for Germany's invasion of the likes of Czechoslovakia, Poland and Yugoslavia. Many such films were in a documentary style and featured real footage of Germany's powerful military machine in action during its invasion of those countries.

On the other hand, once Hitler had torn up his non-aggression pact with Stalin and attacked the Soviet Union on 22 June 1941, new films were released or old films re-released to justify, retrospectively, the reasons for the invasion and to emphasise the threats posed by the Bolshevik 'menace'.

Films bemoaning the treatment of German minorities abroad

Released in 1933, one of the first feature films to focus on the plight of German minorities who had emigrated to the east was *Flüchtlinge* (*Refugees*). Set on the Soviet Union–Chinese border in war-ridden Manchuria in 1928, the film mocks the inability of the High Commission, chaired by an Englishman, to reach a decision as to how the Volga-German refugees caught up in the struggle should be treated. The Bolshevik soldiers in particular are shown to be ruthless murderers who have no hesitation in machine-gunning innocent civilians blocking the route of their truck, and who are intent on capturing a specific group of forty-five Volga-German refugees. It transpires that an English-speaking officer from the International Settlement, played by Hans Albers, is really a German who had turned his back on the old Germany. He eventually takes pity on the refugees and, by working together, they succeed in repairing the railway line and just manage to escape by train before the Bolsheviks can catch them. It is quite a mournful tale but has an uplifting ending as the refugees leave in good spirits, singing joyfully together to the tune of 'Pack up your troubles in your old kit bag'. Romance also flourishes between one of the refugees and Albers, who, as he hugs the girl, makes a moving final comment about returning home to their (beloved) Germany.

As will be seen, such inspiring and nostalgic thoughts of '*Heimat*' were a common feature in all the films set in the east. Special emphasis was often given to the close blood and racial ties between emigrant Germans and their original German homeland. The Nazis were keen to use such films to underline the differences between the superior Aryan race and the coarse and inferior Slav races. The propaganda element intended to affect the audience in two different ways. First, it encouraged native Germans to welcome their 'cousins' back into the fold, justifying military action to rescue German minorities from a cruel existence at the hands of inhuman and inferior races. Second, for ethnic Germans living outside Germany, there was an encouragement to return to the new, improved Germany under Hitler. As will be explained later, the most famous film falling into this category was *Heimkehr* (*Homecoming*), where the Poles rather than Bolsheviks are portrayed as the evil oppressors.

Films specifically identifying the Bolsheviks as a threat to Germany

The campaign against Communism had been a key pillar of Nazi ideology since 1924, and gradually the distinction between Jews, Marxists, Bolsheviks, Soviets and Slavs all became rather hazy as they merged into an image of one cruel, repressive, sub-human enemy of Germany and the Western world.

Cartoon from the satirical magazine *Kladderadatsch*, August 1939. *Top*: Polish police are shown attacking a German school in Poland. *Bottom*: Chamberlain is shown speaking in the House of Commons – 'I can only admire the remarkable calm and intelligent restraint of the Polish Government.' (*Randall Bytwerk*)

The first film specifically concentrating on the Bolsheviks as a direct threat to Germany was produced in 1934. *Um das Menschenrecht* (*For the Rights of Man*) is set in Germany at the end of the First World War. It recounts the experiences of four soldiers who had fought together in the war and their return to Germany which is in the grip of revolution. Uncertain how to respond to the new Germany, one of the soldiers simply tries to escape the turmoil by returning to his farm in the hills, two join the rioting communists ('the reds') and

Hans Albers and Käthe Nagy as the heroes of
Flüchtlinge. (Deutsches Filminstitut/FWM)

one joins the Freikorps ('the whites') – basically ex-soldiers who try to maintain order – easily identifiable by their distinctive steel helmets encircled by a white band.

As fighting on the streets between both sides becomes a regular occurrence, the invariably drunken, womanising, Bolshevik-loving communists are portrayed as being responsible for various acts of theft and murder against ordinary civilians. A doctor who speaks out to defend a woman seized by the communists as a hostage is questioned as to what a member of the bourgeoisie knows about human rights. When he responds that he has been speaking to comrades who had fought at the front and not to Jews, he is marked down as being dangerous, and two men are dispatched to murder him. After a number of fighting scenes, the four comrades become reunited and, thoroughly disillusioned with life at home, they decide to seek their fortune outside Germany.

This was to be followed in 1935 by the even more hard-hitting *Friesennot* (*Frisians in Peril*), which was to precede the Nazis' direct campaign against Bolshevism in Germany.

Once again, the story is about a Volga-German community which is being oppressed by the Soviets. This time the life of a peaceful, God-fearing village, which has deliberately kept itself remote from the rest of the world, is thrown into turmoil with the arrival of a detachment of Soviet soldiers. On the orders of the new Bolshevik authorities, the villagers are forced to hand over their corn and livestock, which they are told will be used to help the starving masses in the Soviet Union.

At first, the Soviet commissar seems a reasonable man, falling in love with one of the village girls, Mette, and even admitting to her that the Soviet Union is an unhappy place. However, resentment soon grows against these rough, intoxicated soldiers who deny the existence of God and defile the villagers' church with gambling and debauchery, and Mette is eventually expelled from the village for flirting with the commissar. In revenge, the Soviet soldiers ransack the Frisians' church and homes, and rape one of the girls.

Driven to despair, the leader of the community reluctantly lays down his Bible and unwraps two pistols with which he then murders the commissar and all the soldiers. Fatally wounded in this action, the leader's dying words to his people are that they should look for a new homeland, and the film concludes with the villagers setting fire to their own homesteads and heading out of the village in their wagon trains. The moral is clear: Bolshevik Russia is a desperate, ungodly country which is intent on spreading its malevolent influence to the rest of the world.

It is little wonder that the signing of the non-aggression pact with the Soviet Union on 23 August 1939 necessitated the immediate withdrawal of all films with an anti-Bolshevik or anti-communist theme – only for these to be re-released two years later, as soon as the pact had been rescinded.

Illustrierter Film-Kurier film programme for *Friesennot*. (Author's Collection/Verlag für Filmschriften)

ANTI-EASTERN EUROPE FILMS REVIEWED

The two films analysed in detail in this section are *Heimkehr* (August 1941) and *G.P.U.* (August 1942) because they are two of the most well-known films in this genre, were both made after war had commenced, and because they enjoyed contrasting success from a propaganda perspective. The former, which is anti-Polish in nature, was to retain some lasting impact on young viewers, while the latter, which is anti-Soviet, gave such an unconvincing portrayal of the Bolshevik enemy as to be unsuccessful, and was eventually banned from being screened to the young.

Heimkehr recounts how a German community is being mistreated in the Volhynian district of Poland through general harassment and the closure of their school. It specifically follows the plight of a German school mistress and her fiancé, who are attacked in a cinema for failing to sing the Polish national anthem. Polish soldiers indulge in acts of extreme cruelty and murder against innocent, ethnic German civilians who have been thrown into prison, before they are spectacularly rescued by invading German forces.

The GPU was an early incarnation of the Soviet KGB, and the film *G.P.U.* is an exciting spy story which tells of various murderous atrocities perpetrated by its agents across Europe in an attempt to destabilise enemy nations and undermine the war effort against the Soviet Union. The action moves swiftly through Armenia, Finland, France and finally Holland, with the Nazis' invasion of Holland portrayed as being almost justifiable because it allowed innocent civilians imprisoned and tortured in the Soviet Trade Delegation in Rotterdam to be rescued from the hands of their cruel Soviet oppressors.

Enjoying varying degrees of propaganda success, these films were designed to arouse in the German audience emotions of fear, hatred and loathing for an all-encompassing Bolshevik enemy. The films instilled a desire for revenge on an adversary which had allegedly carried out many cruel acts against ethnic Germans, and to help engender support for military action to counter the 'red menace' before it crossed the border and entered Germany.

Film title: *Heimkehr*
Year of release: 1941
Type: Feature film
Primary purpose: Anti-Polish propaganda
Director: Gustav Ucicky
Principal stars:
Attila Hörbiger   (Ludwig Launhardt)
Peter Petersen   (Dr Thomas)
Carl Raddatz   (Dr Fritz Mutius)
Otto Wernicke   (Vater Manz)
Paula Wessely   (Maria Thomas)

INTRODUCTION

Released in August 1941, *Heimkehr* (*Homecoming*) is one of the most vitriolic anti-Polish films produced by the Nazis. Inspired by sketches produced for Himmler of ethnic Germans being re-settled from the Polish province of Volhynia in 1940, the primary purpose of this state-sponsored film was to provoke anti-Polish sentiments and provide retrospective justification for Germany's invasion of Poland to acquire greater 'living space'.

While successful in its aims and even winning an Italian film award at the time, the film is very controversial and generally considered to be one of the vilest examples of blatantly malicious propaganda.

PLOT SUMMARY

The opening captions clearly set the scene by explaining to the viewer:

> This film tells the story of a handful of German people whose forefathers had journeyed to the east many decades previously, because there was no more room for them in their homeland. In the winter of 1939, they returned home ... home to a new, strong nation ... Their experiences were shared by hundreds of thousands who endured the same fate.

The film begins in March 1939 and is set in the district around Luck in eastern Poland. In the opening scenes, some Polish inhabitants in one of the towns are witnessed setting fire to the desks which have been thrown out onto the street from a German school. Maria Thomas, the German schoolmistress and daughter of Dr Thomas, complains about the closure of the school to the town's mayor, but he is unsympathetic, claiming that the school building is required for

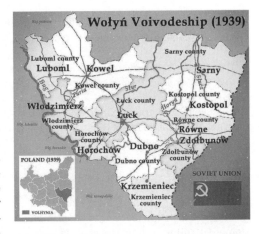

The location of Luck in Eastern Poland. (*Wikimedia Commons*)

other purposes. A bitter argument ensues in which he condemns her for considering herself German rather than Polish, especially as she holds a Polish passport. She is adamant that the Polish authorities should be doing more to protect the rights of the German minority and travels to the city of Luck to raise the matter with the provincial governor. However, delayed by the authorities from making her representations, she eventually goes to the cinema accompanied by her fiancé, Fritz, and Karl, another ethnic German friend who has been called up to serve in the Polish army.

When the three Germans remain silent at the singing of the Polish national anthem, several Poles shout abuse and violently attack the group, during which Fritz is knocked to the ground, badly concussed. Neither the police nor the cinema officials shows any compassion for Fritz and, even when Maria and Karl do manage to transport him to hospital, they are denied access, simply because they are German, and, tragically, Fritz dies of his injuries.

Meanwhile, with the mobilisation of the Polish army and military conscription initiated, apprehension among the ethnic German population continues to mount. Maria's father is blinded by a gunshot from some Polish schoolboys and, when a large group of Germans is caught listening to a speech by Hitler about the oppression by the Poles, they are all arrested and herded off to prison. Some of the prisoners are herded into a flooded cellar, with many mown down by machine-gun fire. Fortunately, liberating German forces soon arrive on the scene, so that Maria, her father and many of the other German prisoners are miraculously

Ethnic Germans hiding from the Polish authorities in a barn. (*Deutsches Filminstitut/FWM*)

saved and joyfully anticipate their return to the safety of their beloved German homeland. The rousing caption appears on the screen:

> Then the day came when they were able to forget all their suffering and were rewarded for their faithfulness ... the day when they could follow the call to their homeland.

The film concludes triumphantly where, to the sound of the German national anthem and the sight of a giant poster of Hitler, a long line of wagons is shown transporting thousands of German civilians back home to Germany.

CRITICAL REVIEW

Heimkehr is a blatant piece of anti-Polish propaganda, designed to portray Germany's invasion of Poland as a mercy mission to liberate thousands of German emigrants from the oppression of the Poles.

The primary focus of the propaganda is two-fold. First, every opportunity is taken to depict the character of Polish people in a poor light, and second, the new Germany is presented as a paradise.

Depiction of the Poles

Every stratum of Polish society is shown to be antagonistic towards those citizens of German descent.

There is the mayor who, in contrast to Maria's more reasoned appeal regarding the fate of the German school, becomes almost apoplectic with anger that she should still consider herself German and that German is still her mother tongue. He threatens her with his rifle, asserting that the Germans will enjoy the same rights as Polish citizens. He categorically

Maria, her father and Fritz trying to go about their business in Luck. (*Deutsches Filminstitut/FWM*)

refuses to be influenced by dangerous doctrines disseminating from what he calls the 'German Territorial Army'. The provincial government official in Luck is equally discourteous towards Maria, deliberately keeping her waiting and ultimately denying Fritz access to the hospital for life-saving treatment.

Poland also had a large Jewish population, and the film is swift to deprecate the character of the Jews. When Maria is walking through the market, a Jewish trader at first seems quite friendly, indicating that he will happily do business with the Germans whom he considers to be a proud and honourable people. However, his attitude soon changes when Maria declares that she does not buy from Jews, and he shouts a tirade of curses after her.

In the cinema in Luck, the three Germans seem quite content to mind their own business and even stand up for the Polish national anthem. However, behaving like a pack of wolves, the Polish general public deliberately provoke a fight, seeking any excuse to throw the Germans out of the cinema. The venomous hatred displayed by the audience is clearly exemplified by the cry of one viewer, 'The German pigs must be wiped out!'

Even the police admit that they are indifferent to Fritz's injuries and demand that the Germans leave the cinema immediately. It also later transpires that Karl is made the scapegoat by the authorities for the whole affair. Instead of assisting the hapless Germans, the cinema officials and the mob outside the hospital continue to crowd the wagon in which Fritz is lying, only gradually dissipating when it becomes obvious that Fritz is motionless. Similarly, when Maria is pleading with the hospital staff to give Fritz assistance, she appeals to their humanity and motions towards the Christian cross on the hospital wall, but all in vain.

In a separate scene, a German woman is attacked by a rough Polish labourer who symbolically rips open her dress and snatches the swastika she is wearing round her neck, holding it up to his colleagues in triumph. She is then stoned to death by children.

The prison guards are shown to be equally sadistic. They smile as they witness the Germans squirming and arguing among themselves in their cramped prison conditions. The guards even joke that the German prisoners should not be prevented from singing together since within an hour, '... they won't be singing anymore!' Finally, a detachment of Polish soldiers seems to have no qualms about murdering their German prisoners, including women and children, with a machine-gun, and even seem to relish the prospect.

In short, all the Poles are portrayed as ungodly and lacking in any form of human compassion, with an almost pathological hatred of the Germans whom they treat little better than animals.

Maria and her German colleagues being berated by angry Poles outside the cinema. (*Deutsches Filminstitut/ FWM*)

Having been herded into a prison by the Poles, the ethnic Germans await their execution. (*Deutsches Filminstitut/FWM*)

The portrayal of the new Germany as a paradise

The extent of the sad plight of the Germans is frequently reinforced by the playing of solemn, funereal music, and one particularly touching scene is where Maria and her father are witnessed in their horse-drawn coach pulling an open wagon containing a bare coffin. The empty streets and the complete lack of any formal funeral trappings to mark respect for the deceased Fritz vividly highlight the desolation and despair of the Germans trapped in this hostile environment.

Against this inhuman world in which they are striving to exist, there is strong religious imagery in which the Germans look to God to save them from their enemies. Salvation is repeatedly depicted as taking the form of release from imprisonment and torture in Poland back to the protection of Germany. The word '*Heimat*' is repeated time and again as an idyllic haven close to the heart of all true Germans.

The most poignant speeches are made by Maria as she tries to raise the spirits of her kinsfolk with warm, optimistic reflections during their period of incarceration:

> How can you really believe that all our lives ... all our suffering ... all our hope has been in vain? ... The one hope is for our return to our homeland ... Why can't we go back home, if that's what we want? Back to good German land. To go into a shop where people don't speak Yiddish or Polish but German ... Not only is everything in our village German, but everything round about as well – the good, warm earth of Germany ... [in our homeland] we live a German life and die a German death and dead we still remain German ...

The modern viewer can't help but draw parallels with the nationalist sentiments of Rupert Brooke's classic First World War poem, 'The Soldier':

> If I should die, think only this of me: that there's some corner of a foreign field that is forever England. (lines 1–3)

Maria's and her father's speeches, which extol the virtues of the new Germany, are certainly just as emotive.

The closing scene, with the prospect of a long trail homeward, is depicted as a pilgrimage towards a better world, and a glorious sun glows across the horizon. To cap it all, the huge portrait of Hitler shows the Führer as a great Messianic figure, who declared that he would save and protect his people and has now delivered on his promises.

The irony of the portrayal of the German emigrants as an abused minority

Yet again, we are presented with a film where the crimes for which the Nazis' enemies are being charged and condemned are almost an exact parallel of how the Nazis had been treating minority groupings in their own country since they came to power. The burning of German property, street attacks on German civilians, the refusal of medical care, incarceration and execution differed little from the harsh treatment which the Jewish minority in Germany suffered at the hands of the Nazis, with the burning of their synagogues and shops, confiscation of their possessions, imprisonment and ultimate death in concentration camps. In reality, there were many more people who wanted to escape the horrors of Nazi Germany than those who wished to enter or return to the country. Consequently, one has to ask whether the ordinary German viewer might not also have quietly recognised these parallels or whether the anger aroused by the cruelty shown towards the ethnic Germans in this film was so great as to rule out any such objective analysis.

POINTS OF NOTE CONCERNING THE PRODUCTION AND CONTENT OF THE FILM

How was the film received?

Shot during the first six months of 1941, the film was premiered in Venice on 31 August 1941, where it won an award from the Italian Culture Ministry before being screened in October in Vienna and Berlin. Goebbels was very satisfied with the film declaring it, 'an educational memo for the whole German people', and he was proud of being able to screen what he regarded as such a magnificent political and artistic success. Having been originally classified by the censors as being of 'special political and artistic merit', by October 1941, *Heimkehr* had been upgraded to the status of 'Film of the Nation'. Despite such commendable credentials, given its lack of any real stars in key roles other than Wessely and Wernicke, and its rather depressing plot, the film was not particularly successful at the box office. However, the emotionally charged, nationalistic monologues by Maria and her father seem to have made a more lasting impression on younger viewers, who, rather surprisingly, named *Heimkehr* as one of their six favourite films in a survey undertaken in 1944.

The fate of the director and key actors associated with the film

Gustav Ucicky was a famous Austrian and German film director, and because of his willing involvement in *Heimkehr* and a number of other propaganda films, he was forbidden from working in cinema by the Allies after the war, although the restriction was subsequently lifted in Austria in July 1947, and he went on to direct a number of other international films.

The best-known performers in this film are Paula Wessely (Maria) and Otto Wernicke (Manz), both of whom were added to the special list of 'God-gifted' German artists in 1944, which absolved them from active military service.

Wessely had been a leading Austrian stage and screen actress since the 1920s and, having been an enthusiastic supporter of Germany's annexation of Austria, her career continued to blossom under the Nazis, with her starring in many of their propaganda films. However, her willing participation in *Heimkehr* was very controversial and, because of her collaboration with the Nazis, the Allies imposed a short ban on her acting career immediately after the war. She later apologised for starring in *Heimkehr* and for not having had the courage to oppose such Nazi propaganda. Wernicke, who had a Jewish wife, actually initially required a special dispensation to allow him to work as an actor, but went on to star in many of the Nazis' best-known propaganda feature films, including *Titanic, Ohm Krüger* and *Kolberg.*

Were the atrocities depicted in *Heimkehr* fact or fiction?

Released in 1941, it is interesting that the film should focus on this particular incident and location in attempting to justify Germany's invasion of Poland to protect the Germany minority.

In the period leading up to war, and as tension grew over the fate of the so-called Danzig corridor, Hitler was keen to list instances of supposed repression and ill-treatment by the Poles towards those inhabitants of German descent. The reality regarding the true extent of such incidents is difficult to assess as there were countless claims of incidents on both sides, many of which were deliberately fabricated.

There is no doubt that prior to the invasion of Poland, such atrocities as 'Bloody Sunday' in Bydgoszcz, Pomerania, where a large number of ethnic Germans were killed, did occur and were investigated at length after the war, although without any firm conclusions other than that such atrocities by both sides often arose through fear, misinformation and revenge. However, the claims of the extensive oppression of ethnic Germans prior to the invasion of Poland might seem more credible to a modern audience if it were not now known that the Nazis had deliberately engineered certain events for their own ends. In a conversation with his generals on 22 August 1939, it is recorded that Hitler indicated that he would give a propaganda reason for starting the war, whether or not it was plausible, since the victor would not be questioned as to whether he had told the truth. Subsequently, history records that the staged attack at Gleiwitz on 31 August 1939 by German soldiers dressed in Polish uniforms was used as an excuse to launch Germany's invasion of Poland.

The Polish city of Luck itself seems a curious choice for the setting of the film. It came under Polish control after the First World War, and the province in which it was situated at the extreme east of Poland was then inhabited by a mix of Ukrainians, Poles, Jews, Czechs and Germans. Under the terms of the Soviet-German non-aggression pact, it was actually conquered by the Red Army in 1939, with the ethnic Germans being allowed to move west, and it was not captured by the German army until June 1941. Despite this, the film clearly shows German forces freeing German prisoners from Polish control in what is supposed to be late 1939. Paradoxically, on taking the city, the Germans were to report the discovery of the massacre of a very large number of the Jewish and ethnic Polish inhabitants by the previous Stalinist regime.

Ultimately, the aim of the film was to provide justification for Germany's invasion of Poland through documenting specific examples of the ill-treatment of the German minority. Whether or not this specific incident occurred was largely irrelevant. All that mattered was that a German audience left the cinema feeling disgust for the Poles, happy that Hitler had acted correctly in protecting the ethnic Germans and believing that Nazi Germany represented the best of all possible nations.

CONCLUSION

Rife with rumours regarding the poor treatment of ethnic Germans in neighbouring countries, *Heimkehr* sought to provide credence to such rumours and provoke feelings of anger among ordinary Germans towards the Poles. The participation of well-known performers such as Wessely and Wernicke undoubtedly gave the film more credibility, even though it must have been evident to the ordinary German cinema-goer that it was unlikely that such a calamitous series of misadventures could have affected this one family, and that the film was full of contrived speeches with a very sentimental image of the new Germany. However, as is apparent from similarly contrived films produced by the Allies, blatant propaganda does not prevent such films being effective, and the miraculous rescue and optimistic finale ensured that German viewers left the cinema more upbeat and certain of the justness of their cause.

Such was the controversial and divisive nature of the film that it was banned by the Allies in 1945, and is still not available for public screening in Germany.

Film Title: *G.P.U.*
Year of release: 1942
Type: Feature film
Primary purpose: Anti-Soviet propaganda/
    entertainment
Director: Karl Ritter
Principal stars:

Andrews Engelmann	(Nikolai Bokscha)
Karl Haubenreißer	(Jakob Frunse)
Wladimir Majer	(CPU Chief)
Will Quadflieg	(Peter Aßmus)
Laura Solari	(Olga Feodorowna)
Marina von Ditmar	(Irina)

INTRODUCTION

Whilst a number of anti-communist films had been produced by the Nazis prior to the war, with the signing of the non-aggression pact with the Soviets on 23 August 1939, all the anti-Soviet films produced until that date were officially banned, and the production of those in course were similarly halted despite the considerable financial loss incurred. These included two films, *Kadetten (Cadets)* and *Legion Condor (The Condor Legion)*, both directed by Karl Ritter.

However, with Germany's invasion of the Soviet Union under Operation Barbarossa on 22 June 1941, a window of opportunity arrived for Ritter to produce a new anti-Bolshevik propaganda film called *G.P.U.*, which premiered in Berlin in August 1942. *G.P.U.* is generally considered to be the only completely anti-Soviet feature film produced by the Nazis. The letters GPU actually stand for '*Gosudarstvennoye Politicheskoye Upravlenie*', the Soviet State Security organisation – an early version of the KGB, with its foreign department charged with liquidating 'enemies of the people' who lived outside the Soviet Union.

PLOT SUMMARY

In common with so many propaganda films of this period, *G.P.U.* begins with a series of frames outlining the background to the film. It is explained to the viewer that:

> Bolshevism is trying to spread anarchy and chaos over all the countries of the world. The tools of this Bolshevik destruction of the world are Kominten and the GPU.

The story continues with a flashback to an incident in the Baltic States in 1919, with a wealthy family being thrown out of its home and the parents and their sons executed by a Bolshevik officer. The action then moves to 1939 and to a concert being organised by the Riga section of the International Women's League for Peace and Freedom, at which the beautiful Olga Feodorowna is playing the violin. One man shouts out that the league is actually financed by Moscow and claims that another member of the audience, the Soviet diplomat, Smirnov, is actually Bokscha, who has been responsible for thousands of murders. As the man is dragged away by some of Bokscha's agents, the pianist alerts Olga that she is certain that Bokscha is the man who had killed her parents and brothers. Later, we see Olga looking at a locket which contains a photograph of her whole family, and the viewer surmises that it was her family who had been murdered at the beginning of the film; we also learn that she is determined to kill him.

The man who had been complaining is subsequently tied up in a crate for transportation to Moscow. A student, Peter, ignorant of the crate's contents, is asked to take it in a truck to the harbour. The next day, he is arrested for kidnapping, as someone had reported to the police that his number plate had been blanked out. Some of the police are actually Bokscha's GPU agents, including a bald-headed thug named Frunse, and they decide to use Peter to assassinate an Armenian nationalist called Aramian. Unaware that he is being used, Peter reluctantly agrees to travel to Kovno to identify the men whom he thought were responsible for the kidnapping, and he is ordered to take a package to Aramian and to be present as the package is opened.

Tension mounts at Aramian's office when his secretary, Irina, takes an anonymous phone call (actually from Olga), warning them that Peter has been sent by Bokscha. When Aramian takes the package into his office it comes as little surprise when the package explodes, killing Aramian. Irina accuses Peter of being a murderer and despite his protests of innocence, Peter is arrested.

In the meantime, we realise that Olga, who is now staying in the same hotel in Kovno as Bokscha, is apparently also a GPU agent, working for Moscow Central Office. It also becomes clear that Olga works for a different section of the GPU and that Bokscha is unaware of her true identity and role. Indeed, Bokscha has become enchanted with Olga and wants to spend more time with her.

Frunse, who had discovered Irina trying to burn the names and addresses of nationalist contacts at her flat, brings her back to be interrogated by Bokscha at the hotel. Simultaneously, Peter is sneaked out of prison by some police who are in the pay of the GPU, and he is also delivered to the hotel. Given that Irina continues to deny that she knows any contact details, another GPU agent from the hotel persuades Olga to speak to Irina 'woman to woman'. She agrees, but on the condition that Frunse is only told the results of her interrogation and not the method by which they are obtained.

Consequently, Olga tries to persuade Irina to trust her and eventually manages to convince her to go to Gothenburg to

Bokscha, played by Andrews Engelmann, gradually becomes infatuated with Olga. (*Deutsches Filminstitut/FWM*)

reveal the identity of a minor contact in her organisation. Olga also gives Irina details of her secret address in Gothenburg. When the contact arrives in the café, Olga rushes to warn him that Bokscha's men, accompanied by Peter, are waiting to pounce. It transpires that Olga has placed some of her own agents in the café, with the result that there is a shoot-out between them and the other GPU agents, and, in the chaos, Peter and Irina escape to take refuge in Olga's secret flat. Realising that Peter was an innocent pawn, Irina now begins to fall madly in love with him, and her feelings are reciprocated. However, Olga manages to persuade Peter to return to Frunse, as it will be the only way of checking what progress the GPU men are making in tracking down Irina.

Having been given fresh orders by Moscow to wreak havoc across the Axis powers, Bokscha is seen teaching agents how to blow up ships with explosives and instructing supporters in Helsinki to assassinate some of their own Soviet citizens in Finland, so that this will give Molotov an excuse to invade Finland. These assassinations are successful, and Bokscha then moves to Paris to arrange for Bolshevik supporters there to inflict similar chaos in France.

Olga, now satisfied that Bokscha definitely was the man who shot her family, agrees to go with him to his secret house in France, where he confesses that he has acquired a French passport and lots of money, and wants to spend the rest of his life quietly with her. Knowing that Olga possesses a hand gun, the viewer half expects Olga to shoot him there and then, but instead she returns to Moscow and informs the authorities, and they subsequently send other agents to execute him at his house in Brittany because of his treachery.

In the interim, Frunse and his men have managed to recapture Irina and Peter, and they are incarcerated in the Soviet Trade Mission in Rotterdam where the GPU continue try to force Irina to give more information about her contacts.

Back in Moscow, Olga is congratulated for her good work in denouncing Bokscha, and she asks to be released from doing any more work for the Central Office. This request is flatly refused, and she then confesses that she has been disrupting GPU's work for years and only ever wanted to see Bokscha killed for murdering her family. She draws her gun and when a shot is fired, we expect to discover that she has shot the Central Office Chief, but instead she has committed suicide and is found on the floor clasping the locket containing the photo of her family.

The action then returns to Rotterdam where the Germans have launched their invasion of Holland and bomb the Soviet Trade Mission. In a very exciting and moving scene, Peter manages to kill Frunse while escaping from his bombed cell, and also manages to release Irina. The film ends with our two heroes both emerging into the bright sunlight, welcoming the arrival of German liberating forces.

CRITICAL REVIEW

It is important to appreciate that by the time this film was being produced, the Nazis had invaded the Soviet Union, and there was a need to discredit the Bolsheviks and make the German population aware of the international activities of the Soviet State Police.

Goebbels had always contended that the primary purpose of feature films should be to entertain, with any propaganda message flowing through naturally from the truth of the underlying story, rather than the creation of a totally contrived plot. In this regard, while *G.P.U.* is certainly a very entertaining film, it is more like a political thriller with so many twists and turns that the plot is more reminiscent of the adventures of John Buchan's secret agent, Richard Hannay.

What does the film actually tell us about the GPU?

It is obvious from the opening credits that, apart from providing entertainment, the film was also designed to shock the viewer with an account of the typical activities of the GPU.

The slogans clearly explain, 'This film only shows *some* of the crimes which the GPU has committed outside the Soviet Union, but it shows enough for the world to see what these three letters mean for the world.' Like something out of a horror movie, and to the accompaniment of dramatic music, wild, jagged lettering appears across the screen, letter by letter:

G　=　*Graven (horror)*
P　=　*Panik (panic)*
U　=　*Untergang (destruction)*

The film gradually reveals how the GPU has a network of secret agents across Europe, and has the ability to organise assassinations, kidnappings and the sinking of ships as it tries to destabilise foreign governments and destroy the power of the Axis nations.

Bokscha explains how their agents consist of idealists, volunteers and people with no choice but to work for the GPU, and it is obvious that once someone works for the GPU, only death will allow release from their grasp. Bokscha and his agents are certainly ruthless thugs who use bribery and threats to achieve their ends, and for whom the lives of even their own people are of little value if it conflicts with the attainment of their ultimate goals. At the end, Frunse is even prepared callously to murder all the prisoners locked in the cells of the trade delegation, rather than allow them to be freed by the advancing German forces.

How does the viewer react to the negative presentation of the GPU?

However, despite the negative portrayal of the GPU, the viewer does not leave the cinema in a particular state of panic. Apart from the dramatic opening slogans and the callous murder of Olga's family, the same feeling of terror is never quite reproduced in the rest of the film. The film has been sanitised of any detailed close-ups which might cause undue distress or alarm. Consequently, we don't actually witness Olga's family being shot, but only the gun being fired four times; we don't observe the actual kidnapping of the man at the concert, and we don't witness Olga's suicide, only the sound of the gunshot.

Bokscha (right) is only one of an army of GPU agents operating worldwide. (*Deutsches Filminstitut/ FWM*)

Indeed, there seems to be confusion as to what the film is trying to achieve. The opening credits lead the viewers to believe that the film is going to be more like a documentary, and that they will be really horrified by everything which is reported about the activities of the GPU. However, because the viewer is distanced from their atrocities and never really sees physical pain being inflicted, it is actually quite difficult to regard the GPU as a serious threat. Also, their shifty appearance, dress and actions are just too stereotypical and unconvincing.

There is their constant bungling, some of which is undoubtedly caused by Olga's anonymous tip-offs, but much of which is also due to their own incompetence, such as when they use Peter to deliver the bomb and he fails to be killed in the explosion, or when they allow Peter and Irina to escape so easily from the café in Rotterdam. There seem to be GPU agents everywhere, but such is their internal secrecy that they don't know of each other's existence.

While Bokscha's GPU agents are certainly brutes, they are not actually shown assaulting Peter or inflicting physical torture on Irina to extract the names and addresses of her contacts. The limit of their persuasive techniques seems to be to shine a bright spotlight on Irina as she is being interrogated. Indeed, they seem quite ineffectual at extracting information, and the closest we get to being given the impression that the GPU might use torture is when Peter, stripped to the waist, is thrown to the floor before Irina in the Soviet Trade Mission in Rotterdam. Frunse explains, 'He is suffering for your lies. That is just the beginning. We have other methods. Then he'll really look pretty.'

Likewise, Bokscha himself is a more complex character and not just a bully. On the one hand, he is quite prepared to arrange for ships to be sabotaged or for Soviet agents to assassinate other Soviet citizens but, on the other hand, he is also someone who does have human feelings. His love for Olga is genuine, and he is enchanted by her playing of the violin. Indeed, when he rushes back from Paris to be with her and we can see his tears as he hears the sound of the violin playing his favourite melody, we almost feel sympathy for him when he is gunned down by the Soviet agents sent to eradicate him. The irony is that he dies without even realising that it was Olga who was responsible for his execution in revenge for the murder of her family.

How does such a potentially depressing film achieve a 'feel good' factor?

What prevents *G.P.U.* from becoming a very depressing and dark film is the fact that the film has at least three real heroes.

First, there is Olga, the beautiful and mysterious GPU agent, who has been scuppering the plans of Central Office for years and whose sole aim is to have the man who murdered her parents punished. The viewer certainly feels empathy towards this compassionate character and totally supports her final outcry against the GPU organisation: 'You will all be liquidated until this whole world will finally be free from your terror.' The only real surprise is that she does not shoot the Central Office Chief, who certainly deserves to die far more than she does. Perhaps there was a feeling that she would lose some of the viewer's sympathy if she had been shown to be no more than a murderer herself. As it is, her heart-rending suicide becomes symbolic of a rejection of the Bolsheviks and that it is preferable to die than live under such a regime.

Further heroism is found in the courage of young Irina and Peter, and their emerging love story. Irina refuses to provide the information which the GPU are seeking, and Peter is prepared to hand himself back to the GPU agents to help protect Irina from being recaptured. In the final dramatic scenes, tension mounts as Peter manages to kill Frunse and escape from his cell, and we share Peter's worries in his frantic cell by cell search to establish if Irina is still alive.

In modern parlance, *G.P.U.* ultimately becomes a 'feel good' film when the viewer witnesses the two heroes emerging safely from the darkness of their cells, relieved to see the arrival of the German forces. The film very much depicts the arrival of German tanks and planes in

The young heroes, Peter and Irina, who are eventually saved from the GPU following Germany's invasion of Holland. (*Deutsches Filminstitut/FWM*)

Rotterdam as symbols of freedom and hope, as if the Nazis are defending the whole world from Bolshevik tyranny. The fact that the Nazis were actually invading Holland, a free sovereign state, for no good reason and murdering thousands of innocent civilians in the process is simply ignored.

Does the film contain any other more subtle elements of propaganda?

It is interesting to spot some throw-away lines and events in the film which are subtly used to reinforce other propaganda messages so favoured by the Nazis.

First, there are a couple of anti-Jewish observations. When the man in the concert hall is warning everyone that the Women's League is controlled by Moscow, he complains, 'The last time they even sent a letter to a Jew named Finkelstein!', as if this is just one more crime for which the Jews can be blamed, namely working hand in hand with the Bolsheviks to overthrow capitalist countries. Likewise, when Olga is trying to find out whether Bokscha really is the person who murdered her family, she is told that, 'he climbed the career ladder although he was neither a Jew nor from the proletariat classes'. This is yet another attack on the perceived insidious influence of Jews in society.

Second, there is a swipe at the English when Bokscha, on receiving a telegram which he believes will mean war, remarks, 'England will never allow Poland to be happy.' This is clearly a reference to Britain's ultimatum that unless Germany withdrew from Poland, Britain would be at war with Germany. Presumably, the German viewer is meant to assume that Poland will be better off being invaded!

Then there is a suggestion that the GPU had even wielded influence over the former French Prime Minister, Léon Blum, who was a Jew and a Marxist, when Bokscha comments that, 'France is going well! That Léon Blum did a good job playing into our hands.'

Finally, when the bourgeoisie are dancing and sipping champagne at a reception in Helsinki, there seems an implicit criticism that the luxurious lifestyle these people were enjoying was far removed from the world of the ordinary citizen.

POINTS OF NOTE CONCERNING THE PRODUCTION OF THE FILM AND ITS RECEPTION

At a cost of 1.5 million Reichsmarks, *G.P.U.* was certainly not one of the most expensive propaganda films produced by the Nazis, although it was filmed in Berlin, occupied Paris, Potsdam and Stettin. While the plot does move along at pace, the film is rather disjointed as it jumps from one location to another, including cities in the Baltic States, Paris, Rotterdam, Helsinki and Moscow. The insertion of documentary footage is also less than convincing. All in all, it is full of stereotypical representations of Soviet spies as men with shaved heads, wearing leather raincoats and displaying evil smiles. The plot is a little too contrived and certainly has more in common with a tongue-in-cheek thriller like *The Thirty Nine Steps*.

In theory, *G.P.U.* did at least meet some of Goebbels' criteria for a good propaganda feature film in that it was certainly entertaining and the messages were simple and repeated, even if the anti-Soviet propaganda elements are laid on a bit thick. However, this was not a view shared by Goebbels who considered the film to be a disaster and disparagingly declared it to be an inferior piece of work produced by an amateur. He also condemned Karl Ritter's shallow portrayal of political and military issues, and for showing all the GPU men to be clichéd Asiatic torturers. The film was not awarded any political classification, which speaks for itself. External opinion on the film is divided. Some feel that it was the worst type of propaganda film because it deliberately tried to rewrite history by distorting the influence of the GPU. Others feel that it was just a poorly produced film. Whatever the truth, Goebbels certainly felt that Ritter had been a failure, and it is notable that Ritter was employed to direct only one other propaganda film for the Nazis, namely *Besatzung Dora* (*The Crew of the Dora*). However, even this film was ultimately banned by the Nazis, because changing war circumstances rendered its screening inappropriate by the time of its completion in 1943.

Karl Ritter, the unfortunate director of the film. (*Deutsches Filminstitut*)

CONCLUSION

With its fast-moving action, a beautiful double agent and an underlying love story, the plot of *G.P.U.* is rather far-fetched, but it certainly succeeds in entertaining, and does promote anti-Soviet propaganda at the same time.

Paradoxically, throughout the war, a number of films were released in the Allied countries in the style of exciting comic book thrillers mostly set in Germany or occupied Europe. British agents, often played by handsome Hollywood stars, successfully pit their wits against the Nazis who are characteristically portrayed as ruthless, devious thugs. Whatever sacrifices had to be made, 'good always triumphed over evil' and the fact that it was pure fiction was irrelevant. The viewer left the cinema entertained and uplifted, in the firm belief that the wicked Germans would ultimately lose the war. It was a very successful propaganda formula for the Allies and is evident in such films as *Night Train to Munich* (1940) and *The Adventures of Tartu* (1943).

Against this background, *G.P.U.* is rather an enigma. On the surface, it adopts a similar style and plot, with the difference that it is the GPU agents who are the brutal thugs, and the heroes are the young couple from the Baltic States and the beautiful violinist who has always sought to undermine the dastardly plans of her Bolshevik masters. It is somewhat ironic, therefore, that the film was considered a failure by Goebbels for the very reasons that he did not like the stereotypical presentation of the GPU as torturers, and that it was too lightweight on actual political detail. Presumably, Goebbels wanted the viewer to take the overall threat of Bolshevism more seriously, but this was something which was always going to be difficult to achieve given the timing of the release of the film.

In the summer of 1942, the German military was still seemingly invincible in its campaign against the Soviet Union and had reached the gates of Moscow the previous year. Even if they understood the meaning of Bolshevism, the Soviet Union would still have seemed a very distant threat for most ordinary Germans who were still largely unaffected by the horror of war, and, therefore, *G.P.U.*'s propaganda potential was rather limited. Nevertheless, the film is still banned in Germany today.

Chapter VII

German Feature Films:
Nationalistic and Pro-Nazi Propaganda

Background

Apart from films specifically commissioned to convey a negative representation of Germany's internal and external enemies, several feature films were produced with a distinctly pro-Nazi and pro-German focus.

Kampfzeit films

This series of films was released to commemorate the period before the Nazis came to power, known as the *Kampfzeit* (the time of struggle), when they were frequently involved in open street fights with the communists to gain control of German hearts and minds. The three classic films of this period are: *S.A. Mann Brand*, *Hitlerjunge Quex* and *Pour le Mérite*.

Released in June 1933, *S.A. Mann Brand* (*Storm Trooper Brand*), had actually been in production before the Nazis came to power and recounts the history of the Brown Shirts and, in particular, the life of Fritz Brand from 1932 to 1933. In speaking out for Germany and exposing the exploitation of the proletariat, the Brown Shirts are obliged to endure unprovoked abuse from the communists, and their organisation is even banned by the authorities for a period of time. Fritz is wounded in an assassination attempt and his young neighbour, Erich, is shot by the communists while on a street march. In a moving

1940: Pro-German, Nazi Party poster emphasising the contribution made by civilian and soldier alike to the war effort. 'Front and Homeland – the guarantors of victory.' (BArch, Plak 003-029-045/Mjölnir, S.)

Film poster for the *S.A. Mann Brand* film. (BArch, Plak 003-022-002/Ottler, O.)

Heini in discussion with his father in *Hitlerjunge Quex*. (*Deutsches Filminstitut/ FWM*)

scene, Erich faces death bravely in the firm belief that he has sacrificed himself for the glorious Fatherland.

The film has a very uplifting ending with fate finally swinging in their favour as Hitler is swept to power. There is a joyous rendition of *'Die Fahne hoch!'* (The flag on high!), and fond remembrance of fallen colleagues murdered by the communists as they march in spirit within their ranks. The film portrays communists as lazy drunkards controlled by Moscow, while the Nazis are depicted as innocent victims. Brand is seen as a model German, always displaying courage and compassion in the face of danger.

As the title suggests, *Hitlerjunge Quex* (*Hitler Youth Quex*) (1933) tells the story of the young Heini Völker, nicknamed Quex, who is the son of an unemployed communist supporter played by the famous Heinrich George. Much to his father's distress, Heini is more attracted to the activities of the Hitler Youth than the rabble of rebellious children who belong to the Internationale. He warns the Hitler Youth about a bomb plot, and they eventually welcome him into their fold, having initially feared he was a traitor. The communists contrive to attack Heini when he returns to distribute leaflets in their district and, in a plot reminiscent of *Hans Westmar*, he is eventually murdered by them. However, he does not lose faith, and his moving final words 'Our banner flutters before us' explode into one final triumphant rendition of the chorus from the Nazi Youth anthem of the same name as the film concludes.

Throughout the film, great effort is taken to emphasise that the communists do not have Germany's best interests at heart, and it becomes apparent that even Heini's father is starting to reconsider his position, remembering that both his birthplace and the place where the very beer they are drinking is brewed is *their* Germany and not the Soviet Union.

Somewhat reminiscent of *Um das Menschenrecht* (*For the Rights of Man*), a film already mentioned in Chapter IV because its plot combines a number of National Socialist themes, is *Pour le Mérite* (1938). Set in the First World War, it tells the story of a brave squadron of German fighter pilots who, feeling betrayed by the German communists who seized power at the end of the war, find it difficult to adjust to life in the Weimar Republic and secretly yearn for the sort of strong government which the Nazi Party represents. The comment, 'A miracle must happen one day!' sums up the mood of the film in which a 'miracle' does eventually occur in the closing scenes when Hitler assumes power and a strong air force is re-established. The date of the release of the film, 1938, is certainly not insignificant.

Military action films

Particularly during the war itself, a number of pro-German action films were produced featuring the exploits of the fighting men at the front. However, these were relatively few in number, and the quality was generally rather poor, often devoid of meaningful dialogue and incorporating a great deal of newsreel footage. Three well-known films, all released in 1941, were *Kampfgeschwader Lützow, Stukas* and *U-Boote Westwärts!*

Kampfgeschwader Lützow (*Battle Squadron Lützow*) follows the exploits of a bomber crew, first in Poland and then in the Battle of Britain. In the Polish campaign, they cause much damage and fend off Polish biplane fighters before passing over a group of ethnic German civilians being escorted along a road by Polish soldiers. In a piece of blatant and rather unconvincing propaganda, the bomber crew happens to witness a Polish soldier shooting dead a German civilian who has collapsed on the road. In revenge, the plane manages to drive off the Polish soldiers and lands beside the civilians, encouraging them to hold out for a couple of days until German troops arrive to save them.

Our heroes are then involved in a daring rescue of another crew that has crashed on territory still occupied by the Poles. Finally, as the war moves against Britain, they successfully sink some British merchant ships and manage to shoot down three fighters, albeit at the loss of some of their own lives. Their damaged plane manages to hobble back across the Channel on one engine, with the pilot finally succumbing to his wounds just as he has succeeded in saving the lives of his comrades by landing the plane. It is all good 'Boys' Own' material and the film ends with the squadron resolutely heading off for yet another attack on Britain to the refrain of their well-known song, *'Wir fliegen gegen Eng[e]land'* (We are flying against England).

In a similar vein, *Stukas* records the day-to-day life of a Stuka squadron. Somewhat repetitive, the action switches between the airmen in high spirits relaxing at their base and various bombing missions against infrastructure targets and even French tanks. Once again, some airmen are killed in these actions, and others display great bravery in landing to rescue comrades whose planes have crashed. Three airmen are captured by the French, and the French are shown mistreating their German prisoners by forcing them to run in front of their tanks. Other downed pilots use their wits to try to escape through the French lines, and the morale of the French soldiers is shown to be very low, as they are seen complaining about their government being controlled by the English and wishing an end to England's war. There is one surreal incident when a recuperating airman, overcome with apathy, is escorted by his nurse

Carl Raddatz as Hauptmann Bork in *Stukas*. (*Deutsches Filminstitut/FWM*)

Scene with U-boat commander from *U-Boote Westwärts!* (*Deutsches Filminstitut/FWM*)

to attend an opera in Bayreuth. He is so moved by the Siegfried music that he immediately rushes back to join his colleagues, and the film concludes with them enthusiastically singing their 'Stuka' anthem together as they fly towards England.

Such films were not restricted to the exploits of the German air force, and *U-Boote Westwärts!* (*U-Boats Westwards!*) was a feature film released in May 1941, which follows the adventures of a U-boat operating off the coast of Orkney. Unlike the two previous films, much of the plot actually centres on the personal relationships of the sailors with their loved ones back home. Despite the war, there is the ability to have a 'marriage at a distance', where the wedding of bride and groom takes place in two different places at the same time, and there is the obvious joy the sailors experience from radio programmes which include requests specifically intended for them.

The main fighting action concerns the sinking of a freighter where the Dutch captain had lied that he was transporting sewing machines and the cargo was actually aircraft propellers. Suddenly surprised by the arrival of a British destroyer, the submarine comes close to being depth charged and is forced to leave some of its sailors trapped in a rowing boat to be captured by the destroyer. Later, the submarine captain has to overcome his personal emotions and torpedo the destroyer, albeit conscious that he might kill his own countrymen. One of the German sailors is badly hurt in the process, but all are brought back on the submarine. The film ends rather abruptly with the wounded sailor proclaiming how good it is to die for the Fatherland and there is an enthusiastic rendition of their song about 'going to battle against England'.

Spy films

There were also a number of pro-German films which fall into the spy genre and which were released throughout the years the Nazis were in power. Generally, the plot is rather predictable and involves foreign agents or German traitors using blackmail, love or financial greed to persuade weak-minded individuals to pass secrets to them. Ultimately, the foreign agents always fail, and the films are as much a warning to the German viewer to be on guard against the inadvertent or deliberate betrayal of secrets, with the underlying moral that such crime never pays.

Three good examples are *Verräter*, *Achtung! Feind Hört mit!* and *Die goldene Spinne*.

Verräter (*Traitor*) concerns a group of agents, whose discoveries are relayed back to an unnamed foreign power which is seeking to establish an overall picture of all the developments Germany has made. In this particular story, the agents are pursuing three specific targets. First and foremost, they have made contact with a Dr Brockau, who is working on an improvement for converting oil into petrol. The agents exploit Brockau's financial problems caused by his wife and persuade him to steal secrets for them. Second, they attempt to blackmail Herr Klemm, a former

Dr Brockau, who will be sentenced to death for treason in *Verräter*. (*Author's Collection/ Verlag für Filmschriften*)

Lotte Koch and René Deltgen working for the British in *Achtung! Feind hört mit!* (*Author's Collection/Verlag für Filmschriften*)

banker who is now serving on military duty with the tank corps, to pass them more secrets. They achieve this by stealing and photocopying information from his notebook and falsifying his signature on a receipt for the payment of 500 Reichsmarks. Finally, they have a contact who is working at an aircraft factory, but who is eventually shot down while trying to steal the Nazis' latest dive bomber. Brockau is apprehended as he tries to steal secrets from a safe and will later be executed for treason. Klemm is eventually praised for reporting the blackmail attempt to his superiors, as this indirectly results in the capture or death of all the foreign agents.

The film is quite remarkable for a couple of reasons. Released in August 1936, it betrays a certain paranoia and exaggerated concern about the disclosure of military secrets at a time when Nazi Germany was trying to convince the world that they had no militaristic ambitions. Also, given that the film was actually shot in early 1936, when Germany was still supposed to be exercising some restraint in the growth of its armed forces, there is no attempt to conceal the vast numbers of tank crews and fighting planes involved in military training at that time. With hindsight, the very conclusion, where some fifty tanks are shown crossing a field and the sky filled with German planes, should have been a rather ominous warning of the dark years of war to follow.

Released in September 1940, *Achtung! Feind hört mit!* (*Watch out! The enemy is listening!*) is about a firm that has invented an especially robust yet lightweight wire which, when attached to barrage balloons, creates a formidable air defence. The plot involves agents working in Germany, supposedly in the pay of the British, using blackmail to persuade a restaurant waiter and draughtsman to steal samples and take photos of documents relating to the invention. One of the agents, Karl, pretends to be in love with a young secretary, Inge, and tries to use her affection for him to obtain a sample of the wire. However, Inge will not betray her country, and the two German traitors are soon arrested and executed for treason. Karl manages to escape in a plane but, rather ironically, soon crashes to the ground when its wing catches on one of the very wires being tested on balloons recently raised above the factory. The moral of the film is clear: careless talk costs lives, those committing espionage will soon be caught and those found guilty of treason will always face the death penalty.

A much later film, *Die goldene Spinne* (*The Golden Web*), was released in December 1943 to alert the populace to the dangers of Soviet agents. In this case, the film begins with two Soviets, Smirnoff and Lisaweta, being parachuted into Germany to uncover the secrets of a new tank which the Germans are developing.

Their methods for gaining information do appear quite plausible. First, they visit the female director of a nightclub with a letter from her daughter in which she pleads with her mother to do all that the Soviet agents ask in order for her life to be spared. The mother agrees to provide introductions for the Soviets, which allows Smirnoff to gain access to the tank factory and Lisaweta to obtain a job as a singer, and then as a worker in the tank factory. Second, using her charm and good looks, she entices an important engineer at the plant, Axel Rüdiger, to her flat and, while they are otherwise engaged, Smirnoff takes copies of the documents in Axel's briefcase. Axel is then blackmailed to provide more information, otherwise Smirnoff threatens to reveal to the authorities what Axel has already done – a crime for which Axel will face certain death for treason.

After several adventures, Lisaweta, disguised as a nurse, is finally arrested while attempting to escape on a train carrying fragments of metal from the tank, and Smirnoff is shot dead as he tries to take some final photographs from within the new tank. The harsh warning to all viewers is again quite clear. Germans who confess to the authorities about any acts of espionage in which they have unwittingly participated may well be spared, but those Germans who continue to work for the enemy will always face the death penalty, as indeed happens to the unfortunate Axel.

While none of the films is a particularly impressive piece of cinematic art and, indeed, all three appear more like 'B' movies, they are all quite exciting adventures, albeit filled with rather obvious propaganda content.

Russian agents Lisaweta and Smirnoff in *Die goldene Spinne*. (*Deutsches Filminstitut/FWM*)

Total war films

Finally, there are those films which were deliberately commissioned to reinforce morale on the Home Front, and to urge civilians to join in the fight as the war threatened to enter German soil later in the war. *Kolberg*, as will be explained, is by far and away the most spectacular film in this category. However, work on what would be the Nazis' final feature film, *Das Leben geht weiter* (*Life goes on*) commenced in 1944. The film was designed to provide a final message of hope that, despite all the damage and suffering they had endured, the Germans would still win the war with the aid of Hitler's wonder weapons, and that an even stronger Germany would emerge from the ashes. The film was never completed, partly because of the difficulty of filming in an increasingly desperate military situation, and partly because of an understandable reluctance on the part of the production team, who realised that the film's completion would mean a return to war service and their probable death on the Eastern Front.

PRO-NAZI AND NATIONALISTIC FILMS REVIEWED

The three films which are analysed in detail in this section are *Hans Westmar* (December 1933), *Wunschkonzert* (December 1940) and *Kolberg* (January 1945). These films have been chosen because they reflect the changing propaganda priorities of nationalistic films which were produced, and because they transcend the whole twelve-year period the Nazis were in power.

Hans Westmar is a romanticised account of the life of the Nazis' most famous hero, Horst Wessel. He was seen as a dangerous agitator by the communists and was eventually murdered in 1930. He was, nevertheless, responsible for penning the lyrics to *'Die Fahne hoch!'* which was to become Germany's co-national anthem until 1945.

Wunschkonzert (*Request Concert*) is a film which strives to create a bond between Germany's fighting forces and the civilians back home. The plot centres on the series of request concerts organised for the troops and broadcast on the radio, and tells the story of a love affair between a Luftwaffe pilot and a young girl whom he met at the 1936 Olympics. While quite a light-hearted story in places, there is some fighting action against the British and the French, and the film has an upbeat ending as our two estranged lovers become reunited. It was a far more popular and well-made film than the three military action films mentioned earlier, although it was actually released one year earlier in 1941.

Lastly, *Kolberg* was the final epic film completed by the Nazis. Delayed in production, it was not released until January 1945 and using tens of thousands of extras it recounts the heroic story of the town of Kolberg which had refused to surrender to Napoleon in 1807. The purpose of the film was to inspire the general populace in 1945 to make one final heroic effort to stand against the Soviet Union, sacrificing their very lives if necessary rather than submitting to a ruthless enemy.

Film title: *Hans Westmar*
Year of release: 1933
Type: Feature film
Primary purpose: Pro-Nazi propaganda
Director: Franz Wenzler
Principal stars:

Carla Bartheel	(Maud)
Heinrich Heilinger	(Camillo Ross)
Emil Lohkamp	(Hans Westmar)
Heinz Salfner	(Maud's father)
Paul Wegener	(Kuprikoff)
Irmgard Willers	(Agnes)

INTRODUCTION

As a record of the Nazis' historical beginnings, *Hans Westmar* is regarded as one of the most significant films of the time, as it relates to the short life story of Horst Wessel, one of the Nazis' early heroes. Wessel was responsible for composing the lyrics to the famous Horst Wessel song, *'Die Fahne hoch!'* (The flag on high!), which became the anthem of the Nazi Party and Germany's co-national anthem until the end of the war.

Hanns Heinz Ewers initially wrote a novel about Wessel, which appealed to Hitler and formed the basis of the script for a film of his life. Ironically, and partly because of internal political jealousy, Goebbels was to declare himself so dissatisfied with the film that it was temporarily banned on the pretext that the heroic figure of Horst Wessel was 'incompletely interpreted', thereby endangering the interest of the state and German prestige. Such was the outcry which Goebbels' ruling provoked that he was eventually forced to reverse his decision, but only after considerable re-editing and the re-naming of the Horst Wessel character as Hans Westmar. The film was eventually released in December 1933.

The screening of the film together with the recitation of the lyrics and the playing of the music of *'Die Fahne hoch!'* are still illegal in Germany today.

PLOT SUMMARY

The film opens in Vienna where a student, Hans Westmar, becomes friendly with a German recently returned from America and his beautiful daughter, Maud, who are on holiday in Europe. Hans tells them that they must visit Berlin but, in an immediate scene switch to Berlin, it is revealed that life there is really quite miserable, with many citizens unemployed and dependent on the welfare system.

Some inhabitants are even heard complaining that life in Moscow is far better and, at a meeting of Soviet-controlled communist leaders, it becomes obvious that most of Germany is under the control of the communists, and that it is they who are responsible for organising many protest marches and civil disorder among the workers.

Having returned to Berlin, Hans, a recognised member of Hitler's Sturmabteilung (SA), is next seen listening rather sceptically to a lecture where a Jewish-looking professor is expounding the merits of the Versailles Treaty for having brought peace to Germany, even though it had meant a retrenchment in Germany's borders.

Hans agrees to show his German-American friend the sights of the capital. His friend is appalled by the changes which have befallen Berlin in the intervening twenty years, and that it is now such a cosmopolitan city that hardly anything German remains. This is clearly demonstrated by their only being able to purchase English beer instead of a German beer, and in the decadent foreign music and promiscuous dancing in the nightclub, which so upsets Hans that he causes a scene and walks out in disgust.

Having watched the impressive demonstrations organised by the communists, Hans is convinced that they are Germany's real enemy, and he agrees to speak at a meeting organised by the communists to promote the National Socialists' views on the reasons for Germany's woes. However, he is soon heckled as he complains about the constant lies which the Bolshevik leaders tell to the German workers, and a fight ensues which ultimately results in one Nazi being attacked and drowned in the river. The Communist Party leader, Kuprikoff, is happy with this outcome, believing that it will serve as a warning to all Nazis to scale down their activities.

However, the murder has completely the opposite effect, with the Brown Shirts deliberately organising a loud procession which concludes in the very square where the communists have their headquarters. Further scuffles and arrests ensue.

The SA on the march. (*Deutsches Filminstitut/Transit Film GmbH*)

Later, Hans is seen assisting a poor girl called Agnes, who is ill-treated by her stepfather, by giving her some money to get away for a few days. At the same time, he is warned by Ross, one of the less ruthless members of the communist leaders, that East Berlin belongs to the Reds and that he should keep to the West. Ross also mocks him for knowing nothing about what the proletariat think or feel. Hans takes this rebuke to heart and, guided by the words of the Führer, resolves to forsake his life as a student to join with the workers, first as a taxi driver and later as a construction worker. He also undertakes to increase the number of Nazi supporters in his district, and the communists are so concerned by his recruiting success that they warn him more forcibly to desist from his activities.

On another occasion, there is a further clash in the streets between the communists and the Brown Shirts, and the communist newspaper, *Die Rote Fahne* (The Red Flag), subsequently claims that the Nazis had been responsible for five deaths and nine wounded workers. However, one of Hans' communist colleagues, who had been present at the incident, is able to report that it was all a lie, that there had been no shooting, and that it was only a car backfiring.

As a result of his recruiting success, Agnes is pressurised to spy on Hans but, because of the kindness which he had previously shown towards her, she warns him that he is being observed and that his life is in danger. In the subsequent elections the Nazi vote increases to 130,000, but Hans is still rather disappointed because the communists and socialists still achieved ten times more votes. The Reds, however, are so upset that they lost 54,000 votes that they determine to murder Hans, with information as to his whereabouts being passed to them by Hans' landlady. Agnes, who has been caring for the physically exhausted Hans, learns of their conspiracy and is able to warn Hans' colleagues so that he is moved to safety just in time. However, when he later returns to his flat to collect his belongings, the communists do manage to shoot him, and he is rushed to hospital badly wounded. Given that there

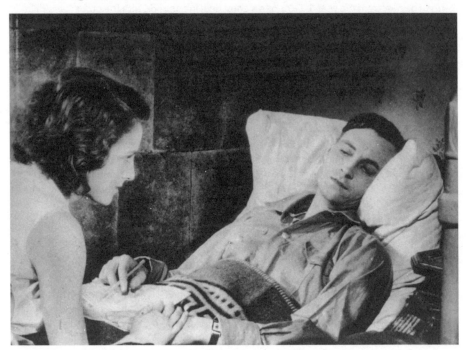

Agnes caring for the exhausted Hans. (*Deutsches Filminstitut/Transit Film GmbH*)

is a risk that he might still survive, the most devious of the communist leaders resolves to have him murdered in hospital, but even Comrade Ross is so appalled by this decision that he alerts the Nazis and they provide Hans with bedside protection. Nevertheless, Hans has been so badly wounded that, in a very moving scene, he silently slips away, uttering 'Germany' as his final word.

His ensuing funeral procession attracts a large crowd and, despite the horse-drawn coaches being attacked by the communists, the coffin, draped in a swastika, does eventually reach the cemetery, where an officer makes an emotional speech which effectively elevates Hans to martyr status:

> Our flags are lowered over you, comrade. But now we raise the flag and the flag will rise higher and elevate you to radiant life. And your spirit will lift with you and it will march with us in our ranks until we achieve power and a glorious Reich!

A shadowy figure in uniform and carrying a Nazi flag, presumably Hans, appears out of the sky. The figure is shown marching purposefully through the heavens and then, to the accompaniment of 'Die Fahne hoch!', the scene dissolves into a series of real marches. All the crowds are cheering, and the film concludes with a final close-up where even Comrade Ross is shown joining in the celebrations and raising his right arm in a Hitler salute.

CRITICAL REVIEW

In both its subject matter and plot, Hans Westmar, which carries the sub-title 'One of many – a German destiny from the year 1929', has a great deal in common with the other classic film of the period, S.A. Mann Brand, which had been released six months previously. Concentrating on the contribution of one particular Nazi hero, both films recount the early days of the Brown Shirts and their struggle for power against the communists.

Where Hans Westmar differs is that, while never mentioned by name except for a fleeting reference in the opening credits, it is based on the true life story of Horst Wessel, whom the Nazis considered one of their greatest martyrs. The film is also far more outspoken in its criticism of the failings of German society in the 1930s. Indeed, it is the intensity and scale of the various marches and crowd scenes which give the film a feeling of authenticity.

It would appear that the real reason for Goebbels' hostility towards the film at the time arose out of jealousy that others in the film industry seemed to wield more influence over Hitler, although he was supposed to be in charge of propaganda. Some foreign critics did consider the Hans Westmar character rather too fanatical at times, and perhaps it is this aspect which concerned Goebbels as much as the notion that no mere film could ever do justice to the portrayal of such an important figure in Nazi folklore.

In terms of pro-Nazi propaganda, there are three key themes which deserve special analysis.

Condemnation of the ruthless behaviour of the communists

From the earliest scenes, the executive of the Communist Party in Berlin is portrayed as a ruthless and dangerous enemy, controlled by Moscow. It is they who are responsible for organising workers' demonstrations aimed at destabilising Germany; they spread false rumours about better working conditions in the Soviet Union, and how everyone there has his own property. Their fat, cigar-smoking, Lenin-like leader, Kuprikoff, admits that misery is their best ally and that it will help to create the commune:

Soviets in Russia, Soviets in Germany and the world belong to us. Poland will be crushed between us and no government in Europe will be able to withstand the Red wave.

One of the most dangerous instigators among the Communist Party's hierarchy has all the appearance of an archetypal Jew, and it is he who openly condemns the fat priests of the Catholic Church, and jokes about how the communists are happy to exploit the Social Democrats to achieve their ends.

Indeed, no crime is considered too vile to stop the communists achieving their objectives of ruling Germany and the whole of Europe. They show no regard for human life, being quite unmoved by the drowning of the Nazi in the river, and they repeatedly threaten Hans with violence if he does not vacate East Berlin. To achieve their ends, the leader is even willing to condone the shooting of Hans and even to try to murder him in hospital when the assassination attempt seems to have failed. The latter is considered a particularly heinous crime as described by the Nazis themselves:

What? Attack an injured man? Nothing is more despicable ... Nothing is impossible for the communists!

The communist leaders show just as little loyalty to their own people by removing the assassins from their party membership lists and sending them away as soon as the attack on Hans has been committed. The overall cause is all that matters.

It is these very communists who are prepared to spread lies about the Nazis through their party newspaper, blaming them for the deaths of a number of workers during their demonstration. Only one of their number, Comrade Ross, and the poor Agnes display any sympathy for Hans.

The communists are so devoid of human decency that they cannot even allow Hans' funeral procession to pass unmolested.

In short, the film aims to convince the viewer that it is the Nazis who are the only party that will really stand up for Germany, in contrast to the treacherous Communist Party, which will stop at nothing for the sake of Mother Russia, or the ineffectual Social Democrats.

Condemnation of social conditions and the loss of German identity

The feeling of despair that Germany has lost its identity and needs to be awakened to the threat of the communists is highlighted on a number of occasions.

First, there is the university professor who asks his students to acknowledge that, despite the fact that Germany has been forced to give up some of its freedom and territory, it is all for the best, and this has meant that Germany has been accepted with equal rights into the circle of civilised nations. It is obvious that Hans is not at all impressed by the grand slogan 'Never again war – down with weapons', especially when he considers the harsh economic environment in which so many of his fellow citizens are trying to survive, and he sits with his arms folded, refusing to take any notes.

The feeling of despair is dramatically brought to a head in the visit with his German-American friends to a Berlin nightclub. Nazi ideology goes far beyond mere nostalgia for the good old days, betraying a heartfelt hatred of foreign influences which are dominating society to the detriment of German culture. There is resentment that a few people have benefited at the expense of others, with 1 million unemployed and a hundred people committing suicide every day from poverty and misery. There is also a real loathing of what is seen as the decadent lifestyles represented by cultural imports from both America and the Latin countries. Ordinary Germans seem to have forgotten the sacrifices of the 3 million Germans who died in the First World War to protect the German lifestyle, and there is a genuine fear that Germany's identity is now also under threat from Soviet Russia.

Above all else, the end of the First World War has been achieved only at great cost, with Germany having to face the disgrace of having its political borders reduced in size.

Religious imagery and the raising of Hans Westmar to martyr status

Religious imagery is a common theme in Nazi propaganda and is often centred on the portrayal of Hitler as a god-like figure. In this film, it is no mere coincidence that the short life of Hans Westmar has so much in common with the life of Jesus Christ.

Hans is idealistic, determined to help the poor in society and a staunch opponent of anything considered decadent or alien to German culture. He renounces the easy life of a student to labour among the workers so as to get to know them better and gain their trust. He does this in fulfilment of the teachings of his beloved Führer who wrote:

> He who wishes to become great among you, must first be a servant.

This quotation could just as easily have been plucked from the Bible.

With no regard for his own safety, he offers practical help to Agnes, even if he has to deliberately walk right into the heartland of the communists, his sworn enemies. Just as Christ spoke out angrily against the money-lenders and the hypocrites in the temple, Hans is fearless when he speaks out against the communists at their own meeting.

Like a celibate priest, he renounces personal physical pleasure out of devotion to the Nazi cause. He undertakes to increase his followers from twelve to 100, and the number twelve is deliberately reminiscent of the number of Jesus' disciples. He is interested only in the salvation of Germany and is eventually murdered by cowards who are the very people he is striving to save from the evil Soviet Union.

His whole life is reminiscent of a crusade against the communists, whom he considers to be the true enemy. Like Christ rising from the dead, the final scenes show the flag-waving Hans rising victorious from the grave to lead his people to greater victories, serving as a triumphant example for all Nazis.

In this way, the whole film depicts Hans and, by analogy, the Nazis, as representing all that is good in society, while the communists and, by inference, the Soviets, stand for everything which is treacherous and evil.

Hans Westmar as
played by Emil Lohkamp.
(*Deutsches Filminstitut/
Transit Film GmbH*)

Is the film a true representation of the life of Horst Wessel?

In his initial condemnation of the film, Goebbels was to explain that he had known Wessel and that 'the figure in the film neither resembles him nor conveys his character.' So who was the real Horst Wessel?

Given the vast amount of religious imagery in the film, it is perhaps fitting to discover that Wessel was the son of an ultra-conservative Lutheran minister. While a teenager, he became a member of the German National People's Party and was frequently involved in street brawls with supporters of the Social Democratic Party and the Communist Party. Having enrolled as a law student at the Friedrich-Wilhelm University in April 1926, he was later to forego his studies to concentrate on his work for the Nazi Party, which he joined in December of the same year, and for a while he did work as a taxi driver and a construction worker. By May 1929, he was appointed leader of SA Troop 34, based in the infamous Friedrichshain district of Berlin.

He was soon to meet Erna Jänicke, a young prostitute in a bar, and they were to live together. Wessel's landlady was the widow of an ex-communist and, on the 14 January 1930, while answering the door to his flat, Wessel was shot in the face by an unknown murderer. Partly because of misinformation circulated by both the Nazis and the Communist Party, doubt remains concerning the identity of the assassin and the real reason for the attack. While it is generally accepted that he was murdered by a communist called Albrecht Höhler, the question remains as to whether Höhler might have been Erna's pimp or even a jealous lover. There is also some speculation that the murder may have been the result of a dispute with the landlady over outstanding rent, or even a revenge killing for Wessel's supposed involvement in the murder of another communist earlier that day, who, ironically, is the same Camillo Ross seen converting to Nazism in the film.

Whatever the truth, it is evident that the more controversial aspects of Wessel's life have been deliberately removed from the screenplay, and perhaps that is another reason why the hero had to be renamed Hans Westmar, since it simply could not be considered an accurate biographical account of Wessel's life.

The reader may also be interested to discover the content of the Horst Wessel song which played such an influential role in the history of the Nazis.

First and fourth verse of the original German version:

Die Fahne hoch! Die Reihen fest geschlossen!
SA marschiert mit ruhig, festem Schritt.
Kam'raden, die Rotfront und Reaktion
erschossen
Marschier'n im Geist in unser'n Reihen mit.

English translation:

The Flag on high! The ranks tightly closed!
The SA marches with a calm and firm step.
Comrades, shot by the Red Front and
Reaction
March with us in spirit in our ranks.

The true life Horst Wessel. (*BArch, Bild 146-1978-043-14/Hoffmann, H.*)

The Nazis' commemoration of the room in which Wessel died in the Horst Wessel hospital in Berlin. (*BArch, Bild 102-15082*)

As a postscript, there are a couple of items regarding the story of Horst Wessel which are particularly worthy of note.

First, the Nazis were so dismayed by the short prison sentences imposed on the murderer and his accomplices that they re-opened the case when they came to power in 1933. With Göring's approval, a pretext was found to move Höhler from prison, and he was immediately executed by the SA in a nearby forest.

Second, while a supporter of the Nazis, Ewers, the writer of the novel on which the film was based, was opposed to their anti-Semitism and had homosexual sympathies. Consequently, by 1934, he had become an outcast, with most of his works having been banned and the bulk of his property and assets seized by the state. He was ultimately to die in poverty suffering from tuberculosis.

Conclusion

Along with *S.A. Mann Brand* and *Hitlerjunge Quex*, *Hans Westmar* was the last of the trilogy of films released in 1933 which were designed to present an idealised account of the Nazis' heroic struggle to come to power in Germany. *Hans Westmar* holds special significance because it is a reworking of the true life story of Horst Wessel.

Despite Goebbels' initial reservations, German critics were generally impressed by the film, and it was reported that cinema audiences were so moved as to stand up during the final scenes at the playing of '*Die Fahne hoch!*'

Nevertheless, Goebbels was always going to have the last word. He had consistently contended that the SA's rightful place was on the streets and not on the stage or cinema screen, and was obviously concerned that the viewer would become immune to the sort of propaganda which the so-called '*Kampzeit*' (time of struggle) films promoted. Hitler was soon to hand complete control of the German film industry to Goebbels, which, in turn, enabled Goebbels to ensure that *Hans Westmar* would be the last of the films in which the plot centred on the exaltation of the early days of the Nazi Party. In any event, the fall from grace of the SA and the execution of its leader, Ernst Röhm, just six months after the opening of *Hans Westmar*, would have always made it more difficult to produce yet another film referring to the Nazis' glorious past without mentioning the contribution of the Brown Shirts.

Film title: *Wunschkonzert*
Year of release: 1940
Type: Feature film
Primary Purpose: Pro-Nazi propaganda/entertainment
Director: Eduard von Borsody
Principal stars:
Joachim Brennecke   (Helmut Winkler)
Heinz Goedecke   (Himself)
Walter Ladengast   (Schwarzkopf)
Carl Raddatz   (Herbert Koch)
Hans Hermann Schaufuss   (Heinrich Hammer)
Hans Adalbert Schlettow   (Max Kramer)
Ilse Werner   (Inge Wagner)

INTRODUCTION

Wunschkonzert (Request Concert) was one of the most successful and influential propaganda films commissioned by the Nazis, combining an entertaining love story with powerful messages which sought to unite the German people in a time of war. Released in December 1940, it was one of Goebbels' favourite films and one in which he had a very direct involvement. Banned by the Allies in 1945 because of its pro-Nazi content, the film has been re-edited a number of times and is now once again available in Germany.

PLOT SUMMARY

The film begins outside the Olympic Games Stadium in Berlin in 1936, with a pretty young girl, Inge Wagner, and her aunt waiting to enter as spectators for the opening ceremony. Inge's aunt discovers that she has forgotten their tickets and while she returns home to retrieve them, Lieutenant Herbert Koch, who happens to have an extra ticket, offers his spare ticket to Inge. A whirlwind romance develops, but is brought to an abrupt halt when Koch is sent to assist Franco in his war in Spain as part of the Condor Legion. While Koch is able to warn Inge that he is being sent on a secret mission, he assures her that he wants her to be his wife and he promises to write whenever he can. However, he is thwarted from fulfilling this undertaking when his superiors inform him that he will not be allowed to send any letters for at least six months.

The action moves swiftly to 6 September 1939, and Germany's invasion of Poland. A number of other soldiers and their families are gradually introduced to the viewer, including the amusing butcher, Max Kramer; the baker, Heinrich Hammer; the teacher, Friedrich; and Schwarzkopf, a pianist who excels in playing Beethoven.

In the interim, Koch has been promoted to a captain in the Luftwaffe and is well-regarded by his men to whom he gives a donation for the *Wunschkonzert*, a popular radio programme

Koch and Inge soon fall in love with each other. (*Deutsches Filminstitut/FWM*)

which plays music requested by listeners. Koch has indicated that he would like the pro-gramme to play the fanfare from the 1936 Summer Olympics, obviously in memory of his meeting with Inge. Meanwhile, Koch takes under his care another young officer, Helmut Winkler, who coincidentally has also become infatuated with Inge and, without revealing her name, even hints to Koch that they are as good as engaged, although this is not the case. Koch and Winkler become good friends and often talk about their girlfriends, little realising that they are both in love with the same girl. Koch explains that he had been in love with a girl but how, because of the demands of duty, the ban on writing and having been wounded, his letters were returned undelivered, because she had moved away.

Having not heard from Koch for three years, Inge starts to believe that he has in fact abandoned her, and is filled with joy when, on listening to the *Wunschkonzert* programme, she hears that a Captain Koch has requested the playing of the fanfare from the Berlin Olympics. She manages to obtain Koch's military address from the programme's producers, sends Koch a letter and they arrange to meet in Hamburg. However, just as Koch is about to leave to meet her, Koch and Winkler are again called into action, having to fly out to search for some British warships. Their plane is shot down, and Winkler is wounded, but they are rescued by a German submarine and taken back to the military hospital at their base. As Koch failed to keep his lunch appointment, Inge decides to track him down for herself and goes directly to Seedorf base to find him.

The action then switches to the land war between the French and the Germans. Friedrich and Schwarzkopf are ordered to shelter in a church, which will serve as a rendezvous point when their colleagues have completed a mission against the French. Although the attack is successful, the German soldiers get lost in fog and are in danger of wandering onto a mine-field. Schwarzkopf comes to their aid by playing the organ, the sound of which guides the other soldiers back to the church, although, in what is a very moving scene, Schwarzkopf is killed as the Allies bombard the church.

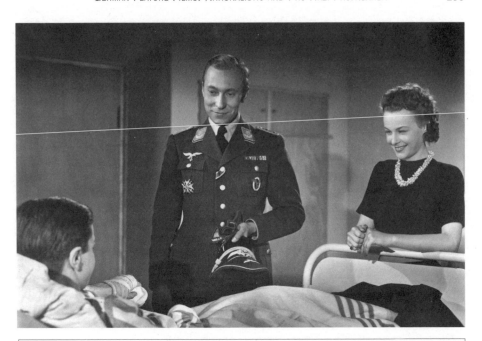

Winkler admits his deception and Inge and Koch are reunited by the end of the film. (*Deutsches Filminstitut/FWM*)

In the meantime, Inge rushes to the hospital when she learns that Koch is visiting the wounded Winkler there. Having by now seen a photo of Inge in Winkler's papers and, given Winkler's earlier claims that he and his girl were virtually engaged, Koch is somewhat distant towards Inge, convinced that she has forsaken him for Winkler.

The bulk of the rest of the film revolves around the *Wunschkonzert* radio programme. The old and the young, mothers with children, soldiers, airmen and workers all prepare to listen intently to the next *Wunschkonzert* broadcast. The programme consists of a live orchestra playing music requested by listeners, and the exchange of messages between soldiers on the front and their loved ones back home, all intertwined with the stars of the day performing song and dance acts. There are some very amusing moments, but also some very poignant scenes about the many sons who have fallen in battle, such as when the viewer discovers that the lady who has requested the song, '*Good night, mother*', is in fact Schwarzkopf's mother.

Back in the hospital, Winkler admits to Inge that he had told Koch that they were as good as engaged, and she immediately understands how Koch had misinterpreted the situation. Winkler confesses the truth to Koch, paving the way for Inge and Koch to be happily reunited.

The film concludes with some inspiring music from the *Wunschkonzert* against background footage of Germany's victorious military forces in action on land, sea and air in the battle against Britain.

CRITICAL REVIEW

Ostensibly, *Wunschkonzert* is a happy love story which, somewhat unusually for German films of this period, is actually set during the war, but its true purpose was to combine entertainment with the promotion of pro-Nazi propaganda.

The *Wunschkonzert* orchestra and choir. (*Deutsches Filminstitut/FWM*)

The film drew its inspiration from the phenomenal success of the real *'Wunschkonzert für die Wehrmacht'* radio programme which was broadcast every Sunday from October 1939. The programme sought to unite civilians and military personnel through the sharing of messages and musical dedications, and was one of the Nazis' major propaganda successes. It is no surprise, therefore, that this film was commissioned by the Nazis to exploit the popularity of the radio programme. Goebbels took a personal interest by providing input for the screenplay and assisting with the selection of well-known artistes for the radio programme scenes. He certainly believed that it was far more than just another feature film, especially as the common bond between so many of the characters harked back to the 1936 Olympics.

In terms of cinematic effectiveness, the film cleverly intertwines archive footage of the Olympics and true war scenes with the events of the screenplay, so as to make the fictitious events in the film appear far more convincing.

Pro-Nazi propaganda

As a piece of pro-Nazi propaganda, the film contains several themes which were of key importance to the Nazis as they sought to engender a real sense of German identity and feeling.

Pride in being German

Hitler's initial appeal to the masses largely arose from the self-belief which the Nazis managed to reawaken in the German nation, where ordinary citizens actually felt a renewed pride in their country. With the opening scenes of the film reminiscing enthusiastically about Hitler's opening of the 1936 Olympics, the viewer is reminded how Germany had been the envy of the world at that time. It was the most spectacular Games which had ever been staged, not only providing much-needed employment, but also proving that German athletes could more than hold their own against the athletes of other nations. There is a particularly touching scene when a young girl in a white dress, sent out to hand a posy of flowers to Hitler, tries to curtsy and give a Hitler salute at the same time. The viewer is also reminded of the competitors of many other nations seemingly saluting Hitler, as if bowing before him in submission.

Respect for famous German cultural figures

German pride extends to the glorification of heroes in the field of the arts. The music of Beethoven is portrayed as something almost divine and so important that it cannot be interrupted. There is an amusing scene where Hammer, Friedrich and others all gradually enter the room where Schwarzkopf is playing Beethoven on the piano, and are so entranced that, one by one, they all sit down and wait until the piece of music has been performed to its conclusion.

Admiration for the German armed forces

Likewise, there is a real feeling of pride in the effectiveness and efficiency of their armed forces.

Koch and his colleagues use their wits to track down the missing British ships and have the presence of mind to send out a signal to their home base before their plane is forced to crash in the sea. However, such is the close co-operation with their naval colleagues that a submarine is immediately redirected to their rescue. Their land forces also carry out a daring attack on the French, and bravery and ingenuity result in their returning safely through the fog.

While there is no attempt to justify why the Germans were secretly assisting Franco in the war in Spain or why Germany has invaded Poland, there seems to be a general acceptance that the war has to be fought, and there is a quiet determination to get the job done. One of the most telling comments comes from the elderly doctor who tries to reassure Friedrich that he will take care of his wife and child, should his wife gives birth while Friedrich is away on war duty:

That is the least I can do while you are removing the cares of the world!

For much of the film, the war seems quite remote and not particularly threatening. The soldiers sing rousing choruses as the train carries them off to war, and life in the trenches seems good-humoured and undemanding. When Max returns home on leave to his butcher's shop, he jokes with customers, as he hacks away with a large hatchet, that this is what he does with the English. There are further comic scenes with Max and Heinrich 'liberating' five French pigs and taking them back to Berlin to the *Wunschkonzert*. Even Koch's and Winkler's experiences in the plane seem more like a 'Boys' Own' account of the war, as although Winkler is wounded, his injuries never seem life-threatening. Indeed, the only real death witnessed is that of Schwarzkopf and, even then, there is no feeling of suffering, only a very moving account of his self-sacrifice for the greater good of his colleagues. It seems only fitting that he should lose his life in a church while playing Beethoven, dramatically falling across the organ keys as he reaches the very final notes of the piece he is playing. It is as if the spirit of Beethoven has reached out from the grave to help save the lives of future generations of Germans by guiding the soldiers away from the minefield.

Koch, Winkler and Schwarzkopf all serve as excellent role models of the good German soldier. There is an unquestioning acceptance that duty always takes priority over personal interests, which is the very reason why the love affair between Koch and Inge is almost thwarted.

Contribution and role of German women

Goebbels had always been impressed with Ilse Werner (Inge), whom he regarded as a model of sympathetic German womanhood. The reward for Inge's tenacity and her faith in Koch is their happy reunion.

However, all the women in the film are portrayed as heroines, ranging from those running the butcher's and baker's in their husbands' absence, to the wife who has to be strong as she is about to give birth, to all the older mothers and wives who may lose their loved ones.

When this film was first screened, the war was just over a year old, but it is already giving clear guidance to the soldiers and civilians alike as to how they are expected to behave during the war, with a general upbeat conclusion that all their sacrifices will be worthwhile in the end.

How was the film received?

Completed in only five months, *Wunschkonzert* (originally named *Das Wunschkonzert*) was classified as being of 'political, artistic and popular worth' and 'suitable for youth'.

It was premiered in Berlin on 30 December 1940, and became the second largest box office success during the Nazi era, with more than 20 million viewers, and yielded a profit of some 4 million Reichsmarks excluding foreign earnings. Its success was only to be exceeded by *Die grosse Liebe*, also a love story set during the war.

Official reports conceded that although the film was enthusiastically received by the general public, much of the success was due to the enormous popularity of the radio show of the same name. The film gave the audience an opportunity to view the performers and locations which they could only imagine from the radio programme, including the host of the radio show, Heinz Goedecke, and celebrated artistes such as Marika Rökk and Heinz Rühmann. In short, it was a film with wide appeal. It moves at pace and includes much comedy, and where there are more serious elements, these are always presented in a heroic and victorious manner, culminating in the upbeat ending to the film.

Key individuals involved in the film's production

The film was directed by Eduard von Borsody, an Austrian who had participated in the production of a number of other Nazi propaganda films before the war, including *Morgenrot* (*Sunrise*) and *Flüchtlinge* (*Refugees*). However, his involvement with the Nazis did not prevent him from continuing to pursue a successful career in the film industry after the war.

Patricia Roc. (*BFI/ ITV Studios Global Entertainment*)

Ilse Werner. (*Deutsches Filminstitut/FWM*)

Having initially declined to participate in this film, Ilse Werner (Inge) was to receive a temporary performance ban by the Allies in 1945 for her involvement in this and other Nazi films. She was actually a Dutch citizen by birth, starring in a number of popular wartime films and musicals. In terms of role, she was more akin to Patricia Roc, who starred in comparable British films of the time such as *Millions Like Us* (1943) as the beautiful, faithful girl whom every soldier wanted to be waiting for him when he returned from the war.

While Carl Raddatz (Herbert Koch) also played roles in two other Nazi propaganda films, *Heimkehr* and *Stukas*, he was said to have been politically opposed to Nazi ideology and continued his acting career after the war.

CONCLUSION

This film was conceived and released while Germany had been at war for only a short period of time, during which it had enjoyed huge military success. At the end of 1940, most Germans still supported the Nazis and felt that the war was justified; however, it was important for Goebbels that a film was produced which reinforced Nazi thinking, made the people feel united as a nation, and provided guidance for soldier and civilian alike as to how they were expected to conduct themselves during wartime.

Being able to exploit the success of the *Wunschkonzert* radio programme was a real bonus, and wrapping up all the propaganda in an entertaining love story with popular musical hits and scenes of German triumphs, both at the Olympics and in the war, was always going to be a recipe for box office success. One can well imagine that, with roles reversed, such an early film would have been just as successful in Britain, before the real horrors of the war and its true cost in lives had become too apparent.

The film was eventually cleared for screening again in 1980, on the condition that the sections which included close-ups of Hitler and the background singing of militaristic melodies about 'going to war against England' were removed.

Film title: *Kolberg*
Year of release: 1945
Type: Feature film
Primary purpose: Pro-German propaganda/
    entertainment
Director: Veit Harlan
Principal stars:

Horst Caspar	(General Gneisenau)
Gustav Diessl	(Leutnant Schill)
Heinrich George	(Bürgermeister Nettelbeck)
Kristina Söderbaum	(Maria Werner)
Paul Wegener	(Stadtkommandant Loucadou)
Otto Wernicke	(Bauer Werner)

INTRODUCTION

Filmed in glorious Agfacolor, *Kolberg* was the most expensive feature film produced in Germany during the time of the Third Reich, requiring many thousands of soldiers and other resources to be diverted from the war effort for its lavish battle and crowd scenes.

It has become one of the most famous Nazi feature films, not only because it was one of the last great films to be completed but also because it displays a different type of propaganda, one where the intention was to motivate the German viewers so that they would be prepared to fight to the death rather than suffer the shame of defeat.

In recognition of the significance of the film, *Kolberg* was the final film to be awarded the title 'Film of the Nation', the most prestigious film rating awarded by the Nazis, reserved for films which were considered to be of exceptional merit in both a political and artistic sense.

PLOT SUMMARY

The action begins in Breslau in 1813, where General Gneisenau is imploring the King of Prussia to utter a proclamation for a call to arms, so as to allow the townspeople to join in the war against Napoleon. Initially reluctant to accede to this request, as the King believes that war is a matter for the army alone, he is, nevertheless, impressed by Gneisenau's explanation that when he had served at Kolberg a few years previously, it had been the actions of its citizens' army which had helped save Prussia from Napoleon.

There is then one long flash back to Kolberg in 1806, and the camera focuses in on its huge church bell, on which are inscribed the words, 'I call the living. I mourn the dead. I break lightning'. This turns out to be an appropriate summary of the whole story of Kolberg.

In the town there is great merriment as all the citizens celebrate their annual festival. However, the mayor, Nettelbeck, quietly confides to his niece, Maria, and her father that the war against Napoleon has been going badly, and that with the loss of Prince Louis Ferdinand in battle, the Prussians are defeated. Maria's brother, Frederick, then arrives home from the war accompanied by a wounded Leutnant Schill. Maria soon falls in love with Schill, and the joy and pain evoked by their relationship becomes one of the underlying themes of the film.

Nettlebeck is determined to prepare for war by introducing rationing and dispersing the town's food supplies. He soon becomes a thorn in the side of Kolberg's cowardly military commander, Loucadou, who has let the town's cannons rust through disuse and firmly believes that the war will never reach such an unimportant town as Kolberg. Despite his misgivings, however, Loucadou can do nothing to prevent Schill training the townspeople to be soldiers.

The seasons pass, and a letter is received from Napoleon demanding that all military commanders hand over their fortresses to the French and pledge allegiance to the French Emperor. The town council debates the matter at length, with several believing that it is better to surrender than have their houses and possessions destroyed. Nettlebeck, however, contends that there are many good reasons for not surrendering, including preventing the French from using their artillery elsewhere such as in Danzig or Tilsit. So, when a French officer arrives demanding to know their response, Nettlebeck sends him away with the defiant answer:

The free citizens of Kolberg would rather be buried under the rubble of the walls than break their oath to the King of Prussia!

Napoleon laughs at their impudence and orders the city to be attacked and no mercy to be shown. As we move into 1807, many thousands of French troops are shown marching towards the city. In frustration, Nettlebeck takes matters into his own hands and manages to secure some new cannons from Sweden, but is so incensed when Loucadou blurts out, 'Surrender is better than suicide', that the mayor has to be arrested.

Nettlebeck's charming niece, Maria, soon falls in love with the dashing Leutnant Schill. (*Deutsches Filminstitut/FWM*)

The action then moves to the Bullenwinkel farm, owned by Maria's father, which some French soldiers have captured. Maria's father is so angry when he sees his other son, Klaus, drinking a toast to the French Emperor that he dashes out of the farmhouse and smashes the glass. He is about to be killed by a French officer for his insolence when Schill and a small band of men arrive to save him. However, Schill explains that the farmhouse will still have to be destroyed because it offers too much protection for the French. Maria's father is so horrified by his son's actions in drinking to the health of Napoleon that he has lost the will to live and he later sets fire to the farm himself, perishing in the process. When Maria visits Nettelbeck in prison to explain what happened to her father, Nettelbeck persuades Maria to deliver a letter to the King in Königsberg, appealing for the appointment of a new commander for Kolberg. Meanwhile, Loucadou has declared martial law and is determined to execute Nettelbeck for his insubordination. However, after representations from Schill and the town council, and conscious of the growing anger of the townspeople, Nettelbeck is eventually pardoned and released.

While Maria is denied an audience with the King in Königsberg, she is given an opportunity to speak to the Queen. In a very dramatic and moving scene in which Maria is so tongue-tied that she is unable to speak, the Queen has to take the initiative and, embracing Maria, declares, 'There are few jewels left in our crown. Kolberg is one of them.' She realises that Maria has brought a letter for the King, and the Queen promises to pass it to the King that very day.

The action then switches back to Kolberg where the siege of the city is well underway. Nettelbeck rushes in to complain to Loucadou about a ditch which is being dug up in the middle of the road, and discovers that Gneisenau has been appointed the new commander.

After initial disagreement, Gneisenau explains that he is keen to work with Nettelbeck because he appreciates that Nettelbeck 'loves his country better than himself!' and they become close friends. Gneisenau then decides that the best means of defence is attack. Charging out of the town, they win the first skirmish against the French, and a further victory is achieved when the attacking French force, caught between Schill's volunteers and Gneisenau's artillery, is forced to retreat.

Gneisenau explains that the city is still exposed to the south and that the sluices must be opened and the fields flooded. In so doing, it is recognised that the citizens are being asked to make a great sacrifice and that it will mean hundreds of families will be left homeless. Maria helps the citizens dig ditches to redirect the water, and then witnesses her brother being killed by stray cannon fire as he tries to rescue his violin from his flooded house. Soon

Loucadou (left) is the complete antithesis of the dashing Gneisenau (right) who rouses the people of Kolberg to resist Napoleon. (*Deutsches Filminstitut/FWM*)

afterwards, Maria also has a tearful farewell scene with Schill and, in a fateful premonition, she declares that Stralsund will be his grave.

Despite the destruction and loss of life being inflicted on the town, the citizens still refuse to surrender, and the siege continues, with the mayor sharing the same plight as his people when his house is struck by cannon fire and burnt to the ground. As if the loss of her father, brother, and the presumed death of Schill were not enough, Maria then endures even further despair with the death of her other brother, Frederick, in battle.

When it is reported to Gneisenau that another 20,000 French soldiers are arriving from Danzig, he seems to suggest to Nettelbeck that there is no sense in continuing to resist. However, in one of the most emotional scenes of the entire film, Nettelbeck, on his knees, makes an impassioned plea to Gneisenau not to surrender. Gneisenau explains that this is exactly what he wanted to hear and while embracing him declares, 'Now we can die together!'

All hope seemingly lost, the French infantry are ordered to charge through the flooded fields to the south of the city, but such is the loss of French life that the French generals argue among themselves, and the artillery is eventually ordered to cease fire rather than risk more men being lost trying to capture the town. Out of the ensuing silence, the townspeople are heard singing in the church, and Nettelbeck tries to comfort Maria as she looks out to sea in the vain hope of seeing Schill again. There is a heart-rending final speech from Nettelbeck in which he praises Maria for all the sacrifices she has endured.

The flashback comes to an end and the action returns to Breslau in 1813. The King is duly persuaded by Gneisenau's account of what happened at Kolberg and sits down to write the proclamation for war, duly inspired by Kolberg's uplifting example. The film concludes with Gneisenau's rousing words:

From the ashes and rubble, like a phoenix, a new people will rise ... a new nation!

Tens of thousands of extras were employed in the spectacular battle scenes. (*BFI/FWM*)

CRITICAL REVIEW

Propaganda Purpose

Released in 1945, *Kolberg* stands out from all the other feature films produced by the Nazis because the motivation for the film derives from a tacit acceptance that the Second World War, if not lost, is certainly going badly for the Germans and is increasingly going to be fought on German soil. The primary propaganda aim of this film is no longer to decry all the Nazis' enemies, but rather to appeal to the inner soul of all Germans and persuade them that it is better to make huge sacrifices, such as the loss of possessions, the death of friends and relatives or being killed themselves, than lose their freedom and submit to the enemy.

However, the ultimate purpose of the film is not just to motivate the viewer to sacrifice, but also to provide guidance to a German audience as to how they should conduct themselves in the war. This guidance is to be provided by the actions of the principal heroes in the film and their emotionally stirring lines.

It would be difficult to find any propaganda feature film produced during the Second World War with a greater number of poignant, 'punch-packed' lines designed to influence the viewer. Their lines are not simply directed to the person in the film with whom they are speaking, but rather to the viewing audience as a whole. There are three characters whose roles deserve particular mention, namely Gneisenau, Nettelbeck and Maria.

Gneisenau as a symbol of the New Order

In Gneisenau, we have an example of the spirit and character of the new Nazi order. He is the dashing, fearless officer, who is respected by all and whose rousing pronouncements dominate the story.

When Gneisenau is asked what he and the King can offer the people, his inspiring response, 'Faith ... in justice, strength and victory' has echoes of the 'blood, sweat and tears' speeches of Churchill.

Gneisenau reflects the general enthusiasm of the Breslau townspeople who have been rushing so purposefully in their thousands through the streets, and he repeats the chorus of their marching song, 'The people rise ... the storm breaks'. Even in these early lines of the film, Gneisenau is preparing the viewer to expect great events. 'In Kolberg, I experienced the birth of German freedom, when princes and kings had deserted the people!'

When appointed as the new commander at Kolberg, there is no doubt that Gneisenau, as a symbol of Nazi authority, is in command, even in his dealings with Nettelbeck: 'Lack of discipline will be punished severely. You wish to lead and can't obey ... I will listen to you when you report you have executed my order.' Even Nettelbeck has to accept that '*Befehl ist Befehl*'(orders are orders).

Portrayed as a benevolent dictator, Gneisenau is also the master tactician, improving the defences of the city and leading daring attacks against the French. In his final dialogue with the mayor he declares his resolve to die rather than surrender. As Gneisenau addresses Nettelbeck, his words sound like those of a god, testing the mayor and tempting him to admit defeat: 'It is all over, Nettelbeck. There is no sense in going on any more. We can't hold the city ... surrender?' Such religious undertones emerge throughout the film, such as in prayers, views of the church, the ringing of bells and the singing of choirs, and it creates a general feeling that God is ultimately on Kolberg's side.

Gneisenau neatly tops and tails the whole film, so that when the flashback ends and we return to Breslau, it is Gneisenau who repeats many of the same lines which he used at the start of the film. He returns to the chorus of the song which proclaims that 'the storm is breaking loose and the people rise', and asserts that a new nation will rise from the ashes.

Gneisenau agreeing with Nettelbeck about the honour of non-surrender. (*Deutsches Filminstitut/FWM*)

Nettelbeck, a symbol of the German Nationalist

If Gneisenau is portrayed as a god-like military leader, then Nettelbeck is depicted as the ideal citizen and leader of civilians. He might be rather uncouth, but he speaks his mind with the wisdom of maturity and it cannot be doubted that he is firmly committed to the cause.

When Napoleon's letter declares that it is his sole wish to ensure Europe's happiness and prosperity, it is Nettelbeck who warns the others, 'You are not falling for that? You can only fight cannons with cannons, not with sentimentality.' He cannot see why they should be prepared to let themselves be ruled by someone else just to safeguard their property: 'Why become vassals when we can be masters?'

It is Nettelbeck, the man of action, who seizes the initiative from the ineffective Loucadou by deciding where their food should be stored and how it should be rationed. He is responsible for Schill training a force of citizen soldiers and for procuring more cannons for the city. Indeed, it is his rousing words which ultimately persuade the town council to support his refusal to surrender to the French, although it might cost them their possessions and houses. He uses logic to convince them that they can help other German cities by diverting French cannon and soldiers to fight in Kolberg, and appeals to their nationalistic feelings of identity:

> What would happen to a Prussian that said to Napoleon, come and swallow us up? What would become of a people who think and talk like that? They would destroy themselves and would deserve nothing else!

When he sees his house of twenty years destroyed by cannon fire, Nettelbeck stoically declares that life goes on, and it is obvious from his argument with Loucadou that surrender is not an option: 'If anyone mentions surrender, I'll run him through with my sabre!'

It comes as no surprise that his position hardens even further in his final moving scene with Gneisenau, when asked whether they should think about surrendering. In a slow, deliberate tone, he responds in horror, 'Like Magdeburg, Erfurt, Küstrin, Spandau ... They'll have to hack off our hands or beat us to death one by one ...'

Maria, a symbol of German womanhood

If Nettelbeck endures a great deal of personal tragedy, then it is nothing compared to the losses suffered by Maria. One by one, she has to suffer the loss of her father, her two brothers, her lover and even her home. However, she is the real heroine of the story and, through countless tearful scenes, she continues to devote all her efforts to the cause as she cares for the wounded, acts as an envoy, digs ditches and fights fires. Her strength and commitment in the face of such adversity make her more than human, and it seems likely that her name has been deliberately chosen as another religious symbol.

Ironically, she does not make many moving speeches herself, but is the focus of the emotional outbursts of others who often say what the viewer is thinking – for example in Nettelbeck's final summing up of her contribution: 'You remained firm and did your duty and did not fear death. You too have conquered, Maria.'

In the early days of Nazi Germany, the role of women was primarily to serve as mothers to their children and to be supportive spouses for their husbands. It was only as the war progressed that increasing numbers were to become involved in military tasks, although most women would still have been remote from the horrors of actual fighting and death. As the war turned against Germany, death was going to become a new experience for German women, and in the glorious example of Maria they are being warned about the sacrifices they might have to suffer and how they should respond.

Parallels between the situation in 1807 and 1945

Although *Kolberg* makes no reference to the Second World War, the film is full of symbolism and, time and again, the action of the film parallels the reality of life in Germany in the mid-1940s.

When the town council is debating the pros and cons of surrender, and several determine that they don't want to see their houses destroyed nor to die as heroes, it is obvious that these same thoughts must have been passing through the minds of many Germans watching the film, who were about to be faced with the same terrible decision in the face of Soviet, British or American soldiers.

When Gneisenau makes his impassioned speech to the citizens in the town square, his words also serve to remind all Germans in 1945 of the reasons why they are fighting: 'No love is more sacred than love for one's own fatherland. No joy is sweeter than that of freedom. We must fight ... whatever the sacrifices ... unless we want to cease to be Prussians and Germans.'

In another scene, as thousands of additional French troops arrive and the outlook for Kolberg looks increasingly hopeless, Gneisenau's summary of the situation could equally have applied to Germany in 1945: 'It is a wonder we are still alive ... in this hopeless time of complete darkness over Germany. One star still glows ... Kolberg ... and when that light goes out ...' The prospect of defeat seemed too dire to contemplate.

Likewise, when Gneisenau states to the King that the citizens of Breslau in 1813 are taking heart from what happened at Kolberg, the appeal is really to all German citizens in 1945 that they should take their lead from the glorious example of Kolberg.

Was there any truth in this story of the Siege of Kolberg?

Throughout the film, hardly any mention can be made of Kolberg to an influential outsider without them being almost struck dumb in admiration for what happened there and the role of the citizens' army. However, and as we have already witnessed in several of the other films which are analysed in this book, as soon as the opening credits state that the plot is based on historical fact, then the warning bells should start to ring. So what is the truth about Kolberg?

Kolberg lies on the Baltic coast of modern Poland, and was indeed laid siege to by the French from March to July 1807, during the Napoleonic Wars. The Prussian armies had already been defeated at Jena and Austerlitz, and Kolberg lay in the way of Napoleon's soldiers as they marched towards Königsberg. Kolberg was able to withstand the siege largely because it continued to be supplied through its port, and it is true that Nettelbeck's citizens' army did play an important role in the defence of the town. Schill was indeed one of the officers involved in the town's defence, and Major Neidhardt von Gneisenau did replace Loucadou as commander in April 1807.

While Gneisenau's forces of around 5,700 men were indeed smaller than those of the French, Napoleon's forces were never as large as the 35,000 suggested towards the end of the film and, at the height of the siege, the defending forces were probably never outnumbered by more than two to one. Nevertheless, and despite the loss of more than 800 lives, Kolberg did manage to stand firm until the Peace Treaty of Tilsit was signed between Prussia and France on 2 July 1807.

Even so, what the film fails to disclose is that, although Kolberg successfully avoided being captured during the war, Prussia itself was still forced to surrender to the French, thereby negating Kolberg's achievements and undermining the heroic sacrifices of its citizens. This was obviously not a truth which the Nazis wanted to convey to an audience in 1945 and was, therefore, deliberately omitted.

POINTS OF NOTE CONCERNING THE PRODUCTION OF THE FILM AND ITS RECEPTION

On 18 February 1943, following the German army's disastrous defeat at Stalingrad and the surrender of 100,000 soldiers to the Soviets, Goebbels felt obliged to make what is now known as his 'total war' speech in Berlin, calling for the absolute commitment of all Germans to the war effort. It is certainly not coincidental that this speech should conclude with almost exactly the same rallying cry as in this film: 'Now People arise! Let the storm break loose!'

Therefore, it comes as no surprise to learn that Goebbels was closely involved in the creation of *Kolberg* and, as early as June 1943, had written to the director, Veit Harlan, that he wanted him to produce a film which, through the example of the town of Kolberg, would show that soldiers and citizens could unite to overcome any opponent. Such was the perceived

Goebbels' Total War speech: Total War – Shortest War! (*BArch, Bild 183-J05235/Schwann, E.*)

Harlan claimed that 187,000 soldiers and 6,000 horses were diverted from the war effort for the production of the film. (*BFI/FWM*)

importance of the film that Goebbels indicated that no expense or resource should be spared and, at a cost of 8.8 million Reichsmarks, it was the most expensive film produced during the Third Reich.

Harlan was selected primarily because of his excellent work in a number of other propaganda movies such as *Jud Süss* and *Der grosse König*, and because he was one of the first directors to become experienced in working with the Agfacolor technology. While Goebbels was disappointed with Harlan's original screenplay, as it devoted too much attention to Maria (played by Harlan's wife, Kristina Söderbaum) rather than Nettelbeck, whom Goebbels considered central to the whole plot, he was still very happy with the overall project. Goebbels kept Hitler closely advised as to the progress of filming and was to note that Hitler had been 'moved to tears' when he was told of the content of some of the scenes. Once filming was complete in November 1944, Goebbels was persuaded it was a true masterpiece of the director's art, although he subsequently insisted on the film being shortened and on the removal of the more gory scenes of death and destruction, so as not to deter Germans from going to view the film or interpreting it as a call to pacifism.

Even by modern standards, the battle and crowd scenes are very impressive visual spectacles and were produced without the aid of any special effects. One example of the extent to which no expense was spared is that a hundred railway wagons were employed to bring salt to the film set in Pomerania for the winter snow scenes. After the war, Harlan continued to exploit the notoriety associated with *Kolberg*, apparently making greatly exaggerated claims that some 187,000 soldiers and 6,000 horses were diverted from the war effort to take part in this film. It is generally agreed today that his comments were probably misinterpreted since he also made direct reference to only 10,000 uniforms and the need to use toilet paper instead of leather shoulder belts in the background shots of 'French' soldiers. Consequently, while still a very significant number, in reality probably no more than 20,000 extras, of which only a portion were German soldiers and sailors, were actually employed on any one day of filming.

Goebbels and Harlan had originally hoped that the film would reach the cinemas by December 1943, but, given the scale of the venture with filming in both Kolberg and Berlin, and constant delays because of Allied air raids, they hopelessly underestimated the production time. The film was eventually premiered simultaneously in the Tauentzien-Palast cinema in Berlin and to the German military in La Rochelle[5] on 30 January 1945. It was also subsequently released in other large and blockaded cities across Germany, and it continued to be screened in Berlin until April 1945.

However, despite both Hitler's and Goebbels' great expectations for the film, it was not a box office success. One of its principal failings is that it is over-endowed with clearly propagandistic dialogue and slogans, especially in the early scenes. It was also released too late to have any significant impact in raising public morale. Many cinemas had already been destroyed and, even if an undamaged cinema could be found, people preferred to watch the more light-hearted *Münchhausen* which was being screened at the same time. The final irony is that the town of Kolberg itself was to fall to the advancing Soviet and Polish troops on 18 March 1945, rendering any subsequent screening of the film a propaganda 'own goal'.

CONCLUSION

Goebbels and Hitler recognised the propaganda value of the cinema and they firmly believed that a cleverly composed film could inspire the viewer to make one last, united effort for the Nazi cause. In terms of dramatic impact and visual splendour, *Kolberg* was a true epic and deserves to be remembered as such. However, the real lesson of *Kolberg* is that even limitless resources and an inspiring script cannot guarantee a successful propaganda film.

The appeal to self-sacrifice was never going to be an attractive message for the viewer, especially since, for so long, the Nazis had deliberately concealed the true state of the war. One inspirational film would not change public opinion and, if such a sacrificial message were to be conveyed, then it needed to be delivered earlier and more frequently, and by using more convincing examples of previous historic victories. Ordinary Germans were reluctant to view a film which was going to remind them of the fate which awaited them. By 1945, all they wanted was for the war to end as quickly as possible and with the least disruption to their lives.

Emotional appeals alone would not win the war and perhaps Goebbels and Hitler would have done better to pay attention to Nettelbeck's own observations about the war with Napoleon:

You fight cannons with cannons, not with sentimentality!

Ultimately, the Nazi leaders were the only ones to listen to their own propaganda. The appeal for mass suicide rather than inglorious surrender was never going to be adopted by all, even if Goebbels and Hitler were going to lead by example, only some four months after the film was released.

The film was banned from being screened in Germany at the end of the war and, although it was subsequently broadcast on television in 1998 on an arts channel, *Kolberg* is still not available for general purchase in German shops. Sensitivity surrounding the film is still so great that, even in 2000, permission for the film to be screened to under eighteen-year-olds was still refused on the basis that the film glorifies heroism and resistance at any price.

---

5   The film canister had to be dropped by parachute as La Rochelle was being blockaded by the Allies.

Chapter VIII

German Feature Films for Entertainment

Background

The Nazis came to power in January 1933, and, between that date and the collapse of the Third Reich, more than 1,300 feature films of every possible description were produced.

Understandably, there was a marked difference in the number of films produced before 1939, namely an annual average of 105, compared to an average of only seventy-five between 1939 and 1944. Although, given the increased costs of production and difficulties in obtaining virgin film and other materials, the fact that films were being produced at all during the war illustrates the importance placed on this medium by the Nazis.

From the examples analysed earlier in this book, the reader would be mistaken in concluding that all the films produced during this period had some dark propaganda purpose. In fact, only around a hundred feature films were actually commissioned by the state and although all films produced were subject to Nazi censorship, only around 10 per cent might be considered purely political films. Subject to some overlap between the categories, around half of the films

The Nazis recognised the importance of the cinema from the moment they assumed power. In this photo, Hitler and Goebbels are seen enjoying a tour of UFA's studios at Neubabelsberg in January 1935. (*BArch, Bild 183-1990-1002-500*)

can be classified as light-hearted comedies or love stories, and around a third were what might best be described as dramatic thrillers.

In reality, as soon as the negative effects of war started to impact on the everyday lives of German citizens, Goebbels acknowledged that there was a need to provide attractive films which would encourage the populace to attend their local cinemas. An entertaining film would raise morale and provide a distraction from the horrors of war, while the nation's attendance at the cinema would still allow Goebbels to assert a more subtle influence on the viewer through the upbeat, propagandistic newsreels which would accompany such films. Cinema attendance increased almost threefold during the war years and, by 1944, the average number of annual cinema visits by an individual had increased to fourteen.

While many of the films did not contain any overtly propagandistic message, they still had a propaganda value and sometimes in the least obvious of ways. There is a strong argument that even the most innocent of films might serve some sort of propaganda purpose, even if only in the choice of subject matter. There are throw-away lines which often do convey some more sinister purpose, but we can only surmise whether many of these comments would have been consciously registered by the ordinary viewer who was more interested in the whole cinema experience than analysing every last detail of every scene or speech. In any event, Goebbels would have argued that unless the propaganda message is simple and consistent, then any impact would be lost. Nevertheless, we do know that the producers of films did spend an inordinate amount of time agonising over the inclusion or exclusion of certain scenes, and Goebbels, himself, was to rewrite some of the more meaningful speeches in key films. State control was still absolute and the censors were often to ban films for the most spurious of reasons.

The very mixed commercial success of films designed primarily for entertainment is reflected in three notable films from the period, all of which revolved around the theme of love.

Zarah Leander as Hanna in *Die grosse Liebe. (Deutsches Filminstitut/FWM)*

The most financially successful film was *Die grosse Liebe* (*The Great Love*). Released in 1942, it is a romantic melodrama about a Luftwaffe pilot, Paul Wendlandt, and his relationship with a Danish singer, Hanna Holberg, who is played by Zarah Leander.

While on leave in Berlin, Paul is so entranced by Hanna's stage performance that he determines to win her affection, and the unexpected intervention of an air raid eventually allows him to spend the night with her. While his love is fully reciprocated, Paul's initial unwillingness to reveal the fact that he is a pilot and his subsequent need to keep restricted war information confidential leads to a series of misunderstandings. This causes Hanna to suffer a rollercoaster of emotional highs and lows as they are regularly separated from each other, and their wedding plans are repeatedly postponed. The film is interspersed with Hanna's performance of a number of famous songs, including the final song, '*Ich weiß es wird einmal ein Wunder geschehn*' (I know that a miracle will happen some day), and its optimistic sentiments are to be turned into reality when it transpires that Paul escapes with only minor injuries when his fighter plane crashes.

There is an uplifting ending when they realise that the recuperation period for his injuries will mean that they can spend three weeks together and finally get married. While this scene of bliss is somewhat tempered by the sight of fighters flying overhead and the recognition that he will eventually have to return to battle, this time it is a reality which they both accept, and they go forward in hope. Hanna's eventual acceptance of the situation allows her to serve as a role model to all German women and the sacrifices which they must be expected to endure in wartime. Likewise, Paul is a model German soldier in that he ensures that his military duty always transcends the pain which he feels when separated from Hanna.

Ironically, the Army High Command complained about the film for the reason that romance really only blossoms because of the rather ungentlemanly approaches of a Luftwaffe officer, who takes advantage of an air raid to spend a night with an actress. It was not exactly the sort of example which might have been expected from an honourable Aryan. Göring disagreed and was indignant about the Army High Command's prudish attitude, a reaction shared by Goebbels who had no intention of having the film banned. In any event, whatever qualms there may have been regarding the morality of the film, it certainly enjoyed wide public appeal, especially at a time when the war was still going fairly well for the Germans, and it was the top box office success of the war with takings of 8 million Reichsmarks.

However, not all films designed for entertainment enjoyed such outstanding success. Also set in the war, *Besatzung Dora* (*Crew of the Dora*) is a film about the crew members of a German reconnaissance plane. The crew enjoys a great reputation at its base, and morale is high as they set about their various tasks. The genre lies somewhere between an action film and an entertaining love story, as at least half the film is devoted to the crew's amorous pursuit of three women and their leisure activities when they are home on leave. In many ways, the love interest and the various scenes of the women going about their day-to-day duties as a tram conductress, farm labourer and doctor respectively combine to appeal to a female audience.

Despite this, the film was destined to be a failure. Completed early in 1943, the film did not receive Goebbels' approval. Given its war setting, he judged that it was not really a National Socialist film, and the sight of scantily clad girls in their hockey outfits and half-dressed dancers in Africa did make it a rather frivolous film, especially at a time when the war was turning against Germany. This stance seems rather at odds with his *laissez-faire* attitude towards the rather risqué romance featured in *Die grosse Liebe*. The main tension arises when the plane runs out of fuel on a mission in Africa and is forced to make an emergency landing in the desert, and it is a question of whether the crew will be rescued before they die of thirst. Of course they are just saved in the nick of time, and the film ends happily with a couple of marriages, while the other two pilots, undeterred by their romantic rebuffs, resolve to pursue other women.

Two of the crew of *Besatzung Dora* on patrol. (*Deutsches Filminstitut/FWM*)

Despite several attempts to remove inappropriate scenes, the film was eventually formally banned in November 1943, by which time its subject matter had simply not kept pace with the progress of the war. First, there is a scene where one of the aircrew asks his girlfriend to imagine the scene when the war is over and they have a farmhouse of their own in the east. But given that the German army had already been defeated at Stalingrad in February of that year, the notion of Germany still establishing colonies in the Soviet Union seems rather far-fetched. Likewise, it was rather unfortunate that the crew is shown being rescued by Italian forces, given that North Africa had already fallen to the Allies by May 1943, and the Italians had deposed Mussolini and sided with the Allies shortly thereafter. With Goebbels' special permission, the film did eventually receive its first formal showing in February 1945, but only to air force personnel.

If Goebbels had been upset by the frivolity of *Besatzung Dora*, it is difficult to see how he could ever have approved of the plot of *Grosse Freiheit Nr.7 (No.7, Great Freedom Street)*, a film set in the red light district of Hamburg. While the film is shot in stunning colour, depicting the liveliness of that part of the city, the brightness of many of the scenes cannot conceal the underlying sordid existence of the women of the street, and the empty lives of many of the sailors, intent on escaping from the drudgery of their emotional troubles by returning to sea. Starring the famous Hans Albers, who was paid a fortune for his appearance, the film is a sad love story about a sailor, Hannes, who, in taking pity on his dead brother's girlfriend, Gisa, invites her to come and stay with him in Hamburg. Hannes soon falls in love with Gisa, but, torn between the call of the sea, his life as a musician in the Hippodrome on Grosse Freiheit Street and a possible call to the theatre, he delays in formally proposing to her. As a result, she falls in love with another deckhand and the film ends with Hannes escaping to sea again, still seeking the true love of his life.

While work on the film started in May 1943, production in Berlin and Hamburg was constantly interrupted by air raids, and there was the added difficulty of presenting a Hamburg port untouched by Allied bombing. The title itself had to be altered from *Die grosse Freiheit* to *Grosse Freiheit Nr.7* since any title containing the word 'freedom' during the war years tended

Hans Albers as Hannes and the ubiquitous Ilse Werner as Gisa in *Grosse Freiheit Nr. 7.* (*Deutsches Filminstitut/FWM*)

to be unwelcome. If production delays and disputes over the title were not enough, a large number of cuts were also requested by the censors, resulting in the film never being premiered in Germany until after the end of the war, although it was considered suitable for screening to non-Germans in Prague in December 1944.

Despite some witty dialogue and a superficial glimpse of the seemingly carefree life of the port district of Hamburg, it is ultimately a rather depressing love story. Given that the original intention of the film had been to raise the morale of the viewing audience, it is difficult to comprehend how a tale where the hero loses his girl and instead heads off to sea to escape the emptiness of his personal life could ever have done much to inspire German civilians. Indeed, Hannes' personal doubts and frustrations seem more symbolic of a Germany which was standing at its own crossroads and running away from the truth.

ENTERTAINMENT FILMS REVIEWED

It is impossible to comment on every type of film which was ever produced, so the detailed analysis in this section has been restricted to three quite different films, one even released before the war. All of the films were primarily produced for entertainment, but with varying degrees of more subtle propagandistic purpose and value. It is often thought, quite inaccurately, that the Germans do not have a sense of humour, so the three films which have been chosen are all, to a lesser or greater extent, comedies and provide a pleasant diversion from the heavy political tones of many of the films examined in the earlier sections of this book.

In chronological order, the three films which are analysed are *Der Mann, der Sherlock Holmes war* (July 1937), *Münchhausen* (March 1943) and *Die Feuerzangenbowle* (January 1944).

Der Mann, der Sherlock Holmes war (*The Man who was Sherlock Holmes*) is a very amusing tale starring two of Germany's most famous actors, Hans Albers and Heinz Rühmann, and is about two private detectives who are quite happy to be mistaken on their travels abroad for the 'real' Sherlock Holmes and Dr Watson. Rather surprisingly, the film contains virtually no anti-British asides, and the Nazis' lack of using Sherlock Holmes for propaganda purposes in the mid-1930s contrasts sharply with the frequent use the Allies made of the character in the 1940s, where, in a revision of some of Holmes' most famous cases into a twentieth-century setting, the Nazis become his evil nemesis.

The incredible adventures of the infamous Baron Münchhausen have been the subject of a number of films, but the Nazis' *Münchhausen* version was specifically commissioned to commemorate the 25th anniversary of the UFA film company. Filmed in colour and packed with special effects, this epic film was as spectacular as anything which Hollywood could produce at the time, and its true propaganda impact lay as much in this achievement, at the height of a major war, as in any more subtle propaganda messages it might have contained.

Finally, *Die Feuerzangenbowle* (*The 'fire-tongs' Punch*) is a rather peculiar, although highly entertaining comedy about a successful writer returning to school disguised as a pupil, so as to comprehend the joy of making fun of teachers – a joy of which he had been deprived through private tuition. Ironically, the education authorities were so alarmed by the content of the film that they almost succeeded in having it banned, and it was only because of a direct appeal to Hitler by the leading actor, Heinz Rühmann, that the film was allowed to be screened. Curiously enough, the film still retains cult status among the younger German film-going audiences of today.

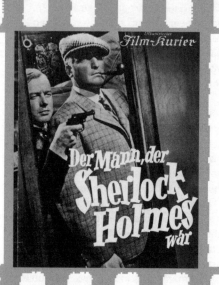

Film title: *Der Mann, der Sherlock Holmes war*
Year of release: 1937
Type: Feature film
Primary purpose: Entertainment
Director: Karl Hartl
Principal stars:

Hans Albers	(Morris Flynn)
Paul Bildt	(Sir Arthur Conan Doyle)
Marieluise Claudius	(Mary Berry)
Hansi Knoteck	(Jane Berry)
Heinz Rühmann	(Macky McPherson)
Siegfried Schürenberg	(Monsieur Lapin)
Hilde Weissner	(Madame Ganymare)

INTRODUCTION

Der Mann, der Sherlock Holmes war (*The Man who was Sherlock Holmes*) was released in 1937 and is generally regarded as one of the funniest German musical comedies ever produced. It starred two of Germany's best known actors, Hans Albers and Heinz Rühmann, and the film was so popular that a separate record was released of the title song, '*Jawohl, meine Herr'n*' (Yes, indeed, gentlemen), which they sing as a duet while bathing in separate bathrooms in their hotel suite.

The censors classified the film as being of 'artistic merit' and indeed it has no evident propaganda content whatsoever. It is, however, worthy of a short analysis both because of the Sherlock Holmes theme, which, paradoxically, was manipulated by the Allies for propaganda purposes, and its timing – only two years before the outbreak of war and at the height of the political tensions.

PLOT SUMMARY

The film begins with two characters waving down an express train en route to Paris. Given that the taller man, played by Hans Albers, is wearing a 'Scottish' cap and chequered coat, and carries a pipe and violin case, the train officials and almost everyone with whom they come into contact assume that these two gentlemen are none other than Sherlock Holmes and Dr Watson. The ruse is given added credibility through the fact that they conduct themselves like the 'real' detectives and address each other as 'the Master' and 'Doctor'. It gradually emerges that their real names are Morris Flynn and Macky McPherson, and that they are 'down on their luck' private detectives, dressing like Holmes and Watson in the hope that they will be employed to solve some cases.

Their surprise arrival on the train results in two petty criminals fleeing, and Flynn and McPherson take the opportunity to acquire the vacated first-class sleeping accommodation

Hans Albers and Heinz Rühmann.
(*Deutsches Filminstitut/FWM*)

for themselves. They also make the acquaintance of the pretty Berry sisters who are in the next compartment and travelling from Britain to Paris to acquire their inheritance from the recently deceased Professor Berry.

On arriving at the Palace Hotel in Paris, our heroes are again mistaken for Holmes and Watson by the hotel detective and, because of their very request that their identities should be kept secret, the rumours spread quickly, and the police engage them to help locate four rare Mauritius stamps which have been substituted with forgeries. In the meantime, the trunks of the two criminals on the train are delivered to the hotel and, while the detectives are helping themselves to the clothes in the trunks, they discover secret papers and hundreds of thousands of French francs. The bosses of the criminals are also staying in the hotel and threaten to expose Flynn and McPherson as phonies if they don't hand over the stolen goods.

Feeling obliged to investigate the case of the missing stamps for the police, their investigations take them to the house of the deceased Professor Berry, where they uncover a secret room full of printing equipment. They realise that Professor Berry was the master forger behind the missing stamps and was also forging bank notes. The address of a pawn shop on a piece of paper leads them to the headquarters of the criminal gang, but our heroes are captured and locked in a coal cellar, although they are eventually released because of the intervention of the Berry sisters who had fetched the police.

The action moves to the courtroom where the two detectives are being tried for impersonation. The basis of their defence is that they had never actually claimed to be Holmes and Watson and that they had, in any event, solved the case which the police had asked them to investigate. Furthermore, they are able to produce the four missing stamps from a pocket watch which they had taken from the boss of the criminal gang. Sir Arthur Conan Doyle then appears in court and claims that since his detective characters had never really existed, the two accused could not be charged with impersonation. In any event, he is pleased that they have brought his fictional characters to life and wants to write their story. The case is dismissed, and the tale has a happy ending as the two detectives look likely to be offered more cases to solve and will soon become betrothed to the Berry sisters.

CRITICAL REVIEW

This film was produced for purely entertainment purposes and was a very successful musical comedy, even if the plot occasionally falls short. There are bound to be some inconsistencies when a film about British detectives is set in France, and is produced in Germany with German actors.

Much of the humour derives from the complications caused by Flynn and McPherson assuming the characters of Holmes and Watson, and from the way they try to use deductive

Image from *Illustrierter Film-Kurier* film programme showing Flynn and McPherson emerging from their incarceration in a coal cellar. (*Author's Collection/Verlag für Filmschriften*)

logic to solve the case of the missing stamps. For example, McPherson is very taken with the Berry sisters and would like to know them better, but Flynn gently reminds him why they can't pursue the girls: 'Have you ever seen Holmes with women?' and McPherson is reluctantly obliged to respond, 'No. So, we will not see the girls again? ... Shame.' The viewer shares their disappointment.

Later, there is McPherson's gentle rebuke for what Flynn has ordered for a meal, namely goulash and beer. However, Flynn successfully convinces him that this is exactly the sort of food which someone like Sherlock Holmes would have ordered.

Likewise, when they are told that three men want to employ their services, they set off full of enthusiasm for what will be their first case. When Flynn realises that the men waiting below are detectives, he steps back, convinced they are to be arrested for impersonating Holmes and Watson. 'I thought you would come but not so soon!' he exclaims in an aside. Fortunately, the police are not aware of their true identities at that stage and were genuinely seeking their assistance.

Acting as perfect British gentlemen, Holmes and Watson do not take advantage of the vulnerable Berry sisters. (*Deutsches Filminstitut/FWM*)

The film is also full of visual humour, such as their panic to hide the money they find in the luggage or their dance routine before they sing their famous song about having no worries and doing what they please.

Why is there no Nazi propaganda in this film?

The film was released in July 1937, when political tensions were rising. To redress the iniquities of the Versailles Treaty, the Nazis had already ordered militarisation of the Rhineland in 1936, and Hitler had also hinted at the further reoccupation of former German territory.

It is, therefore, somewhat surprising that this film neither contains any Nazi propaganda nor seeks to mock any of the British characters. Indeed, the exact opposite is often the case. The two detectives are generally shown to uphold strong moral values and to be brave and resolute. They do not take advantage of the Berry sisters in the train, but instead show compassion for them, returning their money and, when told that one had pretended to be a countess, giving them the amusing and ironical advice: 'Never pretend to be what you are not – it never comes out well!'

When asked in court what they expected to gain from their impersonation of the famous detectives, they claim that all they ever sought was to help 'the victory of justice', and this seems an accurate appraisal given that they return the stolen stamps and do not keep them for themselves.

Even the criminal bosses use the term 'fair play' when speaking to our heroes, so that the British are still recognised as upholding this honourable trait.

There is even an anti-Nazi allusion in an early scene, where a small uniformed man with a moustache is running around the room shouting and ranting like Hitler as he admonishes each of his underlings for not carrying out his orders. The irony may not have been missed by the German audience of the time!

Der Mann, der Sherlock Holmes war was not the only German film with a Sherlock Holmes theme released during the 1930s. There was *Der Hund von Baskerville* (*The Hound of the Baskervilles*) in 1936, and *Sherlock Holmes – Die Graue Dame* (*Sherlock Holmes – The Grey Lady*), released in 1937. The latter is also fairly humorous in parts and is supposedly set in London, notwithstanding a number of continuity errors such as a car's steering wheel being located on the left side of the vehicle. Indeed, detective films as a genre were very popular and *Mordsache Holm* (*The Holm Murder Case*) (1938) was a film which received special

An early scene in which Flynn and McPherson fear that their ruse has been discovered by the police. (*Deutsches Filminstitut/FWM*)

praise from the Nazis because of the exemplary manner in which modern policing methods were used to solve the crime. Interestingly, none of these films had any anti-British bias.

So, why was no use made of the propaganda opportunity presented by the Sherlock Holmes character? It can only be assumed that because Hitler had no intention of going to war with Britain at that time, there was no harm in allowing these films to be screened for the purpose for which they were intended, namely to provide hard-working people with innocent entertainment. With unemployment falling, the German public was beginning to feel proud about being German again, and they deserved some light diversion.

The use of the Sherlock Holmes character by the Allies in anti-Nazi propaganda

In sharp contrast to this non-political use of the character of Sherlock Holmes by the Nazis, there is the famous series of movies starring Basil Rathbone and Nigel Bruce, released between 1939 and 1946. Several of those produced during the war years, namely *Sherlock Holmes and the Voice of Terror* (1942), *Sherlock Holmes and the Secret Weapon* (1942) and *Sherlock Holmes in Washington* (1943) all contained overt anti-Nazi propaganda.

In each case, there is a final postscript to the film which contains some emotive words uttered by Sherlock Holmes to the accompaniment of stirring nationalistic music. He admits he is often quoting from speeches by Churchill, which poetically extol the democratic virtues of the USA or Britain in their struggle against the tyranny of Nazi Germany, and as they strive for a free and safe future for the whole world. Some of the more poignant lines from these films are recorded in Chapter IX of this book.

Point of note concerning the release of the film

Did this film ever have permission from the estate of Sir Arthur Conan Doyle to be released? To give the film some sort of authenticity, the opening credits claim that it was released with the permission of the heirs of Sir Arthur Conan Doyle. This was simply not true. Sir Arthur had actually died in 1930, and, in 1939, lawyers acting for his estate took the matter to the German courts. The intervention of the war meant the case had to be dropped, only to be raised again in 1954. The case dragged on until 1957, with the German courts eventually finding in favour of UFA, the company which had produced the film, primarily on the grounds of the unreasonable delay which the estate lawyers had taken in bringing the matter to court again after the war. This is undoubtedly one of the reasons why the scenes featuring Sir Arthur Conan Doyle were not actually broadcast on German television until the 1970s.

CONCLUSION

While *Der Mann, der Sherlock Holmes war* was not the only detective film released during the Nazi era, it was undoubtedly one of the most amusing films produced at the time, principally because of its musical interludes and the well-known actors playing the leading roles.

In many ways it is reminiscent of a film such as *The Lady Vanishes* (1939 version) or a Marx Brothers' farce. It is pure entertainment and was produced at a time when Britain was not really considered an enemy. Indeed, Britain had been more willing than France to turn a blind eye to German breaches of the Versailles Treaty.

Given how the Allies adapted the Sherlock Holmes stories into anti-Nazi propaganda movies, it would certainly have been interesting to see what difference it would have made to the tone and content of this film if it had been produced in Germany after 1939. Fortunately, however, this was not the case and consequently the world has been left with a charming comedy.

Film title: *Münchhausen*
Year of release: 1943
Type: Feature film
Primary purpose: Entertainment
Director: Josef von Baky
Principal stars:

Hans Albers	(Baron Münchhausen)
Wilhelm Bendow	(The Man in the Moon)
Marina von Ditmar	(Sophie von Riedesel)
Käthe Haack	(Baronness Münchhausen)
Brigitte Horney	(Catherine the Great)
Ferdinand Marian	(Count Cagliostro)
Marianne Simson	(The Woman in the Moon)
Hermann Speelmans	(Christian Kuchenreutter)
Ilse Werner	(Princess Isabella d'Este)

INTRODUCTION

Münchhausen was undoubtedly the most extravagant film produced during the time of the Third Reich. It was commissioned by Goebbels in 1941, and eventually premiered in Berlin in March 1943 to celebrate the 25th anniversary of the founding of UFA, one of Germany's greatest film companies.

At a cost of 6.5 million Reichsmarks, it is a fascinating epic starring no less than forty-five established film actors in a cast of thousands. Above all, it was only the fourth German film to have been made in colour and contained a series of stunning special effects which, in terms of quality, would not be out of place with any film produced today. In a speech to members of the film industry in 1933, Goebbels stated that blatant ideological messages should be ignored when producing a film, and *Münchhausen* was generally conceived to be for entertainment purposes without political motivation. However, the very production of such an expensive film, at that time, was bound to have some propaganda impact.

PLOT SUMMARY

Through a couple of extended flashbacks, the plot revolves around the current Baron Münchhausen telling two friends, Sophie and her fiancé, Fritz, about the adventures of his eighteenth-century ancestor. The tale proceeds at speed, as Münchhausen, accompanied by his faithful servant, Christian, move from one exotic country and unbelievable adventure to another. Münchhausen is an unashamed womaniser and seems irresistible to women. Catherine the Great of Russia is no exception and she is so enchanted by him that she makes him her adjutant general on the basis that they will remain together 'until one of us wants to be free'. During his travels, he encounters the mysterious Count Cagliostro who possesses magical powers. He gives Münchhausen a special ring which, when worn, will give him the power of invisibility for an hour.

Münchhausen's spectactular ride on a cannonball. (*Deutsches Filminstitut/FWM*)

He also wants to reward Münchhausen for warning him about a plot to arrest him but, realising that Münchhausen is not motivated by power or money, he asks, 'If you could make an impossible wish what would it be?' Münchhausen responds, 'I would always wish to remain as young as I am today until I myself ask to become old!'

The granting of this quasi-immortality by Cagliostro becomes the key driver for Münchhausen's actions and emotions throughout the rest of the film. Catherine eventually becomes frustrated with a Münchhausen who never ages, and she sends him off to war. His enemy, Potemkin, fires him across the skies on a cannonball, and he smashes into a tower in the fortress of Ochakon which they have been besieging. Emerging unscathed, he is held prisoner by the sultan in Constantinople.

There, he falls in love with a beautiful Italian princess, Isabella d'Este, who is also being held hostage. By winning a wager, he manages to secure his own release and that of two of his comrades and, having been cheated by the sultan, uses his magic ring to free the Italian princess. They are deeply in love with each other, but she has already been promised to a much older viscount by her parents, and she is recaptured and sent off to become a nun. After a duel with her brother, Münchhausen and Christian escape in a hot air balloon which takes them to the dark side of the moon where they meet the Man and Woman in the Moon. The moon is an odd place where all the seasons of earth pass in twenty-four hours, so that a day on the moon is the equivalent of a year on earth. Consequently, Christian ages quickly and dies.

Returning to the present, the current Baron Münchhausen explains how his ancestor returned to earth and had many more adventures, but kept having to relocate as people became frightened of someone who never grew older. Then, in the presence of his wife, and to the amazement of his two guests, he declares, 'In 1900 he married a beautiful girl and there she sits!' Realising that the modern Baron Münchhausen and his ancestor are one and the same, they all rush off in fear!

Münchhausen testing the gun invented by Christian which can fire accurately over a hundred miles. (*Deutsches Filminstitut/FWM*)

Then, the final moral of the story becomes clear. Münchhausen explains to his wife, 'I don't want to be young when you are old. I don't want to live on when you die. I love you. Eternal youth makes you a demi-god but only half a man. I want the whole of life. I want the rest.'

He then commands fate to allow him to age and the word 'Ende' appears out of smoke. It is a moving finale, tinged with both sadness and happiness in the realisation that the possession of eternal youth by one individual alone will never provide true happiness.

CRITICAL REVIEW

The use of special effects and creative concepts

Apart from the stunning Agfacolor – Germany's answer to 'glorious' Technicolor – and a plot which moves at a tremendous speed, what really captures the viewer's attention in this adult fairytale is the multitude of special effects and imaginative ideas. Many of these special effects were well ahead of their time and really have to be seen to be appreciated, as they would not look out of place in a modern movie.

In terms of special effects, key examples include: the magical way that Count Cagliostro fills his glass with wine from an adjacent glass carafe without lifting it; the ability of the count and Münchhausen to achieve invisibility by using a magic ring; how rabid clothes are seen to float round a room and have to be shot; the way Münchhausen appears to fly through the air on a cannonball; the duel scene where several swords overlap on the screen at the same time to give a feel for the intensity and speed of the thrusts; the impression of the hot air balloon gradually slipping away from blue sky to darkness, with escaping smoke making it appear even more authentic; and finally, the detachable head of the girl on the moon which Münchhausen seems able to turn.

In terms of creative ideas, there is the ointment Christian brings back from Paris which makes hair grow instantly by at least five centimetres; the rifle invented by Christian which will fire accurately over a hundred miles; the messenger who can run at 200 times normal speed; furniture appearing in and out of the floor of Catherine the Great's apartments; food hanging from trees and wine flowing from wells in Petersburg; and the idea of someone being so wealthy that a servant can offer each guest a precious stone to round off his meal. Finally, there is the girl in the moon with a detachable head: 'So more practical – my head can talk to you while my body does the housework.' At various stages in the film, there is also a deeper, philosophical analysis of the advantages and disadvantages of eternal youth.

Humour

The special effects and creative ideas provide both amazement and amusement. Humour, and a type of humour which would appeal to more than a German audience alone, is a surprisingly recurrent theme in the film. The director plays with his audience from the very opening scenes. The film begins in what looks like a ballroom set in the eighteenth century, so that the viewer is caught completely unawares when Münchhausen switches on an electric light, and the girl runs out of the house to drive away in a car. We then realise that it was only a costume ball!

However, there is also much wit in the throw-away lines between the characters. An officer rebukes Christian for not accompanying his master on a reconnaissance mission by questioning, 'You let him ride alone?', and Christian quickly retorts, 'Well, he lets me sit here alone!'

The brother of Isabella d'Este, whom Münchhausen defeats so convincingly in the duel, wants to kill himself out of the shame of having been left only wearing his breeches, but his friends actually agree when they finally see Münchhausen escaping in the balloon: 'Okay, Heaven will kill him, *now* you can shoot yourself!'

The film also contains a good deal of amusing sexual innuendo, such as when Münchhausen is tucking into food in Catherine's boudoir, he exclaims, 'First the hors d'oeuvre and then the main course!' The viewer knows exactly what is implied.

Monumentality of the production

The scale and grandeur of many of the exotic scenes and locations is truly breathtaking. During the banquet in the palace in Petersburg, for example, it seems that there are countless guests at the tables, with whole cooked animals and fish paraded around the hall on trays, and a huge pastry cut open to reveal a costumed dwarf playing a harpsichord. There is also remarkable attention to detail in that valuable Meissen dishes and real gold and silver cutlery were used. However, many of the extras in this scene were actually played by SS guards, who it was felt would be less likely to steal the valuable props. One point of interest for a British audience is that Catherine is shown to be surrounded by advisors from all over the world, including one colourful gent adorned in red tartan, sporting a kilt and an impressive sporran, who is obviously meant to be Scottish.

Then, there is the harem in Turkey with countless topless girls swimming in a pool – a some-what risqué scene for the period – accompanied by a host of impressively dressed African servants. The colourful carnival scene with flags and streamers on the canals in Venice is similarly impressive, but perhaps rather wasted since, although many of the background shots on the canals were specifically filmed for this movie, the actual scene which includes our heroes is quite short and does look as if it has been filmed separately. Likewise, despite the general attention to detail, it is surprising that no attempt is made to re-shoot a particular scene where one of the girls in the harem drops her fan while she is being served food.

Does the film contain any propaganda?

Primarily, this film was intended purely for entertainment purposes without political undertones and, indeed, it is hard to find more than a couple of political allusions which would have held any significance for a Nazi audience.

Certainly, there is a scene where Münchhausen recognises that duty calls, before clicking his heels and lifting his hat in a manner which is reminiscent of a Nazi salute. Later, in a scene with the sultan, Münchhausen does display a real sense of loyalty towards his homeland: 'If you come from Bodenwerder you can't become a Turk! ... Everyone has their own *"Heimat"*, just as they have their own mother.' As has been mentioned throughout this book, the belief in the importance of the '*Heimat*' was a recurrent Nazi theme.

Illustrierte Film-Kurier film programme for Münchhausen.
(Author's Collection/Verlag für Filmschriften)

Baron Münchhausen, himself, can be seen as a very acceptable Aryan figure. He is blond and blue-eyed, dutiful and brave, even if a bit of a womaniser, and yet can show real compassion and eventually places the value of true love above the gift of eternal youth.

Perhaps, there is also an oblique anti-foreigner and even anti-freemason reference in the dark and mysterious character of Count Cagliostro (played by Ferdinand Marian, who starred as the hated Jew in *Jud Süss*), when Münchhausen says to Christian that the count, 'lends people his imagination at an exorbitant rate of interest!'

However, it would be naïve to conclude that simply because there were not more obvious elements of Nazi propaganda, the film did not serve a propaganda purpose. Goebbels had been impressed by the great colour film productions which were emerging from Hollywood and Britain at that time, such as *The Wizard of Oz* (1939), *Gone with the Wind* (1939), *The Thief of Bagdad* (1940) and *Jungle Book* (1942). He was determined that he could demonstrate both to the German nation and to the world at large that just as Nazi Germany could produce the biggest and best airships, bridges, motorways and indeed machines of war, they could also produce films which were as spectacular, if not more impressive, than anything produced by the rest of the world. In this regard, it was a truly successful propaganda 'weapon' at home and abroad.

Whatever the truth, the Soviets certainly believed that the film contained anti-Soviet propaganda. In January 1946, following protests from the Soviets, the British authorities agreed to forbid further screening of the film in the British Zone, since the Soviets considered that the film portrayed the Soviet people in a poor light, and that it contained a number of historical inaccuracies.

POINTS OF NOTE CONCERNING THE CONTENT AND PRODUCTION OF THE FILM

Baron Münchhausen was undeniably a true historical figure who lived in the eighteenth century. He was a German officer famed for his exuberant boasting and tall tales. He was born in Bodenwerder and did, indeed, travel to Russia and Turkey before his death in 1797.

Erich Kästner was chosen to write most of the script for this movie; however, given that he was a banned author who had had his books burned by the Nazis,[6] he was permitted to proceed only on the basis that he wrote under a pseudonym, and so the name Berthold Bürger appeared on the list of credits.

Yet, even though Kästner may have had to be careful about the content of the script and some of it was subsequently discarded, it would appear that at least one controversial comment escaped the attention of the censors. When it is realised how quickly time passes on the moon, Christian remarks to Münchhausen, 'Either your watch is broken or time is broken.' Münchhausen responds that, 'Die Zeit ist kaputt!' (Time is broken). This could be interpreted as a more general political criticism of the 'broken times' in which they were living in 1940s Germany.

CONCLUSION

Given the massive budget supporting the film, the swashbuckling movie of the life of Münchhausen with all its special effects, exciting locations and underlying love story, could not fail to impress, and it was no surprise that it was an instant box office success, diverting the German viewing public's attention away from the reality of the war. Ironically, the very cinema in Berlin in which it was premiered was to be destroyed in an Allied bombing raid shortly after. The film would certainly have had a positive propaganda impact on a German audience, proud that their country could produce such a high quality film about a renowned German character. There is no doubt that movie producers from other countries were also similarly impressed, not least by the quality of the colour photography and special effects.

In all events, it is perhaps only fitting that Joseph Goebbels, the Nazi Propaganda Minister, should have chosen Baron Münchhausen, a character who was also renowned for his lies and tall stories, as a suitable subject for this commemorative film. At the very moment when Germany was reeling from the defeat at Stalingrad, it is rather typical of tyrannical governments that Hitler was actually diverted from such urgent military considerations to agree the precise titles to be awarded to film personnel in this celebration of UFA's 25th anniversary. It would seem that the German High Command was already living in its own fairytale world and was just as remote from reality as anything which would appear in the Münchhausen film.

---

6   The writer of the book which inspired the film Jud Süss was also a banned author.

Film title: *Die Feuerzangenbowle*
Year of release: 1944
Type: Feature film
Primary purpose: Entertainment/oblique propaganda
Director: Helmut Weiss
Principal stars:

Lutz Götz	(Dr Brett)
Paul Henckels	(Professor Bömmel)
Karin Himboldt	(Eva Knauer)
Hans Leibelt	(Headmaster Knauer)
Erich Ponto	(Professor Crey)
Heinz Rühmann	(Dr Johannes Pfeiffer & Hans Pfeiffer)
Hilde Sessak	(Marion)

INTRODUCTION

Die Feuerzangenbowle (*The 'fire-tongs' Punch*) is a comedy set in a grammar school and, released in 1944, it was a great box office success. Its primary purpose was to provide entertainment and to help divert the German civilians' attention away from the grim reality of the war. Based on his own school experiences, the film was adapted from a book by Heinrich Spoerl, first published in 1933, and from which an earlier film had been produced in 1934.

However, this film is notable for a number of other reasons. First, the film was almost prevented from being released at all because of complaints from the education authorities, and it took a direct appeal to Hitler to have it approved. Second, there are a number of seemingly innocent pieces of dialogue in the film which would certainly have held a much deeper significance for the German audience at the time. Third, this film has become a cult movie amongst the student population in modern times, attracting the same sort of interest as films such as *Casablanca* in the UK, albeit for totally different reasons.

PLOT SUMMARY

As with many comedies, the plot is fairly simple and straightforward. It begins with a group of old friends meeting in an inn and drinking a toast to one of their recently deceased former teachers. They are seated around a warm-wine punch bowl, from which the film *Die Feuerzangenbowle* takes it name.

While they are reminiscing about good old times, Dr Johannes Pfeiffer, now a famous writer, joins the proceedings. He complains that being educated privately had deprived him of the enjoyment of the pranks and jokes which his friends had experienced in the days of their youth. As they continue to drink, however, it is agreed that he will now disguise himself as a young student and return to school to find out for himself.

Pfeiffer causes confusion and uproar throughout the school. (*Deutsches Filminstitut/Terra*)

The scene then fades to his arrival at the school, and the bulk of the film is devoted to a series of short episodes where the pupils carry out a variety of innocent pranks on their teachers. All the teachers have been given good-natured nicknames such as Professor Crey, whom they have nicknamed Dr Schnauz ('*tash*'), because of his prominent moustache.

When Pfeiffer, who has changed his first name to Hans, is asked by his teacher if his surname is spelt with one '*f*' or two, he responds that it is actually spelt with *three* '*f*'s, one before the '*ei*' and two '*f*'s after the '*ei*', which all his fellow classmates find hilarious.

Later, we are taken to the class of Professor Bömmel, whose very name suggests someone who bumbles along. He is giving a lesson about the steam engine, but his delivery is boring, and the short attention span of the pupils is not helped by the fact that he admits that, 'everything I say is in the book!' They hide one of his shoes and, as the period comes to an end, there is a bit of a stand-off as he indicates that he won't leave until he gets it back. The one notable exception among the teachers is the new history master, Dr Brett. He is younger and more worldly aware. The pupils jump to attention when he enters the classroom and rush to return the stolen shoe to Professor Bömmel. Brett speaks frankly to them: 'With me it's quite different. I look after my class. I give them a choice of war or peace.' He also boasts that he is familiar with all the tricks they are likely to practice, so they will not fool him. Pfeiffer decides to put this to the test, using a small mirror to reflect sunlight onto a map behind the teacher to help one of his colleagues answer questions about the history of the Goths. Notably, this *is* the only teacher they are unable to fool. Brett knows all about the mirror, awarding poor marks to both the pupils and leaving Pfeiffer lost for words when he mockingly remarks, 'Do you call that something new? What would you do if it rains?'

Meanwhile, Pfeiffer manages to find a way of being excused from music classes and uses the time to pursue a female pupil. He also masterminds pranks in the chemistry class of Professor Crey by arranging for all his classmates to pretend they are intoxicated after only one small gulp of alcoholic fruit-juice. He is locked away in a room for punishment where he is visited by three girls who are keen to meet the pupil who has caused so much mayhem. He teases them and eventually goes out with Eva, the headmaster's daughter.

His next piece of tomfoolery is to erect a sign outside the school gate which states that the school is closed because of building work, and results in all the students going back home when they arrive for school. There is a great debate among the teachers as to how to capture the culprit and, to avoid loss of face, they eventually agree to pretend that there really had been some building work at the school. One of the pupils is resolved to inform on Pfeiffer, but when it is announced that there had indeed been building work, he shouts out that it is all a swindle!

Pfeiffer's real-life girlfriend, the flirtatious and demanding Marion, travels from Berlin to visit him at the school. There is a suggestion they enjoy some tender moments in his bedroom as

Pfeiffer arrives in class seemingly suffering from toothache. (*Deutsches Filminstitut/Terra*)

she closes the curtains, notwithstanding that he has already been making advances towards the fair and far more innocent, Eva. Marion tries to persuade him to leave and return to the real world in the city, and he seems to yield, but then changes his mind at the last moment because he is enjoying himself too much in class.

During another period, one of the pupils draws what is obviously a naked lady on the blackboard, but Pfeiffer, who arrives late in class claiming to be suffering from toothache, comes to the rescue by claiming that it is actually a drawing of a boy which is not yet finished.

In the meantime, he turns back the alarm clock of Professor Crey by one hour and disguises himself as the chemistry master, taking the lesson himself. In the interim, the school inspector arrives to bestow some honour on the chemistry master for his teaching methods, which consist of 'Knowledge mixed with humour'. In the circumstances, Pfeiffer is instructed by the headmaster to continue imitating Professor Crey and he will not be punished. This is exactly what he does and all ends well, even when the real teacher eventually arrives. Pfeiffer is actually exasperated that the headmaster is prepared to keep his word and won't expel him:

Must I kill someone or run off with the head's daughter to get expelled?

Eva can't control her emotions any longer and leaps across the desks to say she will run off with him with or without his *Abitur* (school leaving certificate), still not accepting that he is really a famous author.

Pfeiffer then reveals to the whole school that he already has his *Abitur* and degree, and shows them his income tax return. There is real concern by the school that he will write about his experiences, turning these into a film. Pfeiffer admits that he has already done so, but it is so exaggerated that the school will never be recognised:

Such a school with such teachers and such prankish kids simply does not exist.

For the first time in the film, Pfeiffer speaks directly to the viewer, explaining that 'everything in the film has been invented – teachers, pupils, even myself. Only the beginning with the punch bowl was real. The memories we carry, the dreams we concoct, the yearnings which drive us – we should content ourselves with all of these.' It is a charming comedy, which never loses sight of the fact that 'school days are the best days of your life', whatever the pranks and whatever the quality of the teachers.

Karin Himboldt, as Eva, who was to fall foul of the Nazis for failing to give a Hitler salute at the film's premiere. (*Deutsches Filminstitut/Terra*)

CRITICAL REVIEW

Effectiveness as a work of entertainment

If the primary purpose of the film is to entertain and provide a German audience with some light-hearted escapism from the rigours of the war, then it certainly succeeds. Beginning with jolly music, the credits state: 'This film is meant to be in praise of the school but perhaps the school won't recognise it.'

It combines comedy with a gentle love story and causes little offence to anyone, except perhaps teachers. The whole plot is obviously rather far-fetched. How could Heinz Rühmann, who was forty-one years old at the time, ever pass himself off as the young student, Pfeiffer? The irony is that an earlier version of the film had been released in 1934 and that Rühmann also played Pfeiffer in that version. The fact that the action takes place in a make-believe world is clearly reinforced by the final scenes, when Pfeiffer talks directly to the camera and explains that everything has been invented. Consequently, we can't really find fault with the film for any apparent inconsistencies. Ultimately, the film was a great box office success, undoubtedly aided by the high quality of the cast.

Enigmatic character of hero

One of the more obvious inconsistencies surrounds the character of Pfeiffer himself. In the tavern he seems quiet and boring, yet when he appears in the classroom he is completely transformed. He is the chief trickster, full of ideas for causing mayhem. On the one hand, he is quite an honourable chap, prepared to confess when it looks as if a teacher will get into trouble for a trick he has played, on the other hand, his treatment of Marion and his readiness to abandon her for the younger Eva make him appear less worthy. Indeed, when questioned by Eva as to whether he has ever been in love with anybody else, he claims that he has always restrained himself, which is obviously a lie. However, he is still a likeable character, if rather full of himself.

Special significance to an audience in Germany in 1944

Although the majority of the script is fairly transparent, apart from the strong accents and idiomatic speech of the various teachers, there are a number of scenes which would have had a far deeper significance to an audience in Nazi-controlled Germany. When the teachers are debating how they might find out who was responsible for putting up the sign indicating the school was closed, one of them suggests that, 'often a dear friend might be found'. The idea that someone might be prepared to betray the culprit would have certainly struck a chord with the viewer at the time, when all Germans were being encouraged to report neighbours who showed any reluctance to follow the Nazi Party line. Indeed, it is surprising that some mild criticism of this regime is detected when Brecht responds, 'Hopefully, not in our establishment!'

Likewise, there is a serious moment later in the film when two teachers discuss which teaching methods are correct? Brett, the enthusiastic and seemingly all-knowing teacher, responds, 'Those where a teacher is a friend of his pupils and his pupils respect him. A *new time* has *new methods*! Discipline must be the band that binds young people like binding young trees.' Brett is clearly identified as symbolic of the new Nazi order, where discipline is all and influence over the young is the very key to success.

POINTS OF NOTE CONCERNING THE CONTENT AND PRODUCTION OF THE FILM

Given the light nature of the film, it is somewhat surprising to learn that the film was very close to being banned before it was even released. The then head of education, Bernard Rust, had asked for the film not to be released on the basis that it would damage the authority of schools and teachers. It was difficult enough to maintain discipline in the classroom at a time when there was a shortage of teachers because of the war, without needlessly encouraging pupils to act in this way. The film undoubtedly leaves the impression that most teachers were dreary, bumbling old souls who might be masters of their subject and well-disposed towards their classes, but pupils showed them little real respect.

Consequently, it was only because of the last-minute personal intervention of Heinz Rühmann, who made a special trip to visit Hitler at his headquarters in the Wolf's Lair, that it was eventually announced by Göring and subsequently by Goebbels that the film would be allowed to be released after all. Rühmann was indeed fortunate that Hitler knew him well and liked him as an actor. However, perhaps the real reason why the film was allowed to be released is that Rühmann was able to highlight a very significant change from the original book and earlier film version, with the introduction of a younger and more dynamic teacher, Dr Brett, as the history master. It is perhaps no mere coincidence that this respected teacher with new ideas should be a history master, as anyone who had read *Mein Kampf* would have known – more than 6 million copies had been sold in Germany by 1940 – Hitler had been very unhappy at school and hated most of his teachers. Ironically, the only teacher for whom Hitler had had any respect was the history master, a devout nationalist.

Ackermann, the class leader, clicks his heels and stands to attention when Brett enters the room, and if the film had been set when Hitler was in power, he would have been bound to raise his arm in salute. This is the key propaganda element, and Brett can be seen as representing the discipline of the new order. He is clever, interesting and enjoys the full respect of both his pupils and fellow teachers; he is a 'fine chap'. The pupils rarely play tricks on him and if they do, he soon finds them out.

Die Feuerzangenbowle was filmed in two schools in Baden Württemberg and at Babelsberg's Potsdam studios between March and June 1943. In order to delay the call-up of some of the younger actors as long as possible, it is reported that some of the scenes were deliberately

Heinz Rühmann was one of Hitler's favourite actors. (*Deutsches Filminstitut*)

re-shot again and again. Nevertheless, by the time of its premiere in Berlin on 28 January 1944, several of the actors had already died in action.

What became of the principal actors in the film?

Heinz Rühmann (Pfeiffer) had been a famous comedian and singer before the war, and he starred in thirty-seven films and directed four others during the Nazi regime, although he tried to distance himself from politics. In 1938, he divorced his Jewish wife who survived the war in Norway, and he was accused by some of doing this to safeguard his acting career. However, there is some doubt as to whether this was the case as his re-marriage shortly afterwards to a wife who had a Jewish grandfather caused him considerable difficulties with the authorities. In March 1946, a stage ban imposed on him by the Allies at the end of the war was lifted and he continued to pursue an active career as an actor and director.

Despite having been a supporter of the Nazis and appearing in a number of propaganda movies such as *Die Rothschilds*, Erich Ponto (Professor Crey) also managed to continue in the film industry until his death in 1957, including a role in *The Third Man* in 1949 with Joseph Cotton.

Karin Himboldt (Eva) had worked on earlier films with Rühmann, but after refusing to give the Hitler salute at the premiere of *Die Feuerzangenbowle* (she was married to a half-Jew), her film career in Nazi Germany faded out, and she was never quite able to recapture her earlier success after the war.

CONCLUSION

It is easy to understand why the education authorities wished this film to be banned. However, the introduction of the character of Brett explains why the Nazis eventually permitted its release, and the fact that it is a charming comedy ensured it would enjoy considerable box office success.

Indeed, the amusing and escapist nature of the film has given it a lasting appeal, and it has now become a cult movie, especially among student audiences, for its general theme of 'rejoicing while we are young'. Viewers are often able to recite key lines off by heart and carry numerous props such as alarm clocks into the cinema, which are then brought into action during appropriate scenes in the film. It is often also projected onto a large screen outdoors around Christmas, with the viewers being invigorated with glasses of warm mulled wine. *Die Feuerzangenbowle* is one of the few films of the Nazi period which is still readily obtainable in shops in Germany today.

Anti-British propaganda: The front cover of a large map of Britain and its colonies which accompanied the special edition of the *Illustrierter Beobachter* blaming England for provoking the war. The caption reads, 'England's Guilt' and shows a British NCO with a whip being carried by natives from Britain's colonies. (*Randall Bytwerk*)

Anti-British propaganda: The front cover of *Das Programm von Heute* film programme for *Der Fuchs von Glenarvon* showing Irish freedom fighters carrying the bodies of their fallen colleagues through the treacherous swamplands. (*Author's Collection*)

Anti-British propaganda: The front cover of *Das Programm von Heute* film programme for *Das Herz der Königin* featuring the ill-fated marriage of Mary, Queen of Scots and Lord Bothwell. (*Author's Collection*)

Anti-Jewish propaganda: A poster issued in September 1940 to promote Fritz Hippler's infamous documentary, *Der ewige Jude*. (BArch, Plak 003-020-030/StS)

Anti-Jewish propaganda: A 1943 poster designed to illustrate the Jewish influence over Germany's enemies – 'Behind the enemy powers: the Jew'. (BArch, Plak 003-020-021/Hanich, B.)

Anti-American propaganda: The front cover of the *Film-Kurier* film programme for *Der verlorene Sohn*, a film starring Luis Trenker which paints a depressing picture of life in recession-hit New York. (*Author's Collection /Verlag für Filmschriften*)

Anti-American propaganda: The front cover of *Das Programm von Heute* film programme for *Sensationsprozess Casilla*, a film which mocks the sensationalism of the American legal system. (*Author's Collection*)

Pro-Nazi propaganda: A poster issued to promote Leni Riefenstahl's documentary, *Der Sieg des Glaubens*, about the 1933 Nazi Party Congress held in Nürnberg. (*BArch, Plak 003-022-022/ Mjölnir: [Schweitzer, H.]*)

Pro-Nazi propaganda: A poster issued in April 1933 to promote the feature film *S.A. Mann Brand*. (*BArch, Plak 003-022-002/Ottler, O.*)

Home Front propaganda: The front cover of the *Film-Kurier* programme for *Verräter*, a film which gives a stark warning about the dangers of traitors and the fate which awaits them if caught. (*Author's Collection/Verlag für Filmschriften*)

Home Front propaganda: The front cover of the *Film-Kurier* programme for *Achtung! Feind hört mit!*, a film which warns Germans about the devious methods used by spies to obtain secret information. (*Author's Collection/Verlag für Filmschriften*)

Left and opposite: Home Front propaganda: Respective posters produced by the Germans and the Allies warning their citizens of the dangers of loose talk. The caption from the 1939 German poster reads: 'Watch out for Spies. Be careful when you are talking!' The poster in English was produced in 1943 by the Office of War Information in the United States. (*BArch, Plak 003-027-030/Matejko, T. & North Western University Library/Office of War Information*)

Films for entertainment: Two stills from the spectacular 1943 colour epic version of *Münchhausen*, starring Hans Albers. (*BFI/FWM*)

CHAPTER IX

COMPARATIVE ANTI-NAZI PROPAGANDA IN THE ALLIES' FEATURE FILMS (1938–44)

Having reviewed in detail various examples of the content and nature of the feature films released during the Nazi era, it is interesting to compare and contrast this with the approach of two of the English-speaking Allies (Britain and the United States) and, in particular, in respect of films set during the war.

BACKGROUND

While Hitler may well have been impressed by the Allies' use of propaganda during the First World War, any advantage which the Allies may have once possessed was soon lost in the subsequent years.

Struggling with the impact of the Great Depression, the Allies strove to avoid another war, and there was certainly a marked reluctance by the Americans and, even to a large extent, by many of the British to do anything which would unduly upset the Nazis. Considerable support existed for Germany within the United States from those of German descent, and it was hard to argue effectively against the Nazi regime's internal policies given that Hitler had seemingly been so successful in revitalising Germany and in reducing unemployment. Nor did his regime seem to pose any direct threat to the United States. In Britain, many believed that Germany had been unfairly penalised by the Treaty of Versailles and, rather than risk another war, the British Prime Minister, Neville Chamberlain, was prepared to support a limited policy of appeasement, turning a blind eye to the Nazis' re-occupation of the Rhineland, annexation of Austria and invasion of Czechoslovakia. Indeed, the likes of Winston Churchill and his supporters were branded as war-mongers for highlighting uncomfortable truths about the real nature of Nazi Germany.

Anti-Nazi film propaganda in Britain

When it came to the medium of film, the British government did not exert any direct influence on subject matter in the 1930s, other than in accordance with normal censorship requirements. British feature films released before the war were primarily designed to provide entertainment, and any mention of Germany or political activity in mainland Europe was generally vague and devoid of malice. While the 1938 version of *The Lady Vanishes* hints at a secret world of political intrigue within central Europe, no specific mention is made of Germany's involvement. Even

Above: The unlikely secret agent in the form of the elderly Miss Froy (centre) in *The Lady Vanishes*. (*BFI/ITV Studios Global Entertainment*)

Right: The viewer cannot help but feel a certain sympathy for Conradt Veidt as the U-boat commander outwitted by British agents in *The Spy in Black*. (*BFI/ITV Studios Global Entertainment*)

The Lion Has Wings –
Britain's first Second World
War propaganda feature
film which was released on
3 November 1939, starring
Sir Ralph Richardson.
(*BFI/ITV Studios Global
Entertainment*)

the plot of *The Spy in Black*, which relates to a bold plan by the Germans to sink British ships in Scapa Flow during the First World War, and which was released in the UK in August 1939, may show the Germans as being passionate in their cause, but it also arouses the viewers' sympathy for the death of their commander when their mission fails.

Nevertheless, Britain was not entirely unprepared for a propaganda war. It had secretly been making arrangements for the launch of a government department responsible for handling the control of information and propaganda in the event of a war from as early as 1935, and consequently the Ministry of Information (MOI) was officially created on 4 September 1939, the very day after Britain had declared war on Germany.

Recognising the significance of the film industry for the promotion of 'the national cause', the MOI would suggest subjects which producers might wish to incorporate in their films, and would also advise on the suitability of ideas which the producers themselves were planning to develop. In the early years of the war, even feature films could be financed or directly sponsored by the MOI. Key themes were the justification for Britain being at war and the acceptance of the need for sacrifice.

The earliest Second World War propaganda feature film to be released by the British was *The Lion Has Wings*. It was produced by Alexander Korda, who had made a promise to Churchill that he would release a film within a month of war being declared, although it was not actually released until 3 November 1939. It is really a part-dramatised documentary explaining why Britain is at war, and then shows the RAF in action, both on bombing raids and in defence. The film is quick to distinguish between the freedom-loving British and the regimented order of Germany where Nazi philosophy crushes the role of the individual. Much of the film is pure propaganda, and whether cinema audiences really did believe that Britain had sufficient military resources to fend off its enemies and that fighter planes really could operate in the dark at that time is open to question. The dialogue is rather contrived, and the acting stilted and unconvincing, but the film was still a box office success.

Anti-Nazi film propaganda in the United States

Across the Atlantic, the origins of anti-Nazi propaganda in the cinema were far more complicated.

The United States did not formally enter the Second World War until after the attack on Pearl Harbor on 7 December 1941, and it was only in June 1942 that the United States Office of War Information (OWI) was established to oversee all government information services. Under its remit, the Bureau of Motion Pictures (BMP) was created to work pro-actively with Hollywood producers in the creation and completion of films which would 'help to win the war'.

In the 1930s, however, just as in Britain, there was a marked reluctance in the United States to do anything which might antagonise the Nazis, and this view was shared by the majority of the American film production companies. Recognising that foreign film sales represented as much as 50 per cent of their income, they could not run the risk of having their films banned from being screened across much of Europe by the Nazis. Consequently, they were disinclined to produce films with a particularly anti-Nazi stance and were supported in this approach by the then head of censorship, Joseph Breen, who was reported to have an anti-Jewish bias.

One notable exception was Warner Brothers, who produced a whole series of anti-fascist films in the 1930s. Having descended from a persecuted Jewish family who had emigrated from Poland to the United States in 1883, Harry and Jack Warner were committed to fighting against all aspects of fascism and anti-Semitism. Given that Hollywood's own censorship board, the Production Code Administration, prevented film companies from producing films that were hostile to foreign governments, Warner Brothers discovered that one way of circumventing this code was to make films which related to true incidents.

This allowed them to release the first anti-Nazi feature film, *Confessions of a Nazi Spy*, based on the capture and trial of a real Nazi spy-ring operating in the United States. Fearful that the screening of this film might well result in all American films being banned by the Nazis, the other American film companies did all in their power to have production halted, but Warner Brothers pressed ahead, and the film was eventually released in April 1939.

The film takes great pains to emphasise the dangers of a well-organised group of Nazi supporters active across America, working to secure the support of the millions of American Germans who believed in 'a German destiny for America'. Unsurprisingly, the film aroused a considerable amount of opposition both from within America itself and across the world. In the United States, a number of cinemas screening the film in cities with pro-German sympathies were actually attacked by angry citizens, while the German government filed official objections on the basis that the film was pernicious propaganda which poisoned relations between the United States and Germany. Predictably, it was not only banned from being screened in Germany and Italy, but also in Holland, Norway, Ireland, Switzerland and several Latin American countries.

While Warner Brothers continued to produce anti-fascist films, most of the films which pre-dated the United States' entry into the war produced by other companies were far more restrained in their direct criticism of Nazism.

Foreign Correspondent, released in the United States in August 1940, generally restricts its focus to events in London and Holland, but its closing bombing scenes were obviously designed to alert Americans to what was happening in Europe, with the warning that, unless they took the threat seriously, the same fate could befall the United States.

Even films such as *Saboteur*, released in April 1942 and more than four months after the United States was at war with Germany, still simply make oblique references to the evil threat of totalitarian nations. It is far more concerned with the notion of influential and opportunistic fifth columnists intent on destroying American infrastructure for personal gain. However, it was *Mrs Miniver*, supposedly set in England but filmed entirely in America with American actors and released in June 1942, which did more than any other film to win the sympathy and support of the American public for Britain's undesired war with Nazi Germany.

The attitude of American films towards the Nazis certainly hardened as the war progressed. Through the character of Rick, as played by Humphrey Bogart in *Casablanca* (November 1942), there is merely a gentle reinforcement to American viewers that they could not remain neutral and were justified in joining the battle against Nazi oppression. However, by the time Bogart appears as Lieutenant Rossi on convoy duty to the Soviet Union in *Action in the North Atlantic* (May 1943), all are agreed that the Nazis are evil murderers who delight in the death and destruction of their enemies, and the film concludes with a moving speech by President Roosevelt about there being nothing which will prevent the Allies' final victory.

General differences in the films being produced by the Nazis and the Allies

There are some basic differences in the style and content of the films produced by the Nazis and the Allies. Whereas the Nazis took complete control of all aspects of communication with their citizens as soon as they came to power, including the cinema, the Allies did not exert any obvious control over the sort of information being conveyed to their citizens until war had actually been declared.

For both sides, the bulk of films produced during the period were for entertainment purposes and shared common genres such as sentimental romances, detective thrillers and fantasy stories. Nevertheless, given the strict censorship rules introduced by the Nazis, no German film would be released with content that was likely to be contrary to Nazi ideology, and most German films would, therefore, serve some propaganda purpose, however obscure.

Likewise, although the Allies had no requirement to produce films to justify to their own nations why their respective forms of democratic government were in control, the Nazis' early years in power were dominated by a whole series of films designed to extol the virtues of Hitler and to emphasise the sacrifices which had been made in the struggle against the communists for the Nazis to come to power.

While the majority of the Nazis' more direct propagandistic feature films involved a reinterpretation of historical events to paint all their internal and external enemies in a poor light, the

Vivien Leigh and Laurence Olivier in *That Hamilton Woman*, where Nelson's romance is set against the background of Britain's war with the dictator Napoleon. (*BFI/ITV Studios Global Entertainment*)

Allies did not seek to use history to give a negative depiction of the Germans. The only slight comparison in respect of historical movies was seen in the likes of *That Hamilton Woman* or *The Young Mr Pitt*, which drew oblique parallels between Britain's previous confrontation with the dictator, Napoleon, and the current war with Hitler.

Against this general background, and by concentrating on films which were actually set in the war, a number of interesting trends do emerge concerning how each side approached common themes, and also the extent to which the themes and styles employed were to differ.

Treatment of common themes

Portrayal of the enemy

In their attempts to instil a real hatred for the enemy, it is quite remarkable how both sets of film-makers arrived at the same vile descriptions of their opponents.

The historic German films concentrated on Britain's imperial past, condemning the English/ British as being devious liars, cunning cheats and ruthless murderers as they strove to exploit other nations. Americans are shown to be lacking in compassion and driven by capitalist greed, and rather than being a virtue, democracy is blamed for weakening their country. Likewise, the Soviets are charged with being guilty of murder, senseless destruction and even rape.

However, while the Nazis' vile description of the enemy tends to be reserved for films set outside the war years, the Allies' description of the Nazis or fifth columnists in films is firmly set during the war or in the years leading up to the war. The Nazis are also charged with breaking promises, lying and cheating to achieve their ends, and given that the MOI was convinced of the need to emphasise the brutality of the Germans in their handling of occupied countries, it is little wonder that the Allied condemnation of the Nazis goes much further.

Insane fanatics

Time and again, the Nazis and their followers are portrayed as insane fanatics, driven by a senseless dedication to their cause. *49th Parallel* includes a quote from Göring: 'It doesn't matter if we have only one plane and one man left so long as victory is ours!' *The Day will Dawn* contains a comment from a journalist that Hitler had displayed a mad laugh when he invaded Austria, and even in *Mrs Miniver* the downed German pilot seems filled with fanatical and irrational hatred when he declares, 'We will annihilate you all!' However, the deepest disgust is reserved for fifth columnists whose fanaticism is invariably driven by megalomania or financial greed, as in *Confessions of a Nazi Spy* and *Saboteur*.

Cruel oppressors and ruthless murderers

The Nazis are invariably shown to be unnecessarily cruel and ruthless. This can range from the mere slapping of a boy in *Cottage to Let*, to children being killed through being forced to give blood transfusions for German soldiers in *The North Star*, to rape and the planned execution of hostages in *Edge of Darkness*.

Nor do they have any compunction about murdering unarmed opponents such as in the murder of priests in *Went the Day Well?* and *Edge of Darkness,* or the shooting of the Eskimos in *49th Parallel*, or the repeated strafing of sailors in a dingy during *In Which We Serve*. Even in *Went The Day Well?* there is the ultimate irony of one of the Germans disguised as a British soldier caught bullying a boy being described as 'no better than a German – that's what you are!'

Stereotyped representation

Apart from the emphasis of their more ruthless traits, several films are content to rely on orthodox perceptions of the Nazis. In *Night Train to Munich* and *The Silver Fleet*, the Nazis

49th Parallel exposes the ruthless fanaticism of the Nazis during their flight across Canada. (*BFI/ITV Studios Global Entertainment*)

are perceived as having little sense of humour, being snowed under with paperwork, wearing monocles and being full of their own importance. In *49th Parallel*, they are reduced to mindless thugs, responsible for the senseless destruction of modern art and books which do not conform to their ideology.

However, there is an occasional attempt to distinguish between Nazis and 'good' Germans, such as in *Freedom Radio* which follows the plight of an internal resistance movement against Hitler and whose leader declares, 'I believe your party is destroying this country like a cancer destroys one of my patients.' Likewise, in *49th Parallel*, the one German sailor who has turned against the ways of his Nazi colleagues is eventually executed by the others for treason.

Portrayal of the Allies

The British
When it comes to the British at war, Allied films give conflicting interpretations of the true character of the British. On the one hand, there is the image which the British had of themselves – the clichéd image shared by most of the rest of the world and which is most apparent in *Night Train to Munich*. Rex Harrison, disguised as a German officer, is shown to be cool, brave and resourceful and always keeps a stiff upper lip. There is a dogged determination to get the job done, and innocent civilians, here in the ubiquitous form of Charters and Caldicott with their charming cricket analogies, are just as willing to play their part when required. Likewise, in *One of Our Aircraft is Missing*, the elderly pilot who is shot as the RAF men make their

The Way Ahead demonstrates how a diverse group of reluctant civilians can be moulded into an effective fighting force. (BFI/ ITV Studios Global Entertainment)

daring escape by boat, typically downplays his wounds and continues to man the rudder until they are free from danger.

On the other hand, there are films which admit that this heroic image of the British character is rather overplayed. In *The Way Ahead*, it is recognised that most of the men called up for military service are thoroughly unenthusiastic about having to undertake the various training tasks which they have been set and would much rather not be at war. However, when it comes to the actual fighting, they are all shown to be just as brave, resourceful and committed as anyone could have expected in the fulfilment of their duty.

The Americans

The fighting American is always shown to be brave, resilient and determined to win through whatever the cost, but even before the United States' entry into the war, American civilians are shown to have no time for the Nazis when it is the fate of their own country which is at stake. 'When our basic liberty becomes threatened, we wake up!' and 'This ain't Europe … we'll soon show them!' are quotations from *Confessions of a Nazi Spy* and are typical American responses to fifth columnists operating in the United States. In *49th Parallel*, the American customs officials are only too willing to find an excuse to send the German officer back to Canada rather than allow him to seek refuge in the neutral United States.

However, once America had entered the war, their films are far more direct in their condemnation of everything related to Nazism. When the merchant ship is sunk in *Action in the North Atlantic*, the American sailors are quite outspoken in their abuse of the Nazi submarine which rams their lifeboat: 'I swear to God our time is coming … we'll pay you back!' and later it transpires that the son of one of the sailors is actually fighting with the RAF in England.

Other enemies of the Nazis

All the occupied nations are depicted as having large numbers of brave and imaginative Resistance fighters determined to find ways of outwitting the Nazis and regaining freedom for their respective countries, even if it means putting their own lives on the line.

The brave rebuke in *Edge of Darkness*: 'the individual must stand against you like a rock!' is typical of the contention that the Nazi occupiers will never succeed in converting the local populace to their way of thinking. Even fifth columnists frequently see the folly of their ways and often turn against their Nazi 'friends'.

Religion

In striving to win the hearts and minds of their respective cinema audiences, religion and, in particular, the appeal for justice to some divine Christian authority, are recurrent themes. Just as many of the Nazis' films, especially in their condemnation of the historical activities of Britain, gave the clear impression that God was on the side of Britain's victims, there is hardly a war film produced by the Allies during the war which fails to claim that God is, in fact, on the side of the Allies.

The use of religious devices can range from mere appeals to a divine authority to stand with the Allies, such as the church service on board the ship in *In Which We Serve* where the simple prayer is, 'Preserve us from the violence of the enemy', to the far more dramatic, if perhaps less convincing, events exemplified in *Edge of Darkness*. Here, the Norwegian priest, having just called on God for peace, is so incensed by the crimes of the Nazi occupiers that he picks up a machine-gun and shoots the German soldiers who are about to execute the leaders of the Norwegian Resistance in his village.

The most emotive speeches are uttered by priests or ministers and tend to carry more weight because they are speaking as God's representatives on earth. In the closing scenes to *Mrs Miniver*, the vicar's sermon incorporates a long justification as to why the British are fighting to defend freedom and concludes with the firm declaration:

With God's help – we cannot and shall not fail! ... This is the People's war – fight it and may God defend the right.

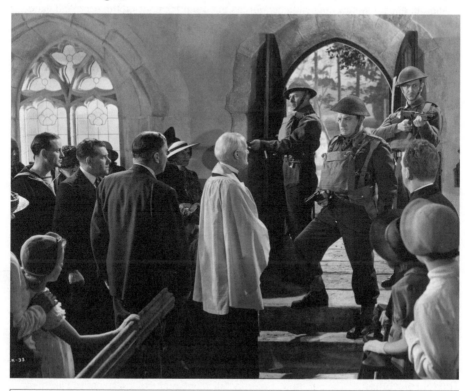

Disguised as British soldiers, the German paratroops are shown to have no qualms about desecrating the sanctity of the village church in *Went the day Well?* (*BFI/Canal + Image UK Limited*)

In *Went The Day Well?* the Nazis' disrespect for the church goes much further. Not only do the German paratroopers desecrate the sanctity of the church where the villagers are attending their Sunday morning service, but they murder the vicar in cold blood after he has uttered the following condemnation and then bravely attempted to ring the church bell:

> You ask me to bow down before the forces of evil – here in this house of God? I will take no orders from those who are the enemies and oppressors of mankind.

Indeed, the heinous murder of men of the cloth by the Nazis is a common occurrence in Allied films. In *Freedom Radio*, a German minister is shot in the pulpit of his very own church for daring to preach against the Nazis, while in *The Cross of Lorraine* (1943) a French priest is shot as he takes a memorial service for a fallen comrade in the knowledge that religious services in the prison camp have been forbidden. He dies having uttered the powerful lines:

> Let not the spirit of evil, which has made thieves, criminals and murderers disguise themselves as soldiers and judges, prevail in this world. Let us live in fear of no man but only in fear of Thee!

The impact of such poignant incidents is frequently enhanced by the accompaniment of the music from inspiring hymns such as 'For Those in Peril on the Sea', 'Onward Christian Soldiers' or 'Land of Hope and Glory'.

Another aspect is how each side condemns the other for abusing the trust and goodwill which people show to men of the cloth. In *49th Parallel*, the Canadians condemn the Nazis for sending a supposed missionary among the Eskimos, who had actually spent his time sketching detailed maps of Canada for the Nazis. (This has direct parallels with *Ohm Krüger* where the British missionaries are accused of handing out guns to the natives along with Bibles.) The bulk of the Nazis are shown to be totally irreligious, having no other 'God' other than their Führer and not even recognising the comfort which rosary beads could bring to a wounded Catholic civilian. The one Christian Nazi in the film is so inspired by the example of the Hutterites that he decides to stay, and he is eventually executed by his comrades for his lack of dedication to the Nazi cause.

While both sides incorporated religious themes and imagery in their films, there is little doubt that when it came to films actually set during the war, it was always going to be more difficult for the Nazis to justify invoking the assistance of God, since it was their soldiers who were on the offensive and the Nazis were already at odds with many churchmen at home and abroad. Conversely, it was for easier for the Allies to appeal to God against a cruel enemy who, in murdering innocent women and children, was intent on removing the freedom of not just Britain and France but the whole civilised world.

Consequently, rather than the inference that God is specifically pro-German, religious reference in Nazi films tends to focus on a condemnation of the unchristian actions of other nations or races, such as in the historical anti-British films or in the treatment of ethnic Germans by heathen-like Soviets or Poles. Indeed, German films set during the war hardly mention religion at all. Notable exceptions are the Polish prison monologue in *Heimkehr*, and *Wunschkonzert* in the dramatic scene where a German soldier is killed by an enemy bombardment while playing the church organ to guide his stricken colleagues through the fog to safety.

The role of women

While major female roles occur in both the films of the Allies and the Nazis, and invariably provide additional romantic interest, when it comes to films set in the war, there is a marked difference in what both sides expected of their respective womenfolk. All films recognise that women have to be supportive of spouses called up to fight, be ready to take over their daily work and even be prepared to suffer the loss of loved ones. Much is also made of ordinary women having to hide their true feelings and show an acceptance that, whatever the hardships and setbacks, life must go on. However, as will be seen from the following examples, it is really only the Allies that ultimately raise the profile of women to a quite different level in their feature films.

Role as civilians

In *Mrs Miniver*, not only is the primary heroine expected to show loving support for her husband and son caught up in the war, but she also manages to deal with an armed German pilot in a quite measured manner and succeeds in handing him over to the authorities. Her daughter-in-law's fatalistic attitude to her marriage to Mrs Miniver's pilot son, whose life is very much at risk, also serves as a shining example to all women:

> I know I may lose him ... he may be killed any day, any hour – if I must lose him, there will be time enough for tears.

The notion of the extreme sacrifices expected of civilian women is a common theme. In *Casablanca*, where the heroine is caught between her love of Rick and her feelings for her husband, she knows that her duty lies with her husband in his heroic resistance to the Nazis. In *Five Graves to Cairo*, the servant girl, Mouche, is prepared to sacrifice her own honour if the Germans will free her brother from captivity but, on realising that she has been cheated, she is tragically executed for continuing to assert that the British will return. Set in an internment camp for British women in France, *Two Thousand Women* tells the story of how the women, with little regard for their own safety, use their ingenuity, guile and female charms to conceal three downed

RAF pilots before arranging for their daring escape from the camp and their return home via the French Resistance.

The most graphic illustrations of the expectations of ordinary women in any British war film are to be found in *Went The Day Well?* When the public eventually revolt against the ruthless German paratroopers who have invaded their quiet, English village, the womenfolk are immediately drawn into the full horrors of war. First, the old shopkeeper throws pepper in the face of a German soldier and then bludgeons him to death with her axe, before being bayoneted herself by another soldier. Next, the minister's daughter, with single-minded determination, shoots down her fiancé who turns

No other British war film was to demand as much courage and determination from its womenfolk as *Went the day Well?* (BFI/ Canal + Image UK Limited)

out to be a fifth columnist and, finally, the lady of the manor unhesitatingly grabs a grenade thrown by the Germans, thus saving the lives of the children in her care, but tragically losing her own life in the process.

Role in the services

British feature films, in particular, contained plots specifically designed to highlight and praise the invaluable contribution which women were making to the war effort. In films such as *Millions Like Us* (1943) and *The Gentle Sex* (1943) they assume roles previously reserved for men, such as working in armaments factories or serving as truck drivers. Despite belonging to very different social backgrounds, the films emphasised the camaraderie which the women eventually experienced in these demanding roles – camaraderie which even helped them survive the sad news of loved ones killed in battle.

It was certainly a 'People's War' and great care was taken to acknowledge that life for women would change forever and for the better after the war:

> The world you are helping to shape is going to be a better world, because you are helping to shape it. (*The Gentle Sex*)

Role as spies

As if enduring the hardships of civilian life, enrolling in the services and working in the munitions factories were not sufficient, in Allied films women are repeatedly portrayed as operating as courageous government agents, saboteurs or Resistance leaders. In films like *Contraband*, *The Spy in Black*, *The Lady Vanishes*, *Yellow Canary*, *The Adventures of Tartu*, *The Day will Dawn* and *One of Our Aircraft is Missing*, women invariably put their lives at risk for their cause and occasionally do lose their lives in the process.

Ironically, the fact that the Germans might be confronted with so many female agents working against them is reinforced by the content of the bulk of German films, where, with only one or two exceptions, the female spies are almost invariably working against Germany, such as in *Achtung! Feind hört mit!* (*Beware! The Enemy is Listening!*) or *Die goldene Spinne*. For their part, the Allies are far more ready to accept that the Germans are just as capable of having dangerous female spies or agents in their service, as is apparent in films such as *Cottage to Let*, *Two Thousand Women* and *The Spy in Black*.

The Allies' films were far more ready to accept that the Germans could have female agents working for them. Among all the interned women in *Two Thousand Women*, the girl seated fifth from right is a German agent. (*BFI/ITV Studios Global Entertainment*)

The role of the armed services

Both Britain and Germany produced feature films with content which recognised the contribution of their respective armed forces to the war. Just as the Germans produced *U-Boote Westwärts!* (submarines), *Stukas* (air force) and *Wunschkonzert* (air force and infantry), the British took pride in such classic films as *In Which We Serve* (navy), *The Way Ahead* (army) and *One of our Aircraft is Missing* or *The First of the Few* (air force).

This is one of the few categories of films where the Nazis and Allies both produced films which were largely fictional, set in the war and designed to inspire both the servicemen themselves and the viewing public.

Similar to the Nazi films, the Allied films had many touching moments and provided many examples of self-sacrifice by servicemen and civilians alike. *In Which We Serve* has one particularly poignant moment when one sailor on learning that his wife has been killed in an air raid stoically remarks, 'I'll just go out on deck a bit'. The film concludes with a moving speech by the captain that despite losing their current ship, they will each take up the battle in other ships with an even stronger heart!

Spies and fifth columnists

One theme which occurs time and again in the feature films produced by both sides is that of spies, secret agents and fifth columnists. This topic allowed films to be made which were both entertaining and practical, in that they warned their respective citizens to be ever watchful for anything that might appear out of the ordinary and to distrust everyone. For example, who would ever have guessed that the downed RAF pilot played by John Mills in *Cottage to Let* would turn out to be a German spy? A noticeable contrast is that the German-produced films usually only feature foreign spies working against Germany, rather than vice versa, while the British and American films devote far more attention to the role played by Allied agents or Resistance groups working against the Germans.

Often the clandestine activity involves groups of agents working to convey valuable information back to their home country or undertaking general sabotage missions, and the precise details of the missions are not clarified. But where such information is detailed, it is interesting to compare the respective secrets each side is trying to obtain or the missions on which they are involved.

In *Contraband*, there are two sets of spies in a battle of wits against each other. The British agents are trying to secure the names of German merchant ships sailing under false neutral names, while the Germans are deliberately trying to feed false information to the British authorities, with the hope of engineering a diplomatic incident between the British and the Americans. In *Five Graves to Cairo*, the British soldier becomes an agent intent on discovering how Rommel is able to supply his advancing tanks as they cross North Africa. In *Freedom Radio*, disillusioned Germans are acting as fifth columnists in trying to undermine support for Hitler through their regular radio broadcasts. In *Night Train to Munich*, the British are trying to prevent a Czech scientist's armour plating secrets reaching the Germans. In *Sherlock Holmes and the Secret Weapon*, the aim is to prevent the Nazis acquiring the details of a new bombsight. In *The Adventures of Tartu*, the mission is to destroy the Nazis' poison gas plant. In *The Lady Vanishes*, the task is to convey details of a vital clause of a secret pact between two European countries back to London. In *The Silver Fleet*, the Dutch Resistance is working to prevent the Nazis acquiring two submarines which the Dutch have been forced to complete. *The Spy in Black* involves foiling a devious plot by the Germans intent on sinking Britain's fleet in Scapa Flow during the First World War. Likewise, Nazis are prevented from blowing up the ships in the port of Halifax, Canada in *Yellow Canary*.

Sir Ralph Richardson conspiring against the Nazis in *The Silver Fleet*. (*BFI/ITV Studios Global Entertainment*)

These wide-ranging activities seem rather impressive when compared with German-produced films, where the information which foreign spies are trying to obtain about German inventions is generally rather more mundane, such as the secret of a special wire for barrage balloons (*Achtung! Feind hört mit!*), secrets of a new tank (*Die goldene Spinne*) and a secret for improved petrol production (*Verräter*).

Morale-boosting speeches and patriotic imagery

Above all else, the war films produced by the Allies were designed to be morale-boosting, and this was often achieved through the insertion of a series of particularly inspiring speeches and musical or visual flourishes. While such devices were also employed in the Nazi films, and their patriotic lines and images could be very effective, there is no doubt that, even to an English speaker today, the key lines and final speeches included in a number of the Allied films seem particularly inspirational, largely because they were quoting from recognised speech-makers such as Churchill and Roosevelt.

Some of the most uplifting and moving speeches by individuals are contained in the following examples, although the full impact is only achieved when seen in their entirety and delivered by the original speaker:

Mrs Miniver – '*It is a war of the people, of all the people and it must be fought not only on the battlefield but in the cities and the villages, in the factories and on the farms, in the home and in the heart of every man, woman and child who loves freedom.*' (Henry Wilcoxon as the vicar)

The Silver Fleet – '*When our country is in danger, it does not count how big we are, what counts is to love our country and be brave – we must never give up!*' (Sir Ralph Richardson as Jaap van Leyden) (While this film was designed as inspiration for the Dutch, it is ironic how by the end of the war the Germans were making similar appeals to their own people in Kolberg.)

To Have and Have Not – '*That's the mistake the Germans always make with people they try to destroy. There will always be someone else!*' (Walter Szurovy as Paul de Bursac)

Here are some of the closing speeches and quotations from the Allies' war films:

Edge of Darkness – *'If there is anyone who still wonders why this war is being fought let him look to Norway. If there is anyone who has any delusions that this war could have been averted let him look to Norway. And if there is anyone who doubts the democratic will to win again I say let him look to Norway.' (President T. Roosevelt)*

Sherlock Holmes in Washington – *'In the days to come the British and American people will, for their own safety and the good of all, walk together in majesty, in justice and in peace.' (Sir Winston Churchill)*

Sherlock Holmes and the Voice of Terror – *'There is an east wind coming ... such a wind as never blew on England, yet it will be cold and bitter and a good many of us may wither before its blast. But it's God's own wind nonetheless and a greener, better, stronger land will lie in the sunshine when the storm has cleared.' (Basil Rathbone as Sherlock Holmes)*

Sherlock Holmes and the Secret Weapon – *'Things are looking up. This little island is still on the map'. – 'Yes – this fortress built by nature. This blessed plot, this earth, this realm – this England.' (Adapted from Shakespeare: Richard II)*

Foreign Correspondent – *'Death is coming to London. It's too late here ... as if the lights were all out everywhere except in America. Keep those lights burning there. Cover them with steel. Ring them with guns. Build a capacity of battleships and bombing planes around them. Hello Americans. Hang on to your lights. They are the only lights left in the world.' (Joel McCrea as Huntly Haverstock)*

Basil Rathbone as Holmes, Evelyn Ankers as Kitty, and Nigel Bruce as Watson working together to thwart the Nazis' invasion plans in *Sherlock Holmes and the Voice of Terror*. (BFI/Universal Pictures)

The endings of most war-related films produced by both sides were deliberately designed to inspire audiences and, in addition to rousing speeches, they were invariably treated to the proud sight of their national flags and the sound of rousing patriotic songs as they left their respective cinemas.

The First of the Few ends with a squadron of Spitfires flying victoriously into the heavens with bright rays of sunshine emerging from behind the clouds, and in The Cross of Lorraine, the suns shines out of the clouds as the villagers set fire to their own houses and take to the hills rather than collaborate with the enemy. Respectively, these each have direct echoes of the endings of Stukas as the squadron flies off joyfully towards England and Heimkehr where the ethnic Germans escape from Poland to the sun-filled Fatherland led by the Führer. The Way Ahead concludes with triumphant music as the soldiers march off determinedly into the smoke of battle – somewhat reminiscent of the endings of the early Nazi films such as Hans Westmar where fallen Nazi martyrs rise again to wave their flag in battle.

Nature of differing propagandistic themes and styles

Identification with oppressed nations

For the Nazis, the focus was on producing films which highlighted either the destructive nature of their internal enemies such as the Jews or the communists or the oppressive nature of their external enemies such as the British, Poles and Soviets.

In contrast, the Allies deliberately produced a large number of films which sought to identify with fellow nations fighting against Nazi oppression, such as The Cross of Lorraine, Tomorrow We Live, Casablanca (all pro-France), The Silver Fleet and One of our Aircraft is Missing (pro-Holland), Chetniks! The Fighting Guerillas and Undercover (pro-Yugoslavia), Edge of Darkness and The Day will Dawn (pro-Norway), The Adventures of Tartu (pro-Czechoslovakia) and The North Star (pro-Soviet). Even Freedom Radio aims to provide reassurance that there is organised resistance against Hitler from good people within Germany itself.

Such films were often made with the assistance of representatives of occupied governments living in Britain. While these films were never to be screened in the occupied countries to which they referred, they still provided inspiration to the citizens who had escaped from those countries and were fighting with the Allies, and were also good for raising morale in the cinema audiences in Britain and America.

Humour

Finally, one aspect which does distinguish Allied and, in particular, British films from the German films set during the war is the former's use of humour when the situation looks particularly unpromising. This does not mean that there is not humour in Nazi war films, but rather that it is rare for it to coincide with the most dramatic moments. For example, in Night Train to Munich, the cool exterior of our heroes and the frequent use of expressive cricket analogies such as 'bowling on a sticky wicket' or 'crooks don't play for the Gentlemen' all serve to lessen the perceived threat from the enemy.

The British tendency for understatement when the outlook is bleakest also serves to lessen the tension. In The Way Ahead, with buildings collapsing around them and the enemy's onslaught imminent, the officer is still able to joke, 'Breakfast may be a bit late this morning!' Such humour is not restricted to the British; when the merchant ship is 'running silent' to try to evade the Nazi submarine in Action in the North Atlantic, one American sailor whispers to another, 'I wish I was in Times Square … I'd catch the subway home!'

Even the German characters can be used for comic effect. In Night Train to Munich, having been reported for making unpatriotic remarks, a civilian tries to persuade a German officer that the phrase he had used had been misinterpreted. Rather than having sarcastically

In *The Way Ahead*, faced with the dangers and uncertainty of battle, the humour provided by the likes of Peter Ustinov and David Niven serves to lessen the tension. (*BFI/ITV Studios Global Entertainment*)

complained, 'This is a *fine* country to live in!' he claims that he had actually praised Germany with a positive emphasis on the word *'this'*. Less than convinced, the German officer later repeats both versions of the lines to himself and then whispers under his own breath, 'This is a bloody awful country to live in!' It is a sentiment which the Allies would have hoped was true for all non-Nazi supporting Germans.

However, whenever comedy is employed, the Germans are rarely depicted as fools. Even in the 1944 farce, *Bell Bottom George*, it is actually George Formby who plays the hapless idiot for most of the film rather than the German spies. The overall moral is that Germans represent a dangerous enemy who should not be underestimated even if they can be outwitted, and the Nazis do always come off second best by the conclusion of every film. An exception to this general rule is Charlie Chaplin's *The Great Dictator*, which was an extreme satire on Hitler and life in Nazi Germany, released in October 1940 before the United States was at war with Germany. Nevertheless, the film had a serious message, and Chaplin's final six-minute epic speech provides a remarkable vision of hope for a better world where everyone can live in harmony and peace irrespective of race or colour. Chaplin later admitted that if he had known the true state of conditions within Nazi Germany at the time, he would never have produced such a film, presumably because the satirical nature of the film made the Nazis seem less menacing.

CHAPTER X

NAZI DOCUMENTARIES (1933-45)

BACKGROUND

As in Britain and the United States, vast arrays of documentary and information films were produced by the Nazis, containing open or discrete propaganda material covering a wide range of subjects. Such films often complemented observations on similar topics found in the press, in posters, on the radio and even in full-length feature films. The precise content of these films was to alter as the priorities and objectives of the Nazis changed, especially after the war had commenced.

As it is impossible in a book of this size to provide a comprehensive summary of every type of documentary ever produced, the content of this chapter has had to disregard the role played by, for example, news reports and public information films and instead concentrate on a number of key documentaries which provide an overview of the types of propaganda material which were being created during this period.

Promotion of race and country

In their early years, the Nazis produced a number of seemingly innocent documentaries designed to arouse passion for the very soul of Germany. These included *Blut und Boden* (1933) and *Ewiger Wald* (1936), both of which might be best described as partially dramatised documentaries.

Against a background of increasing farm bankruptcies in the late 1920s and early 1930s, *Blut und Boden – Grundlagen zum neuen Reich* (*Blood and Soil – Foundations for the new Reich*) follows the plight of one poor family during the Weimar Republic who could not obtain state assistance to purchase a new threshing machine. In one of the narrator's many interjections away from the main plot, all German citizens are encouraged to help the farming sector by buying foodstuffs produced within Germany rather than purchasing foreign goods. Farmers themselves are discouraged from moving to the cities where all that awaits them is unemployment and squalid living conditions. Dramatic statistics are employed to demonstrate how urbanisation leads to the death of a nation, with Berlin's population forecast to reduce from 4 million in the 1930s to 90,000 by 2050. Nevertheless, the film concludes on a positive note

1933/34 poster encouraging the purchase of home-produced goods to reduce unemployment – 'Hitler is re-building. Help him. Buy German goods.' (*BArch, Plak 003-023-027/Nagel, G.*)

by featuring the construction of a new farm built under the Nazi regime and a seeming return to idyllic country life for everyone.

Ewiger Wald – Bedeutung der Natur im Dritten Reich (*Eternal Forest – Meaning of Nature in the Third Reich*) is a much longer film which begins with an atmospheric presentation of the forest as it changes through the seasons, and the narrator claims that the eternal fate of the forest and the German people are intertwined.

The film then transports the viewer on a dramatised journey through German history. The power of nature is shown to conspire to help the Germans defeat the Romans, and accounts are given of other enemies and challenges which followed. The wood from the forest is employed to build great churches and cities, and mention is made of the success of the Peasants' Revolt which arose because of the exploitation of the farmers. Equilibrium is eventually restored and, under Frederick the Great, new forests are planted line-on-line like ranks of soldiers. Throughout the film, defeat and despair are symbolised by the felling of trees and especially by the presentation of the outcome of the First World War where images of black, French soldiers are superimposed over shots of the destruction of lines of tall trees. Arising from the shame of defeat in that war, hope for Germany eventually emerges in the form of rows and rows of Nazi flags, a new summer forest and its Aryan soldiers and civilians gathered around maypoles. Both films are good examples of the Nazis' wider 'blood and soil' belief that all people of German blood should maintain the right to live on the land of their forefathers.

Promotion of Hitler and record of key events in the life of the Nazi Party and Germany

From his early days spent watching communist marches, Hitler had recognised the propaganda value of organising large gatherings of supporters. Not only did these gatherings serve to raise the morale of those very supporters through the comradeship and shared sense of purpose which such events engendered, but they also had an inspirational impact on watching crowds. Acknowledging the importance of the coverage of such events being conveyed to as large an audience as possible, Goebbels appreciated that the cinema provided just such an opportunity and, even more importantly, that the wide cinema screens would ensure that the dramatic scale of such events would not be lost on the viewing public.

Consequently, in 1933, Leni Riefenstahl was to make a film of the fifth Nazi Party Congress called *Der Sieg des Glaubens* (*The Victory of Faith*). While the film was a box office success, it was not an outstanding film, largely because it simply recorded what had occurred, warts and all. It was not rehearsed, and the actions of the participants were too spontaneous.

When Hitler is moving around the arena there is some confusion as to the direction in which he should proceed, with the result that the procession of officers behind him comes to an abrupt halt, and other soldiers almost fall over each other rather than cross Hitler's path. The scene is quite comical and hardly portrays an image of an omnipotent, infallible master race.

Riefenstahl learnt from these mistakes and eventually agreed to make a film of the 1934 Congress, which was subsequently released as *Triumph des Willens* (*Triumph of the Will*). The film is generally regarded as a far more impressive piece of propaganda, portraying Hitler in such

Illustrierter Film-Kurier film programme for *Triumph des Willens*. (Author's Collection/Verlag für Filmschriften)

Illustrierter Film-Kurier film programmes for *Olympia Fest der Völker* and *Olympia Fest der Schoenheit*. (*Author's Collection/Verlag für Filmschriften*)

a way as almost to give him divine status. This film is analysed in detail in this chapter along with another of Riefenstahl's master-pieces, *Olympia*, which documented the spectacular 1936 Olympic Games in Berlin. All these films could not have failed to leave any viewer lost in admiration for German organisation and commitment, and for the reawakened pride the German people had for their country. While such feature-length documentaries extolling the achievements of the Nazis were not unusual, German cinema audiences were normally subjected to much shorter films, such as the 1938 film, *Wort und Tat* (*Word and Deed*) which precisely details increased production levels and the success of the Nazis' various employment programmes, contrasting current living conditions with the uncertainty and decadence of the previous regime.

Military campaigns

Apart from regular newsreels about the war, the Nazis produced a number of feature-length documentaries designed to justify the reasons for the war and to emphasise the success of their military campaigns. The films were not always designed purely for internal consumption, and subtitled versions were frequently created in other languages for wider distribution, often with the deliberate intention of intimidating countries in their path into an early surrender rather than witness their countries razed to the ground by Germany's military might.

One of the longest and most successful of these documentaries was *Sieg im Westen* (*Victory in the West*) released in March 1941. The film is split into two parts and begins by giving a

fascinating insight into the reasons for the First World War. The film explains how Germany has always had to fight to defend its borders, and that it was England's fear that its world dominance was being threatened by the growth in Germany's army and navy which led to the outbreak of the First World War. Germany was victorious in that war on all fronts, and it was only England's enforced hunger blockade against women and children which forced Germany's surrender. The Versailles Treaty brought further misery to Germany, causing unemployment and inflation until Hitler emerged with new ideas for Germany's salvation. The outbreak of the

Illustrierter Film-Kurier film programme for *Feldzug in Polen*. (*Author's Collection/Verlag für Filmschriften*)

Illustrierter Film-Kurier film programme for *Der ewige Jude*. (Author's Collection/Verlag für Filmschriften)

Second World War is simply presented as Germany's justifiable right to regain lost territory, and its attack on French and English forces as a pre-emptive strike against a belligerent France and England who posed a continued threat to Germany's sovereignty. It is a version of history unrecognisable to any unbiased observer of the period.

The bulk of the film is devoted to a detailed analysis of Germany's military campaign against British forces, including Britain's disastrous defeat at Dunkirk. Notably, the film does not record how many British prisoners were taken or how many British soldiers escaped back to the UK. The rest of the two-hour film concentrates on the details of the defeat of France. While it is reported that the large French army did fight bravely, such an admission simply made victory seem all the more complete and creates a picture of the invincibility of the German fighting machine. It must have served as a sobering lesson to all who continued to resist German occupation, as well as proving a real morale booster for the German viewing public.

This film followed upon the success of *Feuertaufe* (*Baptism of Fire*) in April 1940, which documented the devastating effectiveness of the Luftwaffe in the campaign against Poland. As with *Sieg im Westen*, the early part of the film seeks to justify the war against Poland by explaining the threat posed by Poland's expansionist ambitions and highlighting the mistreatment of ethnic Germans within its borders. The film then gives a detailed description of the total destruction wrought by the Nazis' incessant aerial bombardment. This film was itself a sequel to the first major military documentary released by the Nazis in February 1940, called *Feldzug in Polen* (*Campaign in Poland*). The content of this film, which focuses on the army's contribution to the conflict, is analysed in detail in this chapter.

Documentaries to support internal policies towards Jews and other unwelcome minorities

This book has already examined a number of the anti-Jewish feature films produced by the Nazis, and this chapter now turns its attention to *Der ewige Jude* (*The eternal Jew*) which,

A film crew taking motion pictures at the Theresienstadt camp. (*US Holocaust Memorial Museum, courtesy of Ivan Vojtech Fric*)

despite its feature length, deliberately tries to deceive the viewer by appearing as a factual documentary. It is one of the most infamous anti-Jewish documentaries ever produced. However, with regard to their handling of the Jewish question, there is one other documentary, *Der Führer schenkt den Juden eine Stadt* (*The Führer gifts a city to the Jews*), which the Nazis authorised and deserves special attention, not least because it paints the Jews in a much better light and deliberately attempts to present a misleading account of the Nazis' treatment of the Jews in imprisonment. The film was eventually released to a limited audience in March 1945, and is examined in detail.

Euthanasia and sterilisation propaganda

Between 1935 and 1937, the Nazis' *Rassenpolitisches Amt* (Office for Racial Policy) was responsible for releasing six short films on the subject of mental illness, and the promotion of compulsory euthanasia and sterilisation to prevent the spread of hereditary diseases, with a law to this effect having actually been passed shortly after the Nazis came to power. However, it was only in late 1939, with the world distracted by the war and the urgent need for hospital space for military purposes, that their *Aktion T4* euthanasia programme actively swung into action.

The most well known of these films are *Das Erbe* (The Inheritance), *Erbkrank* (Hereditary Ill), *Opfer der Vergangenheit* (Victims of the Past) and *Alles Leben ist Kampf* (All life is a Struggle). These films tended to be screened in the cinemas between main features or to groups of Nazi supporters. *Alles Leben ist Kampf* uses the example of the animal world, where only the strongest and fittest survive, to try to justify the compulsory extermination of those members of the human race suffering from mental or physical illness.

Portrayal of Germany's external enemies

The character assassination of Germany's external enemies was certainly not restricted to the feature film and, once at war, documentaries became quite common. *Soldaten von Morgen* (*Soldiers of Tomorrow*) was an eighteen-minute anti-British film produced in 1941, which compares the decadence of the lazy, intoxicated, public school-educated English boys against the healthy, clean-living German youths whose sporting activities are deliberately designed to give them the training they need to turn them into effective soldiers. These parallels are shown to be reflected in their elders, and particular care is taken to mock the fat, alcohol-dependent Churchill as a stereotypical plutocrat. *Gentlemen* was another 1941 film

which cast both the British political leaders and ordinary soldiers in a poor light. The British concept of 'playing fair' is seen as no more than empty words designed to conceal Britain's true aggressive tendencies. Its armed forces are shown to be little better than brutal thugs in firebombing civilian houses and causing the deaths of 1,250 French sailors in their unprovoked attack on the French fleet at Oran following France's capitulation.

The late entry of the United States into the war also provided a propaganda target for the Nazis, although this was primarily against its leaders and the capitalist way

The concepts of American freedom and democracy as symbolised by the Statue of Liberty are continually derided in *Rund um die Freiheitsstatue*. (*Library of Congress*)

of life, rather than the ordinary man in the street. Produced in 1943 from actual American newsreel, *Herr Roosevelt Plaudert* (*Mr Roosevelt chats*) is a typical example which contrasts Roosevelt's claims about the success of the American way of life, with numerous examples of the ranks of the unemployed, decaying machinery and shanty towns, and where strikers are fiercely attacked by the police and army. It highlights the vast differences which exist in the United States between the rich and the poor, and the influence of the Jewish-dominated Stock Exchange, which can manipulate the price of cotton in a matter of seconds for monetary gain. The film concludes with a threatening image of Roosevelt poised over a globe which he is eagerly carving up with his knife and fork.

Similar films were produced to provide a negative image of life in the Soviet Union. As an accompaniment to an anti-Soviet exhibition held in Berlin, the Nazis produced a short film in 1942 called *Das Sowjetparadies* (*The Soviet Paradise*). There is a general condemnation of Stalin for the godless state which the Soviets have created. Churches are shown to have been converted into vodka factories and power stations. The peasants live in poverty and in fear of being tortured and killed by the Soviet Secret Police, and there are harrowing images of starving children lying unattended in hospitals. In contrast to this oppressive regime, the advancing Germans are seen as saviours and, to illustrate this point, one farm woman is shown holding her crucifix to bless the German soldiers, presumably arriving to save her from the horrors of Stalin's Bolshevik state.

The film chosen to be analysed for its portrayal of Germany's external enemies is *Rund um die Freiheitsstatue* (*Around the Statue of Liberty*), which also condemns Roosevelt for his persistent criticism of Germany when the United States itself was hardly a picture of idyllic bliss.

Hitler stands in the lead car as his motorcade passes through the cheering crowds of Nürnberg. (*Deutsches Filminstitut/Transit Film GmbH*)

Film title: *Triumph des Willens*
Year of release: 1935
Type: Documentary
Primary purpose: Pro-Nazi propaganda
Director: Leni Riefenstahl

INTRODUCTION

Triumph des Willens (*Triumph of the Will*), one of the most famous propaganda documentaries ever produced, is a film about the sixth Nazi Party Congress held in Nürnberg in September 1934. It records the key moments of the congress, ranging from Hitler's triumphant arrival in the city to the impressive daily assemblies held in the Luitpold Arena, and through to the final procession and Hitler's valedictory speech.

As a piece of pro-Nazi propaganda, it is widely regarded as a true work of art for which the director, Leni Riefenstahl, was going to receive many plaudits from within Germany at the time, but stern criticism from a wider world audience for the rest of her life. The film is still banned from being screened in Germany today.

FILM CONTENT

First day

The film opens with Hitler's aeroplane descending through the clouds and flying over the old city of Nürnberg before arriving at the airport. A huge crowd is waiting in anticipation and cheers wildly as his impressive motorcade crosses the Nazi and Imperial flag- bedecked city to the Hotel Deutscher Hof.

Hitler appears briefly on the balcony before the picture slowly fades away to a spectacular evening rally accompanied by marching music, torches and banners, with the swastika being displayed proudly throughout. As there is no added commentary, the viewer is not always sure exactly what is happening, but there is a definite feeling that something meaningful and significant is taking place.

Second day

The mood changes as dawn breaks on another sunny day, and the crowds line the streets again as Hitler's motorcade winds its way through the city towards the Luitpold Arena. The scene soon switches to a huge tented village where the hundreds of thousands of participants who are going to contribute to the day's proceedings are seen washing, eating and generally enjoying themselves. Meanwhile, Hitler meets townsfolk of all ages, dressed in their national costumes. Folk music gradually gives way to more victorious, military music, and tension mounts as people wait for Hitler to speak. Instead, the film fades into darkness again and moves to the Luitpold Hall where Rudolf Hess opens the congress with a short speech extolling the virtues of Hitler.

Official representatives from Japan and Italy are introduced, and a whole host of party members and dignitaries then stand to speak in turn, with two or three key propaganda lines from each of their speeches being included in the film such as:

Sepp Dietrich (No. 2 in the SS) – 'Truth is the foundation on which the power of the press stands and falls. To tell the truth about Germany is our only demand of the press, including the foreign press.'

Fritz Todt (Inspector General for Roadways) – 'The Reich has begun motorway construction in fifty-one places ... 52,000 men are employed on construction ... and a further 100,000 are employed in supplying material.'

Julius Streicher (Gauleiter for Franconia) – 'A people which does not uphold the purity of its race will perish.'

The final speaker, Konstantin Hierl, concludes with the words, 'The German people are now ready for the introduction of the general requirement to work ... We await the Führer's orders.' But still nothing is heard from Hitler at this event.

The action then moves to the huge outdoor arena where Hitler finally speaks; he addresses the Labour Service workers who recite a common oath of loyalty, and then selected representatives from all over Germany shout out their names and home towns. Hitler acts and speaks impressively throughout, although his comment that, 'No one will live in Germany without working for our country' is both exciting and frightening.

Third day

The third day begins with the Hitler Youth parading in the arena, playing their musical instruments and beating their drums. Hitler praises the youth for all they have achieved but warns, 'You must be peace-loving and courageous at the same time.' There then follows a short military tattoo as soldiers charge around on horses and in small, armoured vehicles.

That evening, there is an even more impressive rally with thousands of torch and flag-bearing participants marching towards a colonnaded platform where Hitler gives a further speech. The background is somewhat reminiscent of the Brandenburg Gate, but surmounted by a huge figure of an eagle on a swastika which dominates the whole scene.

Fourth day

The fourth day begins with hundreds of thousands of soldiers lined up in rectangular squares in the huge stadium. In the middle of the ranked masses, three tiny figures – Hitler,

Hitler, Himmler and Lutze saluting the memory of their fallen comrades in the Luitpold Arena. They are surrounded by lines of SA and SS troops. (*BArch, Bild 102-16196/Pahl, G.*)

Himmler (leader of the SS) and Lutze (the new leader of the SA following the murder of the previous SA leaders in 'the night of the long knives') – are seen slowly marching towards the Ehrenhalle (1929 war memorial) accompanied by slow Wagnerian music. It is a very formal occasion where all fall silent as Hitler and his two colleagues give a formal salute to the fallen.

Then, the tone changes to the sound of triumphant trumpets, and hundreds of standard bearers take their places on the esplanade, waiting for another speech from Hitler. The Führer moves among the standard bearers, touching their new party flags with the 'blood banner' (supposedly carried by supporters who died in the Beer Hall Putsch before the Nazis came to power). There is a gentle rendition of *'Die Fahne hoch'* (the Horst Wessel song) in the background with a cannon salute.

A long portion of the film is then devoted to the impressive final massive march through the centre of Nürnberg.

The film closes with a final speech from Hitler, who reminds his audience of the successes of the Nazi Party in the short period since it has come to power. He explains that it is his wish that all Germans will become National Socialists and, as for party members, that he is looking for them to be even more determined and solid in the time ahead.

CRITICAL REVIEW

In principle, *Triumph des Willens* is only a simple documentary about the Nazi Party's sixth annual congress meeting in Nürnberg. In reality, the congress meeting itself is a cleverly stage-managed event, designed to impress participants and spectators alike and to leave everyone full of admiration for Hitler and everything for which the Nazis stand. Leni Riefenstahl's greatest achievement is in using the art of the film-maker to take what was already a propaganda-filled event and to heighten the propaganda impact by making the event appear even more awe-inspiring.

The two greatest themes of the congress are power and unity. These are repeated time and again, both by means of the excerpts which Riefenstahl chooses to feature, and by the way in which Hitler and the Nazis are portrayed.

Portrayal of the Führer

Given that the common aim of the congress and the film is to depict Hitler as a powerful and unifying leader, how is this achieved?

First, the film demonstrates how he is loved by all his people – civilians and military personnel alike. From the opening scenes, great cheering crowds of ordinary men, women and children are witnessed waving enthusiastically from the streets or open windows, having waited for hours in excited anticipation of the arrival of this apparent 'Messiah'.

Second, before Hitler even has a chance to speak, the other party leaders are quick to sing his praises. Hess is like a warm-up act in a music hall, paving the way for the great leader. He cries out, 'You are Germany ... You are a guarantor of peace. *Sieg Heil*!' There is enthusiastic applause between each of his short, sharp statements of approval.

Third, when Hitler does speak, he does so with the apparent authority of a true leader. Unlike those who have preceded him, Hitler does not read from notes and makes great use of his arms and hands in repeating short, key messages – something which he mentions in *Mein Kampf* as being essential for eliciting a successful response from an audience:

> All effective propaganda must be confined to a few bare essentials ... and slogans should be repeated persistently.

To a modern audience, Hitler might appear to rant and rave, but this is all for emphasis, and the viewer is certainly left with the clear impression that here is a man who knows exactly what he wants for Germany; there is no middle ground.

Hitler's speeches make several references to unity, such as in addressing the Labour Service workers when he declares that, 'Work will no longer be a dividing concept, but something that *unites* us all.' In his words to the Hitler Youth, he stresses that, 'We want to be *one* people ... we want to see no more class divisions!' And in his address to the SA and SS men, he emphasises that after the problems that had confronted them, 'They are now standing *together* for a new Germany.'

Fourth, this image of a powerful, unifying authority is reinforced by his portrayal as a god-like father, caring for his people. This is achieved from the very first scenes as Hitler descends like a god to address his creation, and this religious theme is reinforced by other comments in the film, such as at a night rally where he declares that, 'We cannot be disloyal to what has given us sense and purpose ... This order was not given to us by an earthly superior, *but by God*, who created our people.' Similarly, in his final speech he talks of the party being like a religious order, and his very embrace or the shaking of his hand seems to have added significance as if his touch contains some divine power.

Portrayal of the Nazi machine

Apart from providing an inspiring presentation of Hitler, the congress deliberately seeks to impress the viewer with everything that is shown about the Nazi Party. There is a constant reinforcement of the symbols of Nazi power, ranging from the stylish uniforms of the soldiers to the banner and flag swastikas, to huge German eagle sculptures. The scale and number of

The seemingly endless procession of troops through Nürnberg was designed to be an awe-inspiring sight. (*BArch, Bild 183-2004-0312-503*)

such icons is truly impressive: where there are swastika-covered flags and banners, these are hung from every conceivable building and lamp post, and are bigger and more numerous than is imaginable. Where there is a symbol of an eagle astride a swastika, then this has to be the largest conceivable statue of an eagle. Given the eagle, banners and a background of classical columns, easy parallels can be drawn with the might of the Roman Empire.

The monumentality of the assemblies and processions is also truly astounding. The Luitpold Arena could hold around 150,000 people in neat blocks, and Hitler actually mentions a figure of 200,000 taking part in the proceedings. Likewise, the street procession on the final day through Nürnberg must have lasted for hours, with the soldiers marching twelve deep and their columns extending as far as the eye could see. The truth is that it was impossible for the casual observer to calculate just how many people were involved and one can only admire the logistical co-ordination and order in staging such a show without any apparent flaw.

Cinematographic devices employed to intensify dramatic effect

While the very nature and agenda of the congress was to achieve maximum propaganda impact through its concentration on the themes of power and unity, there is no doubt that Riefenstahl adopts a number of clever cinematographic devices to intensify the reactions which it seeks to engender, thereby almost creating fiction out of fact.

Use of music

Although some of the film does simply employ the live music which accompanies certain scenes, such as well-known marching songs during processions or the slow-moving music which accompanies Hitler's long walk to the war memorial, there are other occasions when appropriate background music is deliberately added to the film's soundtrack to intensify the atmosphere of the scene. So, on the one hand, there is moving classical music in the form of Wagner's '*Die Meistersänger von Nürnberg*' fading into a peaceful rendition of '*Die Fahne hoch!*' as Hitler's plane appears out of the clouds and descends slowly across Nürnberg. This helps make him appear even more like a god descending from heaven to visit his people. On the other hand, there is heroic music as Hitler meets the townsfolk, with fast, exciting music reserved for the displays by the cavalry and armoured vehicles. This changes to a more martial-style of music, with trumpets and drums, when Hitler meets the military. The musical accompaniment is carefully chosen to meet specific circumstances and is all the more important when there is no verbal commentary about what is being witnessed; the music dictates how the viewer should react. Riefenstahl had been an important silent movie actress in her day and was more alert than many to the impact of music, which guides the viewer when to laugh or cry.

Use and camera locations

Likewise, Riefenstahl deliberately employs aerial shots, clever camera angles and tele-photo lenses to maximise impact.

Hitler is often viewed from below as if the audience is looking up to a god, or the camera is placed above and behind him as if he is a god looking down on his people. He is made to look larger than life. At one of the evening rallies, the camera concentrates on the tops of the sea of Nazi banners, rather than the soldiers who are carrying them, giving the impression that the party and its symbols of power are more important than the individual party members.

Cameras are often also placed in high locations, such as at the far end of the main arena, to emphasise the huge numbers of people present in the stadium. Likewise, in the final procession through the city, high viewing angles are used so that the viewer cannot fail to be impressed by the scale of the marching columns which seem to stretch for miles.

Variety of the presentation and the building of tension

Given that the film lasts for 114 minutes, there is a real danger that the presentation of the congress could have been rather tedious, but this is certainly not the case with this film.

The very opening credits serve to draw the viewer's attention to the fact that this congress is a momentous event, by highlighting in separate slogans that the congress is 'taking place 20 years after the outbreak of war … 16 years after the start of German suffering … and 19 months after the start of Germany's rebirth!' Appropriate solemn or joyful music accompanies each of these slogans.

The viewer's attention is retained by the speed and variety of the content of the film, and there are no long, boring speeches. In a typical day, actions move swiftly from preparations for the big event to the actions of individual spectators or participants, some key slogans, marches and then an evening presentation. It is like a great variety show where the programme is still being planned.

There is a deliberate heightening of tension as the viewer is repeatedly made to wait for Hitler to speak. So, when Hitler does give his first speech, thirty-five minutes into the film, the viewer is impatient to be impressed and is certainly not disappointed.

Riefenstahl also seeks to make the viewer feel part of the proceedings by concentrating on the human aspects to the film. Much of the film dwells on the happy, inquisitive, emotion-packed faces of civilians and soldiers. When touring the streets or meeting civilians, Hitler is shown to be warm, welcoming and smiling. When he meets the military, he takes time to speak to them and to look people square in the eyes. In short, Riefenstahl is very successful in translating to a cinema audience the enthusiastic feelings of those personally involved in different aspects of the event.

Given that much of the film is so carefully crafted, it is surprising that there are still a number of occasions when everything does not quite proceed as planned. For example, during the morning drive through Nürnberg, there is a moment where the camera is caught between the low sun and the scene it is filming, so that the image of the camera and cameraman is clearly visible on the buildings in the background. Also, there is a speech where a member of the audience stands up and blocks the camera's view as he moves along the row. Given that these scenes could easily have been removed in the editing process, it would seem they have been deliberately retained to make the overall film appear more authentic and less contrived.

Indeed, Hitler's final speech almost acknowledges that the world will conclude that the whole proceedings have been stage-managed. He is keen to stress that although 200,000 people have been brought together for the occasion, they have only come out of a sense of loyalty: 'Other countries who have not suffered cannot understand what brings us together ... it is not a state order. It is not the state which commands us, but we who command the state.'

POINTS OF NOTE CONCERNING THE DIRECTOR AND RECEPTION OF THE FILM

How did Leni Riefenstahl come to direct this film?

Born in 1902, Riefenstahl was a successful silent movie actress, often appearing in films set in mountainous and rugged locations before directing her first movie, *Das blaue Licht* (*The Blue Light*), in 1932. Impressed by *Mein Kampf* and Hitler's appeal as a public speaker, she entered into regular correspondence with Hitler and, as he was also taken by her, it is perhaps not surprising that Hitler eventually approached her to make a film for him of the 1933 Party Congress. Inexperienced in such film-making, she only reluctantly agreed after Hitler explained that he wanted the film to be directed by someone who was not politically aware and who would concentrate on what was most artistically pleasing in terms of the spectacle itself. While the resultant film, *Der Sieg des Glaubens* (*The Victory of Faith*), was a box office success, it had been prepared at short notice in the face of constant squabbles between Nazi Party officials, and also suffered from the fact that one of the main characters featured in the film, Ernst Röhm, the then leader of the SA, was to be executed shortly afterwards. All known copies of the film were then ordered to be destroyed.

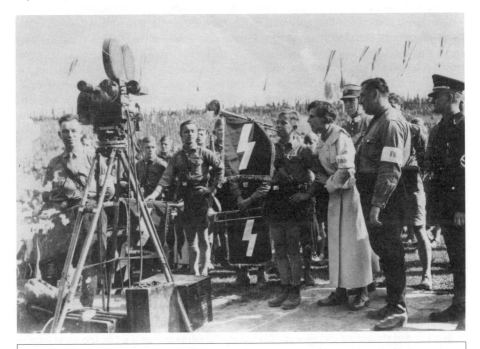

Leni Riefenstahl directing the boy leading the fanfare as to how he should stand before the camera. (*BArch, Bild 183-R80430*)

Despite these setbacks, she again reluctantly agreed to make *Triumph des Willens* of the 1934 Congress for Hitler. Hitler was so pleased with this work that Riefenstahl was also commissioned to direct *Olympia*, also analysed in this chapter.

Although she engaged in little direct film work for the Nazis during the war itself, she continued to work on a non-political film called *Tiefland*, which was to cause her a lot of embarrassment after the war. Apparently, a number of gypsies were forced to work as unpaid extras in the film, and several were sent to Auschwitz concentration camp once filming was complete. Given her apparently close relationship with Hitler, Goebbels and the Nazi hierarchy, Riefenstahl was to continue to be haunted by her Nazi associations long after the war, leading to much of her work being banned and to difficulties in securing funding. As late as 2002, when she was a hundred years old, she was taken to court as part of an investigation into her apparent denial of the Holocaust.

There is ample evidence from interviews, letters and telegrams issued by Riefenstahl during the Nazi period that she was a great admirer of Hitler as a person. Indeed, she told a reporter in 1937, 'Hitler is the greatest man who ever lived. He is truly without fault, so simple and at the same time possessed of masculine strength.'

Until her last breath, she was to contend that she had been a naïve supporter of National Socialism and had never been aware of the atrocities which were being committed. It is certainly true that for at least the first five years during which the Nazis were in power, most Germans were captivated by Hitler, as he provided employment, hope and a reawakened national pride. It is quite plausible that Riefenstahl was swept along in this tide of enthusiasm. However, given that she personally witnessed the murder of civilians in Poland by German soldiers in 1939, and sent an enthusiastic congratulatory telegram to Hitler when he arrived in triumph in Paris in 1940, it is more difficult to accept her later claims of innocence when it is evident that she had become fully aware of at least some of the terrible consequences of Nazism.

She is, however, still widely regarded as the most influential female film director of the twentieth century. She died in her home in Germany on 8 September 2003.

How successful was *Triumph des Willens*?

Given that there was much more time to prepare for this film than for the 1933 Party Congress, and having a much larger budget, with no fewer than 172 crew, including thirty-six cameramen and thirty cameras involved in its production, it is perhaps no surprise that *Triumph des Willens* was a huge box office success in Germany.

However, while the film was to be awarded the German Film Prize, a Gold Medal at the 1935 Venice Film Festival and the Grand Prix at the 1937 World Exhibition, it was widely criticised by many countries for glorifying Nazism, and the film was banned from being screened in most of America.

Was the film a successful piece of propaganda?

The film was certainly very popular with German audiences and continued to be screened until 1945. Riefenstahl herself would deny that there was any deliberate attempt on her part to create pro-Nazi propaganda:

> If it were propaganda, as many say, there would be a commentator to explain the significance and value of the occasion. This was not the case!' (Interview from the film The Wonderful Horrible Life of Leni Riefenstahl, released in 1993)

This very comment, however, betrays an acknowledgement that this is how the film was interpreted by the rest of the world, and Susan Sontag, the New York columnist, had no qualms in declaring, '*Triumph des Willens* is the most successful, most purely propagandist film ever made, whose very conception negates the possibility of the film-maker having an aesthetic or visual conception independent of propaganda.'

Whatever the truth, it would certainly have been difficult for anyone with such fascination with Hitler to have done anything other than create a film depicting Hitler and all that he stood for in the most favourable manner.

CONCLUSION

No one can deny that the chief purpose of the sixth annual Nazi Party Congress was to create an impressive visual occasion which would serve to unite and inspire the faithful, and win more converts to the fascist cause, both from within Germany and the wider world.

The scale of the 1934 Congress was certainly awesome and Riefenstahl not only captured the essence of the occasion in *Triumph des Willens*, but also managed, deliberately or otherwise, to exaggerate many of the propaganda elements and maximise the impact of the event on a much wider audience. In terms of technical skill, it was undoubtedly a work of art and really only failed to achieve everlasting universal acclaim because of the negative associations of the subject it was depicting. It certainly inspired wonder and pride in most Germans at the time, but left much of the world fearful as to where Hitler would lead his people.

Ironically, with such an open display of Nazi strength, even in terms of organisation and the number of soldiers involved, it should have served as an early warning of the potential danger of further military rearmament in Germany, and the rest of the world should have prepared and responded accordingly.

Film title: *Olympia*
Year of release:
  1938
Type: Documentary
Primary purpose:
  Oblique pro-Nazi
  propaganda
Director: Leni
  Riefenstahl

INTRODUCTION

Released in German in April 1938, *Olympia* was a two-part film commissioned by the Olympic Committee to document the 1936 Summer Olympic Games in Berlin. It was the first such film of the Olympics, and was produced and directed by Leni Riefenstahl with the aid of German state-funding. Although *Olympia* received wide critical acclaim in many countries at the time as an innovative work of cinematic art, the film has always suffered from being associated with Riefenstahl, because of her close relationship with Hitler and her involvement in such earlier propaganda-laden films as *Triumph des Willens*.

It would be harsh to class this film in the same category as *Triumph des Willens* because, despite several scenes featuring Hitler and the Nazi elite, the content of the film is actually a fairly accurate representation of what occurred at the Berlin Olympics, and there is little attempt to conceal those scenes which are less than flattering to Nazi ideology and Aryan supremacy.

FILM CONTENT

Divided into two parts, several versions of *Olympia* were produced with an added commentary in German, French or English; each version being slightly different in content. The following analysis is based on the content of the English version:

The Film of the XI Olympic Games
Berlin 1936
To the Honour and Glory of the Youth of the World

The first film, *Fest der Völker* (*Festival of the People*) is just under two hours in length. To the accompaniment of appropriately atmospheric music, it begins by taking the viewer on a fascinating, mystical journey through time. The action moves majestically from the ruins of Greek civilisation and classical athletes performing physical exercises, right through to the Olympic torch being carried by runners across Europe to the great Olympic Stadium in Berlin.

Following the lighting of the Olympic Flame in the stadium's huge cauldron, there is an impressive opening ceremony where the nations participating in the event march around the stadium behind their respective national flags. The film continues by highlighting the key moments of each of the competitions, beginning with the men's discus and concluding with the marathon. The final winners for each event are shown, often to the accompaniment of the winner's national anthem.

The second film, *Fest der Schönheit* (*Festival of Beauty*), is around ninety minutes in length. It opens with athletes training in their countryside bases, and there is an impressive display of what appears to be thousands of young men and women performing gymnastic exercises outside the giant arena, all with synchronised precision. The film continues by reviewing all the other competitions, the bulk of which, such as sailing, boxing, shooting, swimming, cross-country riding and football all take place outside the main arena. Wherever possible, this film tends to dwell on the beauty of human motion, with strength and skill combined in artistic union. The film has a dramatic conclusion as the flags are lowered and the Olympic Flame is gradually extinguished with the smoke merging into the clouds and the glorious evening sunlight above the arena.

CRITICAL REVIEW

Artistic merit

With no such film of the Olympics ever having been previously produced, Riefenstahl certainly succeeded in creating a thoroughly entrancing and exciting documentary about the

The impressive spectacle of endless rows of athletes performing gymnastic exercises in unison outside the Olympic Stadium in Fest der Schönheit. (*Deutsches Filminstitut/IOC*)

1936 Olympics. This was achieved only through a good deal of rehearsal in the months preceding the Olympics and, even during the Games, the film-makers were to receive constant criticism from the organisers for inconveniencing both the competitors and the spectators.

The initial twenty-minute introduction with evocative music and no voice-over makes it appear as if the viewer is drifting back through the mists of time to early Greek civilisation and the ruined temples and statues of the Parthenon, and it paints a vivid picture of the roots of the modern Olympics. The transformation of the statue of a man throwing a discus into a real figure, followed by the appearance of other figures with a spear and shot put, and then three naked female figures dissolving into fire is truly mesmerising, even if a little too long a sequence for the modern viewer.

Employing a number of technical innovations the film was very adventurous for its time, and Riefenstahl, already a well-known actress, was even to play the part of the main female figure exercising elegantly before the camera.

Special effects with graphic representational images are employed to illustrate the progress of the torch through Bulgaria, Yugoslavia, Hungary, Austria and Czechoslovakia towards the present day, and to the crowd-filled stadium in Berlin where a huge bell, emblazoned with a German eagle, is ringing out to the youth of the world to attend the Games.

The coverage of the individual events is concise and objective, with cameras carefully positioned to reflect the nature of different competitions. Whenever possible, the camera is located very near to the action, so that the viewer can appreciate the extent of the challenge which faces the competitors, and share in the emotion with close-ups of the athletes' faces and of the reactions of the crowd, including Hitler and his entourage. Much of the close detail in the stadium was achieved by placing one of the cameras on rails alongside the running track. In the marathon, there is real drama as the race draws to a finale with very dramatic music and shots of the shadows of the runners serving to increase the tension and emphasise the physical effort which is required of the competitors.

Effectiveness as a work of propaganda

Unlike *Triumph des Willens*, which was undeniably produced with a number of specific propaganda objectives in mind, *Olympia* is far less obvious as a vehicle of Nazi propaganda.

Contrary to popular belief the film does not actually conceal the victories of black athletes such as Jesse Owens. (*Deutsches Filminstitut/IOC*)

Undoubtedly, the viewer cannot fail to be impressed by the scale of the arena, the huge numbers of participants and the organisational skills required for the Games to be run so efficiently. It was a massive triumph for the Nazis that they could be seen to undertake this task so effectively, broadcast the event live on television within Germany and, ultimately, produce a film of the event which could be viewed by the whole world. It is only fitting, and presumably deliberate, that the first words spoken in any language in the film are those of the uniformed Adolf Hitler, as he formally declares the opening of the Eleventh Olympiad.

Most of the film, however, is purely dedicated to the provision of an objective report of what actually happened at the Games, rather than any attempt to inspire awe or fear for the Nazi regime behind the organisation of the Games, or indeed to concentrate on the prowess of the German competitors alone. Admittedly, many of those appearing on the winners' podium are Germans, but just as many are not, and the national anthems of other countries are given equal prominence to that of the German anthem. Indeed, there are occasions when the viewer is shown events which must have been truly embarrassing for the Nazis. A good example is the women's 400 metres relay; the German team seems set to win easily, but then their penultimate runner drops the baton at the final change-over. It shows that even Nazi-trained athletes are human and just as prone to make mistakes as anyone else. Likewise, the 8-1 defeat to India in the hockey match must have been discomforting. This is hardly the performance of an omnipotent race and, if the Nazis had so desired, such scenes could easily have been omitted from the final film.

It has often been said that Hitler was apoplectic with anger when Jesse Owens and other black American athletes won events, given that Hitler had always expounded the superiority of the Aryan race. While this may well be true, and there is no doubt that disappointment is etched on Hitler's face each time a German athlete is defeated, the film, or at least the English version of the film, does not try to conceal the victory of the black athletes. Indeed, it almost goes to the opposite extreme. A great deal of time is spent talking about Owens both during the 100 metres and the long-jump events, all of which is very complimentary and almost raises *him* to god-like status. Likewise, in the final of the 800 metres, much mention is made of the giant American 'Negroes' as favourite to win. There is no underlying criticism of their appearance or of their training methods. Even if the German version of the film does make more racist reference to some competitions being a battle between black and white runners, it still does not conceal the eventual result of those races.

The swastika emblem was clearly visible on the vests of the German competitors. (*Deutsches Filminstitut/IOC*)

In practice, if the film had really been intended to glorify the Nazi regime, then it could have gone much further by, for example, bestrewing the stadium and any other events with huge swastika flags, and Goebbels and Göring could have appeared in uniform rather than in their non-threatening civilian dress. Riefenstahl could have concentrated on those events where German competitors were victorious and made negative comments about the others.

In reality, in 1936, the Nazis were still not ready for war and, while they were keen to prove that Nazi Germany could successfully organise an event like the Olympics, their primary aim was to persuade the rest of the world that their intentions were honourable and, consequently, any doctoring of the events and the presentation of overt Nazi symbolism had to be kept to a minimum.

Other points of interest from an historical perspective

When the film is viewed with the knowledge that the Second World War was going to begin within three years, it contains a good number of incongruous and paradoxical occurrences.

At the opening ceremony, doves are released as a sign of peace, but to the sound of cannon fire. Similarly, most of the German competitors appear in suits of white, another symbol of peace, and yet they are led by a number of officers in their striking Nazi uniforms.

When the competing nations march past Hitler's box during the opening ceremony, it is interesting that the German, Austrian and Italian competitors give a Nazi salute as they pass, while the Americans and British do not. While this was perhaps predictable, what is more surprising is that the French and Greeks also appear to give a Nazi salute, which is a rather interesting political decision given what was to follow. However, some confusion may have arisen because the official Olympic salute could easily be mistaken for a Hitler salute, and perhaps this served as a convenient coincidence for some countries.

Nevertheless, there is no doubt as to who is in power in Germany. The vests of the German competitors all carry a small swastika emblem. As for the officers in uniform who take part in the initial opening procession, we can only assume from later coverage that it is these same soldiers who will participate in such events as the pentathlon, where specific shooting and riding skills are as important as physical fitness – skills which were soon to be employed for far less peaceful ends.

How was the film received?

While the film was classified by the Propaganda Ministry as being 'politically and artistically especially worthy', Goebbels was deeply frustrated that it took almost two years for the film to be completed. It was screened to Hitler on the occasion of his 49th birthday on 20 April 1938, before being premiered in

Cameras were situated in the most unlikely of locations to capture the actions and emotions of the competitors. (*Deutsches Filminstitut/IOC*)

Riefenstahl's attention to detail made the film of the 1936 Olympics a true work of art. (*BArch, Bild 146-1988-106-29*)

nineteen European capitals where, other than in Britain, it was generally very well received. It was to win a number of prestigious awards including the German Film Prize for 1937/1938 and the Mussolini Cup as best foreign film at the 1938 Venice Film Festival.

Its reception in English-speaking countries was less favourable, and opinion divided as to the true worth of the film, especially given its glorification of the physical body, a concept closely identified with Nazi ideology. Riefenstahl was not helped by the fact that the premiere in New York in November 1938 occurred only three days prior to *Kristallnacht*, when Jewish synagogues and shops were destroyed in Germany, and many Jews arrested and sent to concentration camps. This resulted in the Anti-Nazi League organising a boycott of the film in the States.

CONCLUSION

Whatever its underlying propaganda value to the Nazis, *Olympia* was a remarkable film in terms of the use of innovative cinematic techniques. It brought alive the whole wonder and excitement of the Olympic Games to a world audience, and it deserves to be honoured for that achievement alone.

It was probably inevitable that the evils of the Nazis blinded several commentators to the fact that the admiration of physical prowess had been promoted by the ancient civilisations long before the Nazis ever adopted the concept for their own ends, and that the intrinsic worth of the film as a work of art should not be dismissed simply because it was produced by a sympathetic Nazi director in 1936. While the film might have engendered a feeling of pride among Germans and admiration among other nationalities for an assured Nazi-led country which was able to stage such a dazzling Olympic Games, *Olympia* does not hide the fact that German Aryan athletes were conquerable. The film was certainly not as blatantly propagandistic in structure and content as it could have been, and does generally reflect an accurate record of the proceedings.

Time is a great healer and has certainly been more forgiving to Riefenstahl. The film's technical merits were to be highly praised by the British press at the time of Riefenstahl's death in 2003, and *Time Magazine* declared the film to be 'one of the 100 best films of all time' in 2005.

Film title: *Feldzug in Polen*
Year of release: 1940
Type: Documentary
Primary purpose: Pro-Nazi and anti-Polish propaganda
Director: Fritz Hippler

INTRODUCTION

Feldzug in Polen (*Campaign in Poland*) is a seventy-minute propaganda documentary, first released in Germany in February 1940, which explains the reasons for Germany's declaration of war on Poland and highlights key aspects of the campaign. It was directed by Fritz Hippler, a loyal Nazi supporter, who ran the film department in the Propaganda Ministry until March 1943. While the original film contained a commentary in German, several foreign language versions were also produced for wider distribution, including a shortened thirty-three-minute version in English. Banned by the Control Commission at the end of the war because of its objectionable commentary, both versions of the film are now widely available from specialist retailers and can be viewed on the Internet.

This review concentrates on the content of the English version and also hypothesises as to why certain items have been omitted from the original German version.

FILM CONTENT

To the accompaniment of classical music, the film begins with impressive scenes of the medieval architecture of the city of Danzig, and the narrator explains how, as far back as the times of the Knights Templar, the city had been a German stronghold against the east. It is then reported how German sections of the city have been ruthlessly persecuted by the Poles, who have been closing their schools and seizing their possessions. Pictures are shown of civilians of all ages, often in tears, forced to flee from Polish terror and seeking protection in German refugee camps.

The narrator continues to explain how repeated attempts by Hitler to find an acceptable solution, including the construction of a highway to reconnect East Prussia with the rest of Germany, and the return of Danzig to the German Reich, had been rejected. As a result, he claims that as Poland had been massing its forces on Germany's eastern border and continuing provocation against ethnic Germans, Hitler had no alternative other than to 'fight force with force' and launch an attack on Poland on 1 September 1939.

Much of the remainder of the film shows Germany's motorised units, cavalry brigades, air force and artillery in action. Danzig is soon 'liberated' from the Poles, and there is an exciting action scene viewed from a camera attached to a Stuka bomber as it attacks a railroad junction. Mention is made of the fact that the German air force was in complete control within a few days, with 800 Polish planes destroyed or captured. There is also praise for the endurance and efficiency of the German infantry divisions which had to march for up to 37 miles a day.

Scenes are shown of Polish murderers being confronted by eyewitnesses, and special mention is made of one Polish officer who is accused of having tortured wounded German soldiers in a most bestial manner.

By 13 September, a ring was closing round the final remnants of the Polish army and, by 21 September, 170,000 prisoners, 320 heavy guns and forty tanks had been captured. There are numerous scenes of the utter destruction of land and property, and thousands of rifles and helmets discarded on the ground. Finally, with all offers by the Germans to save the civilian population of Warsaw having been rejected, the narrator explains how the Germans were forced to bombard the city for several days before its eventual surrender on 27 September.

The film concludes with columns of German soldiers marching past Hitler in triumphant celebration through the streets of Warsaw and, from the perspective of any non-German, a final chilling comment from the narrator:

Germany ought to feel safe under the protection of such an army!

CRITICAL REVIEW

Apart from the full-length film being screened in German cinemas and on television, the film was also released to the governments of Denmark and Romania shortly after Germany's campaign in Poland had concluded, partly as a warning to those governments as to what was likely to happen to their countries if they did not capitulate.

A shortened version with narration in English was produced at the same time. The English accent is impeccable, and the film gives the impression of being an objective documentary. The English version seems to have been designed to achieve a number of different propaganda objectives, some of which are certainly at odds with the reaction which was desired from a German audience.

The primary aim of the shortened film is to justify Germany's attack on Poland. Given Germany's reported reluctance to go to war, the second purpose is to stress how Germany is conducting the war in a most measured and gentlemanly manner. Finally, the film seeks to impress the viewer with the strength and efficiency of the German military machine, albeit in a 'defensive' capacity.

Justification for attack on Poland

From the earliest scenes, the film stresses how Danzig had always been German and even looked German in appearance, and there is an implied criticism that the Treaty of Versailles should ever have handed the port and the corridor of land south of it to Poland. The film certainly aims to arouse the sympathy of the viewer for the ethnic German population when it is reported how their property and belongings have been seized by the Poles, and lines of innocent civilians are shown weeping as they are forced to flee the country.

Against such provocation, Germany is portrayed as having displayed considerable restraint. In their negotiations with the Poles regarding a possible solution, there is frequent use of the words 'offered' or 'suggested' rather than 'demanded' or 'forced'. For example, Hitler is reported as having 'suggested' that Danzig should be incorporated back into the German Reich and, in return, the Poles would be given free access to the port, a twenty-five-year non-aggression pact could be signed and the Germans would acknowledge the existing German–Polish borders as legitimate:

Acceptance would have no doubt brought peace and order to Germany's eastern border.

The whole commentary sounds so reasonable and beguiling.

There is a condemnation of Britain and France for trying to persuade the Soviet Union to side with them and almost a note of triumph that the Germans had actually succeeded in signing a non-aggression pact with the Soviet Union themselves, much to the dismay of the Western powers.

Scenes are shown of burning buildings and against a background of dramatic music, the comment is made that Polish gangs are systematically attacking the German population and tearing down their homes. Germany's sole aim is to bring the days of terror for ethnic Germans to an end. If the treatment of Germans in Poland were not sufficient reason to start a war, then the final straw is the revelation that, behind the scenes, the Poles are reported to have expansionist aims and are talking of the pending destruction of the German army.

Germany's conduct in the war

Having given the impression that Germany was always reluctant to start the war, but was 'obliged' to do so to protect both its people and its own borders, it was important for the Nazis to show that their conduct in the war itself was morally impeccable.

As a result, the narrator stresses that it is the Poles who have been destroying the roads, bridges and general infrastructure to delay the German advance and that it is the Germans who are trying to repair such damage. While it is mentioned that the German air force was soon in complete control, it is emphasised that attacks on non-military objects were carefully avoided,[7] and it is explained that most houses and farms in the path of the advancing Germans have actually been destroyed by the Poles themselves. It is also reported that wherever there are ethnic Germans, the German troops receive a hearty welcome.

Responding to criticism that the Germans had destroyed the famous painting of the Black Madonna of the Bright Mount in the town of Czestochowa, the narrator is keen to demonstrate that such claims are lies by revealing the painting of the Madonna undamaged and even showing German soldiers leaving a service in the church.[8]

If the German soldiers always conduct themselves in a most dignified manner, then this is in strict contrast to the fearful Poles who are reported to have been murdering German civilians and torturing wounded German soldiers by gouging out their eyes (a level of detail curiously omitted from the English version). The defeated Polish soldiers are depicted as cowards, apparently emerging from hiding in cellars dressed in civilian clothes.

The film is also keen to counter any criticism of the German attack on Warsaw by stressing how the Germans had done all in their power to avoid civilian casualties:

---

7   In reality, the German army did little to avoid civilian casualties with frequent bombings of Polish cities.
8   Notwithstanding these claims, it is recorded that, on 4 September 1939, large numbers of the town's civilians, including 150 Jews, were shot by the Germans.

Hitler was prepared to stand for hours saluting the columns of victorious German soldiers. (*BArch, Bild 183-S55480*)

With a view to sparing the population of Warsaw the misery and hardship of siege, the German High Command demanded they should capitulate in 12 hours. When the demand remained unanswered they made another suggestion that at least the civilians should be allowed to escape, but this offer too remained unanswered.

Therefore, the implication is that the responsibility for all the damage and civilian casualties in the city lies with the Poles themselves.

Invincibility of German army

While the Germans may have been unwilling to fight, it is felt necessary to impress the viewer with the quality of their organisation, the scale and variety of weapons and their fighting prowess, presumably with the aim of intimidating other nations which might try to stand in their way. Such was Hitler's pride in the army's achievements that he was prepared to stand and salute the passing columns of troops for hours on end.

To what extent is this documentary a piece of propaganda?

In any film where there are lines of weeping civilians or buildings on fire, the viewer has no way of telling who the victims really are, where the event is taking place or who is responsible for the damage being done. Furthermore, in this film, the commentary often goes far beyond what is even being shown, and the viewer is simply asked to accept without question that everything reported by the narrator is absolutely true.

On the face of it, much of what is reported appears perfectly plausible and might even be true but, with the benefit of hindsight, the modern viewer has to be more sceptical, since it is now known that the film does not tell the whole story and that at least some of the script and film had been deliberately manipulated to evoke certain responses from the viewer. Such propaganda techniques are even more evident in this film, as it is possible to compare the differences between the German and English versions.

Modern historians generally agree that any attacks on the ethnic German population were far less frequent than suggested, and there is firm evidence that the Nazis deliberately manufactured a number of incidents as the outbreak of war drew near, including the infamous Gleiwitz incident where Germans wore Polish uniforms and inmates from Dachau concentration camp were used as the corpses of German and Polish soldiers.

The film makes no mention of the fact that Germany's invasion of Poland was instantly condemned by most of the world and that it led to Britain and France declaring war on Germany. Likewise, the film conceals the fact that Von Ribbentrop's non-aggression pact with the Soviet Union included an understanding that the Soviets would simultaneously invade Poland. Protecting one's own people was one thing, but entering another country with the aim of conquering that country and dividing it with a neighbour is quite a different story from the version of events provided in this film.

Finally, the film gives the impression that the German army was invincible and that the Poles surrendered without much of a fight, despite possessing large numbers of modern war machines. In reality, most of Poland's aeroplanes were old-fashioned and their fighters far slower than their German counterparts. The Poles also had far fewer armoured vehicles, relying on the mobility of cavalry brigades. The Poles did have some minor successes, but their defence strategy was based on early assistance from the French and the British; the unexpected simultaneous attack from the Soviet Union made all their plans unworkable, and the swift defeat of the Polish army was inevitable.

Notable omissions from the English version

The English version of the film is half the length of the original German version. In many instances, the longer version simply shows more archive footage of the German military in action, but a number of other items have obviously been deliberately removed so as not to cause undue offence or alarm to an English-speaking audience.

First, there is a deletion of scenes showing Britain and France actively preparing for war and the omission of a joke about Churchill's claiming that England would fight on against Germany to the last Pole, and then to the last Frenchman. Indeed, all reference to imperialist Britain and France being at war with Germany, or of Germany having forces on its western front is removed, so that the English version can concentrate on Germany's seemingly justifiable frustration with the Poles.

Second, the English version removes the more exaggerated claims as to the size and losses of the Polish army in terms of men and equipment. For example, the German version claims that the Poles had 1,000 planes ready for action when, in reality, they had only around 600 modern aircraft, and many of these were not mobilised in time. While it was presumably acceptable to emphasise or exaggerate the extent of the victory to its own people, it was felt inappropriate to create too much antagonism towards the West when, after all, Germany was meant only to be defending its people and had further expansionist aims.

Third, all reference to the Soviet Union attacking Poland from the east and the division of Poland between the two powers is presumably removed because the film did not want to give the impression that the campaign was pre-planned and was prompted by any other reason than the protection of ethnic Germans.

However, the most telling difference is in the conclusion. While the English version stresses that Germany should feel safe under the protection of its army, i.e. its role is defensive, the

German version emphasises the strength of the German army which will guarantee 'final victory', i.e. its role is far more aggressive. The German version concludes with a large swastika embedded in a map inscribed as Great Germany, incorporating Poland and beyond, and there is a final rendition of the German national anthem which had been banned by the Treaty of Versailles.

CONCLUSION

Feldzug in Polen is a very interesting piece of documentary propaganda which served a number of purposes. For German viewers, it helped reinforce the reasons for Germany's attack on Poland, portrayed the Poles as unworthy and murderous opponents, instilled joy in the viewer at the liberation of their terrorised German kinsfolk in Poland, and generated pride in the efficiency of their armed forces. For the rest of the world and particularly for English-speaking viewers, the shortened film also sought to justify the attack on Poland as being a 'mercy' mission designed to put an end to the oppression of the ethnic German population in Poland, while at the same time demonstrating that, although Germany had an army capable of defending itself, it would always conduct itself in an honourable fashion.

It is interesting that both versions of the film lose track of reality and ignore or exaggerate certain aspects, creating a convenient blurring of the divide between fact and fiction. These were skills which the same director, Fritz Hippler, was soon to put to even more devastating effect in his production of the infamous anti-Jewish film, *Der ewige Jude.*

Film Ttitle: *Der ewige Jude*
Year of release: 1940
Type: Documentary
Primary Purpose: Anti-Semitic propaganda
Director: Fritz Hippler
Narrator: Harry Giese

INTRODUCTION

Der ewige Jude (*The eternal, or wandering, Jew*) is one of the most disturbing and venomous anti-Semitic propaganda films produced by the Nazis. This hour-long production was also
directed by the infamous Fritz Hippler, fresh from his production of *Feldzug in Polen*. The idea
for this film had actually been conceived as early as October 1939, largely as a response
to Hitler's criticism that German films 'had not dared to attack the Jewish Bolsheviks' but,
because of repeated amendments, it was not finally released until November 1940.

Through a series of archive film footage, historical and statistical presentations and extracts
from foreign feature films, *Der ewige Jude* gives the impression of being a factual documentary, but it evokes such feelings of disgust and repugnance that it is designed to leave the
viewer very negatively disposed towards the Jews.

The film is still banned from public screening in Germany, other than for formal educational
purposes.

FILM CONTENT

To the accompaniment of sombre music, akin to something from a horror film, *Der ewige Jude*
opens with pictures of Jews on the narrow streets of the Polish ghettos. The narrator explains
how these shots 'show us the Jews as they really look, before they hide themselves behind the
mask of civilised Europeans'. The viewer is told that although Jews have been in business for
decades and have sufficient money to live in better properties, they choose to live in dark, filthy
properties with bugs and insects crawling all over the walls. The scenes are truly disgusting.

Furthermore, it is explained that the Jews will rarely indulge in any useful work such as farming or physical labour, and are really only in their element when they are 'buying' or 'selling'.

Indeed, it is claimed that the Jewish religion makes cheating and usury a duty. The reporter claims to quote from the fifth Book of Moses, 'You can lend to a non-Jew upon usury but not thy brother, that the Lord might bless them in all their dealings!'

The commentary suddenly becomes even more vitriolic, 'Where the body of a nation shows a wound – the Jews anchor themselves and feed on the decaying organism and they make business out of the sickness of nations.'

It is asserted that, from time immemorial, the wandering Jew has always been a 'free-loader' and that the Jews in Poland are no different from those in Palestine. Their homelessness has been a matter of choice and, for 4,000 years, they have moved from land to land mercilessly looting culturally superior inhabitants. A map appears which shows how the Jews gradually spread first into Egypt then into the Promised Land, along North Africa and through the countries of Europe back into Russia, and then across the whole world; it is explained that everywhere they went, they were unwelcome immigrants.

The Jews are described as parasites and are compared to rats carrying disease, plague, dysentery, cholera, leprosy and typhoid, and this image is reinforced by a series of hideous scenes of hordes of rats scurrying in and out among bags of corn. These are certainly very disturbing images. At times, the commentary seems deliberately ambiguous, so that the viewer is uncertain as to whether subsequent comments refer to rats or Jews, especially when it talks about them being cunning, cowardly and cruel. However, all doubt is removed with the final comment, 'They represent subterranean destruction among animals just as the Jews do among mankind.'

The 'racial assassination' continues with the stark statement that Jews are responsible for a large part of international crime, and some very alarming statistics are quoted from the crime figures for 1932 to support this allegation. Whereas Jews represent only 1 per cent of the world's population, they are reported to account for 34 per cent of drug dealing, 47 per cent of robberies, 47 per cent of crooked games of chance, 82 per cent of criminal organisations and 98 per cent of dealings in prostitution.

There is then a return to one of the common themes of the film, that when the Jew leaves his Polish haunt to exploit the rest of the world, he hides his true appearance by removing his

beard, hair, skull cap and caftan, so that only sharp-eyed people can identify his true racial origin. To illustrate the claim, the producer has employed a number of Jews who are first filmed in their natural state, and then these images are overlaid with pictures of the same people with their hair cut and wearing suits.

The attack is brought even closer to home with the warning that second and third generation Jews in Berlin, and even those who have interbred with non-Jews, might give the impression of acting like the 'host' race, but that it is all an act, and that the true

Example of what is described as grotesque Jewish art. (BFI/DFG)

Hitler was to deliver his infamous anti-Jewish speech at the sitting of the Reichstag on 30 January 1939. (*BArch, Bild 183-2005-0623-500*)

German must guard against being deceived by such appearances. Members of the Rothschild family are specifically detailed as examples of the aristocratic class who fall into this category. This reference is then used as an excuse to show excerpts of an early English-language film with German subtitles, produced by American Jews, about the history of the Rothschild family. The action opens in the middle of a scene where a rich Jew, on being warned that the tax collector is approaching, rushes to hide his silver and his roast meat, and feigns poverty by pulling on torn clothes, having his wife occupied with her sewing and the children made to look hungry, all to avoid paying taxes.

Ironically, the tax collector is not so easily duped and it is not revealed how that scene concludes. Instead, the action jumps to another scene where the head of the Rothschild family, apparently on his death bed, is explaining to his five sons the power they can wield by acting together, and commands them to establish banks in Paris, London, Naples, Vienna and Frankfurt. Nations will entrust gold to them in time of war, and it is this reliance on the Jews which will enable the Jews to wield great international influence over their host nations.

The narrator continues by explaining how, by the beginning of the twentieth century, the power of the Jews had so increased that they were able to terrorise world opinion and politics. Apart from naming specific Jewish families such as the Warburgs and the Oppenheimers, the film proceeds to name influential Jews in New York with a number of seemingly libellous descriptions of those individuals.

With a return to the Home Front, the film reminds the viewer how the Jews had behaved when the German nation lay helpless in November 1918. When it came to the elections to the National Assembly, some Jews had promised 'castles in the sky' while others had incited the masses to rebel against civil order. The narrator condemns the Jewish influence over the press and publishing houses in Germany, and lists Jews who hold important positions in such institutions as the foreign ministry, finance and the police.

Like a lecture, more dramatic charts are produced to illustrate how, despite the fact they only accounted for 1 per cent of the population, the Jews held a disproportionate share of influential posts in Berlin in 1933:

For every 100 state prosecutors	15 were Jews
For every 100 judges	23 were Jews
For every 100 lawyers	49 were Jews
For every 100 doctors	52 were Jews
For every 100 merchants	60 were Jews

Furthermore, although the average German's annual income was only 810 Reichsmarks, the average Jewish income was 10,000 Reichsmarks and, while Germans became unemployed, the Jews became wealthier through a combination of usury, swindling and fraud. Also, apart from reference to the Jews' destructive influence in business and state affairs, the viewer is then warned that the Jews are really at their most dangerous when allowed to meddle with culture and religion.

The viewer is presented with a number of grotesque artworks by Jewish artists and sculptors which are described as 'the fantasy of sick minds' and, given that Jewish actors are reported to have a penchant for cross-dressing and performing in controversial stage and film productions, this section reaches the conclusion that 'the Jew is instinctively interested in everything abnormal and depraved!'

Finally, the film focuses on the nature of the religious practices of the Jews. It declares that religious painters through the ages have deliberately altered the appearance of Jews to make non-Jews more benevolently disposed towards them and their religion. The viewer is also warned that, both in the schools and the synagogues, Jews do not receive *religious* education from peaceful theologians, as the Rabbis are, in fact, *political* educators. One striking example is said to lie in the five lessons which Canaan taught his sons, namely, 'Love one another, love pillage, love excess, hate your master and never tell the truth.'

This is one of the more measured images in the film as most of the Jews are shown to be unkempt, with long hair, beards and wearing ragged clothes. (*BFI/DFG*)

Historic film footage of a service inside a synagogue is used to illustrate how the Jewish religion is full of strange, ambiguous symbols and an incomprehensible language. Conducting financial business during a service is certainly not seen as disrespectful, and it is even claimed that he who teaches the Torah will succeed in business. Furthermore, the Torah is claimed to reveal God's anger towards non-Jews and how only the sons of Israel are the righteous.

The final denigration of their 'so-called' religion is detailed in how the Jews slaughter animals because Jews are not allowed to drink blood. The viewer is warned, 'Sensitive people are recommended not to watch the following pictures', and there is no doubt that the ensuing pictures are truly graphic and very distressing.

It is reported how Judaism demands that animals to be used as food have to be allowed to bleed to death while conscious rather than killed with one blow. Various cows and sheep are displayed having their throats cut, and the panic and suffering of the animals as they slowly die is clearly visible.

It does look barbaric, and the narrator explains proudly how, despite condemnation from the Jewish press for interfering with time-honoured religious customs, on 21 April 1933 Hitler passed a law forbidding such practices so that all warm-blooded animals had to be given an anaesthetic before slaughter. Consequently, 'Jewish thinking and Jewish blood will never again pollute the German nation ... under the leadership of Adolf Hitler Germany has raised the battle flag against the eternal Jew.'

The film concludes with an impassioned speech delivered by Hitler to the Great German Reichstag on 30 January 1939:

> There is plenty of living space in the world but the notion that the Jewish people were chosen by God to live off the productivity of other people will finally have to go. Jews will just have to get accustomed to the idea of undertaking some respectable constructive activity like other people or sooner or later they'll face undreamt of trouble. But if the Jews involved in international finance, inside and outside Europe, succeed in pushing people into another war, the result will not be a victory of Jewry but the destruction of the Jewish race in Europe.

Not surprisingly the speech is greeted with great applause from Hitler's supporters, and the tone of the film changes dramatically, with stirring music and archive footage of handsome Aryan men and women in uniform marching purposefully in step into the future.

The film is particularly critical of Jewish religious practices, including their chanting and the reading of laws written on scrolls. (US Holocaust Memorial Museum/ Owen, E.)

CRITICAL REVIEW

Masquerading as a factual documentary, *Der ewige Jude* is actually well produced, and, unlike a number of other rather disjointed propaganda documentaries, this film is compulsive viewing, even if there are several scenes which are likely to cause offence.

Taking us on a journey from their nomadic Middle Eastern origins to their influence in the world and in German affairs in the 1930s, the film is devoted to a complete character assassination of the Jewish race, and the director's aim is to alienate the German viewer from the Jews by emphasising the differences between Jews and non-Jews.

Basis of anti-Jewish assault

There are five key areas where the film is highly critical of the Jews:

Appearance

Whereas in 1914 we [the Germans] just thought that the Jews had a comical or grotesque appearance we now realise that they represent a plague.

Jews are consistently shown to be rather unkempt in appearance, with long hair, beards and wearing ragged, dark clothes. Many of the innocent souls who pose for the camera do seem to be mentally ill.

Character

The Jew is the demon behind the corruption of mankind – Richard Wagner

The film portrays the Jews as lazy parasites who live off their neighbours rather than contributing or producing anything worthwhile themselves. There is a graphic comparison of Jews and rats, which have always carried disease across the world. Furthermore, the excerpts from films about the Rothschilds and Polish Jews depict the Jewish race as being mean, cunning and vengeful, and responsible for virtually all world crime.

Business Practices

For the Jew only one thing is of value ... money. How he gets it makes no difference!

In business, they are shown to be deceitful and usurious, and are condemned for wielding far too much influence relative to their proportionate population in the world. There is an implied criticism that Jews profited from the Stock Market crash in the 1930s and that they were the cause of civil disorder when Germany was in difficult times after the First World War.

Contribution to the arts

The concept of beauty of Nordic man will always be incomprehensible to the Jews.

In artistic pursuits, the Jews are blamed for producing grotesque modern art and decadent music, and for having a fondness for anything which is abnormal, unnatural or immoral. Peter Lorre and Charlie Chaplin are subjected to particularly venomous criticism.

Religious Practices

Not a religion but a conspiracy against all non-Jews by a sick, deceitful, poisonous race.

Above all, the film is particularly scathing about their religion. Not only does Judaism involve odd incantations, strange bobbing motions and laws written on scrolls, but the impression is also given that much of what their religion stands for is the pure exploitation of the non-Jewish community.

The fiercest attacks surround the Jewish requirement that meat can come only from an animal which has been allowed to die by bleeding to death. The vivid, disturbing pictures of cows and sheep being slaughtered in this way is repellent to all viewers and is likely to have the greatest impact on an impartial viewer.

The emphasis of the difference between the Aryan and the Jew

Apart from the general attack on Jews, and that for which they stand, the film seeks to accentuate the difference in body and soul between the Jew and the true native German (and, by implication, the bulk of the viewers). This differentiation is constantly highlighted by the use of 'us' and 'them', and even more evocatively by a concentration on the word 'Aryan' and the importance of retaining the purity of the Aryan race:

> *They don't have the idealism that our children have. With them the egoism of the individual is not in the service of higher common goals, instead Jewish morality, in contrast to Aryan ethics, proclaims the unreserved egoism of every Jew to be Divine Law.*

> *Aryan men attach a sense of worth to every activity ... he wants to create something worthwhile.*

> *Judaism ... is against the moral laws of Aryan peoples.*

Distortion of truth for propaganda impact

While it cannot be denied that the film is very effective in the implementation of its anti-Jewish propaganda, it is obvious that that there are a large number of contradictions even in the five key areas of attack which the film pursues.

Appearance

On the one hand, the film complains about the dirty and strange appearance of the Jews in the Polish Ghetto, thereby stressing how much they differ from non-Jews. However, on the other hand, the film also complains when Jews clean up their appearance, cut their hair, wear smart clothes and mimic the lifestyle and appearance of non-Jews in Germany. It does not seem to matter how the Jews appear, they will always be in the wrong.

Character

Compelling statistics are provided to demonstrate how the Jews are responsible for the majority of organised crime and the promotion of pornography. In truth, history shows that the Jews were heavily involved in these activities and particularly in the United States, but the actual percentages quoted are certainly exaggerated. For example, virtually all the crime syndicates in the United States at that time consisted of multi-ethnic gangs whose roots owed more to the common bond of poverty, deprivation and unemployment than any specific ethnic origin. It would be a gross distortion to blame all the world's ills on the Jews.

Business practices

The iniquitous nature of the criticism is also evident in the analysis of the Jewish attitude to work. At first, the film mocks the Jews for being averse to physical labour and interested only in bartering and self-aggrandisement. Yet, the film is equally critical of the Jews for having too much influence in the media, on stage, in government and for representing a disproportionate number of lawyers, doctors and civil servants. They are also seemingly condemned for their entrepreneurial spirit in gradually progressing from being mere street traders to owning shops and warehouses. Such achievements are hardly convincing arguments that all Jews are scroungers and ne'er-do-wells.

Contribution to the arts

The general attack on their role in the arts is also very one-sided. No mention is made of famous classical Jewish composers or the fact that the Jewish performers they name have also played countless roles in less controversial productions. Nor is any mention made of the Jewish contribution in the fields of science and medicine.

Religious practices

Likewise, the attack on the Jewish religion is very unbalanced. In many ways, their practices are no more unusual than those found in other religions and, in specifically choosing a couple of quotations from Jewish writings which are likely to cause offence, the film ignores the fact that there are countless instances in the religious writings of Christians or Muslims where certain passages, if quoted out of context or without regard to modern interpretation, might appear to be just as heartless or at odds with the general tenets of their respective religions.

The word 'usury', for example, has become corrupted over the years to mean the charging of an excessive rate of interest for credit, whereas originally it simply meant the charging of interest, and Jewish laws never proposed that a profit should be made out of lending money to people who were 'down and out'.

There is no doubt, however, that the ritual slaughter of animals for food does appear to cause undue pain and distress to the animal concerned, but medical evidence is seemingly divided as to whether this is the case or indeed whether the slaughter of animals using other methods is any more humane. Regardless, this section is the most visibly distressing for the viewer and possibly the one anti-Jewish message which carried the most persuasive propaganda impact.

Effectiveness of the film as a piece of anti-Semitic propaganda

By the late 1930s, Hitler was demanding more anti-Jewish films and, having agreed the format of *Der ewige Jude* with its experienced director, Fritz Hippler, Goebbels was certain that it would prove to be a first class propaganda film. Goebbels had originally insisted that it should be completed within four weeks but, because Hitler took a personal interest in its production and insisted on a number of revisions, it was not premiered until 28 November 1940. Consequently, one can clearly detect as much a note of frustration as relief in Goebbel's diary entry for the 11 October 1940: '*Der ewige Jude* is now finished, at last. It can come out without any misgivings now. We've been working on it long enough as well.' The delay meant that its release would overlap with the screening of the two famous anti-Semitic feature films, *Jud Süss* and *Die Rothschilds*.

Acknowledging the danger of cinema-goers feeling swamped by yet another anti-Jewish film, the *Illustrierte Wochenschrift* of 30 December 1940 emphasises the continuing interest in the still unresolved Jewish question in Germany and notes the box office success of the other films. It continues by stressing that the presentation of the Jews in the film is 'how they really are' rather than some cinematic portrayal. However, given the shocking content of the film with its graphic scenes of rats and the slaughter of animals, it is not surprising that this documentary film was not particularly well received by the general public and, when compared with the two anti-Semitic feature films, was certainly a box office failure. It was even noted that some spectators left the cinema in disgust. Instead, it was primarily viewed by Nazi Party organisations, including the Hitler Youth. Nevertheless, many of the general public were certainly aware of its dramatic content and accepted that this was a fair representation of the Jews and their religion. The film did succeed in stoking up further resentment against the Jews and creating an even greater gulf between the Jews and other Germans.

CONCLUSION

For centuries, the Jews had been labelled as being greedy and fond of money, but by going far beyond this traditional stereotyping, through the use of dramatic pictures and often venomous commentary, *Der ewige Jude* has to be regarded as one of the vilest anti-Jewish documentaries ever produced. The constant repetition of highly emotive words such as 'parasite' and 'usury', and the shocking images of hordes of rats and the uncensored slaughter of animals leave a lasting impression on any viewer, and many would have left the cinema feeling physically sick.

As with much Nazi propaganda, there was a slight degree of truth in what is presented, but the facts are deliberately manipulated to create maximum revulsion for the Jewish race. The anti-Jewish arguments are full of contradictions and ignore any positive contributions which the Jewish race has made to society. There is no acknowledgment that other races may appear just as strange to anyone who does not belong to that race, and that other religions often have just as many peculiarities as those found in Judaism.

The chilling final comment from the narrator is that 'keeping one's own race pure will be the legacy of the National Socialist movement'. The affirmation of this goal was to be repeated time and again, with Göring declaring in October 1942 that the meaning of the war was to decide whether the German and the Aryan would prevail or whether the Jew would rule the world. The terrible measures that the Nazis would employ to realise this goal was only to become fully apparent after the war.

Film title: ***Der Führer schenkt den Juden eine Stadt***
Year of release: 1945
Type: Documentary
Primary purpose: To paint a false and idyllic picture of
life in a concentration camp
Director: Kurt Gerron

INTRODUCTION

As the war progressed, increasing numbers of alarming reports were emerging about the conditions in Nazi concentration camps. Following repeated questioning by the Danish government as to the fate of its Jewish deportees, Adolf Eichmann, the Transportation Administrator of European Jews, eventually agreed in June 1944 to allow a Danish delegation and representatives of the International Red Cross to visit the camp at Theresienstadt, north of Prague.

The camp was first established in 1941 within the grounds of the former fortress, and, at any one time, held tens of thousands of inmates. It was primarily a transit camp, only ever designed to accommodate 7,000 people, and the conditions were so poor that many thousands were to die from hunger and disease. In the months prior to the official visit, great care was taken to improve the appearance of the camp. All the buildings were freshly painted and the streets were repaired. There was a feverish period of construction of cafés, businesses, a children's play area, extensive garden plots and even a bank. The 'make-over' included the removal of 7,500 of the inmates to Auschwitz, so that the camp would appear less crowded.

The subsequent reports produced by the Red Cross were so favourable that the local SS took the decision to produce a film about the camp with the intention that the resultant propaganda film would be distributed worldwide and, in particular, to international humanitarian institutions and neutral countries.

Kurt Gerron, a well-known German film actor and director of Jewish parentage, who was an inmate in Theresienstadt, was 'persuaded' to direct the film, albeit under close SS supervision. Unfortunately, undertaking this task for the Nazis did nothing to improve Gerron's fate since, shortly after filming was completed, he and his wife were also transported to Auschwitz.

Although filming had been completed by September 1944, the final version of the film, with added music and voice-over, was not completed until March 1945. Consequently, given the success of the Allied landings in Normandy in June 1944, the purpose for which the film had

Jewish spectators seemingly enjoying themselves at a soccer game in the courtyard of the Dresden barracks in the Theresienstadt ghetto. *(US Holocaust Memorial Museum, courtesy of Ivan Vojtech Fric)*

The garden plots outside the fortress walls, where additional food could be grown by the inmates, were greatly enlarged for the sake of the film. *(US Holocaust Memorial Museum, courtesy of Ivan Vojtech Fric)*

A young Jewish woman reclining outside on a hospital bed with a book in the Theresienstadt ghetto. (*US Holocaust Memorial Museum, courtesy of Ivan Vojtech Fric*)

originally been designed was largely overtaken by events. It was going to be increasingly difficult for the Nazis to arrange for copies of the film to reach nations favourably disposed towards Germany, and the film's credibility was soon to be called into question as the Allies gradually liberated other camps which revealed the true horrors of the gas chambers.

The ninety-minute film was only ever screened in Prague and also to humanitarian institutions on subsequent visits to Theresienstadt in April 1945. The film disappeared after the war, and the footage which has survived today has been spliced together to produce a film of around twenty-three minutes in length. The remaining film has come to be known, ironically, as *Der Führer schenkt den Juden eine Stadt* (*The Führer gifts a city to the Jews*), although this was not a title adopted by Gerron, who more often referred to it in his notes as *Theresienstadt: Ein Dokumentarfilm aus dem jüdischen Siedlungsgebiet* (*Theresienstadt: a film documentary from the Jewish settlement area*).

FILM CONTENT

As much of the original film did not survive the war, it is only possible to review the excerpts which do exist.

On this basis, the film which remains begins rather abruptly in a hall in which rows of reasonably well-dressed people, whom it will later be discovered are all Jews, are listening intently to a classical concert. The film then switches to give the viewer a short, picturesque history lesson about Theresienstadt, a fortress designed by Vaubin between 1780 and 1790, which lies in Bohemia at the point where the Elbe and Elge rivers meet.

The narrator then returns to the camp where people of all ages are shown enjoying themselves and participating in a whole host of leisure activities in the grounds of the fortress. The inmates are playing cards, reading, walking, kicking a ball, doing keep-fit exercises or just lying and relaxing. The whole activity is summarised neatly in the commentary, 'On the old grounds of the fortress, people happily while away some of the leisure hours in the sunshine.'

The viewer is then taken to a hospital ward where a nurse and doctors are doing their rounds, and there are even many rows of beds arrayed outside in the sun where a smiling nurse is taking food to a patient.

It is explained that a children's convalescent home is situated on the edge of the city, and children are shown enthusiastically tucking into a plate of buttered bread. There is a huge area where children can play in the sand pits, paddling pools or on swings; there are plenty of toys. Finally, a large group of children is shown performing a musical to the rapturous applause of hundreds of other children.

Jews watching a performance in the Theresienstadt ghetto – perhaps betraying a slight defiance. (*US Holocaust Memorial Museum, courtesy of Ivan Vojtech Fric*)

Having devoted so much of the film to leisure activities and the facilities for the children, it is also recognised that work plays an important part in the daily activity of the camp. Fast, lively music accompanies the scenes of a blacksmith shoeing an ox, and the music turns into a lively 'can can' as other blacksmiths take it in turn to hammer pieces of metal. It is explained that workshops are required for blacksmiths, locksmiths, mechanics and technicians to maintain the various pieces of camp machinery. Artisans and craftsmen are shown making vases and sculptures of all sizes, including a huge water fountain. Indeed, water is a common theme throughout the film. It is also explained that people are trained according to their skills and retrained if necessary. There are purse-makers, tailors, seamstresses and stitchers.

However, the film soon again returns to leisure activities, as people finish their daily work. Much footage is spent covering a seven-a-side soccer match and the municipal baths which are available to all. There is also a large library and evening lectures on a host of scientific and arts topics. Apart from another musical performance, inmates are shown tending their allotments where they can grow additional food.

Having made clear that there are special accommodation facilities for single women and girls, a camera moves slowly through one of the huts revealing groups of people chatting and playing games on the tables which are situated between each of the bunk beds. Young women are combing their hair in front of mirrors, and some inmates are writing letters. In short, Theresienstadt is a picture of contentment, with the conditions seemingly more akin to those of a holiday camp.

CRITICAL REVIEW

It is impossible for the modern viewer to analyse this film without being influenced by the knowledge of what was actually occurring in this and so many other concentration camps at that time. It is even more difficult to be objective when it is known that the film was specially commissioned by the Nazis and one is aware of the fate of the inmates and director once the filming was completed.

However, by setting the historical context to one side, it is still possible to review the film with some degree of detachment.

What impression does the film wish to make on the viewer?

The film-makers were faced with conflicting priorities. Ever since the Nazis came to power in 1933, all the documentaries produced about the Jews for internal consumption portrayed the Jews as dirty, lazy, corrupt and promiscuous. Now, Gerron was being asked to produce a film which, on the one hand, would show the Jews being well-treated but, on the other, as still basically unattractive as a race. Consequently, the playing of jazz music (which the Nazis judged to be associated with decadence), girls showing too much leg as they exercised, the lack of enthusiasm and general air of laziness shown by all inmates were all features included in the movie to depict the Jews in a negative light, but without any criticism being directed towards those responsible for their containment in the camp.

Above all else, the film attempts to paint a picture of normality. It strives to show that this is no camp with barbed wire fences and machine-gun towers, but rather a splendid old fortress, located in an idyllic setting in which the inhabitants are well treated. The scene which explains the background to the fortress is described in such a 'matter-of-fact' manner that it makes the Jews' current occupation of the site all seem like just a natural progression of history.

Ostensibly, people of all ages are shown with lots of spare time and free to indulge in a vast variety of leisure activities. While there may be a need for many to work during the day, this is no different from the outside world, and people are given jobs to which they are best-suited or are retrained as appropriate. Good care is apparently taken of children who are free to play outside in the lovely grounds, and the hospital seems to offer unrivalled facilities. Many beds are located outside, so that patients can enjoy the sunny weather. The children appear well-fed, and some of the grown-ups even have the opportunity to grow more fruit and vegetables in the allotments they have been allocated. There are modern washing facilities and an extensive library which caters for all tastes.

In short, conditions in this internment camp seem almost luxurious, with no apparent reason for complaint by any of the internees. There are several images of people laughing and smiling; the sun is always shining; and the internees seem to enjoy a quality of life perhaps more akin to what one would have expected for aliens interned in camps in Britain or America during the war.

However, given that the film was not primarily intended for domestic consumption, but rather to persuade the wider world that Germany was taking good care of its Jewish internees, it has to be questioned whether the film actually succeeds in delivering its propaganda objectives.

How effective is this film as piece of propaganda?

The very fact that the film had to create a largely imaginary world to achieve its propagandistic objectives has resulted in a number of scenes and incidents which catch the viewer's attention. These can be analysed in four categories:

The content of many of the scenes which are depicted

There is an almost obsessive concentration on leisure activities such as the football match, gardening and other outdoor activities. Why bother showing such activities in such detail unless this was in response to criticism that the internees had to spend all their time working indoors? Or, when adults or children are shown watching a concert, the audience appears nervous and just a little too intent on what is happening. Many of the faces are quite empty of emotion and, where older adults are filmed, few are smiling and some are even sitting with arms crossed, perhaps betraying a silent sign of defiance.

The exaggerated way in which certain items are featured

It is just too convenient that the children are sharing a plate which is piled high with buttered bread, although even this film can't hide the fact that several children seem to be devouring the bread very quickly, as if they are quite hungry. In particular, there is a close-up of two girls eating their bread. In the initial shot, they both look quite sad and drained of emotion. Suddenly, they both burst into smiles which are almost too good to be true. On closer analysis, you can see that someone else is talking to the children. Did this person genuinely make them laugh or were they forced to smile? In either event, the smile is clearly designed for the camera.

In the hospital, it does seem quite noticeable that the nurse making her rounds is accompanied not by one, but three doctors. Nor can this hide the fact that the hospital actually appears quite crowded. Similarly, having one or two beds outside might seem admirable, but there is a scene where several scores of beds lined up outside under the trees seem to be devoid of occupants. This hardly seems plausible or practical. Where were all the other patients and what was going to happen when the weather changed?

Inconsistencies and questions which emerge from some of the accompanying dialogue

In the hospital, the commentator adds that, 'It is equipped with all necessary supplies'. Is this not what we would have expected? And what does 'necessary' actually mean?

When people finish work for the day, it is proudly reported, 'People can use their free time as they like'. The surprise for the viewer would have been if this were not the case, since in theory they were only internees.

On returning to the concert hall the viewer is informed, 'Musical performances are happily attended by all'. Why is there a need to insert the word happy? Are they forced to attend?

Likewise, the commentator mentions, 'even the work of a Jewish composer is performed in Theresienstadt'. In fact, all of the classical music used in the film is the work of Jewish composers. The commentator obviously feels a need to stress this point since the performance of Jewish works in Germany was generally forbidden, but it is more likely to instil anger in a non-German audience that such discrimination was the norm.

Questions which are not answered or items which are not featured

It might well be that some of the following might have been included in the complete film, but they are certainly all worth deeper consideration:

◊   There is no explanation as to why there is a need for this camp at all and why the Jews are imprisoned there.

◊   There is no sign of any guards or gates, so why would people stay in the camp?

◊   Where do the inmates actually eat and what was the quality of the food?

◊   It is mentioned that there is special accommodation for single women and girls, so where were the married couples housed?

◊ If it is such a wonderful place, why are there no interviews with some of the inmates who can voice their appreciation, even if these would have been staged interviews?

◊ Why is there a need for so many children to be in a convalescent home?

◊ The film goes to great lengths to feature inmates who are well dressed and it is only in the scenes in the accommodation huts that we see more evident signs of the Star of David which is sewn onto the clothes of some of the women. Was it deliberate policy that several scenes feature people whose clothes are not marked in this way?

◊ Many of the 'inmates', who are only ever described as 'people', are very old. Why was there a need for them to be held in such a camp?

In short, any enquiring mind would have detected that this was a work of propaganda, although, contrary to popular belief, Goebbels apparently had no hand in the production of this film. While Goebbels generally had absolute control over propaganda activity, the one area over which he had no influence was propaganda undertaken by the SS.

Goebbels was always of the mind that the best propaganda comes from how reality is interpreted and portrayed, rather than by creating pure fiction which he believed would fail to impress as it would be obvious that it was contrived. It is unlikely that he would have been satisfied with the finished product on this occasion.

POINTS OF NOTE CONCERNING THE PRODUCTION OF THE FILM AND THE FATE OF THE DIRECTOR AND THOSE IN THERESIENSTADT

In agreeing to direct the film, it is believed that Gerron may well have thought that at least some of the Jewish prisoners would be allowed to remain in the improved conditions in Theresienstadt, or that their deportation to Auschwitz would be delayed. However, this was a forlorn hope and despite any assurances which might have been given, once filming was completed, Gerron and his wife were transported to Auschwitz on 28 October 1944 for elimination in the gas chambers, as indeed were most of the inmates of Theresienstadt.

Those few inmates who were present at the filming and survived the war were able to testify about the hoax which the Nazis had tried to play on the world by producing such a film about Theresienstadt. Paradoxically, they would attest that much that the film portrayed at that particular moment was actually true, although the inmates were forced to smile for the camera and to take part in the various activities which were featured. Like most propaganda, *Der Führer schenkt den Juden eine Stadt* simply failed to tell the whole story. Nothing was mentioned about the tens of thousands of deaths through disease or starvation, nor of the slave labour conditions in which they worked to supply the German war machine, nor of the vast number of deportations to Auschwitz.

Following the visit by the Red Cross in June 1944, a further 18,000 prisoners were to be shipped to Auschwitz before the end of the war. The Danish delegation who had visited the camp were less easily persuaded by what they had been shown and eventually managed to obtain the release of their 450 Jewish citizens from Theresienstadt before they could be moved further east. In February 1945, the Red Cross did manage to negotiate the safe release of a further 1,200 Jews to Switzerland before the camp was finally overrun by the Soviets on the 8 May 1945.

CONCLUSION

Of all the documentary films produced by the Nazis, *Der Führer schenkt den Juden eine Stadt* is unique in that a Jew was not only responsible for both directing and writing the script for the film, but that this same Jew was actually an inmate in the camp about which the film was being made. Whether or not he willingly co-operated in the making of the film, Gerron did undoubtedly put a great deal of effort into the production and was obviously well aware of the false impression of the camp which he was helping to create, and of the purpose for which the film would be intended. If he had hoped that his work would save Jewish lives by delaying or rescinding deportation altogether, then he was sadly mistaken, as is only too evident by his own swift execution.

If the film was to have any meaningful propaganda value in the wider world, then it was imperative that it was released without delay. The elimination of the director by the Nazis before the film was complete was utter madness, as this simply served to delay its eventual release. By the time it was complete, the war was lost and its only remaining purpose was to try to convince the Allies that at least Theresienstadt had been a model camp.

The film itself was never going to be persuasive, and the few remnants which survive simply highlight how difficult it is to make a convincing propaganda film if it is based on fiction, is overly stage-managed and involves human beings with real feelings and emotions.

In short, the costly facelift to the prison, the accelerated exodus of thousands of prisoners and the very production of the film turned out to be a complete waste of time, and took place at a time when they might have done better to concentrate their resources on trying to win the war. The Nazis' obsessive preoccupation throughout Europe, first with the elimination of the Jews and later with their attempts to conceal their crimes, undoubtedly influenced the outcome and duration of the war.

The film roundly condemns President Roosevelt for meddling in German affairs when life in America is far from idyllic. (*Library of Congress*)

Film title: *Rund um die Freiheitsstatue: Ein Spaziergang durch die USA*
Year of release: 1942
Type: Documentary
Primary purpose: Anti-American propaganda
Director: Fritz Hippler

INTRODUCTION

Rund um die Freiheitsstatue (*Around the Statue of Liberty*) was a short documentary produced by the Nazis in response to President Roosevelt's continuing attacks on the lack of freedom which existed in fascist Germany. Only fifteen minutes in length, the film splices together excerpts from actual newsreel distributed by American news agencies around the world, but with the aim of creating a negative picture of life in the United States, in what the narrator mockingly describes as 'the most free democracy in the world'.

As early as January 1939, Hitler had threatened that he would make anti-Semitic films in revenge for the anti-German films which the Americans were producing. Indeed, by April 1940, such was the concern about the content of American feature films that Goebbels actually banned the screening of all American films in Germany. With Germany's declaration of war on the United States in December 1941, the Nazis were prepared to be even more aggressive in their propaganda campaigns, and while only a handful of feature films with any anti-American bias were produced during the whole period that the Nazis were in power, this hard-hitting documentary was released early in 1942.

FILM CONTENT

The film, with a subtitle that reads *Ein Spaziergang durch die USA* (*A walk through the USA*), begins with a close-up of the Statue of Liberty in New York and explains how the statue, gifted to the United States by the French, is meant to be a symbol of the light of freedom. However, the narrator continues by bemoaning the fact that this happened a long time ago and that, in the meantime, the notion of freedom in both countries has fundamentally changed. Scornful of Roosevelt for his speeches about freedom and democracy in America, the film then uses archive footage of a number of news events to illustrate what life is really like in America.

First, there are disturbing scenes of soldiers using tear gas to control a strike by ordinary citizens. The film's sympathies clearly lie with the strikers, who are said to work for starvation wages for a handful of Jewish millionaires, and the authorities are roundly condemned for using such hard-line tactics to break up strikes and demonstrations. However, the film also shows the damage caused by strikers attacking their own factories and the waste resulting from the 1939 milk strike, with farmers pouring milk onto the street which could otherwise have provided much-needed nourishment to the children and the sick.

Next, the film attacks the Jewish businessmen who are responsible for keeping the American masses under control, and accuses Roosevelt of attacking life in National Socialist Germany as a means of diverting attention from the activities of the Jews and the pitiable lifestyles which ordinary workers and farmers have to endure in America. The narrator makes sardonic reference to the sort of human culture which Roosevelt has promoted in America, and photos are used to illustrate examples of villains from the gangster world, criminals, mass murderers and child kidnappers, all of whom have blossomed in Roosevelt's free society.

Then, the film concentrates its ire on Mrs Roosevelt:

Show me your wife and I'll tell you who you are!

Against the previous background of riots, poverty and starving workers, the film shows Mrs Roosevelt modelling furs and other smart dresses financed by her generous clothes allowance. Not only is she reported as having said that higher wages are political nonsense, but she had also endorsed 'swing', a type of dancing favoured by the black population, which her husband had promoted as an integral part of American culture. The film switches to an excerpt of a black man with a head dress surrounded by what appear to be black natives gyrating to some tribal music; the narrator remarks that the scene looks more like Africa than New York. This then develops into a general attack on the type of dancing so favoured by what it calls 'niggers', with scenes which make the dancing appear totally uncivilised. To make matters worse, whites are shown trying to outperform blacks in their own swing endurance competition, and there is the uncomfortable sight of exhausted white dancers having collapsed and having to be assisted from the dance floor.

The film then reverts to an attack on the Jews and especially their abstract modern art, which the commentator declares as not being art at all, but rather speculative folly. The overwhelming influence of the Jews is apparently demonstrated by a procession in front of Jewish Rabbis in New York.

Next, the viewer is shown disturbing pictures of the total immersion baptism of a number of black Americans in a river, with those being baptised seemingly half insane.

Sport is another aspect of American civilisation which is criticised. There are scenes of a bruising wrestling match, where it is claimed that the laws of fairness go out of the window, as all that matters is brute force. The audience behaves like a pack of raging wolves, especially the women who are laughing at the injured or defeated competitors. It is reported that Americans even allow all-women wrestling matches and boxing matches between men and women, and, so as to emphasise the inequality of such a contest, a woman is shown being knocked to the ground by a man. There are further scenes of what appears to be a corrupt and uncivilised society with men fighting in mud or in fish, all of which does look quite disgusting.

Finally, the film switches to a man threatening to commit suicide by jumping from the seventeenth floor of an office block in Chicago. The narrator contends that it would have been quite easy to save him, but no one thinks about that since too many newspaper and film reporters have an interest in seeing him fall to his death, which he eventually does.

The film concludes with a final contemptuous assertion that this is the sort of freedom and culture for which Roosevelt speaks out so enthusiastically and, returning to the Statue of Liberty, the commentator declares that this monument of freedom is actually turning its back on America.

CRITICAL REVIEW

It is obvious that the Nazis had been riled by Roosevelt's criticism of National Socialist Germany, and this anti-American short film was an effective way of retaliating.

Effectiveness of the film

The film is well made and moves seamlessly from one scene to the next, often with clever interconnecting commentary. For example, when reference is made to Roosevelt's praise of 'freedom, democracy and religion in the fresh air of a free country', the commentator is able to contend that the air is not so clean by switching to the scene of a soldier throwing tear gas canisters.

While the validity of the attack on America seems particularly justified because use is made of material produced by the Americans themselves, a host of well-known propaganda devices are also employed to emphasise the points being raised. These include the use of insinuation, generalisation, exaggeration, sarcasm and an exclusive concentration on the specifically negative aspects of American society, as if these are representative of all that was happening in America.

By focussing on the negative aspects of American life, the film successfully draws a picture of a disorderly and corrupt society which any right-minded German would find distasteful and wish to avoid.

Living conditions
It is claimed that the strikers earn only 'starvation wages' which are neither sufficient to allow them to live nor die, and pictures are shown of slum areas and people imprisoned in squalid open air camps. The conditions are probably no different from what might have been found in the poorest parts of any country in the world, but the film gives the impression that these are the living conditions of the bulk of ordinary Americans.

Social unrest
The viewer is shown examples of the brutal dissolution of a series of separate strikes, without knowing the background to those strikes or how frequent the strikes occurred.

Uncivilised culture
There is an undue emphasis on the wild dancing of the black Americans, associated with immorality and decadence, and of their 'strange' baptisms, as if these elements were symbolic of the whole of American culture. However, it is somewhat ironic that many Germans actually liked swing and jazz music and would have gone to view this film simply to hear and see the very types of music which were so difficult to acquire in Germany at that time. Indeed, Goebbels himself was to exploit Britain's fondness for such music by creating his own jazz band in 1940, which re-broadcast the latest musical hits from America to Britain, but with suitably adapted anti-Churchill and anti-Roosevelt lyrics.

Likewise, in terms of sport, there is a deliberate concentration on wrestling and boxing – sports which have always drawn mixed reactions from society across the whole world. There is no recognition that many of the wrestling scenes were contrived and were deliberately staged to be entertaining rather than cause real pain.

Undue influence of Jews
As in the film *Der ewige Jude*, this film is keen to show that much of the ills and corruption of America can be blamed on the Jews, both in terms of the poor working conditions which a handful of Jewish millionaires impose on American workers, and also in the number of gangsters and criminals who roam the streets. While a good number of the millionaire entrepreneurs who ran businesses and those who committed crimes had Jewish roots, it would be completely wrong to claim that the Jews were responsible for all the failings of American society.

Crime
The impression is also conveyed that it is only because of America's free and democratic society that organised crime flourished. America actually had strict and severe penalties for breaking the law, with long prison sentences imposed on those involved in racketeering and organised prostitution and the ultimate threat of the death penalty employed in many states. So, it was not a particularly liberal society.

Negative portrayal of President Roosevelt and his wife
Ultimately, the commentator is keen to depict America's president, while never compared directly to Hitler, as being a weak liberal who outwardly espouses the values of democracy and freedom while ruling over a society which is morally corrupt. It is claimed that he lies and cheats to protect unscrupulous millionaire businessmen, and goes so far as to promote forms of entertainment and sport which are uncivilised and demeaning. Above all else, his wife is shown to take more interest in her own appearance than the fate of the poor workers.

Is the film footage accurate?
While the film excerpts undoubtedly did exist, the accuracy of the accompanying commentary seems more open to question.

The item about the swing endurance competition being held by the whites seems particularly contrived. While this section certainly opens with whites dancing to swing-like music, the clip ends with exhausted performers dancing on what looks like a different floor and to a more sedate style of ballroom dancing. It would appear that two different dance films have been conflated to support the narrator's comments.

Similarly, the viewer does not know what actions were being taken to try to prevent the man jumping from the Chicago office block, nor whether the body which seems to fall in the dark is the same man.

Conclusion

For a very short film composed entirely of archive newsreels, *Rund um die Freiheitsstatue* is actually a very effective piece of anti-American propaganda.

The emphasis on the unusual and extreme elements of American society would have been bound to alienate the viewer, and it is easy to see how a German audience might have been appalled at the sight of the extreme measures used by the authorities to quell riots and strikes. The ordinary German might well have considered that any loss of freedom or democracy in his own country was a price worth paying if it meant stability, employment and protection from distasteful changes to their culture. This documentary was to be followed by others with similar themes such as *Herr Roosevelt plaudert* (*Mr Roosevelt chats*), which was released in 1943.

CHAPTER XI

TELEVISION AS A PROPAGANDA WEAPON FOR THE NAZIS (1934–44)

CONTROL OF BROADCASTING

Hitler had always recognised that communication media exercised an important influence over the mind of the recipient, and that control of such media was fundamental for the promotion and acceptance of National Socialist ideology.

Through a decree issued on 30 June 1933, and only five months after the Nazis came to power, broadcasting became a publicly controlled institution of the Reich's Ministry for Public Enlightenment and Propaganda. Its primary task was to exert influence over as many areas of an individual's day-to-day life as possible.

For the Nazis, such influences included:

◊ The way that specially stage-managed public events such as National Party Days and special events like the 1936 Olympic Games were reported by the media so as to convey the awesome power, order and grandeur of the new regime.

◊ The control of private viewing/listening rooms with the imposition of penalties for listening to foreign broadcasts.

◊ Direct control over all programme content, not just in overtly propaganda-laden educational and instructional films but also, and particularly from 1935–36 onwards, in a more subtle form of propaganda conveyed through seemingly innocent entertainment programmes.

The aim was to create a common mindset among the population that the Nazis' political philosophy was beneficial for Germany and that, ultimately, Germany's expansion into other countries was a logical and justifiable step, even if this resulted in war.

GERMAN TELEVISION DEVELOPMENT

The first broadcasts

While the control of the electronic media was primarily aimed at radio and films, it also applied to the new medium of television. The German National Post Office had been experimenting with television broadcasts for a number of years, but the first public broadcast did not occur until 18 April 1934. By November, the first female announcer, Ursula Patschke, was appointed, and a test broadcast was presented to Hitler in his Chancellery on 18 December.

While the higher echelons of the Nazi Party quickly recognised that television was never likely to exert the same mass propaganda impact on the German nation as could be achieved by radio or film, they did, however, appreciate the international propaganda kudos of standing at the cutting-edge of such technology.

In Britain, the BBC, in conjunction with Baird Television Ltd, had already made its first broadcast on 30 September 1929, and when it was feared that the British might be about to launch a regular service of television programmes, the then State Programme Producer, Eugen Hadamovsky, was determined that Germany would remain at the forefront of television development. Consequently, the Nazis were proud to be able to claim that Germany was the first country in the world to introduce a regular programme service, which commenced on 22 March 1935, and, although using more advanced technology, the British did not actually launch a regular service until November 1936.

The German programmes were transmitted from a small studio in the Charlottenburg district of Berlin by the 'Paul Nipkow' broadcasting station, which took its name from the early German television pioneer. Initial broadcasts were only transmitted three days a week and lasted around a couple of hours at a time. Given that the number of television receivers capable of receiving such programmes did not exist in large numbers, those early broadcasts

were witnessed only by a few hundred chosen viewers, including post office technicians and important Nazi officials, through around seventy-five television sets in the Berlin vicinity.

Television salons

Meanwhile, the National Post Office concentrated on the development of special television salons, located either on Post Office property or in rented shop space, in which small groups of people could watch television. The first television salon was opened in Berlin's National Post Museum on 9 April 1935, and others were gradually opened across Berlin and then in Potsdam and Leipzig. The first television screens

Outside broadcast camera employed in the Olympic Arena in Berlin. (*BArch, Bild 183-G00417/Stempka*)

Roll call of the SA and SS in Nürnberg in 1934 from the film *Triumph des Willens*. *(Deutsches Filminstitut/ Transit Film GmbH)*

were very small – only around 20 x 25cm in size – and the early salons could only accommodate a maximum of twenty to thirty people in four or five rows of seats. There tended to be two television screens in these salons, and a technician would be on hand to adjust the controls should the picture fail. Given the size of the screen and the dark, unreliable picture, the viewer would have had to have had really good eyesight to see much detail from the back row.

In order to attract as many people as possible to this new medium, entrance to the heated salons was free, and the primary focus was on offering the viewer maximum entertainment. Often introduced by a pretty announcer with a Hitler salute, the early schedules contained a variety of 'song and dance' acts together with keep-fit and cooking programmes designed to interest the whole family. Given the poor picture quality delivered by the 180-line system, the initial response from viewers was understandably lukewarm, and the manufacturers awaited further technological advances before committing to the mass production of television sets.

Although two large-screen salons, which could accommodate 294 and 120 viewers respectively, had been opened in Berlin during the first twelve months of broadcasting, there were still only eleven salons in total by early 1936. Development was not helped by the fact that the Propaganda Ministry resisted further expansion in case this should result in competition with the cinemas. In any event, the decision had already been taken that the top priority was for each German family to have access to a reliable People's Wireless, considered a far more cost-effective mass communication and propaganda medium.

The 1936 Olympic Games

Under the auspices of the free time organisation, *Kraft durch Freude* (Strength through Joy), the president of the National Broadcasting Chamber, Horst Dreßler-Andreß, had always sought to make television more widely available so that, 'Germany would be the first country in the world where the whole population would watch television'.

Consequently, it was with some relief to those involved in the industry that the popularity of German television did receive an enormous boost with its broadcasting of the 1936 Summer Olympic Games, staged in Berlin. Dreßler-Andreß was adamant that the technological superiority of Nazi Germany would be demonstrated to a worldwide audience by its successful televising of the Games for the rest of the world.

Three huge new cameras were built to improve picture quality and twenty new television salons were installed for the Games alone, including one in the stadium itself, which could be enjoyed by the competing athletes. It was reported that no fewer than 160,000 people watched the Games from television

Outside broadcasting camera at the opening ceremony of the 1936 Olympics. (*BArch, Bild 102-16140/Pahl, G.*)

A 1933 combined television and radio set manufactured by Telefunken. (*BArch, Bild 183-R26738*)

salons and, at its peak, there were up to eight hours of programming each day, direct from the Olympic Stadium.

The unsuitability of television for the Nazis as a mass propaganda medium

Despite the success of the Olympics and Hadamovsky's desire to 'plant a picture of Hitler indelibly in all German hearts', the Nazi hierarchy never fully embraced television. Goebbels was far from impressed when he saw his own image on television. Portraying the correct representation of Nazism and evoking an awe-filled response from an audience was something for which films were best suited, and especially when many hours could be taken over the careful editing of the final presentation. Films such as *Olympia* and *Triumph of the Will* presented exactly what Hitler wanted to achieve and are fascinating visual documentaries which still impress today.

The greatest drawback with television in those early days was that the scale and grandeur represented by Nazi ideology was never going to be so impressive on a small, flickering television screen. The outside broadcasts were often live, even if delayed by a minute or so through the use of the 'intermediate film technique'. This meant that the viewer saw everything as it happened, warts and all, and that the final presentation could not be effectively stage-managed.

Furthermore, a reliable means of recording live television programmes did not exist at that time, and for many decades there was a dependence on personal recollection and newspaper programme schedules for an impression as to the nature and content of Nazi television broadcasts.[9] However, in 1990, 285 rolls of 35mm film which had been broadcast via television were discovered in the former German Democratic Republic, and these do provide a fascinating visual insight into the sort of programmes which were broadcast on Nazi television.

In one such external broadcast, a young boy can be seen chasing after Hitler's limousine with a ladder so that, when the car stopped, a cameraman could jump on the ladder and take photographs of the event. This amusing distraction from the central character hardly portrayed the omnipotent image of the Führer which the Nazis would have wanted to convey to the world. Likewise, while huge marching parades projected onto a full-sized cinema screen did make an impressive sight, the 'master race' looked more like pygmies when presented on the small screen.

---

9 It is worth noting that the Scottish television pioneer, John Logie Baird, who was involved in a joint venture to establish the Fernseh AG television company in Berlin in 1929 (before the seizure of its assets by the Nazis), had actually invented a way of recording early British transmissions on records as early as 1927, called Phonovision, although the quality was poor.

Even with 160,000 people watching the Olympics, television was never going to reach a mass audience in Germany in the short term. Above all else, the Nazis could not exercise complete control over the hearts and minds of their audiences if people started to watch alone in their own homes, hidden from the eyes of 'Big Brother' and loyal party members who would have been only too willing to inform on anyone who did not show the same absolute dedication to the Nazi cause.

Increasingly politicised programme schedules

After the Olympics, the programme content not only became more varied but also more political. Admittedly, there would be a mix of news reports, debates, nature programmes, plays, short films and variety shows. In addition, however, there were many more programmes with an openly political theme, such as those covering the annual Nazi Party Congress, Party rallies, important speeches, state visits, special occasions like Hitler's birthday and the activities of various Nazi groups such as the Hitler Youth. Seemingly more innocuous programmes, such as reports about the National Wedding School or the latest trends in cooking or the activities of the *Kraft durch Freude* project, actually promoted the same ideological train of thought in the presentation of homeland, marriage and family, and of the value of duty and sacrifice.

Even apparently innocent cultural programmes could contain some hard-hitting propaganda. A good example is the following free translation of some rather threatening comments made by a bow-tied presenter during the interval in a variety show broadcast in 1936:

> I am very pleased that everything today is so harmonious. Granted there are still quite a few people playing out of tune … and maybe even some that would like to march to the beat of a different drum … to the beat of the centre … like the so-called foreign exchange musicians. We don't waste time with them. They are all sent to Concert camps [an obvious pun!] for their further education and they are taught to sing for their supper. And they will stay there until they learn to be more tactful and play along with everyone else!

It was all part of a deliberate process of gradually isolating people with different political views or from different racial backgrounds. Nazi songs and music were often interspersed between traditional folk songs, and a feature on an anti-Bolshevist and anti-Jewish exhibition in 1937, where Semitism is described as a virus, is seen as perfectly normal and acceptable.

Broadcasting during the war years

By 1938, despite a chronic shortage of funds, the Berlin studio managed to move to a larger building in the same district, which possessed no fewer than five production stages, even if these often shared the same cameras. Furthermore, with agreement reached in 1937 for the introduction of a 441-line system and the resultant improved picture quality, the point had been reached when the National Post Office and National Radio Company felt sufficiently confident to turn television into a mass media operation, and the decision was taken to produce 10,000 television sets designed for home use. The FE1 came on the market as 'The People's Television' on 28 July 1939, at a price of 650 Reichsmarks (almost twenty times the cost of a radio), but only fifty of these sets were delivered before production ceased, and industrial capacity was switched to goods which were considered more essential to the war effort. Nevertheless, it is estimated that there were still as many as 500 television sets of various models installed for use in Germany by the outbreak of the Second World War.

Unlike France and the UK, where for the duration of the war television services were suspended, Nazi television was to continue broadcasting well into 1944. Indeed, when the war started, the number of German television technicians actually increased, as many were drafted into the special project for the development of so-called 'wonder weapons' in Peenemünde and other bases. Göring had always believed that television would offer military potential for his air force, particularly for the proposed television-guided anti-shipping bombs such as the Henschel Hs293D. Work was also undertaken on the use of radio-beam guidance in rocket heads such as those for the V2 rockets, the transmission of maps and sketches and the development of cameras for night fighters.

There was an initial suspension of television programmes from 3 September 1939 with the outbreak of war, during which the German Air Ministry took the opportunity to regain control of the broadcasting frequency as a potential jamming signal against enemy aircraft. However, the television salons soon re-opened, and full transmissions recommenced in early November. So, why did such broadcasts recommence? It was primarily to achieve maximum propaganda impact. With the campaign against the Poles proceeding smoothly and with the inactivity of the 'phoney war' in the West, the Nazis were keen to demonstrate to both their own citizens and the world at large the underlying strength and confidence of a German nation which could still afford the luxury of television broadcasting during wartime.

Revised scheduling and programme content

While transmissions continued unabated, the war certainly did have an impact on timings and programme content, as is evidenced by the schedule before and after 3 September 1939, the commencement of war:

Recuperating soldiers enjoying a television broadcast in hospital in March 1942. (*BArch, Bild 146-2006-0196/Orbis-Photo*)

The Eiffel Tower was used as a television transmission aerial from 1943. (*BArch, Bild 183-H28708*)

Sunday, 25 February 1939

8.00pm	*'Zeitdienst' (a mixture of live studio reports and filmed news reports)*
8.20pm	*Sport on Sunday*
8.30pm	*Topical Film Report*
8.45pm	*'From new Operas' (a live musical broadcast)*
9.55pm	*Close*

The most notable immediate change with the outbreak of war was that the two-hour evening transmissions were broadcast increasingly earlier, first running from 7 p.m. to 9 p.m. and then from 6 p.m. to around 8 p.m. It was not that there was any apparent problem with broadcasting outside daylight hours, but since early Allied bombing raids only took place at night, it was felt desirable that broadcasting should be concluded before such raids occurred. This would avoid the embarrassment of being cut-off in mid-broadcast if a bomb happened to fall on the broadcasting studio.

Nevertheless, as can be seen from the following schedule broadcast early in 1940, it was not just the programme times which altered, but rather a focus on more war-related topics:

Sunday, 10 March 1940

3.00pm	*'Feldzug in Polen' (film about the 'Campaign in Poland')*
4.10pm	*Interval*
6.00pm	*'Feldzug in Polen' (a repeat of the earlier film)*
7.10pm	*'Preparedness-Willingness to Sacrifice-Legacy' (a programme of memorial for those who have fallen in the War and for the Nazi Movement)*
8.10pm	*Close*

As the war progressed, the schedule invariably included a half-hour news programme *'Deutsche Wochenschau'*, which was more akin to the Pathé News programmes being shown in Allied cinemas at the time. There were also more military training films and public information films about how people should conduct themselves as good Nazi citizens in wartime, and tips on how to re-use clothes or on collecting food waste which would be used as animal fodder. While television journalists claimed that they did not experience any direct influence over what they reported, they admitted that they would not even have considered criticising the regime of the time, possibly because they had also been won over to the Nazi cause.

Programmes for soldiers and the wounded

Given their small audiences, those involved in producing television programmes were increasingly conscious that there was a danger that television would not be classified 'as essential to the war effort', and so as to avoid their teams being wound up and called to proper military service, they had to find a way of justifying their existence.

Herbert Engler took over as chief producer in June 1939, and it was his idea to change the focus of television so that most of the programmes would be designed to entertain soldiers recuperating in hospital. He had the brainwave of making use of the cable technology, which had been installed in the Olympic Stadium in 1936, to allow programmes to be produced and broadcast live from a large, domed room which accommodated 2,000 spectators.

Among other programmes, the first 'request' concert was broadcast on 14 March 1941 under the title *'Wir senden Frohsinn, wir spenden Freude'* (We send cheerfulness, we give joy), and this popular programme was screened regularly throughout the war. By 1942, some thirty-four military hospitals had been supplied with their own television sets to provide sup-port and entertainment to the wounded, and all the great showbusiness stars of the day took part in these programmes which were a great success.

Although German television was to continue to make technological advances, including the use of broadband cables to take the Berlin broadcasts to a number of new television salons in Hamburg, by the spring of 1943 virtually all broadcasts to the general public had ceased, being replaced by programmes specifically designed to entertain the military. Indeed, from May 1943 to August 1944, regular entertainment programmes in French and German, primarily intended for wounded German soldiers in military hospitals in Paris, were broadcast by means of the Eiffel Tower, which could even be picked up by the French on their own television sets.

One of the last surviving film reports produced for Nazi television features amputees being made fit for service again. It is a rather grotesque film which shows soldiers who have lost limbs still being able to negotiate an obstacle course with great agility. One soldier who has been given two artificial legs is seen dancing with a pretty girl and pronouncing, 'Life is really wonderful'. This was obviously reported for propaganda purposes and to raise the morale of the wounded troops. It is hard to believe that his enthusiasm was genuine or that many soldiers, other than the most fervent Nazis, could have eagerly anticipated being patched up and returned to the front. Most ordinary Germans had realised that, with the entry of America into the war and the campaign in the Soviet Union having faltered, military defeat was only a question of time.

As the war progressed, transmissions did become more erratic and although the Berlin transmitter was eventually destroyed by a bomb on 23 November 1943, broadcasting continued for a while through the use of telephone lines. The station was forced to cease transmitting completely on 21 June 1944.

CONCLUSION

While the Nazis never really sought to exploit the medium of television to its full potential, primarily because of television's early stage of development and limited viewer accessibility, there is no doubt that it still served a useful purpose to the Nazi machine. Overall, the costs of maintaining a broadcasting capability for almost five years of the war were quite insignificant and were more than justified by the worthwhile results which were achieved, even if these would have little effect on the overall outcome of the war.

First, there was the propaganda triumph of being able to launch the first regular program-ming service in the whole world, and this was further enhanced by the spectacular televised screening of the 1936 Olympic Games. By claiming the successful development of television as a specific Nazi achievement, they sought to make their apparent technological supremacy evident to all. Second, continuing with broadcasts and television development throughout the war not only enabled the Nazis to portray an image of 'life as normal' while providing ideologi-cal guidance, but it also contributed directly to the greater war effort under the auspices of the 'wonder weapons' programme.

Finally, the gradual switch from public to hospital broadcasting to boost the morale of the wounded soldiers was a great success, and the propaganda impact of interviews with remarkably enthusiastic soldiers who had just had artificial legs or arms fitted should not be underestimated. Indeed, it even has uncomfortable parallels with the world of today where, in the summer of 2009, a recuperating British soldier, who had lost limbs in a bomb explosion, was quoted as saying, 'I'm raring to get back to Afghanistan to complete unfinished business.'

Chapter XII

Conclusion

The exploding of myths

The purpose of this book has been to tell the truth about the nature of Nazi film propaganda and to provide the reader with a greater understanding of the content and variety of the vast volume of feature and documentary films which were produced during the Nazi era.

As the Second World War becomes an increasingly distant memory, a number of myths have started to emerge regarding the nature of Nazi film propaganda:

◊ First, that the Nazis were masters *par excellence* of the art of film propaganda.
◊ Second, that the bulk of their film production at the time was overtly political and of no interest to the modern viewer.
◊ Third, that all films produced during the Nazi era were lie-ridden, evil pieces of work which should be discounted accordingly.

This book serves to set the record straight and, in so doing, to dispel a number of the myths which have arisen through a more objective analysis of the truths and the lies, the successes and the failures of Nazi film propaganda.

The Nazis were masters *par excellence* of the art of film propaganda

When Hitler explored the causes of Germany's defeat in the First World War, he became convinced that superior propaganda utilisation was one of the primary reasons for the Allies' success and, consequently, he was determined that when the Nazis assumed power, absolute control of all mass media communication including the cinema would be one of their primary objectives. The subsequent creation of the all powerful Ministry for Enlightenment and Propaganda seemed ideally suited to meet this objective. Cinema audiences grew considerably, and the content of the more than 1,300 feature films and countless documentaries which were produced between 1933 and 1945 bear witness to the material which was allowed to be released under such a restrictive regime.

However, film propaganda, like all propaganda, is a somewhat fickle art. Regardless of the level of control which the Nazis exerted over the choice of subject matter and over every piece of dialogue spoken in every film produced in Germany and Austria, and irrespective of the amount of money and other resources devoted to film production, nothing could ultimately guarantee the success of any film either in terms of box office sales or in terms of propaganda impact.

Admittedly, when it came to the promotion of Hitler as a leader who enjoyed the full support of his people, and of Germany as a vibrant and technologically superior country which was the envy of much of the world, there were some notable 'successes'. Having learnt from her earlier mistakes, Riefenstahl's *Triumph des Willens* did more than any other documentary to raise Hitler to god-like status. Likewise, from a cinematic viewpoint, her documentary of the 1936 Olympic Games and colour films such as *Münchhausen* and *Kolberg* do still stand out as epics today. Nevertheless, this book reveals that the Nazis also made a lot of mistakes in their development and use of film propaganda, and a lot of time and resources were often wasted for no good purpose.

In theory, both the subject matter on which the Nazis decided to concentrate film production and the gradual change in this subject matter over time did seem perfectly understandable. In the early days, their top priority was to convince the general populace that the Weimar Republic had failed Germany and that Nazism could make a real difference in people's lives through falling unemployment, improved living conditions and a renewed pride in their country. Along with numerous documentaries and news footage, the '*Kampzeit*' and '*Blut und Boden*' type films all contributed to this purpose and highlighted the sacrifices which the Nazis' followers had been obliged to make to achieve this new Germany.

Defending their internal policies against attacks from other nations such as America necessitated the production of films which would portray such adversaries in a negative light. When it came to war itself, the production of historically based films to depict the likes of the British and Russians as being treacherous and dangerous foes was necessary to justify internally why they were waging war on such a large scale, rather than just recovering land which had been lost after the First World War. As the horrors of war intensified, Goebbels recognised the need for films which would primarily entertain, albeit usually serving some underlying propaganda purpose. As a result, the authorisation of the production of such heart-rending films as *Kolberg,* which was intended to provide inspiration when all seemed lost, appears completely logical and necessary.

So, given that such an approach appeared totally understandable from a Nazi viewpoint, despite the malevolent intention, where does this book propose that the Nazis might be considered to have failed in their manipulation of film propaganda?

There are a number of indications, and one of the easiest ways to list these is to try to distinguish between those consequences which were avoidable and those which were really out of the control of the Nazis.

Avoidable mistakes

Failure to prevent inappropriate films from being completed

For a regime where film scripts had to be cleared before filming could even commence, it is difficult to understand how the Nazis could ever have allowed a situation to develop where more than thirty films were actually permitted to be partially or fully completed before they were banned from being screened. It was hardly a worthwhile use of actors, crews and, most importantly, of the rare resource of celluloid itself.

Failure to predict likely impact of a film on an audience

Apart from the propaganda own goal of screening historical anti-British resistance films to countries outside Germany, one of the Nazis' greatest difficulties was in turning unpalatable documentary films on subjects such as euthanasia, sterilisation and the Jews into films which their citizens would wish to go and watch. The most obvious failure is to be seen in the contrast between the reception of the feature film *Jud Süss*, which was an outstanding box office success, and that of *Der ewige Jude*, where the scenes of animal slaughter were just too gruesome for the ordinary citizen to stomach. The latter film might well have prompted an anti-Jewish reaction in viewers, but as the resultant negative viewing experience reported by early audiences discouraged others from attendance, its propaganda effectiveness was somewhat curtailed.

Unnecessary production delays caused by Goebbels' intervention

Goebbels' blind belief that he should be the sole arbiter as to what might constitute good or bad propaganda, and his constant intervention in scripts and director and cast selection, meant that films took so long to be completed that they often conflicted with the release of other films. Indeed, it could be argued that just as the Nazis' military campaign foundered because it was being fought on too many fronts, their film propaganda foundered because it was required to fulfil too many objectives simultaneously and sometimes gave conflicting messages. Similarly, the rash execution of the directors of films such as *Titanic* and *Der Führer schenkt den Juden eine Stadt* before their films were even suitable for screening resulted in such delays and controversy that these films were either never released or were released to very limited audiences late in the war.

The concentration on historical incidents to stoke up hatred against the Nazis' enemies

Another consideration is the limitation in film styles arising from Goebbels' firm belief that for a propaganda film to be effective, it had to be based on fact and that the viewer should be unaware that it was propaganda.

> *The best propaganda works invisibly, infusing all public life, without the public being conscious of any propaganda programme. (1941)*

Consequently, with only a few exceptions, such as films designed to promote the common bond between those at home and those on the frontline, propagandistic feature films, and especially those aimed at promoting hatred or fear for their enemies, were not set during the war but further in the past. *Wunschkonzert* is one of those exceptions, and its success was as much due to the fame of the radio programme bearing the same name and the quality of the actors in the film.

While some of the historical films were very effective, Goebbels should have perhaps also paid more attention to the success of the myriad of fictional films set in the war which were being produced by the Allies for propaganda purposes at the same time. *Went the Day Well?* and *One of Our Aircraft is Missing* were obviously pure fiction, but audiences still left the cinema inspired, confident that British spirit and resilience would eventually defeat the hideous Nazis. Of course, the key difference for the Allies was that it was easier for them to produce films set in the war because their citizens were fighting for their own survival against a ruthless enemy. Once the Germans' military aggression went beyond simply recovering land previously lost or protecting citizens of German origin, it was always going to be more difficult for the Nazis to produce convincing films set in the war without arousing sympathy for an enemy which was fighting to retain its freedom and independence.

Unavoidable mistakes

Political necessity and the unpredictability of the course of the war

Changing political aims frequently hampered film production and resulted in the subsequent delay in release or even withdrawal of certain films. So, for example, there were the problems caused by understandable indecision as to whether or not Britain should be regarded as an enemy, given Hitler's hope that an accommodation could be found with the British which, at the very least, would prevent their intervention in the war in Europe. This meant that the first truly anti-British films did not appear for more than seven months after war had been declared, and the most ardent were not to appear until the spring of 1941. Likewise, films which were openly anti-communist in outlook were immediately withdrawn when Germany entered into a pact with the Soviet Union in 1939, only to be re-released once the pact had come to an end. Such delays and manoeuvrings hardly served to fulfil the consistent and repetitive approach which Goebbels considered to be the very tenets of successful propaganda.

Given that it could easily take up to twelve months to produce even a fairly straightforward film, it was little wonder that the course of the war would mean that by the time some films were completed, they had to be withdrawn again almost immediately. For the Nazis, *Besatzung Dora* is one such unfortunate example where comments about looking forward to settling down in the lands they had conquered in the east and scenes featuring Italian allies coming to the rescue of German airmen forced to land in the desert were both redundant by 1943, as the Soviets had begun to recover lost territory and the Italians had changed sides.

Difficulty in assessing the true propaganda success of their films

There was an over-reliance by Goebbels on judging the success of films in terms of box office receipts or on the basis of so-called independent observation of cinema audiences. It is fairly easy to identify where a film has been made with the deliberate purpose of promoting some piece of propaganda. It is also possible to identify items in a film which might be perceived as being propaganda whether or not this was the deliberate intention. What is harder to identify is whether propaganda is effective and what makes successful propaganda in the long term.

The most successful films in terms of box office receipts between 1940 and 1942 actually tended to be general entertainment films which, while perhaps helping to raise morale, served little other direct propagandistic purpose. Even well-attended Nazi-commissioned films such as *Ohm Krüger* do not prove that films with an openly propagandistic message could influence the mindset of an audience in the long term. If press criticism of films was forbidden, how could Goebbels be certain that the reports which the SS observers were submitting about the reception of films were correct? It would have been a brave observer who would have given a particularly negative report about a film in which Goebbels was known to have taken particular personal interest.

When the SS reported that the pro-Irish/anti-British films were actually having the exact opposite effect to what was desired when screened in occupied countries, Goebbels let it be known that he never wanted to see another Irish film. However, if these films were actually proving successful in Germany, then surely all he needed to do was to differentiate between the countries in which each film should be screened rather than 'throwing out the baby with the bath water'.

In reality, while their film propaganda may have helped to reinforce existing attitudes, it did little to change people's perceptions and mindset. The negative portrayal of Jewish characters in *Jud Süss* simply confirmed what some Germans already felt about the Jews, even if such wild generalisations were completely unjustified. And while *Kolberg* was a very impressive film in terms of visual impact, its screening still failed to arouse ordinary citizens to take to the barricades in a determined last fight to the death. Ultimately, propaganda tends to be successful only if it coincides with what people want and expect to hear, and if it is so contrary to their real experience of the world in which they live, it will not be effective.

The only Nazi films of any interest to the modern viewer are the Leni Riefenstahl documentaries and a couple of feature films

When mention is made of Nazi film propaganda today, many people are aware only of the Leni Riefenstahl documentaries, a couple of anti-Jewish films and colour classics such as *Münchhausen* or *Kolberg*.

Nevertheless, closer inspection of films such as the 1936 Olympic Games – often considered to be instruments of pure Nazi propaganda – reveals a number of interesting incongruities. The decision to screen both the successes of Jesse Owens and the failures of German athletes hardly serves to promote the notion of the invincibility of the Aryan race.

However, what this book has attempted to do is to reveal that apart from these well-known films, many other feature films and documentaries were produced which are now largely forgotten or, indeed, were unknown to audiences outside Germany, but which were just as influential and in many cases of even more interest to the modern viewer. It is fascinating to observe how the Nazis deliberately manipulated historical events to produce anti-American and anti-British films, which were designed to make German audiences feel ill-disposed towards these nations with whom they were to be at war. Other films such as *Hans Westmar* give an intriguing insight into how the cinema was used to influence German viewers; this was firstly, by acknowledging the debt they owed to the 'martyrs' who had supported a Nazi regime which was so beneficial to Germany; and then through the likes of *Heimkehr* and *G.P.U.* into accepting the need for a war to recover lost lands and to protect ethnic Germans living abroad.

Any films produced during the Nazi era must be lie-ridden, works of evil, which should be discounted accordingly

Given that the Nazi regime was responsible for so many evil deeds and so much death and destruction, it is easy to understand why it is tempting to condemn anything produced during the Nazi era out of hand. Nothing can justify the Nazis' attempted brutal elimination of a whole race or their pursuit of world domination, and there is no doubt that they did employ film propaganda to support the realisation of such objectives. However, the purpose of this book is not to judge the Nazis' policies nor their position in history, but rather to provide an objective analysis of the content of their films.

In the anti-British feature films, history is certainly not clear cut; Mary, Queen of Scots did receive harsh treatment at the hands of Queen Elizabeth; the British did rule Ireland with an iron fist; and the reasons for Britain's involvement in the Boer War were not entirely altruistic. Likewise, in their anti-American films, the democracy of America did not guarantee a life of plenty for all, and this book has shown that not everything that the Germans claimed was false, but rather that they manipulated events and facts to their own ends and frequently neglected to give the other side of the story. Of course, this approach neatly served Hitler's requirement that the way to influence the masses was to produce propaganda which was simple and certain, positive or negative, right or wrong, truth or lies – but never half measures.

Similarly, highlighting controversial issues and statistics which viewers might find disturbing about the history of the Nazis' enemies and about certain Jewish customs was not in itself a crime, but to use such one-sided arguments to reach biased conclusions which were to be used as a justification for total war and the forced extermination of whole races or sections of society was quite another purpose which could never be condoned in a civilised society.

While not every film was specifically commissioned by the Nazis and not even all the commissioned films had deep political overtones, it has to be acknowledged that every film released during the period, however innocent it seemed, was a form of propaganda. The choice of subject matter, the manner in which the subject is portrayed and the censure of all films which did not meet acceptable Nazi criteria all served some purpose, even if it were only to raise German morale or to encourage more of the populace to attend cinemas and, thereby, be subjected to the more openly political documentaries and newsreels which would precede the main feature.

Significance of Nazi film propaganda for the modern world

Notwithstanding some of the Nazis' failures when it came to the effective use and control of film propaganda, the example of the Third Reich, and especially the presentation of Hitler, clearly demonstrates the awesome potential power of propaganda when wielded for evil purposes by a totalitarian regime, and it would be naïve to believe that we are not subjected to similar propaganda methods today, even within our apparently open and democratic existence in the West.

Regardless of the party concerned, every party political broadcast will highlight only the positive aspects of that party's policies and the negative aspects of its rivals. Any television documentary which is produced has a firm conclusion it wishes to reach, and its content will be shaped and presented with this objective in mind; any feature film has the potential to be used as a piece of propaganda, especially if the same message is repeated in a number of films and there are no films produced which give a counter-argument.

In theory, we are fortunate to live in a free society where we have free access to the Internet and where we can compare what is being reported in our country with what is being said elsewhere. We know that many countries in the world do not allow such freedoms and their inhabitants are presented with only a very selective view of events in their own country and in the wider world. However, even this apparent freedom should not lead us to become complacent. With modern visual effects, anything can appear real and it can be difficult to distinguish between what is genuine and something which has been generated by a computer in a film studio. Nor should we believe everything we read on the Internet. Just because it is reported a hundred times that the moon is made of cheese, it does not mean that it is. I am conscious even in researching this book that a number of details about a particular film which were actually quite fallacious were repeated word for word on a number of websites, and it was impossible to trace the source of the original piece of misinformation.

With regard to the films I have reviewed in this book, I would hope that many readers will now be sufficiently interested as to wish to view several of these for themselves. Many of the films analysed are now available with English or German subtitles and can be purchased commercially, primarily from specialist film concerns in the United States and occasionally also from Germany, although with the obvious caveat that these are often shortened, censored versions which were only re-released many years after the war. Be warned that documentaries such as *Der ewige Jude* do make particularly harrowing viewing; however, with the exception of *Ohm Krüger*, *Heimkehr* and *Jud Süss*, it is unlikely that any of the other feature films reviewed in this book are particularly likely to shock or offend, especially when judged against the harrowing content of some twenty-first century films. Indeed, the propaganda of some of the feature films may even cause some amusement to a modern audience because it is so blatant, rather like some of the more obvious moralising and stereotyping of British and American films of the period.

The significance of this book for the modern world is not restricted to its investigation of the use of film propaganda, as the level of current interest in the Second World War, its history and its cinema is still quite astonishing. The commemoration of the 70th anniversary of the Battle of Britain resulted in the release of a whole series of new documentaries about the period, and the production of such feature films as *Valkyrie* starring Tom Cruise in 2008 reveals the fascination which that period still holds for the current generation, although it is ironic that *Valkyrie* also presents a distorted view of history. Undoubtedly, part of the reason for this renewed and increasing interest in the Second World War is that sufficient time has now passed that the period can be examined more objectively and people are less likely to be upset when it is revealed that the general assumptions which had been taken for granted over the years were not always valid.

Even within Germany, the production of films such as *Der Untergang* (released in English as *Downfall*) in 2004 and *Mein Führer* (*My Führer*) in 2007 would have been inconceivable twenty years ago. What is of even more interest in relation to this book is the general release in August 2010 of a new German film called *Jud Süss: Film ohne Gewissen* (*Jew Süss: Film without Conscience*) which is a film about the Nazis' infamous *Jud Süss* production, analysed in Chapter IV of this book. This new film caused a real furore in Germany, with some audiences so upset by the content that they walked out of cinemas in disgust. Apart from anything else, the film reveals how unwilling Ferdinand Marian, who plays the main Jewish character, had been to accept a role which was always going to be controversial. The verdict of one major newspaper was that while the modern German nation may feel comfortable now about producing films which mock or criticise the Nazis, it did not feel it was appropriate to make films which left the viewer feeling sympathy for Hitler's helpers, whatever the extenuating circumstances. It is obvious that the wounds caused both by the Nazis and the 1940 *Jud Süss* film still run deep.

Perfectly understandably, it would seem that Germany's Nazi history is perhaps still too painful and recent for it to permit a completely detached analysis of the true nature of German cinema during the Nazi era.

Select Bibliography

Books in English

Bergfelder, T. *The German Cinema Book.* (British Film Institute, 2002)

Birdwell, Michael E. Celluloid *Soldiers: Warner Bros. Campaign against Nazism.* (NYU Press, 2000)

Brown, P. Hume. *Scotland: A Short History.* (Oliver and Boyd, 1961)

Burrin, P. *Hitler and the Jews: The Genesis of the Holocaust.* (Hodder Arnold, 1994)

Casey, S. *Cautious Crusade: Franklin D. Roosevelt, American Public Opinion and the War against Nazi Germany.* (Oxford University Press, 2001)

Farrington, K. *Secret War.* (Bookmart Ltd, 1995)

Fox, J. *Film Propaganda in Britain and Nazi Germany: World War II Cinema.* (Berg, 2007)

Goebbels, J and Taylor, F. *The Goebbels Diaries 1939-1941.* (Putnam Pub Group, 1983)

Hitler, A . *Mein Kampf.* (Translation – Jaico Publishing, 2009)

Hoffmann, H. *Triumph of Propaganda: Film and National Socialism, 1933–1945.* (Berghahn Books, 1997)

Hull, D.S. *Film in the Third Reich: A Study of the German Cinema, 1933–1945.* (University of California Press, 1969)

—*Film in the Third Reich: Art and Propaganda in Nazi Germany.* (Simon and Schuster, 1973)

Hurd, G. *National Fictions: World War Two in British Films and Television.* (BFI, 1984)

Hyland, G., and Gill, A. *Last Talons of the Eagle.* (Trafalgar Square Publishing, 1999)

Irving, D. *Goebbels: Mastermind of the Third Reich.* (Focal Point Publications, 1997)

Jackall, Robert. *Propaganda.* (NYU Press, 1994)

Kamm, A., and Baird, M. *John Logie Baird – A Life.* (NMSE Publishing, 2002)

Kelson, J.F. *Catalogue of forbidden German feature and short film productions: held in Zonal Film Archives of Film Section, Information Services Division, Control Commission for Germany.* (Flicks Books, 1996)

Koppes. C R. *Hollywood Goes to War: How Politics, Profits and Propaganda Shaped World War II Movies.* (University of California Press, 1990)

Kreimeier, K. *The UFA Story: A History of Germany's Greatest Film Company, 1918–1945.* (University of California Press, 1999)

Leiser, E. *Nazi Cinema.* (Secker and Warburg, 1974)

Lloyd, A. *Movies of the Thirties.* (Orbis, 1985)

Manuel, R., and Fraenkel, H. *Dr Goebbels: His Life and Death.* (Simon and Schuster, 1960)

Opfermann, C. *The Art of Darkness*. (University Trace Press, 2002)

Petley, Julian. *Capital and Culture: German Cinema 1933–45*. (Educational Advisory Service, British Film Institute, 1979)

Reeves, N. *Official British Film Propaganda during the First World War*. (Routledge, 1986)

—*The Power of Film Propaganda: Myth or Reality?* (Cassell, 1999)

Reimer, R.C. *Cultural History through a National Socialist lens: essays on the cinema of the Third Reich*. (Camden House, 2002)

Rentschler, E. *The Ministry of Illusion: Nazi Cinema and its Afterlife*. (Harvard University Press, 1996)

Schoeps, K. *Literature and Film in the Third Reich*. (Camden House, 2004)

Shirer, W. *The Rise and Fall of the Third Reich*. (Pan Books, 1981)

Short, K.R.M. *Film and Radio Propaganda in World War II*. (University of Tennessee, 1983)

Spies, S.B. *Methods of Barbarism: Roberts and Kitchener and Civilians in the Boer Republics, January 1900–May 1902*. (Human and Rousseau, 1977)

Stanley, L. *Mourning Becomes … post/memory, commemoration and the concentration camps of the South African War*. (Manchester University Press, 2006)

Steel, T. *Scotland's Story*. (William Collins, 1984)

Taylor, B., and Van der Will, W. *The Nazification of Art: Art, Design, Architecture Music and Film in Third Reich*. (Winchester Press, 1981)

Tegal,S. *Nazis and the Cinema*. (Hambledon Continuum, 2008)

Thomas, T. *The Cinema of the Sea*. (Thomas Mcfarland and Co., 1988)

Welch, D. *Propaganda and the German Cinema 1933–1945*. (I.B Taurus & Co Ltd, 2007)

Winkel, R.V., and Welch, D. *Cinema and the Swastika: The International Expansion of Third Reich Cinema*. (Palgrave Macmillan, 2007)

Books in German

Bauers, Dr A. *Deutsche Spielfilmalmanach 1929–1950*. (Filmladen Christoph Winterberg, 1976)

Donner, W. *Propaganda und Film im Dritten Reich*. (TIP-Verlag, 1995)

Dustar, B. *Film als Propagandainstrument in der Jugendpolitik des Dritten Reiches*. (Coppi-Verlag, 1996)

Giesen, R. *Hitlerjunge Quex, Jud Süß und Kolberg: Die Propaganda Filme des Dritten Reiches*. (Schwarzkopf und Schwarzkopf, 2005)

Franz, E.G. *Die Chronik Hessens*. (Chronik Verlag, 1991)

Hardinghaus, C. *Filmpropaganda für den Holocaust?: Eine Studie anhand der Hetzfilme "Der ewige Jude" und "Jud Süß"*. (Tectum, 2008)

Hembus, J. *Das Western-Lexicon*. (Carl Hanser Verlag & William Heyne Verlag)

Hickethier, K. *Geschichte des Deutschen Fernsehens*. (Verlag J.B. Metzler, 1998)

Hollstein, D. *Antisemitische Filmpropaganda: die Darstellung des Juden im nationalsozialistischen Spielfilm*. (Verlag Dokumentation, 1971)

Jacobsen, W. *Geschichte des Deutschen Films*. (Verlag J B Metzler, 2004)

Kanzog, K. *"Staatspolitisch besonders wertvoll": ein Handbuch zu 30 deutschen Spielfilmen der Jahre 1934–1945*. (Diskurs-Film-Verlag, 1994)

Kinkel, L. *Die Scheinwerferin: Leni Riefenstahl und das "Dritte Reich"*. (Europa Verlag, 2002)

Kleinhans, B. *Ein Volk, ein Reich, ein Kino : Lichtspiel in der braunen Provinz*. (PapyRossa Verlag, 2003)

Knilli, F. *Ich war Jud Süß: Die Geschichte des Filmstars Ferdinand Marian*. (Henschel, 2000)

Knopp, G. *Damals 1944: Das Jahr des Widerstands*. (Deutsche Verlags-Anstalt, 1994)

Köppen, M. *Kunst der Propaganda: Der Film im Dritten Reich*. (Lang, 2007)

Maiwald, K. *Filmzensur im NS Staat*. (Nowotny, 1983)

Meiners, A., and Taffelt, A. *Träume Bilder. Bilder Träume: Die Geschichte der Ufa von 1917 bis heute*. (Nicolai, 2007)

Moeller, F. *Der Filmminister: Goebbels und der Film im Dritten Reich*. (Henschel, 1998)

Oberwinter, K. *Bewegende Bilder: Repräsentation und Produktion von Emotionen in Leni Riefenstahls* Triumph des Willens. (Deutscher Kunstverlag, 2007)

Prinzer, H.H. *Chronik des Deutschen Films 1895–1994*. (Verlag J.B. Metzler)

Reichert, R. *Im Kino der Humanwissenschaften: Studien zur Medialisierung wissenschaftlichen Wissens*. (Transcript Verlag, Bielefeld, 2007)

Ruhl, K. *Brauner Alltag: 1933–1939 in Deutschland*. (Droste Verlag, 1981)

Sakkara, M. *Kino im Dienst der Propaganda, der Politik und des Krieges*. (DSZ Verlag, 2008)

Wetzel, K., and Hagemann, P. *Zensur – Verbotene Deutsche Filme 1933–1945*. (Verlag Volker Spiess, 1978)

Wildt, M. *Geschichte des Nationalsozialismus*. (UTB, 2008)

Winkler, K. *Fernsehen unterm Hakenkreuz – Medien in Geschichte und Gegenwart*. (Böhlau Verlag)

Wulf, J. *Theater und Film im Dritten Reich*. (Sigbert Mohn Verlag, 1964)

BOOKS IN FRENCH

Bellan, M. *100 Ans de Cinéma Allemand*. (Ellipses Marketing, 2001)

Haver, G. *La Suisse, les Alliés et le cinéma – Propagande et Représentation 1939–1945*. (Editions Antipodes, 2001)

FILM AND TELEVISION MAGAZINE ARTICLES

Friedmann, R.M. *Juden-Ratten – Von der rassistischen Metonymie zur tierischen Metapher in Fritz Hipplers Film 'Der ewige Jude '*. (Frauen und Film, No. 47, 1989)

Horak, Jan-Christopher. *Luis Trenker's The Kaiser of California: How the West was won, Nazi style*. (Historical Journal of Film, Radio and Television, Vol. 6 No. 2, 1986)

Hornshøj-Møller, Stig and Culbert, David. *'Der ewige Jude' (1940: Joseph Goebbels' unequalled monument to anti-Semitism*. (Historical Journal of Film, Radio and Television, Vol. 12 No. 1, 1992)

Netzeband, G. *Feindbilder: Skizzen zur hitlerfaschisten Filmpolitik und Propaganda* (Film und Fernsehen, No. 10, 1988)

Richards, Jeffrey. *Two Titanics* (Focus on Film, No. 28, 1977)

Walker, G. *An analysis of Der Ewige Jude: its relationship to Nazi Anti-Semitic ideas and policies*. (Wide Angle, Vol. 3 No. 4, 1980)

Manuscripts and Essay Papers

Delseit, Wolfgang. *'Der Wandel des "Englandbildes" im nationalsozialistischen Spielfilm'* (Köln University, 1989)

Hallstein, Christian W. *Creating the Enemy: Anti-British Nazi film propaganda*. (West Virginia University, 1994)

Lymberopoulos, Christopher. *Rundfunk und Film als Propagandamittel im Dritten Reich*. (Aachen University, 1989)

Ross, Stephen J. *Confessions of a Nazi Spy: Warner Bros. Anti-Fascism and the Politicization of Hollywood from Warners' War: politics, pop culture & propaganda in wartime Hollywood.* (The Norman Lear Center, 2004)

Other
Deutschland von Heute (Booklet published by Terramare Office, Berlin, 1935)
Terveen, Fritz. 'Erläuterungen und Hinweise zu dem NS-Propagandafilm "Herr Roosevelt Plaudert"' (Hamburg, 1936)
Press and magazine cuttings held in the Frankfurt Film Museum Library Archive
Original film programmes

INDEX

49th Parallel (1941) 198, 199, 200, 202
Action in the North Atlantic (1943) 196, 200, 208
Achtung! Feind hört mit! (1940) 141, 142, 204, 206
Albers, Hans 117, 118, 119, 173, 174, 175, 176, 177, 181
Alles Leben ist Kampf (1937) 215
Allied Control Commission 50, 84, 232
Allied Feature Films 193–209
America
    legal/justice system 97, 110, 113, 114, 115, 116
    portrayal of 21, 27, 67, 92–116, 149, 196, 198, 200, 207, 208, 215, 216, 254–258, 273
    the Great Depression 97, 98, 103, 193
Amerika sieht sich selbst (1942) 96
Anna Karenina (1935) 100
Anti-American films 92–116, 273
Anti-Bolshevik films 117–136
Anti-British films 9, 17, 19, 23–71, 78, 202, 215, 272, 273
Anti-Communist films 117–136, 272
Anti-English *see* Anti-British films
Anti-Polish films 121, 122–128, 232–237
Anti-Semitic films 9, 24, 72–92, 94, 95, 134, 214–215, 237, 238, 247, 255, 271, 273
Aryan 20, 72, 84, 87, 101, 118, 172, 185, 212, 226, 229, 231, 242, 244, 273
Baird Television Ltd 260, 263
Battleship Potemkin (1925) 100
BBC 260
Bell Bottom George (1944) 209
Berge in Flammen (1931) 103

Besatzung Dora (1942-43) 135, 172, 173, 272
'Bloody Sunday' 128
Blum, Léon 134
Blut und Boden (Blood and Soil) 270
Blut und Boden (1933) 210
Boer War 52, 53, 59, 273
Bolsheviks 19, 117, 118, 131, 133, 134, 238
Canada 199, 200, 202, 205
Cap Arcona 70
Carl Peters (1941) 25, 26
Casablanca (1942) 187, 196, 203, 208
Caspar, Horst 160
Censorship 9, 18, 170, 194, 196, 197
Chamberlain, Joseph 52, 53, 54, 55, 57, 60
Chamberlain, Neville 23, 53, 55, 58, 118, 193
Chaplin, Charlie 89, 209, 243
Chetniks! The Fighting Guerillas (1943) 208
Church 10, 11, 30, 31, 32, 39, 42, 56, 101, 105, 119, 149, 154, 157, 160, 163, 164, 216, 234
Churchill, Sir Winston 24, 56, 164, 180, 194, 195, 206, 207, 215, 236, 257
Communists 20, 35, 118, 119, 137, 139, 144, 145–152, 197, 208
Concentration camps 53, 55, 58, 70, 72, 127, 231
    Auschwitz 224, 247, 253
    Dachau 263
    Theresienstadt 247–254
California Gold Rush 97, 107, 109
Condottieri (1937) 109
Confessions of a Nazi Spy (1939) 92, 94, 116, 196, 198, 200
Contraband (1940) 204, 205
Cottage to Let (1941) 198, 204, 205

Danzig 128, 161, 163, 232, 233, 234
Das blaue Licht (1932) 223
Das Erbe (1935) 215
Das Herz der Königin (1940) 25, 26, 36–54
Das Leben geht weiter 144
Das Sowjetparadies (1941) 216
Democracy 20, 89, 116, 198, 215, 255, 257, 258, 273
Denmark 233
Der ewige Jude (1940) 76, 77, 95, 214, 238–246, 258, 271, 274
Der Fuchs von Glenarvon (1940) 25, 28–35, 50, 51, 82
Der Führer schenkt den Juden eine Stadt (1944) 215, 247–254, 271
Der grosse König (1940-1942) 168
Der grosse Sprung (1927) 99
Der heilige Berg (1926) 99
Der Hund von Baskerville (1936) 179
Der Kaiser von Kalifornien (1936) 97, 104–109
Der Mann, der Sherlock Holmes war (1937) 174, 175, 176–180
Der Rebell (1932) 98, 10, 102, 103, 109
Der Sieg des Glaubens (1934) 212, 223
Der Untergang (2004) 275
Der verlorene Sohn (1934) 97, 98–103
Die Fahne hoch! 139, 144, 145, 148, 151, 152, 219, 221
Die Feuerzangenbowle (1944) 174, 175, 187–192
Die goldene Spinne (1943) 141, 143, 204, 206
Die grosse Liebe (1942) 158, 171, 172
Die Nibelungen (1924) 100
Die Rothschilds (1940) 76, 78–84, 192, 245
Die Rothschilds Aktien auf Waterloo (1941) 78–84
Dietrich, Sepp 218
Documentary Films 9, 17, 20, 74, 77, 117, 133, 135, 195, 210–259, 269, 270, 274
Doyle, Sir Arthur Conan 176, 177, 180
Dreßler-Andreß, Horst 262
Edge of Darkness (1943) 198, 200, 201, 207, 208
Education 14, 20, 46, 48, 127, 175, 187, 191, 192, 241, 259, 264
Ehrenhalle 219
Eichmann, Adolf 247
Eiffel Tower 266, 268
Elizabeth I, Queen 26, 36–45, 273
Enemy, portrayal of 14, 19, 23, 34, 88, 118, 121, 144, 146, 148, 198, 201, 202, 209, 271
Engelmann, Andrews 129, 130

Engler, Herbert 267
Entertainment Films 170–175, 176–192
Erbkrank (1936) 215
Espionage see Spies
Ethnic Germans 92, 118, 121–128, 140, 202, 208, 214, 233, 236, 237, 273
Euthanasia 20, 215, 270
Ewers, Hanns Heinz 145, 152
Ewiger Wald (1936) 210, 212
'Fair Play' 49, 179
Fanck, Arnold 94
Feldzug in Polen (1940) 213, 214, 232–237, 267
Feuchtwanger, Lion 89, 90
Feuertaufe (1940) 214
Fifth Column 92, 196, 198, 200, 204, 205
Film see individual film titles
Films
    banned 10, 17,18, 36, 51, 61, 62, 69-71, 91, 95, 96, 97, 103, 104, 116, 121, 128, 129, 135, 136, 145, 153, 169, 172, 173, 175, 191, 196, 217, 224, 232, 238, 255, 270
    box office success 18, 26, 69, 78, 85, 145, 169, 172, 186, 187, 190, 195, 212, 223, 224, 245
    cinema attendance 18, 20, 60, 171, 271
    comedies 74, 75, 89, 95, 158, 171, 174, 176-192
    in colour 10, 160, 173, 175, 181, 185, 186, 270, 273
    production 9, 17, 18, 21, 24, 34, 50, 52, 60, 68, 74, 84, 89, 127, 135, 158, 167, 168, 170, 173, 174, 184, 186, 191, 196, 224, 245, 253, 269, 270, 271, 275
Film industry 17, 18, 20, 35, 81, 100, 116, 148, 159, 192, 195
'Film of the Nation' 60, 127, 160
First World War 9, 14, 17, 23, 24, 27, 50, 55, 101, 118, 128, 139, 150, 162, 193, 195, 208, 212, 213, 243, 269, 270
Five Graves to Cairo (1943) 203, 205
Flüchtlinge (1933) 117, 119, 159
Foreign Correspondent (1940) 196, 207
Freedom Radio (1941) 33, 199, 202, 205, 208
Friesennot (1935) 119, 120
Fünf Millionen suchen einen Erben (1938) 95
Gentlemen (1941) 215
George, Heinrich 85, 91, 110, 112, 116, 139, 160
Germanin - Die Geschichte einer Kolonialen Tat (1943) 26, 27
Gerron, Kurt 247–254

Goebbels, Joseph
anti-Jewish sentiments 24, 73, 74
speeches 17, 100, 131, 135, 167
influence over films 17, 22, 25, 28, 34,
35, 46, 51, 60, 70, 74, 78, 89, 90, 91,
94, 96, 103, 109, 145, 152, 156, 167,
168, 171, 172, 173, 181, 185, 245,
255, 270, 271
views on films 42, 50, 52, 60, 69, 74, 76,
84, 91, 101, 127, 135, 136, 145, 148,
153, 168, 169, 212, 230, 245
views on propaganda 19, 84, 171, 253,
272
Goedecke, Heinz 153, 158
Göring, Hermann 152, 172, 191, 198, 230,
246, 265
Gone with the Wind (1939) 185
G.P.U. (1942) 76, 121, 129-136, 273
Große Freiheit No. 7 (1943-1944) 173, 174
Hadamovsky, Eugen 260, 263
Hans Westmar (1933) 76, 100, 139, 144,
145-152, 208, 273
Harlan, Veit 85, 90, 91, 96, 160, 167, 168
Heimat, concept 87, 98, 101, 118, 126, 185
Heimkehr (1941) 76, 118, 121, 122-128,
273, 274
Heroism 46, 69, 71, 133, 169
Herr Roosevelt plaudert (1943) 216, 258
Hess, Rudolf 84, 218, 220
Hierl, Konstantin 218
Himboldt, Karin 187, 190, 192
Himmler, Heinrich 122, 219
Hinz, Werner 28, 30, 35, 46, 51, 52
Hippler, Dr Fritz 232, 237, 238, 245, 255
History 24, 27, 36, 45, 50, 59, 71, 77, 80, 82,
128, 137, 151, 188, 191, 198, 212, 214,
240, 249, 275
Hitler, Adolf
as a leader figure 20, 58, 89, 94, 101,
108, 118, 124, 126, 128, 150, 159,
179, 210, 220, 222, 235, 258, 270
on America 92
on Aryan superiority 89, 229
on British 23, 24, 55, 84
on Jews 17, 72, 73, 74, 238, 242, 245,
255
on propaganda 11-15, 24, 128, 269,
273
speeches 20, 95, 219, 220, 222, 223,
240
Hitler Salute 148, 157, 190, 192, 230, 262
Hitler Youth 20, 50, 51, 139, 218, 220, 246,
264
Hitlerjunge Quex (1933) 60, 100, 137, 139,
152

Hollywood 10, 60, 74, 94, 95, 103, 136, 175,
185, 195, 196
Holocaust 224
Horst Wessel Song 145, 151, 219
Humour 83, 84, 174, 177, 179, 184, 208, 209
In Which We Serve (1942) 198, 201, 205
International Red Cross 247, 253
Ireland 25, 27, 28-35, 46-51, 74, 82, 196, 273
Ismay, Bruce 62-69
Italy 109, 196, 218
Jannings, Emil 52, 60
Jews
appearance 9, 73, 74, 86, 149, 243, 244
business and finance practices 14, 17,
20, 26, 72, 74, 78-84, 85-91, 96,
216, 245, 256
contributions to art 73, 103, 116, 239,
243, 245, 256
criminal activity 73, 239, 244, 258
religious practices 88, 241, 242, 244,
245, 246
Jud Süss (1940) 76, 78, 85-91, 96, 168, 185,
245, 270, 272, 275
Jud Süss - Film ohne Gewissen (2010) 275
Jungle Book (1942) 185
Kadetten (1939) 129
Kästner, Erich 186
Kampfgeschwader Lützow (1941) 139
Kampfzeit 20, 137
Kimmich, Max 28, 35, 46, 50
Kitchener 32, 53, 55, 56, 58, 59
Kohner, Paul 103
Kolberg (1945) 22, 60, 91, 127, 144, 160-
169, 270, 272
Koppenhöfer, Maria 36, 42
Kraft durch Freude organisation 262, 264
Krauss, Werner 85, 91
Kristallnacht 72, 73, 231
La Rochelle 169
Leander, Zarah 36, 39, 42, 45, 89, 171
Legion Condor (1939) 129
Leinen aus Irland (1939) 74, 76
Lindbergh, Charles 92, 94
Lohkamp, Emil 145, 150
Luitpold Arena 217, 218, 219, 221
Luther, Martin 88
Lutze, Viktor 219
Marian, Ferdinand 28, 35, 52, 60, 85, 87, 91,
181, 185, 275
Marsch der Veteranen 96
Martyrdom 41
Mary, Queen of Scots 26, 36-45, 273
Mein Führer (2007) 275
Mein Kampf 11, 13, 14, 17, 72, 191, 220,
223

Mein Leben für Irland (1941) 25, 35, 46–51
Millions Like Us (1943) 159, 204
Mills, John 205
Ministry of Information 195
Ministerium für Volkserklärung und Propaganda 16-17
Missionaries 49, 56, 60, 202
Morale 22, 92, 140, 144, 169, 171, 172, 174, 206, 208, 212, 214, 268, 272, 274
Mordsache Holm (1938) 179
Morgenrot (1933) 24, 158
Mrs Miniver (1942) 196, 198, 201, 203, 206
Münchhausen (1943) 21, 91, 169, 174, 175, 181–186, 270, 273
Music 16, 31, 62, 74, 99, 126, 132, 141, 145, 155, 157, 176, 180, 190, 202, 206, 208, 217, 219, 221, 222, 226, 228, 238, 247, 257, 264
Myths 10, 269–275
Napoleon 72, 76, 79, 81, 84, 97, 100, 108, 144, 161, 162, 165, 167, 169, 197, 198
Nationalistic Films 137–144, 145–169
Nazism 10, 151, 196, 200, 224, 263, 276
New York 68, 97, 98-103, 225, 231, 240, 255, 256
'Night of the Long Knives' 219
Night Train to Munich (1940) 136, 198, 199, 205, 208
Norway 196, 207, 208
Ohm Krüger (1941) 27, 49, 52-61, 272, 274
Olivier, Laurence 197
Olympia (1938) 213, 224, 226–231
Olympic Games 1936 9, 89, 153, 213, 226, 231, 259, 262, 268, 270, 273
One of our Aircraft is Missing (1942) 204, 205, 208, 271
Opfer der Vergangenheit (1937) 215
Owens, Jesse 89, 228, 229, 273
Paris 62, 70, 131, 135, 176, 184, 224, 240, 268
'Paul Nipkow' 260
Pedro soll hängen (1941) 95, 96
Peenemünde 265
People's War 201, 204
Poland 23, 24, 50, 58, 117, 118, 121, 122–128, 149, 153, 157, 166, 196, 208, 214, 224, 232–237, 239, 267
Ponto, Erich 187, 192
Possendorf, Hans 110
Pour le Mérite (1936) 25, 137, 139
Prädikate 18
Prague 76, 91, 174, 247, 249
Press 14, 16, 17, 35, 69, 96, 113, 114, 210, 218, 231, 241, 242, 272
Pro-Nazi films *see Nationalistic films*

Quadflieg, Will 36, 45, 46, 129
Raddatz, Carl 122, 144, 153, 159
Rassenpolitisches Amt 215
Reiter von Deutsch-Ostafrika (1934) 23
Religion 73, 88, 201, 202, 239, 241, 242, 244, 245, 246, 257
Resistance 25, 50, 169, 199, 200, 201, 203, 204, 205, 208, 270
Rhodes, Cecil 52–61
Riefenstahl, Leni 94, 212, 213, 217–225, 226–231, 270, 273
Ritter, Karl 129, 135
Robert und Bertram (1939) 74, 75
Roc, Patricia 158, 159
Röhm, Ernst 152, 223
Roosevelt, Eleanor 256
Roosevelt, Franklin 95, 101, 116, 197, 206, 207, 216, 254, 255–258
Rühmann, Heinz 95, 158, 175, 176, 177, 187, 190, 191, 192
Rund um die Freiheitsstatue (1942) 96, 215, 216, 255–259
S.A. Mann Brand (1933) 6, 137, 138, 148, 152
Saboteur (1942) 196, 198
Scotland 36–45
Second World War 9, 10, 12, 55, 61, 97, 164, 166, 195, 214, 230, 264, 269, 270
Self-sacrifice 46, 69, 71, 157, 169, 205
Selpin, Herbert 62, 70
Sensationsprozess Casilla (1939) 97, 110–116
Sherlock Holmes 174, 175, 176–180, 205, 207
Sherlock Holmes – Die Graue Dame (1937) 179
Sherlock Holmes and the Secret Weapon (1943) 180, 205, 207
Sherlock Holmes and the Voice of Terror (1943) 180, 207
Sherlock Holmes in Washington (1943) 180, 207
Sieg im Westen (1941) 213, 214
Söderbaum, Kristina 85, 90, 160, 168
Solari, Laura 129
Soldaten von Morgen (1941) 215
Sontag, Susan 225
Soviet Union 22, 58, 71, 104, 108, 117, 119, 121, 129, 131, 136, 139, 144, 148, 150, 173, 196, 216, 234, 236, 268, 272
Spies 92, 121, 135, 141–143, 194, 195, 196, 198, 200, 204, 205, 206, 209
Stereotypes
    national 133, 135, 136, 198, 215
    racial 74, 81

Sterilisation 20, 215, 270
Stranger on the Stairs (1940) 116
Streicher, Julius 218
Stukas (1941) 139, 140, 159, 205, 208
Suter, Johann 97, 104–110
Swastika 34, 125, 148, 217, 218, 220, 221, 229, 230, 237
Television 259–268
   intermediate film technique 263
   programme schedules 263, 264, 267
Terra 18, 188, 189, 190
That Hamilton Woman (1941) 197
The Adventures of Tartu (1943) 136, 204, 205, 208
The Cross of Lorraine (1943) 202, 208
The Day will Dawn (1942) 198, 204, 208
The First of the Few (1942) 205, 208
The Gentle Sex (1943) 204
The Great Dictator (1940) 89, 209
The Lady Vanishes (1939) 180, 194, 204, 205
The Lion Has Wings (1939) 195
The Longest Day (1962) 35
The North Star (1943) 198, 208
'The People's Television' 264
The Silver Fleet (1943) 198, 205, 206, 208
The Spy in Black (1939) 194, 195, 204, 205
The Thief of Bagdad (1940) 185
The Third Man (1949) 192
The Thirty Nine Steps (1935) 135
The Way Ahead (1944) 200, 205, 208, 209
The Wizard of Oz (1939) 185
The Wonderful Horrible Life of Leni Riefenstahl (1993) 224
The Young Mr Pitt (1942) 198
Theresienstadt 214, 247–254
Tiefland (1954) 224
Titanic (1943) 25, 27, 62–71, 271
To Have and Have Not (1944) 206
Tobis 18, 60
Todt, Fritz 218
Tomorrow We Live (1942) 208
'Total War' speech 167
Trenker, Luis 26, 94, 97, 98–103, 104–109

Triumph des Willens (1935) 212, 217–225, 226, 228, 261, 270
Tschechowa, Olga 28, 35
Two Thousand Women (1944) 203, 204
U-Boote Westwärts! (1941) 139, 141, 205
Ucicky, Gustav 122, 127
UFA 18, 170, 175, 180, 181, 186
Ufi 18
Um das Menschenrecht (1934) 118, 139
Undercover (1943) 208
United States Office of War Information (OWI) 195
Valkyrie (2008) 274, 275
Veidt, Conrad 90, 194
Venice Film Festival 60, 85, 103, 104, 109, 224, 231
Verräter (1936) 141, 142, 206
Versailles Treaty 21, 146, 179, 180, 193, 213, 233, 237
Victoria, Queen 53, 54, 55, 57, 59, 60
Von Baky, Josef 181
Von Ribbentropp 24
Von Borsody, Eduard 110, 116, 153, 158
Warner Brothers 116, 196
Wegener, Paul 46, 145, 160
Weimar Republic 20, 139, 210, 270
Wellington, Duke of 78–82
Went the Day Well? (1942) 10, 33, 198, 201, 203, 271
Wenzler, Franz 145
Werner, Ilse 153, 157, 158, 159, 174, 181
Wernicke, Otto 52, 60, 62, 122, 127, 128, 160
Wessel, Horst 144, 145–152, 219
Wessely, Paula 122, 127, 128
White Star Line 62–67
Women
   role of 20, 41, 50, 51, 157, 166, 172, 202, 203, 204
Wort und Tat (1938) 213
Wunschkonzert (1940) 116, 144, 153–159, 202, 205, 271
Yellow Canary (1943) 204, 205

Also by Ian Garden

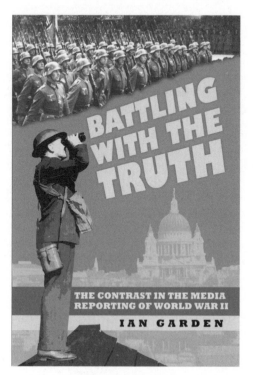

978 0 7509 5632 1

The destination for history
www·thehistorypress·co·uk